AF891396

CIMA

How to access your online resources

Kaplan Financial students will have a MyKaplan account and these extra resources will be available to you online. You do not need to register again, as this process was completed when you enrolled. If you are having problems accessing online materials, please ask your course administrator.

If you are not studying with Kaplan and did not purchase your book via a Kaplan website, to unlock your extra online resources please go to **www.mykaplan.co.uk/add-online-resources** (even if you have set up an account and registered books previously). You will then need to enter the ISBN number (on the title page and back cover) and the unique pass key number contained in the scratch panel below to gain access.

You will also be required to enter additional information during this process to set up or confirm your account details.

If you purchased through the Kaplan Publishing website you will automatically receive an e-mail invitation to register your details and gain access to your content. If you do not receive the e-mail or book content, please contact Kaplan Publishing.

This code can only be used once for the registration of this book online. This registration and your online content will expire when the examinations covered by this book have taken place. Please allow one hour from the time you submit your book details for us to process your request.

Please scratch the film to access your unique code.

Please be aware that this code is case-sensitive and you will need to include the dashes within the passcode, but not when entering the ISBN.

KAPLAN PUBLISHING

Professional Level

Subject E1

Managing Finance in a Digital World

Study Text

CIMA

KAPLAN PUBLISHING

Published by: Kaplan Publishing UK

Unit 2 The Business Centre, Molly Millars Lane, Wokingham, Berkshire RG41 2QZ

Acknowledgements

We are grateful to AICPA® & CIMA® for permission to reproduce past examination questions. The answers to CIMA's CGMA® exam questions have been prepared by Kaplan Publishing, except in the case of CIMA's November 2010 exams and subsequent CIMA's exam answers where CIMA's official answers have been reproduced. Questions from past live assessments have been included by kind permission of CIMA.

This product contains material that is ©Financial Reporting Council Ltd (FRC). Adapted and reproduced with the kind permission of the Financial Reporting Council. All rights reserved. For further information, please visit www.frc.org.uk or call +44 (0)20 7492 2300.

Notice

The text in this material and any others made available by any Kaplan Group company does not amount to advice on a particular matter and should not be taken as such. No reliance should be placed on the content as the basis for any investment or other decision or in connection with any advice given to third parties. Please consult your appropriate professional adviser as necessary.

Kaplan Publishing Limited and all other Kaplan group companies expressly disclaim all liability to any person in respect of any losses or other claims, whether direct, indirect, incidental, consequential or otherwise arising in relation to the use of such materials.

Kaplan is not responsible for the content of external websites. The inclusion of a link to a third party website in this text should not be taken as an endorsement.

Kaplan Publishing's learning materials are designed to help students succeed in their examinations. In certain circumstances, CIMA can make post-exam adjustment to a student's mark or grade to reflect adverse circumstances which may have disadvantaged a student's ability to take an exam or demonstrate their normal level of attainment (see CIMA's Special Consideration policy). However, it should be noted that students will not be eligible for special consideration by CIMA if preparation for or performance in CIMA's CGMA exams is affected by any failure by their tuition provider to prepare them properly for the exam for any reason including, but not limited to, staff shortages, building work or a lack of facilities etc.

Similarly, CIMA will not accept applications for special consideration on any of the following grounds:

- failure by a tuition provider to cover the whole syllabus
- failure by the student to cover the whole syllabus, for instance as a result of joining a course part way through
- failure by the student to prepare adequately for the exam, or to use the correct pre-seen material
- errors in the Kaplan Official Study Text, including sample (practice) questions or any other Kaplan content or
- errors in any other study materials (from any other tuition provider or publisher).

British Library Cataloguing in Publication Data

A catalogue record for this book is available from the British Library.

ISBN: 978-1-83735-089-6

Printed and bound in Great Britain

Contents

Introduction

How to use the Materials

These official CIMA® learning materials have been carefully designed to make your learning experience as easy as possible and to give you the best chances of success in your objective tests.

The product range contains a number of features to help you in the study process. They include:

- a detailed explanation of all syllabus areas
- extensive 'practical' materials
- generous question practice, together with full solutions.

This Study Text has been designed with the needs of home study and distance learning candidates in mind. Such students require very full coverage of the syllabus topics, and also the facility to undertake extensive question practice. However, the Study Text is also ideal for fully taught courses.

The main body of the text is divided into a number of chapters, each of which is organised on the following pattern:

- **Detailed learning outcomes.** These describe the knowledge expected after your studies of the chapter are complete. You should assimilate these before beginning detailed work on the chapter, so that you can appreciate where your studies are leading.
- **Step-by-step topic coverage.** This is the heart of each chapter, containing detailed explanatory text supported where appropriate by worked examples and exercises. You should work carefully through this section, ensuring that you understand the material being explained and can tackle the examples and exercises successfully. Remember that in many cases knowledge is cumulative: if you fail to digest earlier material thoroughly, you may struggle to understand later chapters.
- **Activities.** Some chapters are illustrated by more practical elements, such as comments and questions designed to stimulate discussion.
- **Question practice.** The text contains three styles of question:
  - Exam-style objective test questions (OTQs).
  - 'Integration' questions – these test your ability to understand topics within a wider context. This is particularly important with calculations where OTQs may focus on just one element but an integration question tackles the full calculation, just as you would be expected to do in the workplace.
  - 'Case' style questions – these test your ability to analyse and discuss issues in greater depth, particularly focusing on scenarios that are less clear cut than in the objective tests, and thus provide excellent practice for developing the skills needed for success in the Operational Level Case Study Examination.

- **Solutions.** Avoid the temptation merely to 'audit' the solutions provided. It is an illusion to think that this provides the same benefits as you would gain from a serious attempt of your own. However, if you are struggling to get started on a question you should read the introductory guidance provided at the beginning of the solution, where provided, and then make your own attempt before referring back to the full solution.

If you work conscientiously through this official CIMA Study Text according to the guidelines above you will be giving yourself an excellent chance of success in your Objective Tests. Good luck with your studies!

Quality and accuracy are of the utmost importance to us so if you spot an error in any of our products, please send an email to mykaplanreporting@kaplan.com with full details, or follow the link to the feedback form in MyKaplan.

Our Quality Co-ordinator will work with our technical team to verify the error and take action to ensure it is corrected in future editions.

Icon explanations

Definition – These sections explain important areas of knowledge which must be understood and reproduced in an assessment environment.

Supplementary reading – These sections will help to provide a deeper understanding of core areas. The supplementary reading is **NOT** optional reading. It is vital to provide you with the breadth of knowledge you will need to address the wide range of topics within your syllabus that could feature in an assessment question. **Reference to this text is vital when self-studying.**

Test your understanding – Following key points and definitions are exercises which give the opportunity to assess the understanding of these core areas.

e.g **Illustration** – To help develop an understanding of particular topics. The illustrative examples are useful in preparing for the Test your understanding exercises.

Study technique

Passing exams is partly a matter of intellectual ability, but however accomplished you are in that respect you can improve your chances significantly by the use of appropriate study and revision techniques. In this section we briefly outline some tips for effective study during the earlier stages of your approach to the objective tests. We also mention some techniques that you will find useful at the revision stage.

Planning

To begin with, formal planning is essential to get the best return from the time you spend studying. Estimate how much time in total you are going to need for each subject you are studying. Remember that you need to allow time for revision as well as for initial study of the material.

With your study material before you, decide which chapters you are going to study in each week, and which weeks you will devote to revision and final question practice.

Prepare a written schedule summarising the above and stick to it!

It is essential to know your syllabus. As your studies progress you will become more familiar with how long it takes to cover topics in sufficient depth. Your timetable may need to be adapted to allocate enough time for the whole syllabus.

Students are advised to refer to the examination blueprints (see page P.13 for further information) and the AICPA® & CIMA website, www.aicpa-cima.com , to ensure they are up-to-date.

The amount of space allocated to a topic in the Study Text is not a very good guide as to how long it will take you. The syllabus weighting is the better guide as to how long you should spend on a syllabus topic.

Tips for effective studying

(1) Aim to find a quiet and undisturbed location for your study, and plan as far as possible to use the same period of time each day. Getting into a routine helps to avoid wasting time. Make sure that you have all the materials you need before you begin so as to minimise interruptions.

(2) Store all your materials in one place, so that you do not waste time searching for items every time you want to begin studying. If you have to pack everything away after each study period, keep your study materials in a box, or even a suitcase, which will not be disturbed until the next time.

(3) Limit distractions. To make the most effective use of your study periods you should be able to apply total concentration, so turn off all entertainment equipment, set your phones to message mode, and put up your 'do not disturb' sign.

(4) Your timetable will tell you which topic to study. However, before diving in and becoming engrossed in the finer points, make sure you have an overall picture of all the areas that need to be covered by the end of that session. After an hour, allow yourself a short break and move away from your Study Text. With experience, you will learn to assess the pace you need to work at. Each study session should focus on component learning outcomes – the basis for all questions.

(5) Work carefully through a chapter, making notes as you go. When you have covered a suitable amount of material, vary the pattern by attempting a practice question. When you have finished your attempt, make notes of any mistakes you made, or any areas that you failed to cover or covered more briefly. Be aware that all component learning outcomes will be tested in each examination.

(6) Make notes as you study, and discover the techniques that work best for you. Your notes may be in the form of lists, bullet points, diagrams, summaries, 'mind maps', or the written word, but remember that you will need to refer back to them at a later date, so they must be intelligible. If you are on a taught course, make sure you highlight any issues you would like to follow up with your lecturer.

(7) Organise your notes. Make sure that all your notes, calculations etc. can be effectively filed and easily retrieved later.

Progression

There are two elements of progression that we can measure: how quickly students move through individual topics within a subject (for example within the individual topics of the E1 subject); and how quickly they move from one subject to the next (for example, from E1 to E2). We know that there is an optimum for both, but it can vary from subject to subject and from student to student. However, using data and our experience of student performance over many years, we can make some generalisations.

A fixed period of study set out at the start of a course with key milestones is important. This can be within a subject, for example 'I will finish this topic by 30 June', or for overall achievement, such as 'I want to be qualified by the end of next year'.

Your qualification is cumulative, as earlier papers provide a foundation for your subsequent studies, so do not allow there to be too big a gap between one subject and another. For example, E1 Managing Finance in a Digital World builds on your knowledge of the finance function from certificate level and lays the foundations for E2 Managing Performance and all strategic papers particularly E3 Strategic Management and P3 Risk Management.

Also, it is important to realise CIMA's CGMA® Operational Case Study (OCS) Exam tests knowledge of all subjects within the Operational level. Please note that candidates will need to return to this material when studying OCS as it forms a significant part of the OCS syllabus content.

We know that exams encourage techniques that lead to some degree of short term retention, the result being that you will simply forget much of what you have already learned unless it is refreshed (look up Ebbinghaus Forgetting Curve for more details on this). This makes it more difficult as you move from one subject to another: not only will you have to learn the new subject, you will also have to relearn all the underpinning knowledge as well. This is very inefficient and slows down your overall progression which makes it more likely you may not succeed at all.

In addition, delaying your studies slows your path to qualification which can have negative impacts on your career, postponing the opportunity to apply for higher level positions and therefore higher pay.

You can use the following diagram showing the whole structure of your qualification to help you keep track of your progress. Make sure you seek appropriate advice if you are unsure about your progression through the qualification.

Reproduced with CIMA's permission

Objective test

Objective test questions require you to choose or provide a response to a question whose correct answer is predetermined.

The most common types of objective test question you will see are:

- Multiple choice, where you have to choose the correct answer(s) from a list of possible answers. This could either be numbers or text.
- Multiple choice with more choices and answers, for example, choosing two correct answers from a list of eight possible answers. This could either be numbers or text.
- Single numeric entry, where you give your numeric answer, for example, profit is $10,000.
- Multiple entry, where you give several numeric answers.
- True/false questions, where you state whether a statement is true or false.
- Matching pairs of text, for example, matching a technical term with the correct definition.
- Other types could be matching text with graphs and labelling graphs/diagrams.

In every chapter of this Study Text we have introduced these types of questions, but obviously we have had to label answers A, B, C etc. rather than using click boxes. For convenience, we have retained quite a few questions where an initial scenario leads to a number of sub-questions. There will be no questions of this type in the objective tests.

Guidance re CIMA's CGMA on-screen calculator

As part of CIMA's Objective Test software, candidates are now provided with a calculator. This calculator is on-screen and is available for the duration of the assessment. The calculator is available in each of the Objective Tests and is accessed by clicking the calculator button in the top left hand corner of the screen at any time during the assessment. Candidates are permitted to utilise personal calculators as long as they are an approved CIMA model. Authorised CIMA models are listed on the AICPA & CIMA website. https://www.cimaglobal.com/Studying/study-and-resources/.

All candidates must complete a 15-minute exam tutorial before the assessment begins and will have the opportunity to familiarise themselves with the calculator and practise using it. The exam tutorial is also available online via the Pearson Vue website.

Candidates may practise using the calculator by accessing the online exam tutorial.

Fundamentals of objective tests

The objective tests are 90-minute assessments comprising 60 compulsory questions, with one or more parts. There will be no choice and all questions should be attempted. All elements of a question must be answered correctly for the question to be marked correctly. All questions are equally weighted.

CIMA's CGMA® 2019 syllabus – Structure of subjects and learning outcomes

Details regarding the content of CIMA's new CGMA syllabus can be located within CIMA's CGMA 2019 professional syllabus document.

Each subject within the CGMA syllabus is divided into a number of broad syllabus topics. The topics contain one or more lead learning outcomes, related component learning outcomes and indicative knowledge content.

A learning outcome has two main purposes:

(a) To define the skill or ability that a well prepared candidate should be able to exhibit in the examination.

(b) To demonstrate the approach likely to be taken in examination questions.

The learning outcomes are part of a hierarchy of learning objectives. The verbs used at the beginning of each learning outcome relate to a specific learning objective, e.g.:

> **Calculate** the break-even point, profit target, margin of safety and profit/volume ratio for a single product or service.

The verb '**calculate**' indicates a level three learning objective. The following tables list the verbs that appear in the syllabus learning outcomes and examination questions.

The examination blueprints and representative task statements

CIMA has also published the CGMA® Exam Blueprints, giving learners clear expectations regarding what is expected of them.

The blueprint is structured as follows:

- Exam content sections (reflecting the syllabus document)
- Lead and component outcomes (reflecting the syllabus document)
- Representative task statements.

A representative task statement is a plain English description of what a CGMA® qualified finance professional should know and be able to do.

The content and skill level determine the language and verbs used in the representative task.

CIMA will test up to the level of the task statement in the Objective Tests (an Objective Test question on a particular topic could be set at a lower level than the task statement in the blueprint).

The format of the Objective Test blueprints follows that of the published syllabus for the 2019 Professional Qualification.

Weightings for content sections are also included in the individual subject blueprints.

CIMA's CGMA VERB HIERARCHY

CIMA places great importance on the definition of verbs in structuring Objective Tests. It is therefore crucial that you understand the verbs in order to appreciate the depth and breadth of a topic and the level of skill required. The Objective Tests will focus on levels one, two and three of CIMA's hierarchy of verbs. However, they will also test levels four and five, especially at the Management and Strategic Levels.

Skill level	Verbs used	Definition
Level 5 Evaluation How you are expected to use your learning to evaluate, make decisions or recommendations	Advise	Counsel, inform or notify
	Assess	Evaluate or estimate the nature, ability or quality of
	Evaluate	Appraise or assess the value of
	Recommend	Propose a course of action
	Review	Assess and evaluate in order, to change if necessary
Level 4 Analysis How you are expected to analyse the detail of what you have learned	Align	Arrange in an orderly way
	Analyse	Examine in detail the structure of
	Communicate	Share or exchange information
	Compare and contrast	Show the similarities and/or differences between
	Develop	Grow and expand a concept
	Discuss	Examine in detail by argument
	Examine	Inspect thoroughly
	Interpret	Translate into intelligible or familiar terms
	Monitor	Observe and check the progress of
	Prioritise	Place in order of priority or sequence for action
	Produce	Create or bring into existence
Level 3 Application How you are expected to apply your knowledge	Apply	Put to practical use
	Calculate	Ascertain or reckon mathematically
	Conduct	Organise and carry out
	Demonstrate	Prove with certainty or exhibit by practical means
	Prepare	Make or get ready for use
	Reconcile	Make or prove consistent/compatible

Skill level	Verbs used	Definition
Level 2 **Comprehension** What you are expected to understand	Describe	Communicate the key features of
	Distinguish	Highlight the differences between
	Explain	Make clear or intelligible/state the meaning or purpose of
	Identify	Recognise, establish or select after consideration
	Illustrate	Use an example to describe or explain something
Level 1 **Knowledge** What you are expected to know	List	Make a list of
	State	Express, fully or clearly, the details/facts of
	Define	Give the exact meaning of
	Outline	Give a summary of

CGMA SYLLABUS GRIDS

E1: Managing Finance in a Digital World

How the finance function is organised

Content weighting

Content area	Weighting
A Role of the finance function	20%
B Technology in a digital world	20%
C Data and Information in a digital world	20%
D Shape and structure of the finance function	20%
E Finance interacting with the organisation	20%
	100%

E1A: Role of the finance function

This section examines the roles that finance plays in organisations and why. It describes in detail the activities that finance professionals perform to fulfil these roles. Consequently, it is the foundation of the whole qualification and answers the question: what do finance professionals do and why? It provides links with other topics within the subject and what is covered in other areas of the Operational Level.

Lead outcome	Component outcome	Topics to be covered	Explanatory notes	Study Text Chapter
1. Explain the roles of the finance function in organisations.	Explain how the finance function: a. Enables organisations to create and preserve value b. Shapes how organisations create and preserve value c. Narrates how organisations create and preserve value	• The fast-changing and unpredictable contexts in which organisations operate • Enabling value creation through planning, forecasting and resource allocation • Shaping value creation through performance management and control • Narrating the value creation story through corporate reporting • The role of ethics in the role of the finance function	Describe the increasingly disruptive contexts in which organisations and their finance teams operate and how these contexts shape the role of finance. Take each role and show how finance performs it in a typical organisational setting. The coverage should be introductory and brief. It is meant to set the scene for subsequent sections and draw a link between the roles and the topics that will be covered in other areas of the Operational Level.	1
2. Describe the activities that finance professionals perform to fulfil the roles.	Describe how the finance function: a. Collates data to prepare information about organisations b. Provides insight to users by analysing information c. Communicates insight to influence users d. Supports the implementation of decisions to achieve the desired impact e. Connects the different activities connect to each other	• How data is collected, cleaned and connected by finance • Types of analysis to produce insights • How finance communicates to influence key stakeholders (audiences, frequency, format, etc.) • How finance uses resource allocation and performance management to enable organisations to achieve their objectives • Potential impact of technology	Use 'information to impact' framework to describe the primary activities finance professionals perform. Relate it to how data is generated, transformed and used. Link it to how technology could be used to improve the productivity of finance professionals in these areas and the threat of automation.	2

E1B: Technology in a digital world

This section focuses on the technologies that define and drive the digital world in which finance operates. It provides awareness of the technologies used in organisations and deepens understanding of the impact of the technologies on what finance does. It draws on the issues raised in the previous section about the role of finance and the activities finance performs to fulfil these roles. Given that the digital world is underpinned by technology and the use of data, this section provides a foundation to the next section on data.

Lead outcome	Component outcome	Topics to be covered	Explanatory notes	Study Text Chapter
1. Outline and explain the technologies that affect business and finance.	a. Outline the key features of the fourth industrial revolution. b. Outline and explain the key technologies that define and drive the digital world.	• Characteristics and dynamics of the fourth industrial revolution • Cloud computing • Big data analytics • Process automation • Artificial intelligence • Data visualisation • Blockchain • Internet of things • Mobile • 3-D printing	The aim is to create awareness of the technologies that drive the digital world and how they interact with each other. The technologies outlined by the major advisory firms and the World Economic Forum digital transformation initiative provide the material on which learning and related activities can be based.	5
2. Examine how the finance function uses digital technologies to fulfil its roles.	Examine how finance uses the following to guide how it performs its roles: a. Digital technology b. Digital mindsets c. Automation and the future of work d. Ethics of technology usage	• How finance uses technologies listed above • Areas of finance susceptible to automation and why • New areas for finance to focus on • Digital mindsets for finance • Ethics of the use of technology	Examine how finance professionals use the relevant technologies to fulfil their roles. Explain how the technologies affect various activities finance professionals perform in the 'information to impact' framework. The intention is to move from creating awareness to generating understanding of how finance can use these technologies to increase its value and relevance to organisations.	6

E1C: Data and information in a digital world

This section draws out one of the major implications of using technology in organisations and the finance function – namely the collection and processing of information can be done more effectively by machines rather than by people. It asserts that the role of finance professionals should be to use data to create and preserve value for organisations. Five ways of using data are examined. The key competencies required to use data in these ways are also highlighted. The primary objective is to help finance professionals understand what they can do with data and how to build the skills needed to use data.

Lead outcome	Component outcome	Topics to be covered	Explanatory notes	Study Text Chapter
1. Describe the ways in which data is used by the finance function.	Identify the ways in which the finance function uses data: a. In a general sense b. Specifically in each of the primary activities of finance	Using data for: • Decision-making • Understanding the customer • Developing customer value proposition • Enhancing operational efficiency • Monetising data • Ethics of data usage	Build on the previous section on technology to explain why, in the digital world, finance professionals must place more focus on using information than on collecting and/or processing information. Outline and describe the various uses of information. Link them to the primary activities that the finance function performs and to the topics to be covered in other modules of the Operational Level.	7
2. Explain the competencies required to use data to create and preserve value for organisations.	Explain the competencies that finance professionals need in: a. Data strategy and planning b. Data engineering, extraction and mining c. Data modelling, manipulation and analysis d. Data and insight communication	• Assessment of data needs • Extraction, transformation and loading (ETL) systems • Business Intelligence (BI) systems • Big data analytics • Data visualisation	Highlight and explain the data competencies required in the digital world. Locate where finance has a competitive advantage and where finance will need to work with data scientists.	8

E1D: Shape and structure of the finance function

This section brings together the implications of the previous sections. It reveals how the finance function is structured and shaped. This structure and shape enables finance to perform its role in the organisation and with other internal and external stakeholders. In this sense, it prepares candidates for the next section, which looks at how finance interacts with key internal stakeholders in operations, marketing and human resources.

Lead outcome	Component outcome	Topics to be covered	Explanatory notes	Study Text Chapter
1. Describe the structure and shape of the finance function.	Describe the: a. Evolution of the shape of the finance function b. Shape of the finance function in the digital era	• Structure of the finance function from the roles that generate information to the roles that turn information into insight and communicate insight to decision-makers • Hierarchical shape of finance function • Shared services and outsourcing of finance operations • Retained finance • Automation and diamond shape of finance function	Introduce candidates to the structure of the finance function and outline the broad areas of finance such as finance operations, external reporting, financial planning and analysis (FP&A), decision support etc. Describe the evolving shape of the finance function from the triangle to the diamond shape. Link the description to the impact of digital technology and automation on the finance function.	3
2. Explain what each level of the finance function does.	Explain the activities of: a. Finance operations b. Specialist areas including financial reporting and financial planning and analysis (FP&A) c. Strategic partnering for value d. Strategic leadership of the finance team	• Finance operations to generate information and preliminary insight • FP&A, taxation, corporate reporting, decision support to produce insight • Business partnering to influence organisation to make appropriate decisions • Leading the finance team to create the required impact for the organisation	The focus is the diamond shape and the four levels within this shape. Explain what each level does, the relationship between the levels, and the link between the levels and the basic finance activities covered under the role of finance.	4

E1E: Finance interacting with the organisation

The finance function is not the only area of activity in organisations. Finance joins with others to create and preserve value for their organisations. This section brings together what has been learned in the previous section to describe how finance can interact with other parts of the organisation to achieve the objectives of finance, those other areas and crucially the objectives of the whole organisation. The aim is to show how finance can work collaboratively in a connected (and joined-up) organisation and not in isolation.

Lead outcome	Component outcome	Topics to be covered	Explanatory notes	Study Text Chapter
1. Describe how the finance function interacts with operations.	Describe: a. Main role of operations b. Areas of interface with finance c. Key performance indicators	• Process management • Product and service management • Supply chain management	Describe how finance plays its role by interacting with the rest of the organisation. Bring together the issues raised in the previous sections and link them to what the other areas of the organisations do. For example, address how finance and marketing interact using data and collaborative technology to achieve organisational goals and the individual functional goals of both finance and marketing. Describe how the use of KPIs influence these interactions and how the KPIs of finance and these areas can be aligned to ensure they work together effectively.	9
2. Describe how the finance function interacts with sales and marketing.	Describe: a. Main role of sales and marketing b. Areas of interface with finance c. Key performance indicators	• Market segmentation • Big data analytics in marketing • Channel management • Sales forecasting and management		10
3. Describe how the finance function interacts with human resources.	Describe: a. Main role of human resources b. Areas of interface with finance c. Key performance indicators	• Staff acquisition • Staff development • Performance management • Motivation and reward systems		11
4. Describe how the finance function interacts with IT.	Describe: a. Main role of IT b. Areas of interface with finance c. Key performance indicators	• IT infrastructure • IT systems support • Costs and benefits of IT systems		12

Information concerning formulae and tables will be provided via the AICPA & CIMA website, www.aicpa-cima.com.

Chapter

1

The roles of the finance function in organisations

Chapter learning objectives

Lead	Component
A1: Explain the roles of the finance function in organisations.	Explain how the finance function: (a) Enables organisations to create and preserve value (b) Shapes how organisations create and preserve value (c) Narrates how organisations create and preserve value

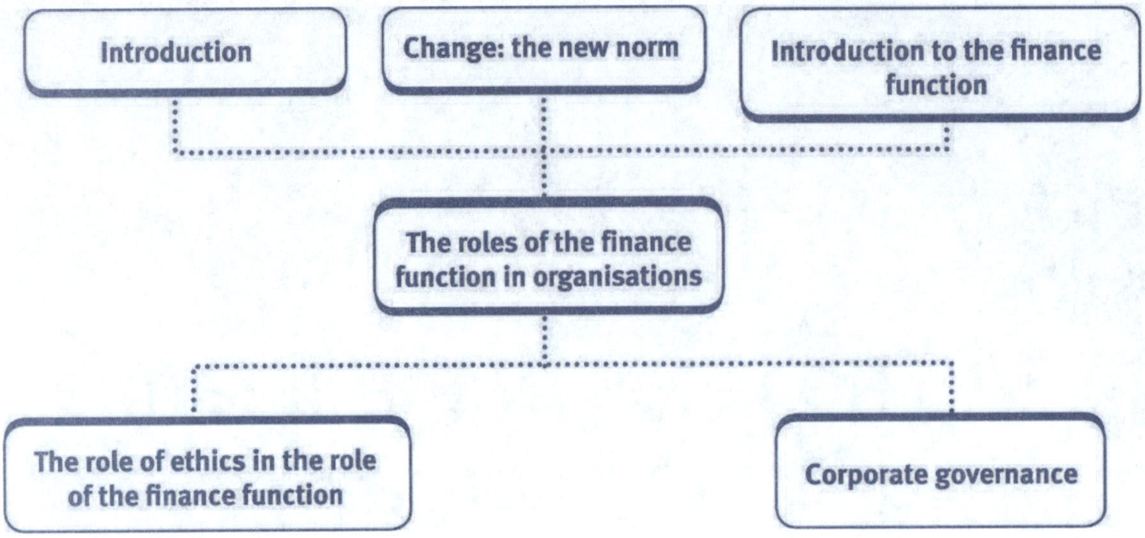

1 Introduction

Before we look at the roles of the finance function in organisations, it is useful to understand the overall purpose of E1 and how it fits within the Professional Qualification.

1.1 The Professional Level Qualification

The Professional Level Qualification will give you the skills that you need to work as a confident and competent management accountant in an age where change is the new norm so that you can guide and lead your organisation's success.

We live in an age of technological advancements and innovation and these factors are transforming the way in which we work and live. The World Economic Forum calls it the **4th Industrial Revolution** and this revolution is having a huge impact on the finance function and, as a result, the skillset of a management accountant.

1.2 The Operational Level

'Finance' runs through the Operational level:

- **P1** – focuses on '**what**' the finance function does
- **F1** – focuses on '**what**' the finance function does and its **implications**
- **E1** – focuses on '**how**' the finance function is organised

The E1 syllabus is very broad in terms of coverage of subject matter (as evidenced by 12 Lead outcomes and 38 Component outcomes). The Operational level will focus on levels one, two and to some degree level three of CIMA's CGMA hierarchy of verbs; the emphasis will be on **remembering** and **understanding** but **some insight** regarding specific problems or situations may also be required. On completion of this level, you will be able to work with others in the organisation to use appropriate data and technology to translate medium-term decisions into short-term actionable plans.

1.3 Subject E1: Managing Finance in a Digital World

There are five connected areas to the syllabus:

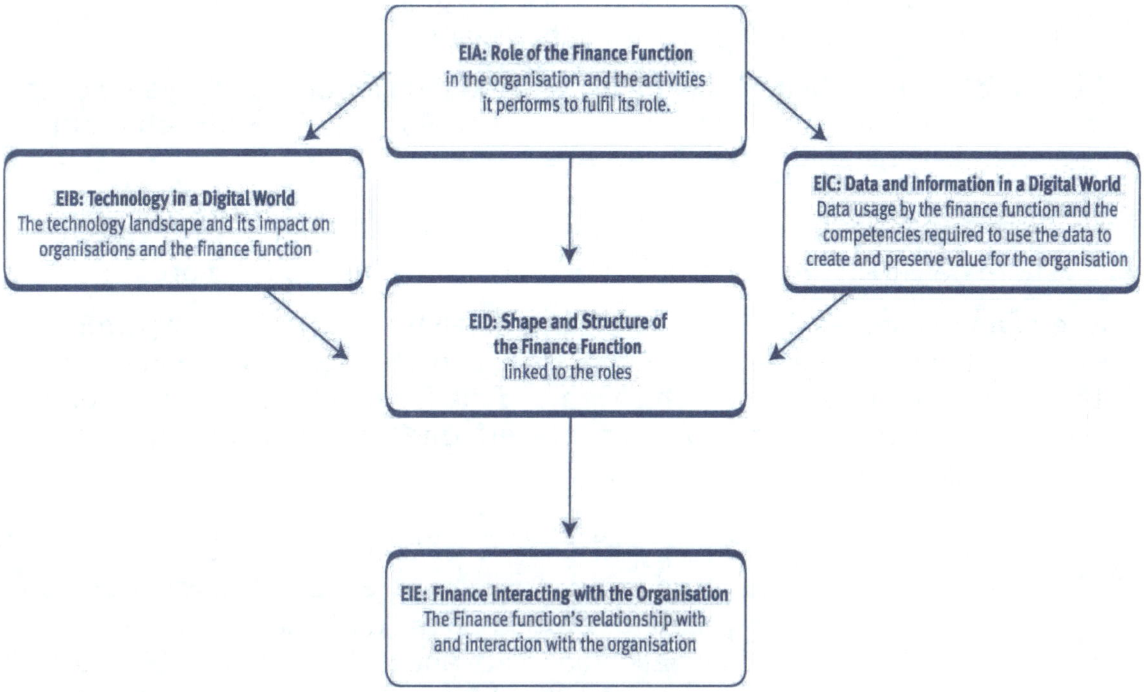

1.4 The roles of the finance function in organisations

This chapter covers **syllabus area A1**, '**explain the roles of the finance function in organisations**'. It describes in detail the activities that finance professionals perform to fulfil these roles. Consequently, it is the foundation of the whole qualification and answers the question 'what do finance professionals do and why?'. It provides links with other syllabus areas and what is covered in other modules of the Operational level.

By the end of this chapter you should understand how the finance function enables, shapes and narrates value creation through its **roles** of:

- planning
- forecasting
- resource allocation
- performance management and control and
- financial (corporate) reporting.

These roles are changing due to the **continuous change** that is impacting all organisations and so before introducing the roles of the finance function we will begin our discussion of this syllabus area by briefly looking at change.

The chapter concludes with a discussion of **ethics**, **corporate social responsibility** and **corporate governance**. These areas are fundamental to an organisation's sustained value and relate directly to the finance function's role in value creation and preservation.

2 Change: The new norm

Change is the new norm in many organisations due to seismic shifts in the level of competition, customers' expectations and the global political outlook combined with a fast pace of technological change.

Although change has been constant in organisations for the last 50 years or so, what is different is the rapidity of change. This **rapid** and often **unpredictable** evolution has resulted in huge **disruption**:

- Organisations are having to plan for a different way of doing business.
- There has been an evolution of the roles of the finance function.

These changes present both risks and opportunities, which will be explored in greater depth in subsequent chapters. Before considering change and its potential impact on both the organisation and the finance function, however, we need to firstly understand the overall roles performed by the finance function within an organisation.

e.g

Illustration 1 – Change and impact on organisations

Extraordinary economic changes are happening at such a fast pace driven by technology innovations and advances. The Fortune 500 (US 'Fortune' magazine's annual list of the 500 top worldwide companies based on revenue) has changed dramatically over the years. In 2024 the list showed that several more banks and financial institutions had entered the top 500 companies. Oil companies had dropped several places while Amazon and Apple amongst others had moved up the rankings. The fastest growing companies included Tesla and Nvidia (computer manufacturing). And of the top 500 companies 17 were British, 125 were Chinese and 139 were US based.

3 Introduction to the finance function

Before focusing on the finance function, it is useful to remind ourselves of the different types of organisations that exist and of the different functions that exist within an organisation.

3.1 Different types of organisation

Every organisation is different, but organisations can be viewed as belonging to one of two main types:

- **Profit seeking organisations, i.e. businesses** include companies (Ltd or plc), partnerships and sole traders. Their primary objective is the maximisation of the wealth of their owners.
- **Not-for-profit organisations (NFPOs)** include public sector organisations (such as schools and hospitals) and private sector organisations (such as charities and non-governmental organisations (NGOs)). These organisations do not see profit as their primary objective but exist to maximise the benefit to beneficiaries.

Throughout the text the concepts that are introduced are done so mainly in relation to businesses. However, it is worth noting that much of the discussion is just as relevant to NFPOs.

Two main types of NFPO

- **Public sector organisations** are operated by the government and exist to provide a service for the population as a whole and the community. Examples include the British Army and the National Health Service (NHS) in the UK.
- **Private sector organisations** are operated by the private sector (i.e. not the government). There are two sub-types:
  - **Third sector organisations** aim to make a difference to society and include charities, community groups/clubs and social enterprises.
  - **Non-governmental organisations (NGOs)** are local, national, or international voluntary groups that aim to address issues (such as health, human rights or the environment) to support the public good. Examples include Amnesty International and Save the Children.

Test your understanding 1

Which THREE of the following are not-for-profit organisations?

A unlisted public limited company

B medical research charity

C local publicly funded hospital

D sole trader who is making a loss

E private limited company

F local government agency

3.2 The functions of an organisation

The main functions of a business are:

- operations
- sales and marketing
- human resources (HR)
- IT and
- **finance**.

This reflects the model of the business as taking three basic types of resource – material, labour and money – to produce goods and services which generate profit.

It is a major part of the finance function's work to look after the business's money. The finance function's role in managing the financial resources of the organisation and providing information to help economic decision making will be integral to the effectiveness of the finance function.

3.3 The roles of the finance function in organisations

The finance function plays **three key roles**:

- **enabling**
- **shaping how** and
- **narrating how**

an organisation **creates and preserving value**.

Value is the achievement of the specified objective(s), most economically and at the required standard of quality and reliability.

The finance function works, both, in **creating value in the short-term** and **preserving value for the longer-term**. Their roles will contribute to sustained and optimum organisational performance.

The three key roles are discussed below. A finance function:

- **ENABLES** an organisation to create and preserve value though planning, forecasting and resource allocation:
  - **Planning:** the finance function will have an important role in preparing plans to assist the organisation in achieving its objectives and formulating relevant strategies. One of the main types of planning carried out at the operational level will be budgeting.
  - **Forecasting:** the preparation of forecasts, for example of future sales or material prices, will be an important role of the finance function at the operational level.
  - **Resource allocation:** an important role of the finance function will be in working out which resources (for example, labour, material, machinery, finance) the organisation will require to achieve its objectives.

  In the Professional Level Qualification, the 'enables' element is encompassed in the Enterprise pillar.

- **SHAPES HOW** an organisation creates and preserves value through performance management and control:
  - **Performance management:** the finance function has an important role in the management of performance and the achievement of the organisation's plans and budgets.

    For example, it will help to prepare information for internal management such as performance measures. These measures will assist in monitoring the performance of the organisation. The performance measures may be quantitative, i.e. numerical (such as sales, profit or units produced) or may be qualitative, i.e. non-numerical (such as customer satisfaction or levels of innovation).
  - **Control:** this will be an important part of effective performance management; actual performance will be compared to planned performance to identify any differences. Variance analysis may be carried out as part of this role. The identification of these differences may result in a reassessment or amendment of the original plans, strategies or budgets.

  In the Professional Level Qualification, the 'shapes how' element is encompassed in the Performance pillar.
- **NARRATES HOW** an organisation creates and preserves value through financial (corporate) reporting:
  - Financial reporting (also called corporate reporting): an important role of the finance function is in preparing comprehensive reports intended to give information to shareholders and/or other interested people about the organisation's activities and performance throughout the year.

  In the Professional Level Qualification, the 'narrates how' element is encompassed in the 'Financial' pillar.

If it plays these roles effectively, then the finance function is valuable to the organisation.

Important note: This is a brief introduction to the roles of the finance function. However, this area is highly examinable and will be returned to and built upon in subsequent chapters. It will underpin much of the discussion in these later chapters.

4 The role of ethics in the role of the finance function

4.1 The ethical responsibilities of the organisation and individuals

As mentioned previously (in section 1.4), ethics will be a fundamental underpinning factor in the organisation's sustained value creation.

The roles that the finance function performs should be carried out in an ethical way, with integrity and professionalism.

The professional accountant has a special role in promoting ethical behaviour throughout the business.

Ethics, business ethics and ethical dilemmas

Ethics is the system of moral principles that examines the concept of right and wrong.

Business ethics is the application of ethical values to business behaviour.

An **ethical dilemma** involves a situation where a decision-maker must decide what is the 'right' or 'wrong' thing to do. Examples of ethical dilemmas can be found throughout all aspects of business operations:

Finance (Accounting) issues

- Creative accounting to boost or suppress reported profits.
- Large remuneration for directors even if the company is performing poorly.

Operations (Production) issues

- The production of certain products, for example guns, pornography, tobacco, alcoholic drinks aimed at teenagers.
- The effects on the environment of its production processes.

Sales and marketing issues

- Price fixing and anti-competitive behaviour.
- The ethics of targeted advertising (such as fast food at children).

Human resource management (HRM) issues

- Employees should not be favoured or discriminated against, for example based on gender, race, religion, age, disability.
- The workplace must be a safe and healthy place to operate in.

Information technology (IT) issues

- The ethics surrounding the collection, storage and use of customer and employee data.

4.2 CIMA's ethical guidelines

Management accountants have a duty to observe the highest standards of conduct and integrity, and to uphold the good standing and reputation of their profession.

The Code of Ethics for Professional Accountants, published by The International Federation of Accountants (IFAC), forms the basis for the ethical codes of many accountancy bodies, including CIMA.

CIMA's Code of Ethics, based on IFAC's five ethical principles, seeks to help management accountants in their day to day role. It helps management accountants to identify areas where ethical pressures may exist and provides a recommended course of action for their resolution.

To achieve the objectives of the accounting profession, CGMA qualified professional accountants must observe five fundamental principles:

Fundamental Principle	Interpretation
Integrity	Integrity means being straightforward, honest and truthful in all professional and business relationships.
Objectivity	Objectivity means not allowing bias, conflict of interest, or the influence of other people to override your professional judgement.
Professional competence and due care	This is an ongoing commitment to maintain your level of professional knowledge and skill so that your client or employer receives a competent professional service. Work should be completed carefully, thoroughly and diligently, in accordance with relevant technical and professional standards.
Confidentiality	This means respecting the confidential nature of information you acquire through professional relationships such as past or current employment. You should not disclose such information unless you have specific permission or a legal or professional duty to do so. You should also never use confidential information for your or another person's advantage.
Professional behaviour	This requires you to comply with relevant laws and regulations. You must also avoid any action that could negatively affect the reputation of the profession.

Test your understanding 2

John is a CIMA Member in Practice and advises a range of individual clients and organisations. John has been asked, by his brother, to prepare the accounts for his brother's company. John's brother says that he wants the reported profit to be as high as possible, as he will soon be applying to the bank for loan finance.

To do this would be in breach of which fundamental ethical principle (according to CIMA's Code of Ethics)?

A Integrity

B Objectivity

C Professional competence and due care

D Confidentiality

E Professional behaviour

4.3 Why business ethics are important

In addition to the professional accountant having a role in promoting ethical behaviour within an organisation, the organisation as a whole, and all the individuals within it, are expected to act in an ethical way.

Businesses are part of society. Society expects its individuals to behave properly, and similarly expects companies to operate to certain standards. Acceptable business ethics may comprise as a minimum:

- paying staff **fair wages** and pensions
- providing **safe working conditions** for staff
- **paying suppliers** in line with agreed terms
- **sourcing supplies** carefully
- using sustainable or **renewable sources**
- being **open and honest** with customers.

However, apart from any moral duty to be ethical, the prime purpose of a company is to maximise shareholder wealth and the chance of this happening is increased by the adoption of ethical behaviour since:

- Ethical behaviour is likely to be favoured by:
  - customers: resulting in higher sales volumes and/or prices.
  - employees: resulting in the attraction/retention of the best employees and increased employee productivity.
  - business collaborators: resulting in increased opportunities for profitable projects.
- Ethical behaviour reduces risk and gives access to cheaper funds which, in turn, increase project profitability.
- Unethical behaviour will, at some point be discovered resulting in a damage to reputation and potential legal charges.

e.g

Illustration 2 – Why business ethics are important

The Fairtrade mark is a label on consumer products that guarantees that disadvantaged producers in the developing world are getting a fair deal. For example, the majority of coffee around the world is grown by small farmers who sell their produce through a local co-operative. Fairtrade coffee guarantees to pay a price to producers that covers the cost of sustainable production and also an extra premium that is invested in local development projects.

Consumers in the developed world may be willing to pay a premium price for Fairtrade products, knowing that the products are grown in an ethical and sustainable fashion.

Test your understanding 3

Which of the following would potentially be ethical concerns for a cosmetics manufacturer? Choose all that apply.

A The amount of chemicals included in their products.

B The quality of the cosmetics.

C How much it pays its staff.

D How much its supplier pays its staff.

E The way the cosmetics are advertised.

4.4 Corporate codes of ethics

Most companies (especially if they are large) have approached the concept of business ethics by creating a written code of ethics (a set of internal policies) and instructing employees to follow them. These policies can either be **broad** generalisations (**a corporate ethics statement**) or can contain **specific** rules (**a corporate ethics code**).

There is no standard list of contents – it will vary between different organisations. Typically, however, it may contain guidelines on issues such as honesty, integrity and customer focus.

It is becoming more commonplace for organisations (particularly those that are larger and/or those that operate in sectors such as finance or healthcare) to appoint **Ethics Officers** (also known as **Compliance Officers**). The Ethics Officer monitors the application of the policies and is available to discuss ethical dilemmas with employees where needed.

4.5 Corporate social responsibility

This follows on from our discussion of ethics but before we review 'corporate social responsibility', we need to define the term 'stakeholder'.

A **stakeholder** is a group or individual, who has an interest in what the organisation does, or an expectation of the organisation.

Stakeholders can be broadly categorised into three categories; internal, connected and external.

Internal

Internal stakeholders are intimately connected to the organisation, and their objectives are likely to have a strong influence on how it is run. Internal stakeholders include:

Stakeholder	Need/expectation
Employees	Pay, working conditions and job security
Managers/directors	Status, pay, bonus, job security

Connected

Connected stakeholders either invest in or have dealings with the firm. They include:

Stakeholder	Need/expectation
Shareholders	Dividends and capital growth and the continuation of the business
Customers	Value-for-money products and services
Suppliers	Paid promptly
Finance providers	Repayment of finance

External

These stakeholders do not tend to have a direct link to the organisation but can influence or be influenced by its activities. They include:

Stakeholder	Need/expectation
Community at large	Will not want their lives to be negatively impacted by business decisions.
Environmental pressure groups	The organisation does not harm the external environment.
Government	Provision of taxes and jobs and compliance with legislation.
Trade unions	To take an active part in the decision-making process.
Competitors	To understand the actions of competitors that will impact organisational performance and influence decision-making. (Note: competitors are traditionally excluded from stakeholder considerations of this nature.)

The needs/expectations of different stakeholder groups may conflict. In the event of conflict, an organisation will need to decide which stakeholders' needs are more important. This will commonly be the most dominant stakeholder. However, not all decisions are this straightforward. Stakeholders interest in a particular decision and their significance as a group are issues to consider and **Mendelow's power-interest matrix** is of relevance.

Level of interest

Level of power	Low	High
Low	Minimal effort	Keep informed
High	Keep satisfied	Key players

By plotting each stakeholder according to the power that they have over an organisation and the interest they have in a particular decision, the dominant stakeholder(s), i.e. the key player(s) can be identified. The needs of the key players must be considered during the formulation and evaluation of new strategies.

Illustration 3 – Stakeholders' influence

The airline, Ryanair, has regular labour relations problems with pilots, cabin attendants and check-in staff. For example, in recent years pilots at Ryanair threatened a mass strike (and possible desertion to a competitor airline) if there were not significant improvements in pay and conditions. Ryanair cannot operate without these employees, so they have great power and have shown that they are willing to exercise that power.

Example of stakeholder management

R is a high-class hotel situated in a thriving city. It is part of a worldwide hotel group owned by a large number of shareholders. Individuals hold the majority of shares, each holding a small number, and financial institutions hold the rest. The hotel provides full amenities, including a heated swimming pool, as well as the normal facilities of bars, restaurants and good quality accommodation. There are many other hotels in the city, all of which compete with R. The city in which R is situated is old and attracts many foreign visitors, especially in the summer season.

The main stakeholders with whom relationships need to be established and maintained by management and the importance of maintaining these relationships is as follows:

Internal stakeholders

The employees and the managers of the hotel are the main link with the guests and the service they provide is vital to the quality of the hotel as guests' experience at the hotel will be determined by their attitude and approach.

Managers should ensure that employees deliver the highest level of service and are well trained and committed.

Connected stakeholders

The shareholders of the hotel will be concerned with a steady flow of income, possible capital growth and continuation of the business. Relationships should be developed and maintained with the shareholders, especially those operating on behalf of institutions. Management must try to achieve improvements in their returns by ensuring that customers are satisfied and are willing to return.

Each guest will seek good service and satisfaction. Different types of guests, for example business versus tourist, will have different needs and managers should regularly analyse the customer database to ensure that these needs are met.

Suppliers should be selected very carefully to ensure that services and goods provided (for example, food and laundry) continue to add to the quality of the hotel and to customer satisfaction. Suppliers will be concerned with being paid promptly for goods. Maintaining a good relationship with suppliers will ensure their continued support of the hotel.

External stakeholders

The management of the hotel must maintain close relationships with the authorities to ensure they comply with legislation. Examples of external stakeholders include fire and safety authorities and food hygiene authorities. Failure to do so could result in the hotel being closed down.

Stakeholder conflict

The needs/expectations of the different stakeholder groups may conflict. Some of the typical conflicts are shown below:

Stakeholders	Conflict
Employees versus managers	Jobs/wages versus bonus payments for managers
Customers versus shareholders	Product quality/service levels versus profits/dividends
General public versus shareholders	Effect on the environment versus profit/dividends
Managers versus shareholders	Independence versus growth by merger/takeover

It is important that an organisation meets the needs of the most dominant stakeholders, but the needs of the other stakeholders should also be considered – nearly every decision becomes a compromise. For example, the firm will have to earn a satisfactory return for its shareholders whilst paying reasonable wages.

Now that we understand what we mean by 'stakeholders' we can introduce the concept of 'corporate social responsibility'.

Corporate social responsibility (CSR) refers to the idea that a company should be sensitive to the needs and wants of all the stakeholders in its business operations, not just the shareholders.

As such, business ethics are just one dimension of CSR.

A socially responsible company may consider:

- the environmental impact of production or consumption, for example due to the use of non-renewable resources or non-recyclable inputs
- the health impact for consumers of certain products, for example tobacco and alcohol
- the fair treatment of employees
- whether it is right to experiment on animals
- the safety of products and production processes.

Traditionalists argue that companies should operate solely to make money for shareholders and that it is not a company's role to worry about social responsibilities.

The **modern view** is that by aligning the company's core values with the values of society, the company can improve its reputation and ensure it has a long-term future due to the following:

- **Differentiation** (making the product/service different from its competitors) – the firm's CSR strategy (for example with regards to the environment, experimentation on animals or to product safety) can act as a method of differentiation.
- **High calibre staff** will be attracted and retained due to the firm's CSR policies.
- **Brand strengthening** – due to the firm's honest approach.
- **Lower costs** – can be achieved in a number of ways, for example due to the use of less packaging or energy.
- The identification of **new market opportunities** and of **changing social expectations**.

An overall **increase in profitability** should be achieved as a result of the above – good CSR should hopefully contribute to an increase in revenue and a reduction in costs in the long-term.

Illustration 4 – Responsibilities of businesses to stakeholders

888.com is an internet gambling site that is listed on the London Stock Exchange. Its headquarters are in Gibraltar and it operates under a licence granted by the Government of Gibraltar.

It has responsibilities to the following stakeholders:

- **Shareholders** – since it is listed on the London Stock Exchange it must comply with the rules of that exchange, including adopting the Corporate Governance Code (the code is discussed later in this chapter).
- **Employees** – to be a good employer to all its members of staff.
- **Customers** – to offer a fair, regulated and secure environment in which to gamble.
- **Government** – to comply with the terms of its licence granted in Gibraltar.
- **The public** – the company chooses to sponsor several sports teams as part of strengthening its brand. The company also tries to address public concerns about the negative aspects of gambling, for example by identifying compulsive gamblers on their site and taking appropriate action.

Test your understanding 4

Requirement:

Why should a gambling company like 888.com voluntarily choose to turn away certain business, for example known compulsive gamblers, gamblers who may be under-age, gamblers in certain countries etc?

Test your understanding 5

Humes plc adopts a socially responsible approach.

This means that the company seeks to:

A Meet the minimum obligations it owes to its shareholders

B Exceed the minimum obligations it owes to its shareholders

C Meet the minimum obligations it owes to its stakeholders

D Exceed the minimum obligations it owes to its stakeholders

5 Corporate governance

The discussion of corporate governance touches upon and builds upon aspects of business ethics and CSR.

5.1 Why corporate governance?

Corporate governance has become a major business issue driven by a succession of public 'scandals'.

In the early 1990's, the collapse of London Stock Exchange listed company Polly Peck International, the Mirror Group collapse (and the associated Maxwell pension scandal) and the liquidation of BCCI (The Bank of Credit and Commerce International) led to the formation of the **UK Corporate Governance Code**.

e.g

Illustration 5 – Why corporate governance?

Polly Peck International

Asil Nadir, the owner of Polly Peck International (PPI) built the company from very little but by the end of the 1980s it was worth over £2bn. However, the company collapsed in 1991 following the discovery of huge theft by Nadir from his own company, totalling £29m.

The Mirror Group

In 1991 the Mirror Group collapsed amid allegations that £440m had been defrauded from the company's pension scheme by its owner, the late Robert Maxwell. An enquiry concluded that Robert Maxwell and his son Kevin had a heavy responsibility for the collapse of the company, but that City Institutions were also to blame.

BCCI

In 1991 BCCI was forced to shut its doors by the Bank of England amid identification of huge fraud. Hard hit were 35 local UK councils who lost approximately £90m in investments.

More recently...

The 2008 financial crisis, which claimed Lehman Brothers, Northern Rock, Bradford & Bingley and many others, saw the code revised and radical changes to how risks are assessed within financial institutions. Other non-financial companies with corporate governance failures include Thomas Cook (travel agency – dubious accounting practices), Volkswagen (cars - emissions scandal) and Sports Direct (sports retailer – working conditions).

The code may change again since the **UK Post Office** scandal where more than 900 sub-postmasters were accused of theft, fraud and false accounting despite some managers knowing the Horizon accounting system was faulty.

The **need for corporate governance** arises because, in all but the smallest of organisations, there is a separation of ownership and control.

The **separation of ownership and control** refers to the situation in a company where the people who own the company (the shareholders) may not be the same people as those who run the company (the board of directors).

This separation can bring benefits (for example, specialist managers can often run the company more efficiently than those who own the company). However, there is a risk that the directors may run the company in their own interests, rather than those of the shareholders and the other stakeholders. This is referred to as the 'agency problem'.

The **agency problem** arises as a result of directors controlling a company whilst shareholders own the company. Directors might not act in the shareholders (or other stakeholders) best interests.

Illustration 6 – The agency problem in a company

The directors of a large, quoted company may hold a board meeting and vote themselves huge bonuses and salaries even if only modest profit targets are achieved and may also put contractual terms in place granting them huge compensation payments if they are sacked. Those votes are in the selfish best interests of the directors, and not in the best interests of the shareholders who own the company and whose interests the directors are meant to be looking after.

5.2 The meaning of corporate governance

Corporate governance is the set of processes and policies by which a company is directed, administered and controlled. It includes the appropriate role of the board of directors and the auditors of the company.

Corporate governance is concerned with the overall control and direction of a business so that the business's objectives are achieved in an acceptable manner by **ALL** stakeholders.

The following **symptoms** can indicate that there is poor corporate governance:

- **Domination of the board** by a single individual or group
- **No involvement by the board, for example** meeting irregularly, failing to consider systematically the organisation's activities and risks, or basing decisions on inadequate information
- **An inadequate control function**, for instance no internal audit, or a lack of adequate technical knowledge in key roles, or a rapid turnover of staff involved in accounting and control
- Lack of **supervision** of employees
- Lack of independent scrutiny by **external or internal auditors**
- Lack of **contact with shareholders**

- Emphasis on **short-term profitability**, leading to concealment of problems or errors, or manipulation of financial statements to achieve desired results
- **Misleading financial statements and information**

5.3 The principles of corporate governance

One of the main debates surrounding corporate governance regulation is whether it should be:

- A set of **best practice** guidelines – as in the **UK** with its **principles based** approach requiring companies to adhere to the **spirit** of the law.
- A **legal** requirement – as in the **US** with its **rules based** approach with appropriate penalties for transgression.

The US Sarbanes-Oxley Act 2002 (SOX)

In 2002, following a number of corporate governance scandals in the US, such as Enron and WorldCom, tough new corporate governance regulations were introduced.

SOX is only applicable in the US and for subsidiaries of US-based companies.

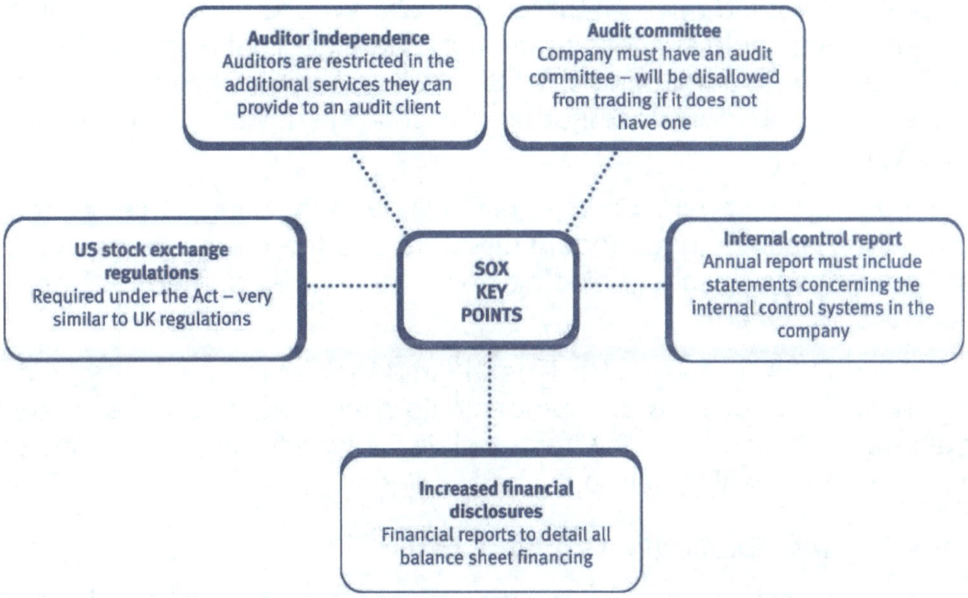

5.4 Features of best practice guidelines

Based upon the UK approach (as an example) the following represent more general features of best practice in relation to corporate governance.

In the UK, company law sets out a great many of the rules on corporate governance, especially with regards to the following:

- **Board leadership and company purpose**
- **Division of responsibilities**

- **Composition, succession and evaluation**
- **Audit, risk and internal control**
- **Remuneration**

The Financial Reporting Council (FRC) is the body responsible for promoting high standards of corporate governance in the UK. All companies listed on the London Stock Exchange are required to apply the principles of the **UK Corporate Governance Code** (last revised in 2024) and must produce a disclosure statement confirming compliance with the code and explaining any departures from it and why.

Smaller listed companies, i.e. those not in the FTSE 350 can take a more flexible approach to applying the code. (**Note:** The Financial Times Stock Exchange (FTSE) 350 is an index of the top 350 companies by capitalisation and includes the more commonly used FTSE 100 index, which contains the top 100 companies and the smaller FTSE 250 combined.)

Use of the AGM

The board should use the annual general meeting (AGM) to construct a dialogue with shareholders.

Board

The company should have an effective board whose role is to promote the long-term sustainable success of the company, generating value for shareholders and contributing to wider society .The Board should have a balance of skills, experience, independence and knowledge, and meet regularly.

The annual report should identify the Chair, Deputy Chair, Chief Executive Officer (CEO), senior independent directors and the members and chairs of the board committees. It should also disclose the number of meetings held and the directors' attendance.

The revised 2024 Code emphasises the importance of effective relationships and participation between the company, its shareholders and its stakeholders. For example, the board is now responsible for workforce policies and practices that reinforce a healthy culture.

Chair and Chief Executive Officer (CEO)

The Chair leads the board and is responsible for its overall effectiveness. The CEO runs the company on a day-to-day basis. These two roles should be separated to ensure that no one individual has too much power within the company. The Chair should be independent on appointment.

Non-executive directors (NEDs)

Directors who are involved in the execution of day-to-day management decisions are called **executive directors (EDs)**. Those who primarily only attend board meetings (and the meetings of board committees) are known as **NEDs**.

Non-executive directors should have sufficient time to meet their board responsibilities. They should provide constructive challenge, strategic guidance, offer specialist advice and hold management to account.

Current guidance is that NEDs should as far as possible be 'independent' so that their oversight role can be effectively and responsibly carried out. NEDs must not:

- have been an employee of the company in the last five years
- have had a material business interest in the company for the last three years either directly or indirectly (for example, as an employee of an organisation that has a relationship with the business)
- participate in the company's share options, performance-related pay scheme or pension schemes
- have close family ties with company directors or senior employees
- serve as a NED for more than nine years with the same company
- hold cross directorship (i.e. two or more directors sit on the board of the same third party company) or have significant links with other directors through involvement in other organisations.

If any of these apply to a NED, their independence will be seriously compromised.

Typical recommendations include:

- At least half of the board (excluding the Chair) should comprise independent NEDs. A smaller company should have at least two independent NEDs.
- One of the NEDs should be appointed the 'senior independent director'. Shareholders can contact them if they wish to raise matters outside the normal executive channels of communication.

Remuneration for all non-executive directors should not include share options or other performance-related elements.

Test your understanding 6

X retires from the post of finance director at AB plc. The company is keen to retain their experience, so invites them to become a NED of the company.

Requirement:

Can X qualify as an independent non-executive?

Nomination committees

The Board should establish a nomination committee to lead the process for appointments, ensure plans are in place for orderly succession to both the board and senior management positions, and oversee the development of a diverse pipeline for succession.

Over 50% of this committee should be made up of independent NEDs. This is to ensure that all appointments are based on merit and suitability and that the composition of the board is balanced. There should be a formal and rigorous annual review of the performance of the board, its committees, the chair and individual directors. The chair should commission a regular externally facilitated board performance review. In FTSE 350 companies this should happen at least every three years. The chair should act on the results of the board performance review by recognising the strengths and addressing any weaknesses of the board.

Remuneration committees

The Board should establish a remuneration committee of independent non-executive directors with a minimum membership of three, or in the case of smaller companies, two.

The remuneration committee should have delegated responsibility for determining the policy for executive director remuneration and setting remuneration for the chair, executive directors and senior management. It is an important principle of corporate governance that no director should be involved in setting the level of their own remuneration.

Levels of remuneration for the chair and all non-executive directors should reflect the time commitment and responsibilities of the role.

Remuneration schemes should promote long-term shareholdings by executive directors that support alignment with long-term shareholder interests. In normal circumstances, share awards granted for this purpose should be released for sale on a phased basis and be subject to a total vesting and holding period of five years or more.

Remuneration committee

Advantages of having a remuneration committee:

- It avoids the agency problem of directors determining their own levels of remuneration.
- It leaves the board free to make strategic decision about the future.

Disadvantages of having a remuneration committee:

- There is a danger that NEDs may recommend high remuneration for the executive directors in the hope that the executives will recommend high remuneration for the NEDs.
- There will be a cost involved in preparing for and holding the meetings.

Test your understanding 7

Requirement:

On what basis should NEDs be remunerated for their service to the company?

Test your understanding 8

Which one of the following can non-executive directors accept as remuneration from the company?

A A fixed daily rate for their time

B Shares

C Pension payments

D Equity options

Audit committees

The board should establish an audit committee consisting solely of independent NEDs (at least three for FTSE 350 companies and at least two for smaller listed companies). At least one member should have recent and relevant financial experience. The committee as a whole should have competence relevant to the sector in which the company operates.

The audit committee acts as an interface between the board of directors on one side and the internal and external auditors on the other side. Their main roles and responsibilities include:

- monitoring the integrity of the financial statements
- providing advice on whether the annual report and accounts, taken as a whole, is fair, balanced and understandable
- reviewing the company's risk management and internal control framework
- monitoring and reviewing the effectiveness of the company's internal audit function
- reporting to the board on how it has discharged its responsibilities.

An audit committee should be the first point of contact for auditors, improving the independence and the overall quality of the audit functions.

Test your understanding 9

Requirement:

Why are the members of an audit committee required to be NEDs rather than executive directors?

6 Chapter summary

Introduction

- The CIMA Professional Qualification
- The Operational Level
- Paper E1: Managing Finance in a Digital World
- The roles of the finance function in organisations

Change: the new norm

Introduction to the finance function

- Different types of organisation
- The functions of the an organisation
- The roles of the finance function in organisations

The roles of the finance function in organisations

The role of ethics in the role of the finance function

- The ethical responsibilities of the organisation and individuals
- CIMA's ethical guidelines
- Why business ethics are important
- Corporate code of ethics
- Corporate social responsibility

Corporate governance

- Why corporate governance?
- The meaning of corporate governance
- The principles of corporate governance
- Features of the UK corporate governance code

Test your understanding answers

Test your understanding 1

The correct answers are:

B – Medical research charity

C – Local publicly funded hospital

F – Local government agency

Test your understanding 2

The correct answer is **B**

By virtue of his family relationship John's objectivity is potentially compromised. There is also an argument that answer A (integrity), and answer E (professional behaviour) are also correct. Do note that this question is in the Study Text to get you to start thinking about these principles. Any questions given in the exam will have a definitive right or wrong answer.

Test your understanding 3

The correct answers are **A, B, C, D and E**

All the issues would be of ethical concern.

Test your understanding 4

Either you could argue that such action was ethically correct (with the company wanting to 'do the right thing'), or you could argue that a concentration on short-term profits is likely to store up problems in the longer term. If under-age gamblers are seen to be gambling on a particular website, then the public reputation of that site will be damaged and its long term profitability could be in jeopardy if governments or customers turn against it.

Test your understanding 5

The correct answer is **D**

A socially responsible organisation seeks to exceed their obligations they owe to all stakeholders not just the shareholders.

Test your understanding 6

It is very unlikely that X can be independent since they have been an employee of the company within the last five years. If the board believes that X is independent despite their recent employment then they must state the reasons for this determination.

Test your understanding 7

NEDs should be paid fees that reflect the time commitment and the responsibilities of the role, for example a fixed daily rate for when they work for the company. Share options should not be granted to the NEDs since this could detract from their independent judgement.

Test your understanding 8

The correct answer is **A**

NEDs should be paid fees that reflect the time commitment and the responsibilities of the role, for example a fixed daily rate for when they work for the company. Share options should not be granted to NEDs since this would detract from the detached judgement that they should bring, and it would also prevent them from being identified as 'independent' NEDs.

Test your understanding 9

NEDs have no day-to-day operating responsibilities, so they can view the company's affairs in a detached and independent way and liaise effectively between the main board and both sets of auditors.

Chapter

2

The activities performed by finance professionals to fulfil the roles

Chapter learning objectives

Lead	Component
A2: Describe the activities that finance professionals perform to fulfil the roles.	Describe how the finance function: (a) Collates data to prepare information for organisations (b) Provides insight to users by analysing information (c) Communicates insight to influence users (d) Supports the implementation of decisions to achieve the desired impact (e) Connects the different activities to each other

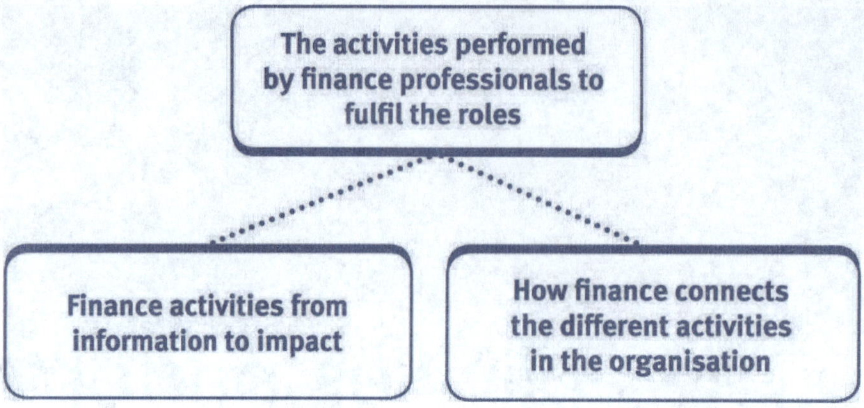

1 Introduction

In the previous chapter we discussed the roles of the finance function in organisations – understanding how the finance function **enables**, **shapes** and **narrates** value creation and preservation through planning, forecasting, resource allocation, performance management and control, and financial (corporate) reporting.

In Chapter 2 we will focus on the **activities** that finance professionals perform to fulfil these roles.

2 Finance activities from information to impact

2.1 The information to impact framework

The structure of the finance function and the activities that finance professionals perform can be best understood in the context of the basic finance activities that form the backbone of all the work of finance professionals.

These basic activities can be summarised using the **'information to impact' framework**.

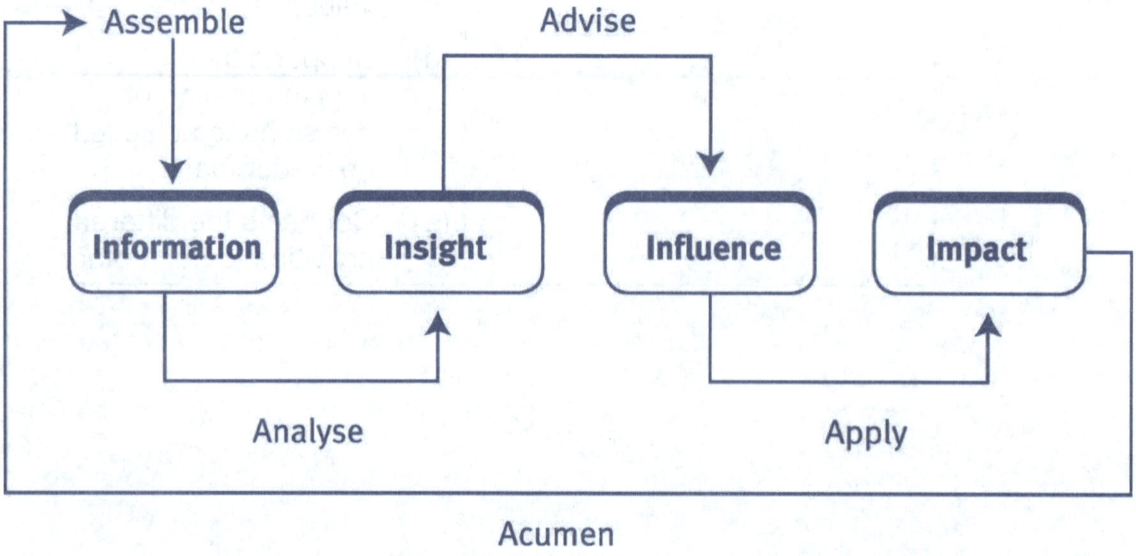

The framework has **four sequential stages to value creation and preservation** and there are **five linking activities** (the **5 A's**):

Finance activity	**Explanation of finance function activity**
Assembling **information**	**Collates data to prepare information about the organisation** Finance professionals collect and assemble data from a range of internal and external sources. Data is defined as facts or figures in a raw, unprocessed form. To become useful in the organisation this data needs to be turned into information. Information is data that has been processed in such a way that is has a meaning and use to the person who receives it. This processing may involve: • cleaning the data, i.e. identifying incomplete, inaccurate or irrelevant data and then replacing, modifying or deleting it • connecting different sources of data. Examples of assembled information would be: • management information in an accessible format for managers • accounts and returns prepared in a prescribed format for external reporting. This activity can also be viewed as the broad role of **REPORTING**.
Analysing for **insights**	**Provides insight to users by analysing information** Finance professionals analyse both financial (for example, sales information) and non-financial (for example, customer satisfaction information) information to draw out patterns and relevant insights for those who use the information. This could take the form of a comparison of the information with budgeted or historical figures. This activity can also be viewed as the broad role of **QUESTIONING**.

Finance activity	Explanation of finance function activity
Advising to **influence**	**Communicates insight to influence users** Finance professionals then: • communicate these insights and • contribute an objective and responsible perspective to influence the organisation's decision making. This activity can also be viewed as the broad role of **DEVELOPING SOLUTIONS**.
Applying for **impact** (also called **'execute'**)	**Supports the implementation of decisions to achieve the desired impact** Finance professionals apply the information to harness value for the organisation through their impact on, for example: • strategic plans • budgeting and resource allocation • performance measures • performance reviews. This activity can also be viewed as the broad role of **DEPLOYING SOLUTIONS**.
Acumen	This is different to the other A's in that it is not one of the four sequential stages to value creation and preservation. Rather, **it connects the different activities to each other and covers the entire framework**. Acumen is the ability to use practical skills and a depth of perception or discernment to make good judgements and accurate, quick and effective decisions. Finance professionals prepare valuable information (such as reports and analysis) on the outcomes achieved from different initiatives (such as investment in new technology or a new product) to help inform decision making and future proposals.

Note: The information to impact framework may not always show 'acumen' but it will always be an important dimension of the finance function.

Test your understanding 1

Requirement:

Using the 'Information to Impact' framework, match the following descriptions to the activities they are describing and put them into the correct order.

Activity	Description
Advising to influence	Providing insights that will be useful for future decisions.
Assembling information	Using information to create value for the organisation.
Applying for impact	Interpreting information to find patterns and trends that may not have been previously known.
Acumen	Processing data into meaningful, useful information.
Analysing for insights	Developing solutions to influence the decisions made by the organisation.

The **information to impact framework can be expanded** as follows:

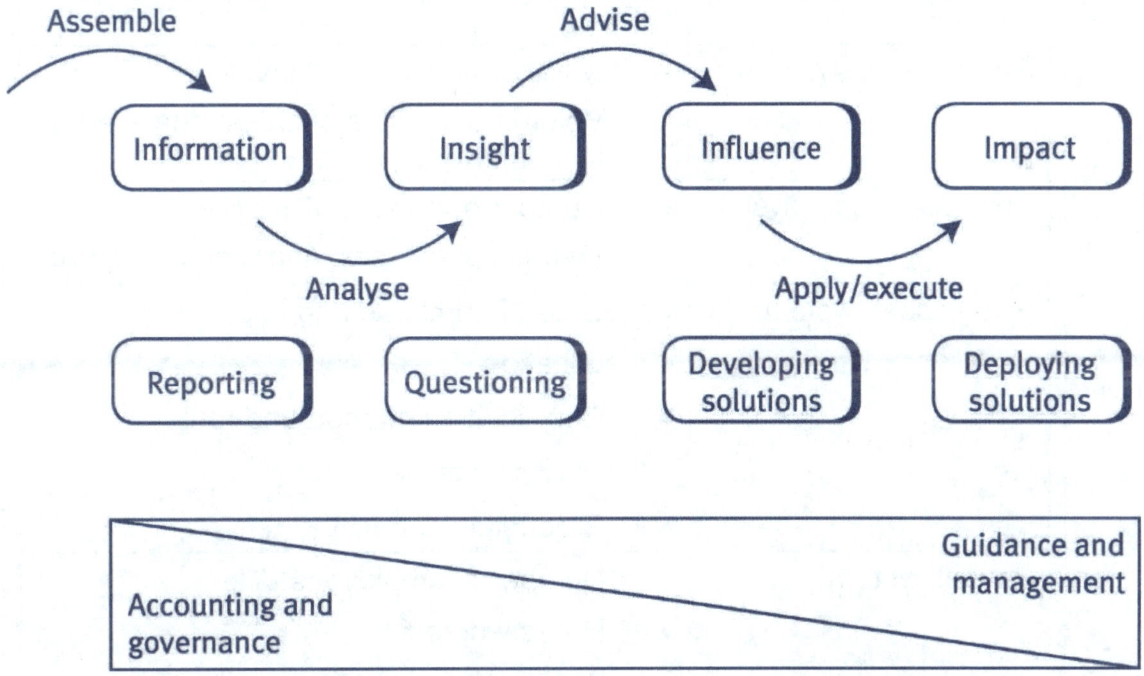

Moving from left to right there is a shift in emphasis from:

- **accounting and governance** – for example, financial (corporate) reporting and management accounting, regulatory compliance, risk management and corporate governance, to
- **guidance and management** – for example, helping the organisation to forecast and analyse trends to reach profitable growth goals.

2.2 Sources of data

Finance professionals **assemble data** from a range of **internal and external sources**. It is worth noting that organisations now have access to vast amounts of (potentially valuable) data in various formats (this is called 'big data', and this will be discussed in Chapter 5).

Internal sources

Internal sources of data may be taken from a variety of areas such as:

- accounting records including sales ledger data (such as the volume of sales), purchase ledger data (such as the value of purchases for each supplier) and fixed asset data (such as the depreciation method and rate)
- payroll data such as the number of employees, total payroll costs and total hours worked
- production data such as the number of rejected units
- sales and marketing data such as market research results or customer feedback.

Examples of internal sources of data

Source	Data
Sales ledger system	• Number and value of invoices • Volume and value of sales, analysed by customer or product
Purchase ledger system	• Number and value of invoices • Value of purchases, analysed by supplier
Fixed asset system	• Date of purchase and cost • Location • Depreciation method and rate • Service history • Production capacity
Payroll system	• Number of employees • Hours worked • Wages and salaries earned • Tax deducted
Production system	• Number of units produced • Number of units rejected
Sales/customer database	• Market research results • Customer feedback

External sources

In addition to internal data sources, there is much data to be obtained from external sources such as:

- suppliers (for example, price lists)
- customers (for example, credit scores)
- the internet and other technology, newspapers and journals (for example, competitor price lists, technological developments by industry, competitor financial statements)
- the government (for example, HMRC website).

Examples of external sources of data

External source	Data
Suppliers	• Product prices and specifications
Customers	• Product requirements • Price sensitivity
Internet and other technology, newspapers and journals	Web browsing, social media, text messages, emails, smart technologies (Chapter 5) as well as newspapers and journals are a source of data such as: • Share price • Information on competitors • Technological developments • Discussion groups
Government	• Industry and demographic statistics • Taxation and inflation rates/policy • Forecasts for economic growth

External data may be limited in its usefulness to finance professionals. The **limitations of using externally generated data** are as follows:

- External data may not be accurate.
- External data may be out of date.
- The source of the published data may not be reputable.
- External data may not meet the exact needs of the business.
- It may be difficult to gather external data, for example, from customers or competitors.

2.3 Information

To become useful in the organisation data needs to be turned into information.

The organisation needs **'good'** information for planning and decision making and to manage and control the organisation effectively.

One way of looking at the qualities of good information is to use the acronym '**accurate**'. This is explained using the illustration below.

e.g

Illustration 1 – Qualities of management reports ACCURATE

The 'accurate' acronym is explained in the context of the management reports produced by an information system. The reports from an information system should allow the organisation to run the business effectively both today and in the future. Management reports should have the following characteristics:

Characteristic	Explanation
Accurate	For example, figures should add up and there should be no typographical errors.
Complete	The reports should include all the information that is needed by the readers of the report and should be aligned to the overall objectives of the report or of the organisation.
Cost < benefit (i.e. **C**ost effective)	The cost of providing the information must be less than the benefit of generating it.
Understandable	The readers of the report must be able to understand the contents and use the contents to fulfil their needs. Presentation should be clear and in line with best practice.
Relevant	Information that is not needed by the reader(s) of the report should be omitted. Information overload can be a huge problem and can detract from the usefulness of the report. The problem of information overload may be overcome using, for example, drill-down reports (providing users with the capability to look at increasingly detailed information about a particular item) and exception reports (which are only triggered when a situation is unusual or requires management action).

Adaptable	The output reports should have the capability of being adapted to meet the needs of the user or the organisation. (Note: this 'A' can also be for '**A**ccessible' meaning that the information is accessible via the appropriate channel of communication (verbally, via reports, via emails, etc.) and is reported to the relevant person).
Timely	The information should be provided when needed and should not be provided too frequently (this can result in information overload and the cost of providing the information exceeding the benefit).
Easy to use	Information should be presented in a form recommended by the industry or organisation's best practice. It should not be too long (to prevent information overload), and it should be sent using the most appropriate communication channel, enabling the user to make decisions quickly.

Technology will play a key role in capturing this information and then displaying it. Automation involving complex machines can now do the collection of data much more effectively and much more efficiently than humans.

Information can now be produced at a press of a button, in real time and in a format the suits the needs of the organisation.

e.g

Illustration 2 – Visualisation

Visualisation is becoming a mainstream feature of many organisations' finance functions. Visualisation is about using technology to turn increasing amounts of raw data into useful information for the organisation. Traditional spreadsheet content is turned into pictures and infographics, enabling the finance function to make decisions more quickly, or to assist in understanding by non-financial users .

Technology should not be viewed by the finance function as a threat but rather as an opportunity. For the finance professional, the automation of repetitive tasks will free up their time to concentrate on creating and preserving organisational value, which is often more interesting.

2.4 Types of information

Finance professionals will **analyse** a range of information to draw out patterns and relevant insights for those who use the information. Information may include the following:

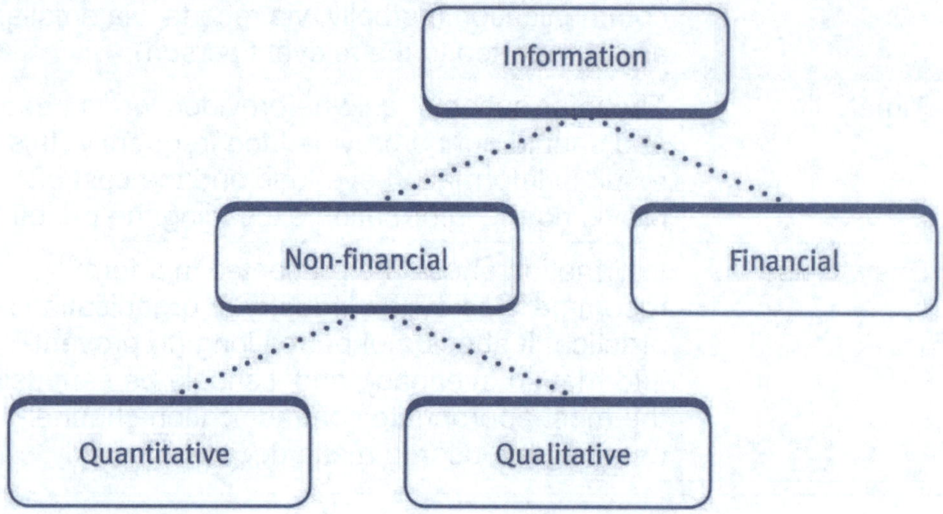

Quantitative and qualitative information will be discussed in a little more detail below.

Quantitative information

Quantitative information is information that can normally be expressed in numerical terms.

Financial information will be quantitative (for example total sales information). Non-financial information may be partly quantitative (for example, number of complaints).

There are several common mistakes that finance professionals could make when analysing quantitative information for insights. For example:

- **Presentation of information** – the choice of, say, graph or chart may be inappropriate. For example, a graph may indicate dramatic changes but only because of the scale chosen.
- **Failure to evaluate the figures using a suitable comparator or benchmark** – finance professionals may report an increase in sales of 20% on the last year but this may indicate poor performance if the market grew by 30% over the same period.
- **Collection of data** – an organisation often uses sampling to collect data and establish statistics. However, it is difficult to collect a random sample or a sample that is big enough to be representative of the entire population. This will result in poor information being produced and then analysed by finance professionals.

Qualitative information

Qualitative information is information that cannot normally be expressed in numerical terms.

Qualitative information is often in the form of opinions, for example:

- **employees** – who will be affected by certain decisions which may threaten their continued employment, or cause them to need re-training
- **customers** – who will be interested to know about new products, but will want to be assured that service arrangements, etc. will continue for existing products
- **suppliers** – who will want to be aware of the entity's plans, for example, a move to a just-in-time (JIT) environment (i.e. holding minimal or no inventory).

The fact that qualitative information is often in the form of opinions presents a problem since the information is **subjective** in nature. For example, in assessing quality of service, customers have different expectations and priorities and so are unlikely to be consistent in their judgements. One way to reduce the effect of subjectivity is for finance professionals to look at **trends** in performance since the biases will be present in each individual time period but the trend will show relative changes in quality.

It is difficult to record and process data of a qualitative nature, but qualitative factors still need to be considered when making a decision. These include:

- **The effects on the environment:** certain decisions may affect emissions and pollution of the environment. The green issue and the entity's responsibility towards the environment may seriously affect its public image.
- **Legal effects:** there may be legal implications of a particular course of action. For example, choosing to set up a subsidiary in another country might expose us to differing employment laws.

  Or a change in law may have been the cause of the decision. For example, any change in data protection law may require a business to rethink its marketing strategy and how it collects and uses customer data.
- **Political effects:** government policies, in both taxation and other matters, may impinge on the decision.
- **Timing of decision:** the timing of a new product launch may be crucial to its success.

These factors must be considered before making a final decision. Each of these factors is likely to be measured by opinion. Such opinions must be collected and coordinated into meaningful information. Qualitative data will often be transformed into quantitative information (for example, by applying a 1 to 5 scale when assessing customer satisfaction). However, it will never escape the problem of being judgemental and subjective.

3 How finance connects the different activities in the organisation

The finance function does not work in isolation. Rather the contemporary finance function **collaborates** with the other functions of the business and helps to connect the different activities that they perform.

- It provides information and insight to other functions **enabling** them to create and preserve value.

e.g

Illustration 3 – Resource allocation

The finance function can use **resource allocation** to enable the organisation to achieve its objectives.

For example, it may assist the sales and marketing function in understanding the potential impact of its promotional spend. The sales and marketing function will need to decide which products/services it should focus promotion on, the potential benefit of the different promotional tools available and the cost of these tools. The finance function can assist in providing this information and in recommending how the resources available for promotional activity should be allocated.

- It works with other functions to **shape how** the function creates and preserves value.

e.g

Illustration 4 – Performance management

The finance function can use **performance management** to assist the organisation in achieving its objectives. 'What gets measured gets done', i.e. the things that are measured get done much more often than the things that are not measured.

For example, finance may work with the operations function to set appropriate performance measures to capture what the operations function needs to do to achieve its objectives. Examples of measures could include the time taken to deliver a customer's order or the percentage wastage rate. The finance function can help to assemble the relevant performance measurement information, report it to those people who need it and question and understand any deviations between the actual and the planned performance. In this way, the operations function (and the organisation) can be assisted in achieving its objectives.

- It works with other functions to achieve the desired organisational impact for this function, **narrating how** the finance function creates and preserves value.

The finance function will communicate insight to influence stakeholders, extracting value from financial and non-financial data to help the organisation:

- make better future decisions
- enhance future operational efficiency
- better understand its customers.

The focus will be very much on what the organisation will need to do in the future to preserve and to create value.

4 Chapter summary

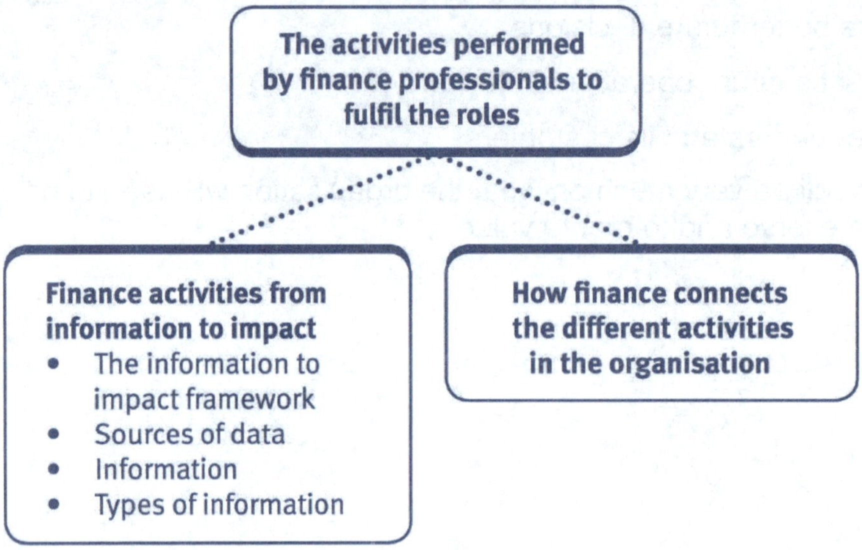

Test your understanding answers

Test your understanding 1

Using the 'Information to Impact' framework, match the following descriptions to the activities they are describing and put them into the correct order.

Activity		Description
1	Assembling information	Processing data into meaningful, useful information.
2	Analysing for insights	Interpreting information to find patterns and trends that may not have been previously known.
3	Advising to influence	Developing solutions to influence the decisions made by the organisation.
4	Applying for impact	Using information to create value for the organisation.
5	Acumen	Providing insights that will be useful for future decisions.

Chapter

3

The structure and shape of the finance function

Chapter learning objectives

Lead	Component
D1: Describe the structure and shape of the finance function.	Describe the: (a) Evolution of the shape of the finance function (b) Shape of the finance function in the digital era

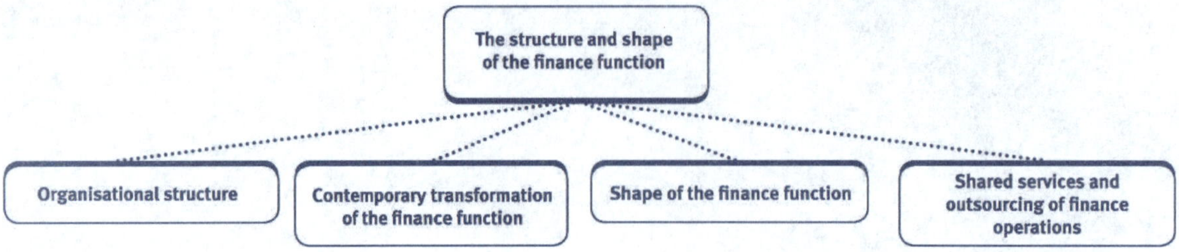

1 Introduction

In the previous chapters we looked at the different roles of the finance function and the activities that finance professionals perform to fulfil these roles. We also discussed the importance of ethics, CSR and corporate governance for an organisation and its people and, more specifically, for the finance function.

In this chapter we are going to continue to learn about the finance function, with a focus on the structure and shape of the finance function and how this enables finance to perform its role in the organisation. We will learn about the traditional shape and structure of the finance function, and we will then look at the contemporary transformation of this shape and structure, linking the description to the impact of digital technology and automation on the finance function.

Before we learn about these areas it is useful to begin by understanding the different structures that the organisation may adopt.

2 Organisational structure

Organisational structure is formed by the grouping of people into departments or sections and the allocation of responsibility and authority.

2.1 Mintzberg's effective organisation

Mintzberg suggested that an organisation can be analysed into **six building blocks** and that effective **co-ordination** will be needed to integrate the building blocks into one cohesive unit.

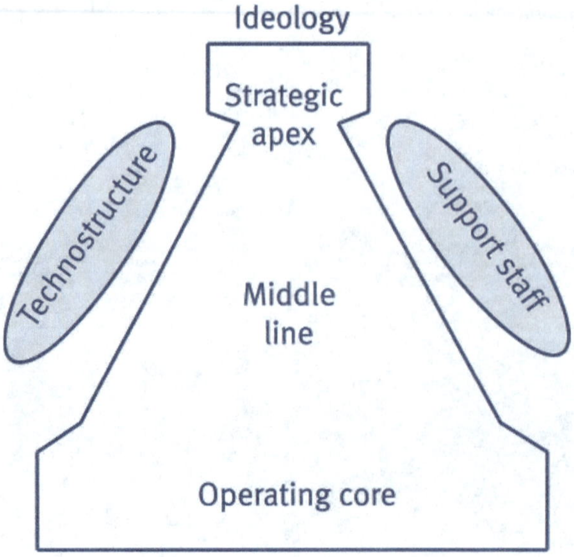

Operating core – this is the basic work of the organisation, i.e. the individuals who perform the task of producing the product or providing the service. In a small organisation this will represent nearly all the organisation, but larger organisations will require more complex arrangements.

Strategic apex – higher levels of management responsible for formulating the strategy and long-term plans.

Middle line – this links the strategic apex to the operating core and includes middle and lower level management.

Technostructure – this is responsible for designing procedures and standards. The technostructure includes accountants, computer specialists and engineers.

Support staff – provide services (such as sales and marketing or human resource management) to the organisation which support operations/ production.

Ideology – this is the organisation's values and beliefs (culture).

Test your understanding 1

The technostructure:

A is dedicated to the technical side of product and process development

B is the board of directors who decide on the financial structure and technicalities of a business

C are departments such as accounting and personnel which provide support for technical structures by co-ordinating and standardising work

D are functions to purchase materials and process them for distribution

Mintzberg's effective organisation

Co-ordinating mechanisms integrate the building blocks into a cohesive unit:

Co-ordinating mechanism	Explanation
1 Mutual adjustment	Co-ordination through informal contact
2 Direct supervision	Co-ordination through a formal hierarchy
3 Standardisation of work processes	Standardisation of work processes and specified operating procedures
4 Standardisation of outputs	Product and service specifications
5 Standardisation of skills and knowledge	Identifies training needs and the necessary skills base to do the work
6 Standardisation of norms	Cultural norms and expectations

The building blocks and the co-ordinating mechanisms vary significantly from business to business. Mintzberg **combined the building blocks and co-ordinating mechanisms in different ways** and identified **five main structural configurations**.

Structural configuration (and example)	Key building block	Key co-ordinating mechanism
Simple structure (newsagent)	Strategic apex	Direct supervision
Machine bureaucracy (heavily unionised organisation)	Techno structure	Standardisation of work
Professional bureaucracy (hospital, Kaplan)	Operating core	Standardisation of skills
Divisionalised (organisation split into business units for each product sold)	Middle line	Standardisation of outputs
Adhocracy/Innovative (advertising agency)	Operating core/ Support staff	Mutual adjustment

Test your understanding 2

According to Mintzberg's structural configurations model, which one of the following structures occur when the middle line is the key building block?

A Machine bureaucracy

B Simple

C Divisionalised

D Professional bureaucracy

2.2 Types of structure

Different categories of structure exist and will be appropriate to businesses at the various phases of their lives. A typical pattern of structural change would be as follows:

- entrepreneurial structure
- functional structure
- divisional structure
- matrix structure.

Entrepreneurial structure

- The structure is built around the owner-manager – typical of small companies (early stages of development).
- The structure is totally centralised with all key decisions being made by the strategic leader (often the owner/entrepreneur in an owner-managed business).

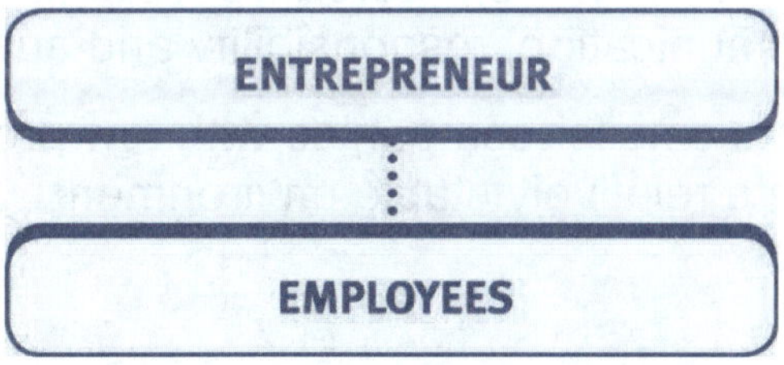

Advantages	Disadvantages
• **Fast decision making** – Only one person is making decisions • **Good control** – The small size and few layers of management means that the entrepreneur has good control over the workforce and all decisions within the organisation, leading to better goal congruence • **More responsive to market** – As soon as an element in the market changes the entrepreneur should recognise it and be quick to react • **Close bond to workforce** – The entrepreneur and employees work closely together.	• **Success is dependent on the capabilities of the owner-manager** • **Lack of career structure** for employees due to the small size of the organisation • **Cannot cope with diversification/growth** – The owner-manager will not be able to cope with, for example, the increased volume of decisions arising from the organisation becoming more successful and therefore bigger.

Functional structure

- This is common in organisations that have outgrown their entrepreneurial structure. It has been decided that employees that undertake similar tasks should be grouped into separate departments.
- A longer chain of command will exist.

The **chain of command** is the series of positions of authority or rank within an organisation that are ordered from top to bottom, creating a formal line of communication, responsibility and authority.

- Most appropriate to smaller companies with few products and locations and which exist in a relatively stable environment.

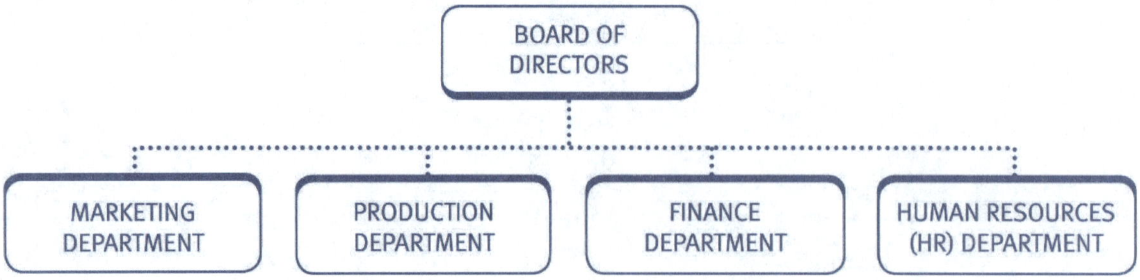

Advantages	Disadvantages
• **Economies of scale** – Roles and activities are grouped together and not duplicated leading to lower costs • **Chain of command** – Creates a formal line of communication, responsibility and authority and makes growth or diversification more manageable (e.g. compared to an entrepreneurial structure) • **Standardisation of outputs and systems** – Similar activities are grouped together resulting in standardisation and a focus on optimum quality • **Specialists more comfortable** – People with similar skills are grouped together and do not feel isolated • **Career opportunities** – Employees can work their way up through the function.	• **Empire building and conflicts between function** – Functional managers may make decisions to increase their own power or that are in the best interests of their function (empire building), rather than working in the best interests of the company overall • **Slow to adapt to market changes** – Decision making may be slow due to a longer chain of command (e.g. compared to an entrepreneurial structure) • **Cannot cope with rapid growth or diversification** – For example, specialists in the production function may not be able to cope with making a new product.

Divisional structure

- This structure occurs where an organisation is split into several **divisions** (strategic business units) – each one autonomously overseeing a **product** line/brand or **geographical** location.
- Headed by general managers who take responsibility for their own decisions and resources.

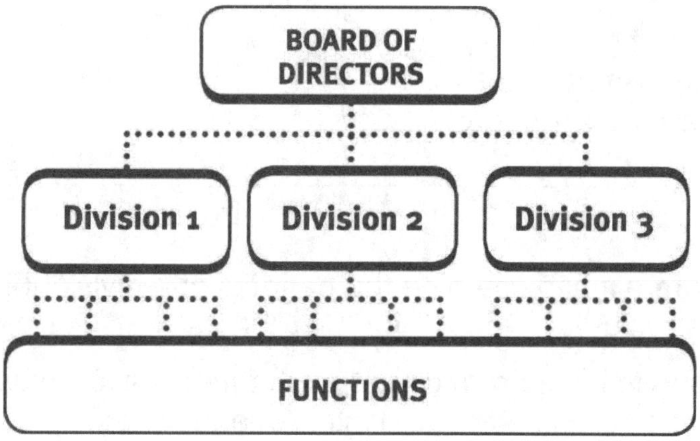

e.g

Illustration 1 – Divisional structure

AB is a company that manufactures two different products – toasters and televisions. The products require different components and require different advertising and sales and staffing.

AB therefore operates a divisional structure, with a toasters division and a television division. Each division has its own sales, purchasing, HR and advertising divisions.

The finance department, however, is still operated centrally. This is a choice made by AB as the finance department could be divisional too.

Advantages	Disadvantages
• **Enables product or geographical growth** – The structure can be easily adapted for further growth and diversification • **Clear responsibility** – Divisional managers should be able to see clearly where their area of responsibility lies • **Training of general managers** – Less focus on specialisation should result in managers having a wider view of the organisation's operations • **Decision making** – Placing responsibility for divisional profitability at the divisional level should improve the speed and (hopefully) the quality of decisions (due to local knowledge) • **Top management free to concentrate on strategic matters.**	• **Duplication of business functions** – Each division will have its own functions. This will result in more managers • **Lack of goal congruence** – Divisions may make decisions to benefits themselves to the detriment of the overall company (empire building) • **Potential loss of control** due to the autonomy given to the divisions and its managers • **Allocation of central costs can be a problem** • **Specialists may feel isolated.**

Matrix structure

- This structure aims to combine the benefits of a divisional structure and a functional structure.
- Usually found in multi-product and multi-functional organisations with significant interrelationships and interdependencies.

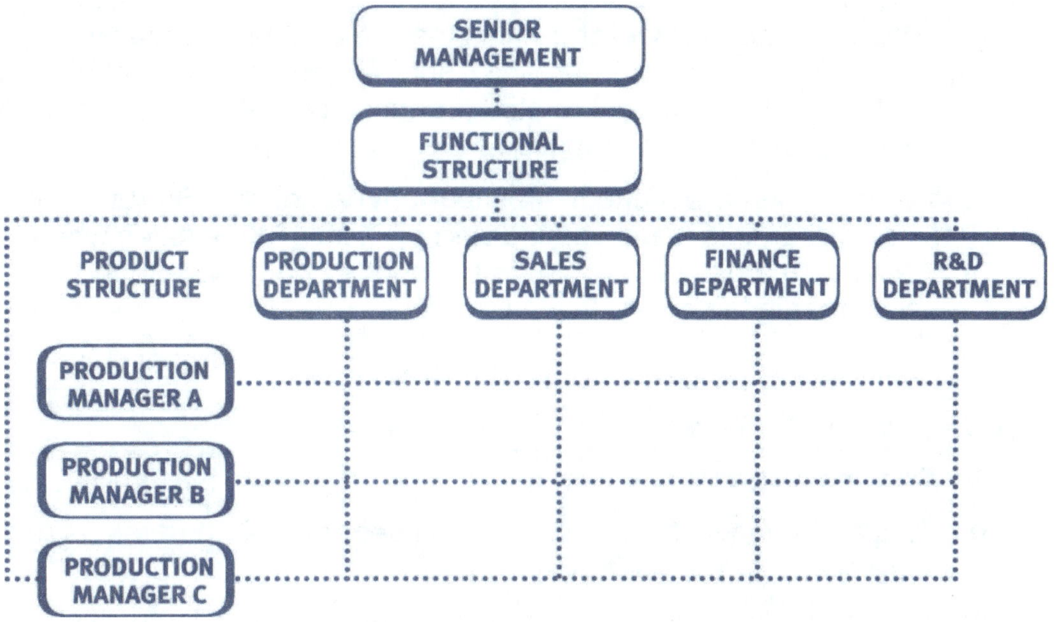

Advantages	Disadvantages
• **Advantages of both functional and divisional structures** • **Flexibility** – The matrix structure offers the flexibility to co-ordinate the tasks and people required in more complex situations • **Encourages teamwork and the exchange of opinions and expertise.**	• **Dual command** – Team members may be answerable to a product manager and a functional manager resulting in potential confusion, stress, conflict • **Dilution of functional and divisional authority** • **Lack of individual accountability** • **Time-consuming meetings.**

e.g

Illustration 2 – Starbucks' matrix structure

Starbucks Coffee Company has a matrix structure with the following four features:

1 **Functional groups** – the company is split into several functions including human resources (HR), finance and marketing. The functions are hierarchical so, for example, the company's HR function implements policies applicable to all of the company's cafes and these are then monitored and controlled by senior management.

2 **Geographical divisions** – these are based on the physical location of operations, with each division head being given the flexibility to adjust strategies and policies to reflect the local market. Starbucks has three geographical divisions: (1) Americas, (2) China and Asia-Pacific and (3) Europe, Middle East and Africa.

3 **Product-based divisions** – this feature enables Starbucks to focus on product development. There are several product divisions including (1) coffee and related products, (2) baked goods and (3) merchandise such as mugs.

4 **Teams** – team working is an important part of how Starbucks is structured. This team working is most visible in the cafes where teams are organised to deliver the goods and service to the customer in the optimum way.

Test your understanding 3

Consider the following statements:

(i) Under the functional structure, each department operates as a strategic business unit.

(ii) The matrix structure will enable rapid decision-making within the organisation.

Which of the statements is/are correct?

A (i) only

B (ii) only

C Both

D Neither

Test your understanding 4

M is a large company that operates in country G. It manufactures several different products, each of which is highly complex and extremely specialised. Its sales have grown significantly over the last several years, with each of its products producing a roughly equal amount of M's overall revenue.

Which organisational structure is most likely to be appropriate for M?

A Geographic

B Divisional

C Functional

D Entrepreneurial

2.3 Centralisation and decentralisation

Another method of analysing structures is by reference to the degree of autonomy or the level at which decisions are made.

In a **centralised structure,** the upper levels of an organisation's hierarchy retain the authority to make decisions.

In a **decentralised structure,** the authority to make decisions is passed down to units and people at lower levels.

Factors affecting the amount of (de)centralisation

The following factors will affect the amount of (de)centralisation:

- **Management style** – for example, managers who want to retain control may operate a centralised structure.
- **The ability of management/employees** – for example, the more able the employees, the more decisions they can be entrusted with and the greater the level of decentralisation.
- **Geographical spread** – this may make central control more difficult resulting in a decentralised structure.
- **The size of the organisation** – small organisations can retain a level of central control relatively easily.
- **Ideology (Mintzberg's organisation)** – the organisation's values and beliefs (culture) may, for example, focus on employee autonomy and empowerment; this would make a more decentralised structure more appropriate.

Most organisations will operate a degree of both centralised and decentralised decision making; the extent of each will be influenced by the factors above.

Illustration 3 – A centralised organisation

A good example of a centralised business would be a multinational fast food chain such as McDonalds or Burger King. Most of the locations of these international fast-food chains are privately owned **franchises** (a franchise is the purchase of the right to exploit a business brand in return for a capital sum and a share of the profit or turnover).

A centralised structure enables control and consistency to be maintained across thousands of outlets thus protecting its brand and reputation, while saving on overheads such as local payroll and accounting functions, through economies of scale.

The advantages and disadvantages of decentralisation are:

Advantages of decentralisation	Disadvantages of decentralisation
• Senior management free to concentrate on strategy • Better local decisions due to local expertise • Better motivation due to increased empowerment of employees and a more defined career path • Quicker responses/flexibility due to reduced bureaucracy and increased autonomy	• Loss of control by senior management and lack of standardisation • Dysfunctional decisions due to a lack of goal congruence • Poor decisions made by inexperienced managers • Training costs • Duplication of roles within organisation • Extra costs in obtaining information since it is stored in several locations

(**Note:** The advantages and disadvantages of centralisation have not been discussed but are largely the opposite of the points above).

Test your understanding 5

Which of the following is not a likely additional cost to an organisation caused by decentralisation?

A Additional training costs are often required in a decentralised organisation

B Duplication of roles, leading to higher costs

C Extra costs of gathering information from various sources and locations

D Lost sales due to a lack of local knowledge and expertise

2.4 Tall and flat organisations

Organisations can also be classed as tall or flat depending on the length of the scalar chain and the breadth of the span of control.

The **scalar chain** is the line of authority which can be traced up or down the chain of command, from the most senior member of staff to the most junior. It therefore relates to the number of levels of management within an organisation.

Illustration 4 – British Army chain of command

The British Army is a good example of an organisation with a long chain of command. There are two main groups of staff with a ranking system existing within each group:

1 **Commissioned officers** are ranked from top to bottom as follows – Field Marshal, General, Lieutenant General, Major General, Brigadier General, Colonel, Lieutenant Colonel, Major, Captain, Lieutenant, Second Lieutenant.

2 **Other ranks and non-commissioned officers** are ranked from top to bottom as follows – Regimental Sergeant Major, Company Quarter Master Sergeant, Company Sergeant Major, Staff Sergeant, Sergeant, Corporal, Lance Corporal, Private.

The **span of control** considers how many people report to one superior.

Factors that influence the span of control

The factors that influence the span of control include the:

- **Nature of the work** – the more repetitive or simple the work, the wider the span of control can be.
- **Type of personnel** – the more skilled and motivated the managers and other staff members are, the wider the span of control can be.
- **Location of personnel** – if personnel are all located locally, it takes relatively little time and effort to supervise them. This allows the span of control to become wider.

Test your understanding 6

Consider the following statements:

(i) The scalar chain relates to the number of people over whom a manager has authority.

(ii) A business with highly skilled, motivated members of staff will tend to have a wider span of control than a business with demotivated employees.

Which of these statements is/are correct?

A (i) only

B (ii) only

C Both

D Neither

A '**tall**' organisation has many levels of management (a long scalar chain) and a narrow span of control.

A '**flat**' organisation has few levels of management (a short scalar chain) and a wide span of control.

e.g

Illustration 5 – A move by organisations to a flatter structure

Many organisations are adopting (and seeing the benefits of) a flatter structure. For example, Google's core values from the beginning were to have a flat organisation, a lack of hierarchy and a collaborative environment. This flatter organisation encourages employees to take initiative without needing approval from multiple managers. They empower employees to take charge, help make decisions and feel responsible for the company's success.

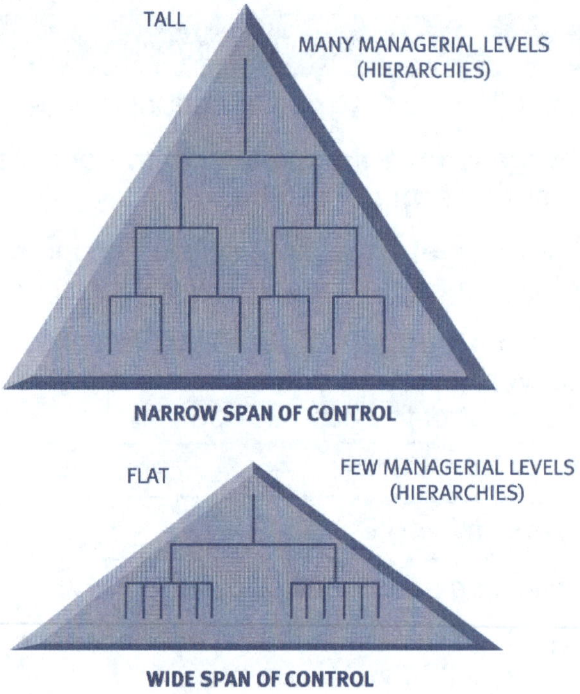

It is worth noting that **tall** organisations tend to be **more bureaucratic** and take **longer to make decisions**, due to the large number of levels of management that need to be involved.

However, **flat** organisations are not without their problems. These organisations tend to have **weaker control** and **fewer chances for employees to progress** or be promoted within the organisation as fewer middle management roles are available.

Test your understanding 7

Requirement:

If a managerial structure has many levels of management, is it likely to have a narrow or wide span of control at each level of management?

2.5 Contemporary transformation of organisations

- It is worth noting that the **discussion above has focused on the historical organisational configurations and structural dimensions** that an organisation may adopt.
- Although much of this is still relevant, the changing expectations of customers, competitive pressures, a changing political and economic landscape and huge technological innovations have changed many of the traditional organisational forms and boundaries.
- Organisations have adopted new forms, for example outsourcing many aspects of the organisation's work to specialist providers and have focused on factors such as flexibility rather than having a more rigid set of organisational boundaries in place.

Illustration 6 – Nike

The sports good manufacturer, Nike, outsources production activities but retains total control over design and quality specifications.

This contemporary transformation will be reviewed in the remainder of this chapter, with a specific focus on the contemporary transformation of the finance function.

Illustration 7 – General Electric

The term 'boundaryless' organisation originated from Jack Welch in the early 1990s when he was Chairman of General Electric. He recognised that the modern environment was subject to continuous innovation and change, thus requiring management to develop more flexible organisations. He aimed to achieve competitive advantage by replacing vertical hierarchies with horizontal networks; linking together traditional functions into inter-functional teams and forming strategic alliances with suppliers, customers and even competitors.

3 Contemporary transformation of the finance function

3.1 Introduction

In Chapter 2 we discussed the finance activities from information to impact. The basic activities of the finance function are still relevant in today's organisations but there has been a shift in emphasis regarding the importance of each of the activities. The broad areas of finance such as financial operations, external reporting, financial planning and analysis (FP&A) and decision support etc. remain.

Historically, the overall mandate of the finance function was to focus on organisational efficiencies and to **reduce operational costs**. This focus has resulted in organisations achieving optimum operational efficiency.

Technology has, to a large extent, replaced the historical mandate of the finance function, with machines being capable of monitoring operational costs and patterns of organisational efficiency.

If we relate this back to the information to impact framework this has resulted in **automation** of much of the '**assembly**' and '**analysis**'.

e.g

Illustration 8 – Automation of the finance function's activities

Advances in technology are providing opportunities to automate many of the activities of the finance function. For example, robotic process automation (RPA) is providing opportunities to automate many routine, clerical 'assembly' activities.

RPA is a software-based approach that replicates user actions to reduce or eliminate human intervention in mundane, repetitive and manually intensive processes.

RPA started off in manufacturing (for example, with robotic vehicle assembly lines) but is now used across other functions such as finance. Rapid strides in the development of this technology mean machines are now encroaching on activities previously assumed to require human judgement and experience, such as **data entry, automated formatting, reconciliations and foreign exchange transactions**.

This allows finance staff to re-focus on **higher value, customer-focused activities.**

Finance professionals should not view this automation as a threat but as an **opportunity**. The core accounting role will still be an essential foundation of the finance function but enabled by new technologies, the function can now be a more influential player in the organisation.

Technology allows the contemporary finance function to refocus its energy on revenue and value creation.

The finance function will no longer work largely in isolation but will **collaborate** with others from across the organisation to drive business transformation that creates shareholder value.

To do this the finance function will need to reallocate its resources to the '**advising**' and '**applying/executing**' activities in the information to impact framework.

Test your understanding 8	
Read the following statements and decide if each one is true or false.	
A	Because of advancements in technology the basic activities of the finance function are no longer relevant
B	Technology allows the contemporary finance function to refocus its energy on value creation
C	Technology has meant that a large amount of the assembly and analysis activities can be automated
D	Technology has meant that a large amount of the advising and applying activities can be automated

3.2 Can the finance function cope with this shift?

Traditionally, organisational finance functions have proved their worth because of particular areas of expertise. These have centred on the generation of information. With digital and technological capabilities increasing, these functions are recognising a need to develop new areas of expertise (for example, communicating insights) and build upon these to develop particular competencies.

However, the finance function is well positioned to meet this changing mandate since:

- it has a unique end-to-end view of the organisation, understanding that every activity has a financial consequence
- its accounting information is trusted and credible
- it already provides a framework for performance management, for example through management accounting
- it brings professional, evidence based objectivity to decision making.

3.3 The information to impact framework revisited

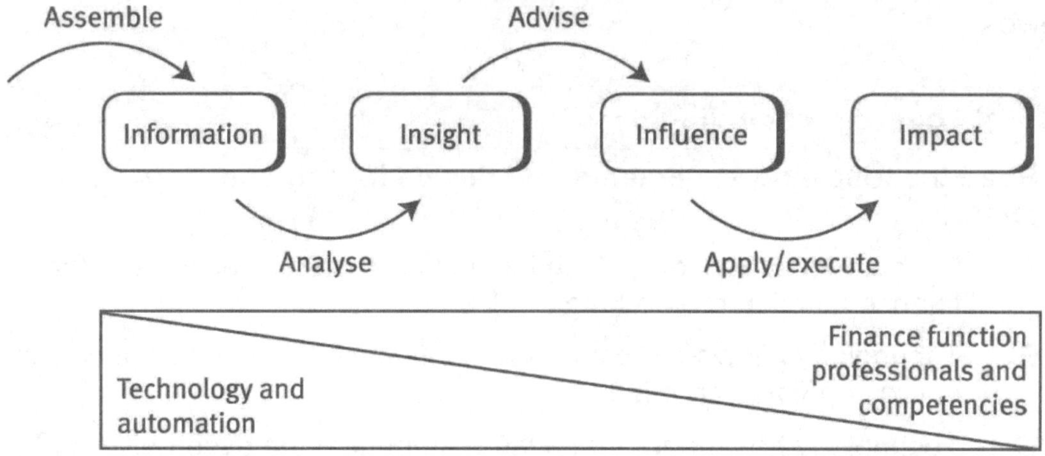

The information to impact framework clearly shows that:

- **Technology and automation** will play an important role in all of the activities of the finance function but will have the largest impact on the '**assembly**' and '**analysis**' activities.
- This will 'free up' the resource of the **finance function professionals** who can now place greater focus on the '**advising**' and '**applying/executing**' activities.
- The finance function will need to develop its **competencies**:
  - firstly, so that it is able to **use the up to date technology** and
  - secondly, so that it has the **necessary skills to provide the influence and impact required**.

e.g

Illustration 9 – New competencies required by finance function

The World Economic Forum published a 'Future of Jobs' report in 2025. The top fastest growing jobs predicted for 2025-2030 were for Big Data specialists, FinTech engineers, AI and machine learning specialists, software and applications specialists...data warehousing specialists...delivery drivers, Internet of Things specialists, data analysts...

The top fastest declining jobs were postal service clerks, bank tellers, data entry clerks, cashiers...

The share of tasks performed by humans would decrease from 47% to 33% whilst technology performing the same tasks would increase from 22% to 34%. (The balance of tasks would be shared between humans and technology.)

The report also stated that the most looked for skill by employers was **analytical thinking** followed by resilience, flexibility, agility, leadership and social influence.

Note: terms such as Big Data, Artificial Intelligence (AI) and the Internet of Things, etc. will be expanded upon more fully later in the text.

Test your understanding 9

Which of the following THREE activities are likely to be the most impacted by technology and automation?

A Processing data into information

B Producing monthly variance reports

C Developing solutions to influence the decisions of an organisation

D Analysing non-financial information for insights

E Using information to create value for the organisation

4 Shape of the finance function

4.1 Introduction

In this section we are going to look at the shape of the finance function and how this shape is evolving because of advances in technology, the changing mandate of the finance function and the changing capabilities of the finance function.

The evolution of the shape of the finance function is as follows:

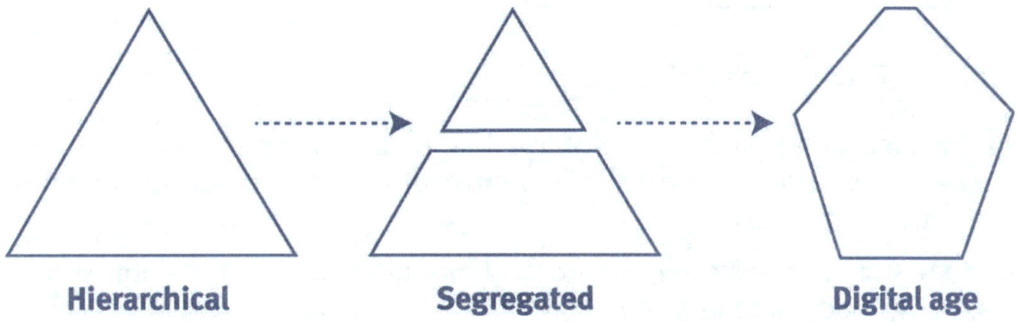

The shape is migrating from:

- **a hierarchical triangle (traditional shape)** – containing a broad base of finance workers reporting upwards to a series of ever narrower management levels
- **to a segregated triangle (last 20 years)** – globalisation and technological advances meant that much of the routine processing of the finance function could be carried out by a shared service centre (i.e. the centralisation of this routine processing into one place). The bottom section of the segregated triangle represents the finance function activity carried out by these shared service centres
- **and finally to the diamond shape (today's digital age)** – the traditional triangular base is being eroded due to automation of many of the basic activities of the finance function.

We will begin by briefly looking at the traditional hierarchical shape of the finance function before looking at how this shape could/has evolve(d) to a diamond shape.

Test your understanding 10

Pick from the following options to complete the sentences below:

Options:

Traditional hierarchy

Legislation

Diamond shape

Globalisation

Boundaryless structure

Technology

Governance

Sentences:

The shape of the finance function has evolved from a ________________ to a ________________ in today's digital age.

This has primarily been driven by ________________ and ________________.

4.2 Traditional hierarchical triangle

In Chapter 1 we learned that the roles of the finance function can be summarised as **enabling**, **shaping how** and **narrating how** the organisation creates and preserves value.

We can understand the traditional hierarchical triangle shape in the context of these roles. In the traditional triangle:

- at the bottom of the triangle, there is a broad base of finance workers carrying out the operational 'enabling' roles of planning, forecasting and resource allocation.
- in the middle of the triangle, there is a narrower set of management level finance workers who are reported to from the level below and who carry out the 'shaping how' roles of performance management and control.
- at the top of the triangle sit a narrower group of senior finance staff. These staff are reported to from below and they concentrate on the 'narrating how' role of financial (corporate) reporting.

4.3 Diamond shape

Evolution into a diamond shape

The traditional hierarchical triangle is evolving into a diamond shape as follows:

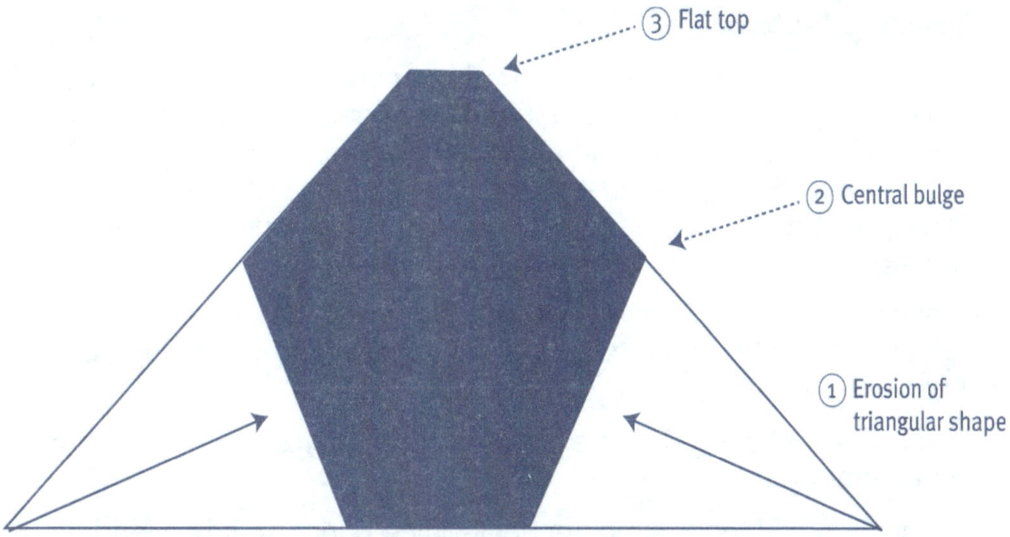

The evolution can be summarised as follows:

1 Technological automation has **eroded the traditional triangular shape** with much of the lower level assembly and processing tasks now being carried out by technology rather than finance professionals.

2 The **central bulge** in the diamond shape is due to many of the higher-value services now being offered by centres of excellence (or shared service centres) where finance professionals will work as part of a multi-disciplinary team, assembled in skills combinations that support the business.

3 The **flat top** of the structure shows a move to a collaborative finance leadership approach – with the chief finance officer (CFO) and other senior finance staff working with and alongside the chief executive officer (CEO).

e.g

Illustration 10 – The diamond shape of the finance function

Industry experts have considered the need to design a finance function that is fit for the future. Some useful quotes highlight the importance of the following:

1 **Tackling technology**

'Finance is actually no different from any other department in our business. The problem facing it can be encapsulated in one word: technology. Automation and all the efficiencies that come with improved technology are removing many of the function's traditional tasks. I think that's a good thing, because they are mundane and no one really wants to do them.'

(Daniel O'Toole, CEO of Retail Merchandising Services, a development company that supports many of the UK's biggest high-street names.)

2 **A focus on strategic decision making and growth rather than historical data**

'Finance is no longer simply a back-office concern. It is a leading function in the business. It's up front, collating the intelligence and presenting it in a way that is easily understood. In the past it was just about reporting financial performance in the preceding year or quarter, but now things are so different. Today it's about combining financial data with non-financial intelligence to get a much wider perspective on how the business has performed and to predict how it will perform – and it's about using all of this to make sound business decisions.'

(Hari Punchihewa, deputy chief executive and finance director at the University of Derby (UK).)

3 **Finance as a business partner**

'Management accountants don't really exist now as they once did. They are being replaced with what I would call finance business partners. Accounting was always seen as the boring part of the business, but the new position of finance business partner is much more exciting and creative.'

(Jim Jordan, finance director at the IoD (Institute of Directors – UK).)

The four levels of the diamond shape

This evolution has resulted in a diamond shape. The diamond can be split into four levels. **Level 1 is at the top** and **level 4 is at the bottom** of the diamond.

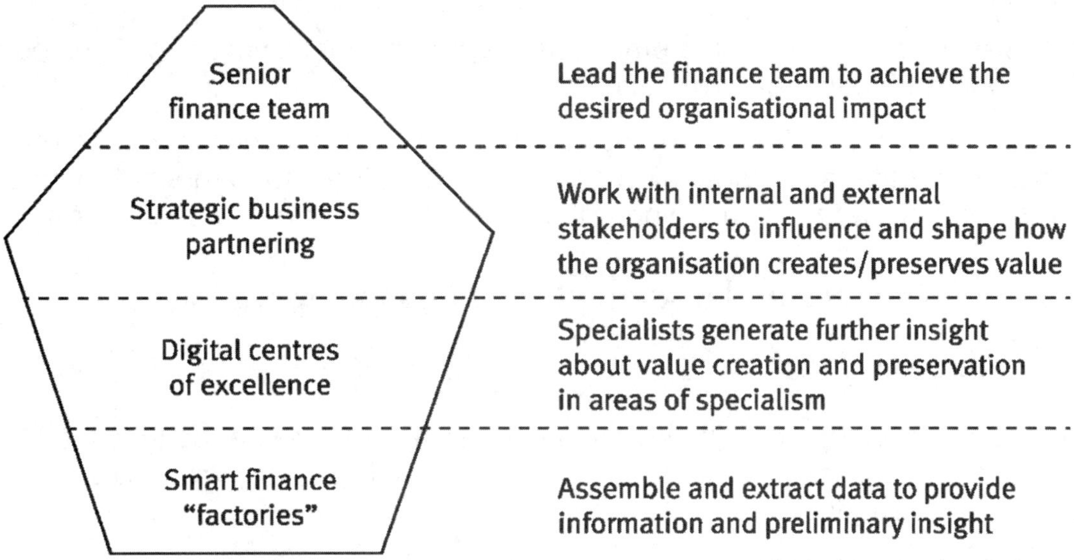

Note: This is an important diagram to learn and to understand for the exam.

Why the shape of the finance function is changing

There are three main reasons why the shape of the finance function is changing:

Reason	**Explanation**
The changing mandate for finance	The contemporary transformation of the finance function better enable the finance function to focus on level 2 'strategic business partnering' and explain why the diamond shape bulges outwards at this level.
Technology	Technology has impacted the finance function in two main ways: Firstly, it has supported the automation of many of the management information processes and much of the reporting performed at level 4. Secondly, it has increased the need for skills at levels 2 and 3.
Finance function capability	The changing mandate for finance combined with advancements in technology have changed the competencies required of the finance function. Level 2 is the focal point of these changes and is another reason for the bulge in the finance function shape at this point.

Will the shape of the finance function continue to evolve?

The shape of the finance function will continue to evolve in response to the changing roles of the function, what is clear is that finance will no longer just be for pure accountants.

- There will be an increasing emphasis on professional level roles requiring support and management skills.
- There will be a continued emphasis on specialist knowledge (for example, in different areas of automation and technology) leading to the formation of **multi-disciplinary teams** who will become members of the finance team.

5 Shared services and outsourcing of finance operations

5.1 Introduction

Contemporary developments in the role and activities of the finance function have for some organisations meant a structural reconfiguration, with solutions based on, for example:

- greater or less centralisation
- offshoring – the relocation of business activities (such as call centres) from the home country to another country
- shared service provision
- business partnering
- outsourcing.

The local variations are endless, but the aim is the same – to make the finance function a valued and worthwhile essential of organisational functioning.

Two of these options, outsourcing and shared service provision, are discussed below.

Outsourcing means contracting out aspects of the work of the organisation previously done in-house, to specialist providers.

A **shared service centre** may be established for a particular activity of the organisation. The term describes a situation whereby, a usually large, multinational organisation with processing centres in all or several of the countries in which it operates chooses to consolidate these activities at one site, or shared service centre. This is sometimes referred to as '**internal outsourcing**'.

5.2 Introduction to outsourcing

The outsourcing of many aspects of business activity is one strategy that has been suggested as a source of adding value and streamlining activities to maintain competitiveness.

In theory, any of the operations that a business performs can be outsourced. However, an organisation will **often outsource its non-core services** to a third party, allowing them to focus on their core competencies which are integral to the organisation's ability to create and to add value.

Non-core activities may include:

- facilities management
- human resource management
- cleaning services
- catering services and
- legal services.

The organisation's core competencies are something that they can do that drives competitive advantage and is very difficult for a competitor to emulate. It **may be unwise for an organisation to outsource activities in which they have a core competence** as this could erode competitive advantage.

e.g

Illustration 11 – Outsourcing in a clothing retailer

In clothing retail, it may be the case that most firms have outsourced production to Asian manufacturers to gain low costs. This outsourcing may be essential just to be a feasible player in the market.

For example, Nike outsources the manufacturing of some of its products to third-party factories primarily located in countries such as China, Vietnam, and Indonesia. These countries offer cost advantages due to lower labour costs and established manufacturing infrastructures.

However, clothing retailers may still retain aspects of the work in which they have a core competence in-house.

For example, Nike can concentrate on its core competencies such as its design and innovation. The company invests heavily in research and development (R&D) to create cutting-edge products and technologies that appeal to consumers.

Test your understanding 11

Canterell is a bank based in country Z. It is considering outsourcing its IT function. Its current IT systems are considered excellent, which is important, as the banking industry in country Z is highly competitive and innovative.

Which of the following statements regarding this proposal is correct?

A Canterell will definitely be able to improve its in house IT expertise as a result

B Outsourcing could cause Canterell a loss of competitive advantage

C It will be easy for Canterell to bring IT back in-house if they are not satisfied with the outsource supplier

D It is not possible to outsource IT

Outsourcing has become increasingly common in organisations. The advantages and disadvantages include:

Advantages of outsourcing

The main reason for outsourcing is that it is cheaper. **Cost advantages** can come from a number of sources:

- A large supplier may benefit from economies of scale in production.
- The firm concerned will benefit from reduced capital expenditure.
- Reduced headcount.
- Research and development expenditure may also be saved.

There can also be **quality advantages**:

- The supplier may have superior skills and expertise. For example, Apple's main reason for outsourcing to China is superior manufacturing capability rather than cost savings.
- Outsourcing may solve the problem of the company having a skills shortage in certain areas.

Other advantages include the following:

- The supplier may have greater production expertise and efficiencies, leading to faster and more flexible supply of components.
- The management of the customer is no longer a distraction, and so management can focus on core business activities.
- The organisation can exercise buyer power over suppliers ensuring favourable terms and conditions.
- The organisation has greater flexibility to switch suppliers based on changing cost/quality considerations.

Disadvantages

- Cost issues – the supplier will want to make a profit margin, suggesting it may be cheaper to do the work in house. In addition, if dealing with a major supplier the organisation may be vulnerable to future price rises.
- Loss of core competence – the service may represent (or contribute to) a core competence for the organisation and therefore outsourcing may lead to a loss of competitive advantage.
- Transaction costs – arise from the effort put into specifying what is required, co-ordinating delivery and monitoring quality.
- Finality of decision – once a service has been contracted out it may be difficult to take back in-house later, for example due to a loss of in-house expertise.
- Risk of loss of confidential information.
- Risk of continuity of supply if the supplier has problems.
- Difficulty agreeing/enforcing contract terms.
- Damage to employee morale if redundancies occur or if organisational culture is eroded.

e.g

Illustration 12 – Outsourcing advantages

Organisations can outsource a wide range of activities and processes.

Robotic process automation (RPA) was discussed earlier on in this chapter. Organisations may want to harness this new technology but do not have the resources or expertise to do so effectively. Therefore, the organisation may outsource this business process to an expert in this field.

This outsourcing will allow the organisation to harness the potential to automate business processes and to enjoy the benefits of RPA including:

- faster processing and improved productivity
- lower costs
- improvements accuracy and compliance
- a focus on higher value, customer focused activities.

Test your understanding 12

Q Co is considering outsourcing its IT function to a third party IT company on a fixed fee basis. Q does not consider IT to be core function. A junior accountant has produced a list of possible advantages of this to the company.

Which FOUR of the following factors are likely advantages of Q outsourcing its IT function?

A It will reduce the probability of other organisations gaining access to Q's information

B It will reduce uncertainty relating to how much the IT function will cost Q each year

C The third party company may have access to IT skills that Q lacks

D If the third party fails to perform well, Q can easily bring the IT function back in-house

E The third party company may have access to more economies of scale for IT, allowing Q to save money on its IT function

F It will reduce Q's dependence on its suppliers

G Q is likely to gain competitive advantage over rivals with its IT systems

H It is likely to allow Q to focus its management time on core activities

Service level agreements

At least some of the potential disadvantages of outsourcing can be controlled though the use of effective service level agreements.

A **service level agreement** (SLA) is a negotiated agreement between the supplier and the customer and is a legal agreement regarding the level of service to be provided.

Content of service level agreements

- A detailed explanation of exactly what service the supplier is offering to provide.
- The targets/benchmarks to be used and the consequences of failing to meet them.
- Expected response time to technical queries.
- The expected time to recover the operations in the event of a disaster such as a systems crash, terrorist attack, etc.
- The procedure for dealing with complaints.
- The information and reporting procedures to be adopted.
- The procedures for cancelling the contract.

Transaction cost theory

Transaction costs are the indirect costs (i.e. non-production costs) incurred in performing a particular activity.

When outsourcing, transaction costs arise from the effort that must be put into specifying what is required and subsequently co-ordinating delivery and monitoring quality.

There are three main types of transaction costs:

- **Search and information costs** – for example, the cost of determining which supplier is cheapest.
- **Bargaining costs** – the cost of agreeing on an acceptable SLA.
- **Policing and enforcement costs** – are the costs of making sure the other party sticks to the terms of the contract and taking appropriate action (often through the legal system) if this turns out not to be the case.

High transaction costs for outsourcing may suggest an in-house solution whereas low transaction costs for outsourcing would support the argument to outsource.

Test your understanding 13

Which of the following statements is/are true?

	True?
High transaction costs will usually lead to a company deciding to outsource	
A robust SLA will prevent the risk of a loss of confidential data	
Transaction costs include bargaining costs	
Transaction costs are incurred when outsourcing is used	
Transaction costs include the cost of production	

Transaction cost theory (Wiliamson and Coase)

Organisations choose between two methods of obtaining control over resources:

- the ownership of assets (hierarchy solutions – decisions over production, supply, and the purchases of inputs are made by managers and imposed through hierarchies) and
- buying-in the use of assets (the market solution – individuals and firms make independent decisions that are guided and co-ordinated by market prices).

The decision is based on a comparison of the transaction costs of the two approaches.

Transactions have three dimensions that determine the costs associated with them:

- uncertainty – the more uncertain the environment the harder it is to write effective long-term contracts and the more likely the acquisition of a supplier is
- the frequency with which the transactions recur; and
- asset specificity – the extent to which the transacting firms invest in assets whose value depends on the business relationships remaining intact. The greater the specificity of the assets involved, the greater the likelihood that a transaction will take place within the firm.

These factors translate into **'make-or-buy' decisions**: whether it is better to provide a service from within the organisation, with hierarchical co-ordination (make), or from outside the organisation (buy), with market co-ordination. Williamson and Coase argue that it is the third dimension, the degree of asset specificity, which is the most important determinant of transaction. The more specific the assets are to a transaction then, all other things being equal, the greater will be the associated transaction costs and the more likely that the transaction will be internalised into a hierarchy (make).

Conversely, when the productive assets are non-specific the process of market contracting is more efficient because transaction costs will be low.

Asset specificity

An asset is said to be transaction-specific if its value to a given transaction is greater than its value in its best alternative use. The greater the gap between these two values, the greater the degree of specificity of the asset. Williamson and Coase suggested six main types of asset specificity:

- Site specificity – suggests that once sited the assets may be very immobile.

  For example, a car components manufacturer locating a components factory near to a large customer's manufacturing plant.

- Physical asset specificity – when parties make investments in machinery or equipment that are specific to a certain task these will have lower values in alternative uses.

  For example, Cadbury (the chocolate bar manufacturer) has bespoke production lines producing certain types of chocolate bar. In their entirety, the production line would be of little use to another chocolate bar manufacturer unless they were to produce an identical bar of chocolate.

- Human asset specificity – occurs when workers may have to acquire relationship-specific skills, know-how and information that is more valuable inside a particular transaction than outside it.

  For example, a consultant may have to acquire detailed knowledge of a client's in-house developed systems, but this knowledge may not be useful on other clients.

- Brand name capital specificity refers to becoming affiliated with a well-known 'brand name' and thus becoming less free to pursue other opportunities.

  For example, an actor may become 'typecast' in a particular role or show.

- Dedicated asset specificity entails investments in general-purpose plant that are made at the behest of a particular customer.

  For example, the car components manufacturer above invests in dedicated machinery to make bespoke components for just one manufacturer. Should the contract be lost, these components may have to be adapted for sale elsewhere.

- Temporal specificity – arises when the timing of performance is critical, such as with perishable agricultural commodities .e.g. milk for cheese, where a farmer may struggle to find alternative processors at short notice.

5.3 Outsourcing the activities of the finance function

Introduction

Outsourcing of the finance function's activities has become increasingly common in organisations in recent times. The emphasis has been on **reducing costs** but outsourcing has also enabled the retained finance function (i.e. the finance function performing the non-outsourced activities) **to focus on strategic change** by working more closely with the business to provide **business partnering** to help improve decision making.

Which finance function activities should be outsourced?

A key consideration is which finance activities should be outsourced.

- Transactional processes (such as accounts payable/receivable, payroll, travel and entertainment and cash management) tended to be very popular to outsource.
- However, improvements in provider capabilities have also resulted in outsourcing of services such as statutory and regulatory accounting, financial reporting and tax, management accounting, budgeting and forecasting.

Relating this back to the '**information to impact framework**' these activities relate largely to the left hand side of the framework and the '**assembly**' and '**analysis**' activities.

Benefits and drawbacks of outsourcing the finance function's activities

<table>
<tr><th>Benefits</th><th>Drawbacks</th></tr>
<tr><td>

- **Cost reduction** – outsourcing can deliver significant economies of scale through the use of standardised processes and leading-edge technology.
- **Radical transformation** – outsourcing can enable broad structural change. Low value, non-core activities can be moved to the external provider allowing the organisation to shift internal resources from operations to innovation, i.e. the 'advisory' and 'application' parts of the 'information to impact framework'.

  Note: A radical transformation and fundamental rethinking of business processes is called business process re-engineering (BPR).
- **Access to superior capabilities, expertise and resources** of the specialist provider.
- **Business partnering** – the retained finance function can concentrate on their role as business partners, working more closely with the business in decision making.

</td><td>

- **Loss of control** – the external provider is relied upon for providing the right level of resource and skill.
- The organisation will need to develop expertise and invest time and money in **managing the outsourced services**.
- Outsourcing **will cause disruption** and may result in significant resistance to change.
- **Risk of intellectual property theft and data breaches.**
- **Erosion of internal knowledge and skills.**

These drawbacks may result in a decision not to outsource all or some of the finance function activities; the non-outsourced activities are described as '**retained finance**'.

</td></tr>
</table>

5.4 Establishing a shared service centre for the finance function

Introduction

Shared service centres have become a well-established model for organisations to drive efficiencies, improve compliance and controls and enable insight into the business.

The scope of services that are provided include **finance**, HR, IT, procurement, and other business support activities.

The **traditional** shape of the finance function was a **hierarchical triangle**, with a broad base and few roles at senior levels. Over the past two decades this shape **evolved to a segregated triangle** with **routine processes** being migrated to and carried out by **shared service centres**.

This change was **driven by two main factors**:

- **Globalisation** – many organisations grew in size and became multinational organisations with operations and processing centres in several countries. The establishment of a shared service centre enabled the consolidation of these activities at one site.
- **Advances in information technology** – enabling automation of many of the lower level tasks carried out by the finance function.

e.g

Illustration 13 – Siemens' finance shared services

Siemens is a German technology company that performs electrification, automation and digitisation activities in nearly all countries of the world. The finance function operates a shared service model. The centre located in North West Europe has historically focused heavily on high-volume, low-complexity tasks. One early transformation used automation to sort and analyse high volumes of data, create automatic journal vouchers and email them to cost centre managers.

The use of automation creates significant efficiency savings by removing low complex roles previously carried out by entry-level employees. This frees up time for more complex and stimulating tasks, resulting in higher engagement among trainee accountants. In addition, error rates for high-volume, low-complexity work have reduced, creating cost savings across the company.

The initial focus of the automation was on repetitive tasks, but the scope has grown to include more advanced uses such as query resolution for cash collection.

The **benefits** of establishing a shared service centre for the finance function are as follows:

- Cost reduction – a shared service centre may reduce costs by up to 50% due to factors such as:
  - a reduction in premises and associated costs
  - potentially favourable labour rates, for example if the shared service centre is based in a country with lower wage rates
  - headcount reductions, for example due to the more routine activities benefiting from economies of scale and a reduction in repetition of tasks
  - systems consolidation
  - potential tax savings.

- Opportunity to standardise processes:
  - resulting in a lower potential for errors
  - making the design and update of the control environment easier
  - allowing for consistent reporting.
- An improved level of service – the shared service centre will view the business to be the customer. The more professional supplier/customer relationship should result in marked improvements in the quality of the service provided.
- A better opportunity to compare trends across the organisation.
- Consolidation of systems, to say one type of accountancy software, makes add-ons such as robotics and greater use of automation easier.

However, there are **risks** associated with the establishment of a shared service centre:

- Has the organisation got the resources required to cover the major set up costs?
- Employee issues – these include the potential cost of making staff redundant plus the impact on the morale of the remaining staff due to the changes made.
- Lack of systems integration across the organisation may make migration of diverse systems complicated, costly and time consuming.
- A shared service centre is often established in a multinational organisation which has operations in several countries. The complexities of these countries including different laws, taxes, languages, cultures, reporting requirements and time zones may make this difficult.

Tips on establishing a successful shared service centre

- A clear vision of how the shared service centre fits into the overall business model.
- Senior management commitment – senior management need a clear vision and strategy and to support the process.
- Integration with other change initiatives.
- Clear scope and boundaries of responsibility.
- Buy-in of operating units impacted by the change.
- Ensuring that the organisation that remains after service transfer is robust.
- Support from those who have implementation experience to help navigate through the challenges faced.
- A strong customer-focused culture.
- A commitment to continuous improvement.

Test your understanding 14

Which THREE of the following are drawbacks of outsourcing the non-core activities of the finance function?

A Loss of control

B Risk of data breaches

C Erosion of internal knowledge

D Increased costs

E Loss of competitive advantage

F Major set up costs

Alternatives to establishing a shared service centre for the finance function

The benefits must be weighed up against the risks before a decision is taken to establish the shared service centre. It may be that a decision is taken to keep the **finance function's activities in several sites** across the business.

An alternative would be to establish a shared service centre but rather than the services being provided in-house a decision is taken to **outsource the provision of the shared services to a third party** who specialises in the provision of such services.

Illustration 14 – Outsourcing of finance shared services

PwC (UK) is a one of the larger providers of finance shared services. The following is taken from their website and illustrates nicely the future of the finance function and how an outsourcing provider could assist with this future:

'You are the CFO sat in a finance shared service centre. There's a wall of screens showing the latest profit forecasts for each of your divisions – changing every few minutes. In the corner, there's a Robotic Process Automation (RPA) hub with a few people studiously monitoring the 50 bots deployed across your finance processes. In the general accounting team it's month end – but there's an air of calm as with your cloud based Enterprise Resource planning (ERP) you can close whenever you want within a few minutes. The brightest monitor in the room is at the back, showing the daily Shared Service Centre's (SSC) huddle board with lots of stars and names up in lights.

At PwC we are helping clients take advantage of new digital tools and ways of thinking to move towards this sort of reality. Whether you're just thinking about shared services or outsourcing or have been established for years and are looking to evolve your SSC further to take advantage of the digital revolution, we can help.'

Shared services and the diamond shape of the finance function

The finance function has evolved from a traditional hierarchical triangle to a segregated triangle with routine processes being migrated to and carried out by shared service centres. The scope of the shared service centre's work was very much on the lower level tasks (level 4 tasks) of 'assembling and extracting data and providing limited insight'.

However, the shape of the finance function is now evolving to a diamond shape. In the diamond shape the level 3 tasks present within 'specialists generating further insights in their areas of specialism' are now offered by shared service centres. Opportunities for business partnering will also be expanded.

Organisations are demanding a higher level of service, capabilities and understanding within their shared service centres. They will be viewed as centres of excellence formed of the key people that are necessary for areas such as reporting and complex accounting and tax. These people won't all be based in the same location but will utilise collaborative tools such as video calls to create more virtual centres of excellence.

In summary, shared service centres whether in-house or operated by a service provider (outsourced) have industrialised the provision of routine management and accounting services, and now offer scope to expand vertically to offer higher value services.

6 Chapter summary

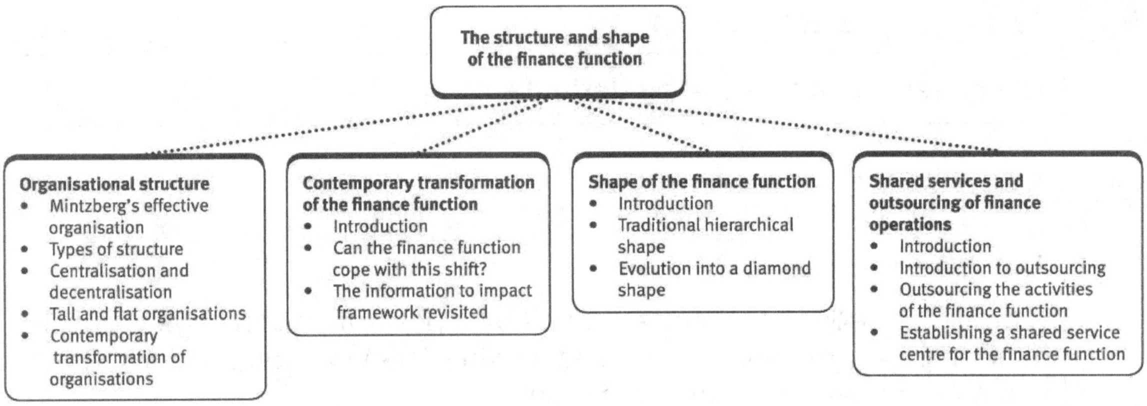

Test your understanding answers

Test your understanding 1

The correct answer is **C – by definition**.

Test your understanding 2

The correct answer is **C**

A divisionalised form is characterised by a powerful middle line in which a there are a large number of middle managers who each takes charge of a more or less autonomous division.

Test your understanding 3

The correct answer is **D**

The separate parts of the organisation operate as SBUs in a divisional structure – not a functional structure.

The matrix structure tends to require time-consuming meetings and has significant overlap of authority between managers. This tends to slow the decision-making process down.

Test your understanding 4

The correct answer is **B**

As M has several complex products, a structure that creates a separate division to look after each one seems the most logical. Functional and geographical structures would struggle to cope with the differing needs of the products. The level of work needed to run a large, complex organisation would also probably be beyond the capabilities of an entrepreneurial structure.

Test your understanding 5

The correct answer is **D**

Decentralisation should result in better local decisions being made since autonomy is devolved to local managers.

Test your understanding 6

The correct answer is **B**

The scalar chain relates to the number of levels of management within the organisation.

Test your understanding 7

Narrow

Test your understanding 8

Answer A: Because of advancements in technology the basic activities of the finance function are no longer relevant – FALSE they are still relevant but there has been a shift in emphasis on the importance of each of the activities.

Answer B: Technology allows the contemporary finance function to refocus its energy on value creation – TRUE.

Answer C: Technology has meant that a large amount of the assembly and analysis activities can be automated – TRUE.

Answer D: Technology has meant that a large amount of the advising and applying activities can be automated – FALSE, although some of these activities can be automated the finance function will need to reallocate its resources to these activities.

Test your understanding 9

A, B, D – these are all assembly and analysis activities, which are more heavily impacted by technology and automation.

C and E are advising and applying activities.

Test your understanding 10

The shape of the finance function has evolved from a traditional hierarchy to a diamond shape in today's digital age.

This has primarily been driven by globalisation and technology.

Test your understanding 11

Answer B is the correct answer – outsourcing is likely to cause a loss of competitive advantage as IT is a core competence within this highly competitive and innovative industry. In addition, Canterell will have no way to create its own unique systems.

Outsourcing IT would be likely to mean the closure of their own IT department, which will mean the loss of skilled staff. This will make it difficult to bring IT back in-house in the future (answer C) and will result in a loss of IT expertise (answer A). It is possible to outsource the IT function (answer D) although this decision may not be in the best interest of the company.

Test your understanding 12

The correct answers are **B,C, E and H**

As it is a fixed fee, Q will know how much the IT function will cost each year (answer B). Outsourcers often have a level of expertise that organisations can benefit from if they have skills lacking in-house (answer C). As outsourcers are providing services for many customers they are able to generate economies of scale, often making outsourcing a cheaper option (answer E). Not having to focus on non-core activities mean that management can focus on core activities which often are the source of competitive advantage (answer H).

Test your understanding 13

	True?
High transaction costs will usually lead to a company deciding to outsource	No – opposite
A robust SLA will prevent the risk of a loss of confidential data	Reduce not prevent
Transaction costs include bargaining costs	✓
Transaction costs are incurred when outsourcing is used	✓
Transaction costs include the cost of production	No

Test your understanding 14

The correct answers are **A, B and C** – The organisation will become reliant on the external provider and will not have as much control over the function being outsourced (answer A). This leads to the erosion of internal knowledge (answer C) and could increase the risk of data breaches (answer B).

Outsourcing should be a cheaper option thereby reducing costs (answer D). Outsourcing the non-core activities means the remaining activities retained within finance can focus on business partnering enhancing competitive advantage (answer E). Major set up costs are a drawback of setting up a shared service centre not a drawback of outsourcing (answer F).

Chapter

4

What each level of the finance function does

Chapter learning objectives

Lead	Component
D2: Explain what each level of the finance function does.	Explain the activities of: (a) Finance operations (b) Specialist areas including financial reporting and financial planning and analysis (FP&A) (c) Strategic partnering for value (d) Strategic leadership of the finance team

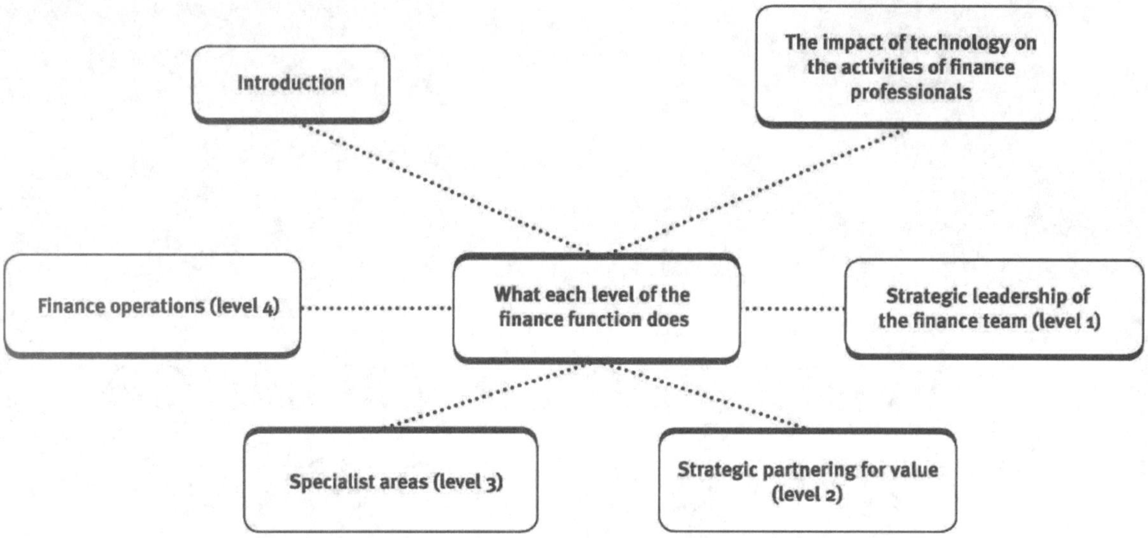

1 Introduction

In Chapter 2 we discussed the basic activities that the finance function performs using the 'information to impact framework'.

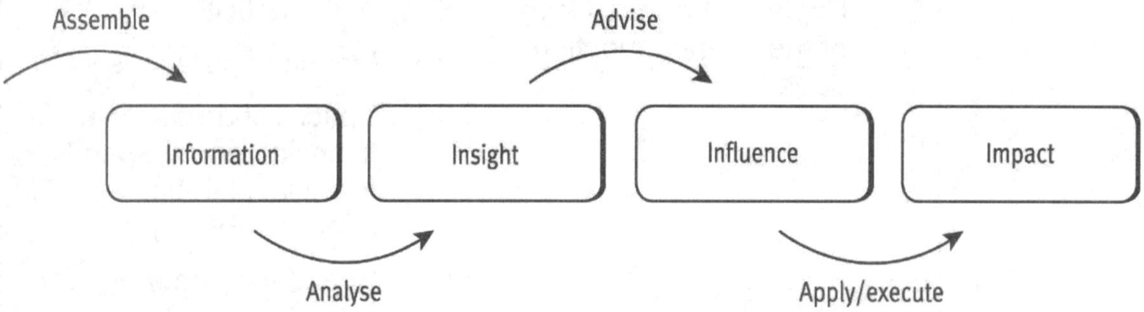

We also **linked these basic activities to the diamond shape of the finance function** (see diagram below).

In this chapter we are going to review each of these activities in more detail, with specific reference to the role of the finance function.

We will also briefly discuss how an organisation could use technology to improve the productivity of finance professionals within these areas and we will discuss the threat of automation.

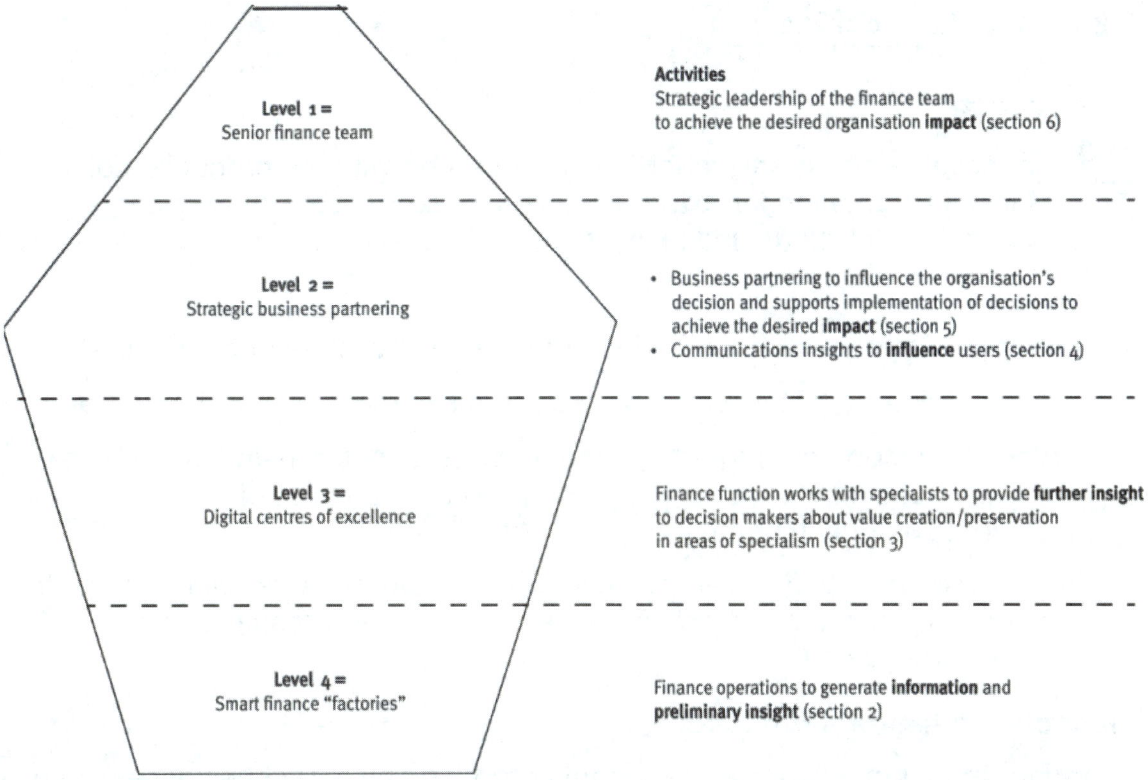

2 Smart finance "factories" (level 4)

2.1 Introduction

In this section we are going to look at the basic components of finance operations (i.e. accounting operations) and how these finance operations generate information and preliminary insight. The information and extracted data provided at this level become the foundations of the work of finance professionals.

Finance operations consist of the following, often inter-related, components:

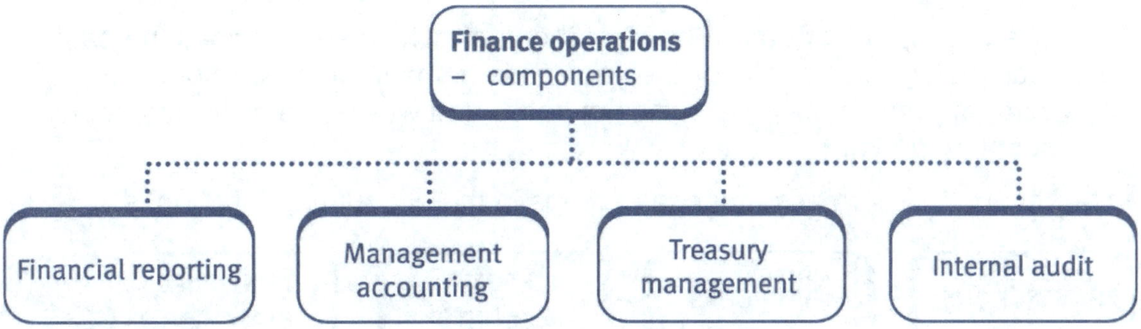

Each of these components will be explored in turn below.

2.2 Financial reporting

Introduction

Financial (or corporate) reporting is concerned with the production of financial information for external users in accordance with relevant accounting standards and legislation.

The financial information may include:

- financial statements (for use, for example, by investors and creditors)
- tax reporting (to HM Revenue and Customs in the United Kingdom) and
- regulatory reporting (regulatory bodies exist for different industries and specify a set of laws, regulations and reporting requirements to the relevant authority that must be adhered to).

The information provided about the business to external users will be useful to them in their decision making and for assessing the stewardship of the business's management.

Financial statements produced

There are three main financial statements produced by most businesses each year:

- The **statement of profit or loss (SOPL)** for the year, which details the income as well as the costs incurred in the period. This allows the business to calculate whether it has made a profit (if income exceeds costs) or a loss (if costs exceed income).
- The **statement of financial position (SOFP)** as at the year end, which shows the assets (business resources such as motor vehicles, buildings and cash) and liabilities (money owed to third parties such as banks and suppliers) of the business. This statement also shows the stake that the owners of the business have in the organisation (or their 'capital'). In a company, this is often referred to as 'shareholder's equity'.
- The **statement of cash flows** for the year, which summarises the cash receipts and payments for the year. This helps to show whether the company is solvent (has sufficient cash) and where the cash has been spent in the year.

In summary, the normal sequence of steps in the accounting function is:

Test your understanding 1

J has been asked to find four pieces of information about FGH Ltd for their manager from the company's statement of profit or loss (SOPL) and statement of financial position (SOFP). They have been asked to find:

(1) The ratio of current assets to current liabilities

(2) Total shareholders' equity

(3) Gross profit as a percentage of turnover

(4) Total rent paid for the year

Which of the following (A, B, C or D) correctly match the information needed with the financial statement each would be found in?

	(1)	(2)	(3)	(4)
A	SOFP	SOFP	SOPL	SOPL
B	SOPL	SOPL	SOFP	SOFP
C	SOFP	SOPL	SOFP	SOPL
D	SOPL	SOFP	SOPL	SOFP

Why do businesses need to prepare financial statements?

The preparation of financial statements is a time-consuming and expensive process. So why do most organisations have a financial reporting component?

The main reason is to satisfy stakeholders who have an interest in the financial performance of the business. These could include:

- **Investors/potential investors** – interested in how profitable the business is and how well it is being run.

Illustration 1 – Investor ratios

Several ratios will be of interest to the investor. These include:

Earnings per share (EPS)

EPS is a measure of the profit attributable to each ordinary shareholder.

$$\text{EPS} = \frac{\text{Profit after tax (less preference dividends)}}{\text{Weighted average number of ordinary shares in issue}}$$

Price/earnings (P/E) ratio

$$\text{P/E ratio} = \frac{\text{Share price}}{\text{EPS}}$$

A high P/E ratio means that investors are paying more for today's earnings in anticipation of future growth.

Dividend yield

$$\text{Dividend yield} = \frac{\text{Dividend per share}}{\text{Current share price}} \times 100$$

- **Managers** – interested in the company's financial situation so that they can plan effectively for the future.
- **Banks** – may wish to see whether the business can afford the repayments on loans and overdrafts.
- **Employees** – interested in the financial position of the company and the impact this will have on their jobs and wages.
- **Suppliers and customers** – may wish to check the financial stability of the business to ensure it will be able to make payments/supply goods as needed.
- **Government** – may wish to check that the business is obeying relevant laws on reporting and taxation.

Companies must send a copy of their financial statements to each of their shareholders at the end of the year. Large and publicly-quoted companies are also required to appoint external auditors each year to give an independent opinion on whether the financial statements have been drawn up properly and whether they give a true and fair view.

2.3 Management accounting

Introduction

Management accounting is the provision of information to help managers and other internal users in their decision making, performance measurement, planning and control activities.

Management accountants will use financial accounting records as a source of data for their work, but they will also use other sources of internal and external data.

While there are no legally required formats for management accounts, there are several key management reports that are common to many businesses. Three of the most common are **cost schedules, budgets** and **variance reports**.

Cost schedules

A **cost schedule** lists the various expenses involved in manufacturing units of a product. This is often shown as a list of the costs incurred when making a unit of each type of product. This may be called a **standard cost card**.

Illustration 2 – Standard cost card

ABC Ltd manufactures toys. One of its products is a wooden train set, which has the following standard costs per unit:

	$
Direct materials (wood and paint)	5.50
Direct labour (time spent cutting and painting)	6.50
Prime cost	12.00
Variable overheads (heat and light)	4.00
Marginal cost	16.00
Fixed overheads (factory rent)	5.00
Total (absorption) cost	21.00

There are several key business decisions that this report can help a business to make:

- **Pricing decisions** – How much should the business sell the products for to ensure it makes a profit?
- **Break-even analysis** – Which products are profitable or loss-making? Is a new product worth producing? Can the business sell enough units to cover the costs of making the product?
- **Key factor analysis** – should products be made in-house or should their manufacture be outsourced to somewhere cheaper?
- **Investment appraisal** – should a new machine be bought to replace an old machine? Should the business begin a new project, such as launching a new product?

Budgets

In addition, once the costs per unit have been identified, it should be possible to produce a budget. This shows the total planned revenues and costs for the business for the coming period. It is based on the cost schedules mentioned earlier.

Budgets are useful for several reasons. A useful memory aid is the acronym **CRUMPET**

- **C**o-ordination – the budget provides guidance for managers and ensures they are all working together for the good of the company.
- **R**esponsibility – the budget authorises managers to make expenditure, hire staff and generally follow the plans laid out in the budget.
- **U**tilisation – budgets (especially cash budgets) help managers to get the best out of their business resources in the coming period.

- **M**otivation – the budget can be a useful device for influencing the behaviour of managers and motivating them to perform in line with business objectives.
- **P**lanning – budgets force managers to look ahead. This may help them to identify opportunities for, or threats to, the business and take effective action in advance.
- **E**valuation – budgets are often used as the basis for management appraisal. Some might consider that a manager has performed well if they have met their budget in the period. Certainly, it is a significant factor.
- **T**elling – also called 'communication', budgets ensure that all members of the business understand what is expected from them during the coming period.

One major drawback of budgets is that they are only estimates of what will happen in the coming period. In reality, most businesses will not perfectly achieve the targets set out for them in their budgets.

This means that they will have to prepare a **variance report** at the end of each period, comparing the budget to the actual results and identifying any differences (i.e. variances) between the two.

Variance reports

A variance report compares the budget to the actual results achieved for the budget period and identifies any significant differences, or variances, between the two.

For control purposes, management may need to establish why a particular variance has occurred. Once the reason has been established, a decision can be taken as to what, if any, control measures might be appropriate to:

- prevent adverse variances from occurring again in the future, or
- repeat a favourable variance in the future, or
- bring actual results back on course to achieve the budgeted targets.

The management accountant will assist and interact with other functions in providing solutions to variances.

The differences between financial reporting and management accounting

	Management accounting	**Financial reporting**
Why information is mainly produced	For internal use, such as managers and employees.	For external use, such as shareholders, creditors, banks, government.

Purpose of information	To aid planning, controlling and decision making.	To record the financial performance in a period and the financial position at the end of the period.
Legal requirements	None.	Limited companies must produce financial accounts.
Formats	Management decides on the information that they require and the most useful way of presenting it.	Format and content of financial accounts must follow accounting standards and company law.
Nature of information	Financial and non-financial.	Mostly financial.
Time period	Historical and forward-looking.	Mainly a historical record.

Test your understanding 2

Consider the following two statements regarding the management accounting function.

(i) Variance analysis enables a business to identify why the actual financial results were different to those predicted by the budget.

(ii) Management accounts follow a set, pre-determined format as laid out in relevant accounting standards.

Which of these statements is/are correct?

A (i) only

B (ii) only

C Both

D Neither

2.4 Treasury management

Introduction

Treasury management is the management of the funds of the business, namely cash and other working capital items, plus long-term investments, short-term and long-term debt, and equity finance.

The key roles of the treasury function include:

Working capital management	The treasury section will monitor the organisation's cash balance and working capital to ensure that it never runs out of money.
Cash management	Preparation of cash budgets and arrangement of overdrafts where necessary.
Financing	The treasury section will monitor the organisation's investments and borrowings to ensure they earn as much investment income as possible and incur as little interest expense as possible.
Foreign currency	The treasury section will monitor foreign exchange rates and try to manage the organisation's affairs so that it minimises losses due to changes in foreign exchange rates.
Tax	The treasury section will try to manage the organisation's affairs to legally avoid as much tax as possible.

Working capital management

Working capital is the capital available for conducting the day-to-day operations of an organisation, calculated as the excess of current assets over current liabilities. Thus:

Inventory	X
Trade receivables	X
Cash	X
Total current assets	X
Less: Trade payables	(X)
Working capital balance	X

The treasury function is responsible for deciding on an appropriate level of investment in working capital for the business.

There are advantages in holding either large or small balances of each component of working capital, as shown below.

	Advantages of a large balance	Advantages of a small balance
Inventory	Customers are happy since they can be immediately provided with goods.	Low holding costs. Less risk of obsolescence costs.
Trade receivables	Customers are happy since they like credit.	Less risk of irrecoverable debts. Good for cash flow.
Cash	Creditors are happy since bills can be paid promptly.	More can be invested elsewhere to earn profits.
Trade payables	Preserves your own cash.	Suppliers are happy and may offer discounts.

Management must decide on the appropriate balance to be struck for each component.

Test your understanding 3

Conservative managers will have a policy of holding a large working capital balance, while aggressive management will hold a low working capital balance.

Which of the following is a consequence of an aggressive management policy?

A Increased bad and doubtful debts

B Increased credit periods attract more customers

C Increased inventory obsolescence

D Increased risk of inventory outages

Financing

The organisation may need additional funding to allow it to grow and invest in new projects. It may therefore need to raise finance from external sources. There are **two main types of external finance**:

- **Debt** involves borrowing cash from a third party and promising to repay them at a later date. Normally, the company will also have to pay interest on the amount borrowed.

  There are various sources of debt that an organisation can raise funds from, including bank loans and overdrafts, venture capitalists and through selling bonds or debentures.

  The main advantages of raising cash through debt finance are:

  – Interest payments are allowable against tax. Note that dividend payments made to shareholders, by contrast, are **not** an allowable deduction.

- Raising debt finance does not change the ownership of the organisation.
- Debt tends to be cheaper to service than equity, as it is often secured against the assets of the company and takes priority over equity in the event of the business being liquidated.

- **Equity** involves selling a stake in the business to raise cash. For companies, this involves selling shares to either new or existing shareholders.

  Raising equity finance has the following advantages:

  - There is no minimum level of dividend that must be paid to shareholders. This means that dividends can be suspended if profits are low and the company cannot afford them. Interest payments on debt finance must be paid each year.
  - A bank will normally require security on the company's assets before it will offer a loan. Some companies may lack quality assets to offer, making equity more attractive as it does not require security.

  The treasury and finance function will weigh up which source of finance best suits the circumstances of the business.

e.g. Illustration 3 – Financial gearing

$$\textbf{Financial gearing} = \frac{\textbf{Long-term debt}}{\textbf{Shareholders' funds}} \times 100$$

A high gearing ratio indicates a high level of risk since debt obligations (such as interest payments) must be met, whereas returns to shareholders (such as dividends) are voluntary.

Test your understanding 4

AHG needs to raise $50m to launch a new product. AHG hopes the new product will be a success, but the returns are highly uncertain, with a 30% chance that the launch will be a failure. The product is expected to sell for around 5 years.

AHG is currently trying to decide whether the launch should be financed using a 5 year bank loan, or through raising equity.

Which of the following statements is correct?

A Equity will be cheaper, as dividends are allowable against tax

B AHG should choose equity due to the risky nature of the project

C Equity should be chosen as AHG needs a permanent increase in its finance

D Debt usually does not require security, meaning it may be easier for AHG to raise

Foreign currency

Companies may have borrowings in foreign currencies, or may have customers/suppliers who will pay/expect payment in a foreign currency. The treasury department will try to manage affairs to minimise the company's exposure to foreign exchange losses.

Managing foreign currency risk

Background

Assume a UK company buys goods costing US$1m from a US company on 1 January 20X1. The goods are due to be paid for on 31 March 20X1.

The exchange rate at 1 January is £1:US$1.5, so the goods will cost £666,667 ($1m/1.5).

However, if the exchange rate changes to, say, £1:US$1.3, then the payment to be made will be £769,231 ($1m/1.3).

Managing the risk

The company can manage this risk by entering into a 'forward exchange contract' at 1 January to fix the rate of exchange at which it can buy $1m at 31 March.

The rate in the forward exchange contract will depend on what the market thinks will happen to exchange rates.

Let us say, for example, that the company can enter into a contract to purchase $1m at the rate of £1:S1.48. The company's cost, in sterling, is then fixed at £675,676 ($1m/1.48).

This is not as good as only £666,667 but not as bad as £769,231, and at least the company knows what it will pay (£675,676) so can budget for it.

Tax

One of the roles of the finance and treasury function is to calculate the business tax liability for the organisation and lawfully mitigate, or reduce, that liability as far as possible.

Illustration 4 – Tax avoidance, tax evasion and tax mitigation

Tax avoidance is the legal use of the rules of the tax regime to one's own advantage, to reduce the amount of tax payable by means that are within the law.

Tax evasion is the use of illegal means to reduce one's tax liability, for example by deliberately misrepresenting the true state of your affairs to the tax authorities.

The directors of a company have a duty to their shareholders to maximise the post-tax profits that are available for distribution as dividends to the shareholders, thus they have a duty to arrange the company's affairs to avoid taxes as far as possible. However, dishonest reporting to the tax authorities (for example, declaring less income than actually earned) would be tax evasion and a criminal offence.

While the traditional distinction between tax avoidance and tax evasion is clear, recently in the UK authorities have introduced the idea of **tax mitigation** to mean conduct that reduces tax liabilities without frustrating the intentions of Parliament. **Tax avoidance** is used to describe schemes which, while they are legal, are designed to defeat the intentions of Parliament. Thus, in the United Kingdom, once a tax avoidance scheme becomes public knowledge, Parliament will nearly always step in to change the law to stop the scheme from working.

Note: Operational level candidates should understand the work and scope of the treasury function but are not expected to understand the detail of matters such as foreign exchange contracts. These matters of detail are explored in later levels of the syllabus.

2.5 Internal audit

What is internal audit?

Internal audit is an independent activity, established by management to examine and evaluate the organisation's risk management processes and systems of control, and to make recommendations for the achievement of company objectives.

The purpose of internal audit

Company directors have a legal requirement to produce true and fair annual financial statements. To help ensure this is done, companies are required to have their published financial statements audited by an external team of experts **(external auditors)**.

Directors also need assurance on other financial matters. This assurance is primarily for their own internal use, although in recent years pressure has grown for increasingly more of such work to be made publicly available.

This additional work is carried out by internal auditors, who may be company employees or (if the service is outsourced) experts from a firm of accountants.

Internal audit is part of the organisational control of a business; it is one of the methods used by management to ensure the efficient and orderly running of the business as a whole, and is part of the overall control environment.

Internal auditors' work has expanded in recent years, and the role of internal audit often now includes:

- helping to set corporate objectives
- helping to design and monitor performance measures for these objectives.

Internal audit as part of good corporate governance

A properly functioning internal audit department is part of good corporate governance, as recognised by all national and international corporate governance codes.

Internal audit enables management to perform proper risk assessments (another central theme of corporate governance codes) by means of properly understanding the strengths and weaknesses of all parts of the control systems in the business.

The UK Corporate Governance Code states that companies without an internal audit function should **annually review the need for one**.

Where there is an internal audit function, the board should **annually review its scope of work**, authority and resources.

Ideally, the internal audit function should be staffed with **qualified, experienced staff**, whose work is closely monitored by an audit committee.

The function of internal audit in the context of corporate risk management

Internal audit has a particular interest in evaluating the company's risk management structures. Internal audit can:

- manage the basic data used by management to identify risks
- identify techniques for prioritising and managing risks
- report on the effectiveness of risk management solutions (for example, internal controls).

Scope of internal audit

Internal audit staff are typically expected to carry out a variety of tasks:

- reviewing internal controls and financial reports
- reviewing risk management systems
- carrying out special assignments e.g. fraud investigations
- conducting operational reviews e.g. into issues of value for money (VFM) and economy, efficiency and effectiveness (3E's) of parts of the organisation.

The purpose of internal audit can be **summarised** in the table below:

Role	To advise management on whether the organisation has sound systems of internal controls to protect the organisation against loss.
Legal basis	Generally, not a legal requirement. However, the UK Corporate Governance Code recommends that if a listed company does not have an internal audit department it should annually assess the need for one.
Scope of work	Determined by management. Covers all areas of the organisation, operational as well as financial.
Approach	The approach is increasingly risk-based. This involves assessing risks, evaluating systems of controls, testing the operation of those systems and making recommendations for improvement.
Responsibility	To advise and make recommendations on internal control and corporate governance.

Test your understanding 5

The internal audit is simply a necessary cost that must be incurred by a company and offers few tangible benefits for the organisation.

Is this statement true or false?

A True

B False

Test your understanding 6

Internal audit may be carried out by employees of the company being audited, or by external accountants paid for delivering this service.

Is this statement true or false?

A True

B False

Test your understanding 7

In a large company, to who do internal auditors normally report their conclusions?

A Executive directors

B Board of directors

C Shareholders

D Non-executive directors

The role of internal audit in preventing and detecting fraud

Fraud is an intentional act involving the use of deception to obtain an unjust or illegal advantage – essentially 'theft by deception'. Fraud is a criminal offence, punishable by a fine or imprisonment.

As far as the financial statements are concerned, fraud comprises both the use of deception to obtain an unjust or illegal financial advantage and intentional misrepresentations affecting the financial statements. It is ultimately up to the courts to decide in each instance whether fraud has occurred, for example:

- deliberate falsification of documents/records
- deliberate ignoring of errors requiring correction
- deliberate suppression of relevant information.

There are three prerequisites that are required for fraud to occur:

- **dishonesty** – relates to a lack of integrity or honesty. An honest employee will be unlikely to commit a fraud.
- **opportunity** – the individual must have the opportunity or opening for a fraud to be committed. These opportunities will often be created due to weak internal controls.
- **motivation** – the individual must feel that the rewards that can be earned by the fraud will outweigh the potential costs if they are caught.

All three are usually required – for example an honest employee is unlikely to commit fraud even if given the opportunity and motive.

Factors that might indicate an increased risk of fraud and error include (amongst others):

- **management domination by one person, or a small group of people** – dominant individuals often find it easy to circumvent controls and procedures.
- **unnecessarily complex corporate structure** – this makes it harder to trace transactions, meaning it is easier for employees to hide fraud.
- **poor staff morale** – if staff dislike the company they work for, it may give them additional motivation to perpetrate frauds.
- **personnel who do not take leave/holidays** – this may indicate that staff members are unwilling to pass their duties over to other members of staff in case they identify fraudulent activities.
- **lavish lifestyles of employees** – if an employee is clearly living beyond their means, it may indicate they are committing fraud to fund it.

- **lack of monitoring of control systems** – for controls to be effective, they need to be monitored on a regular basis.
- **unusual transactions** – in cash, or direct to numbered bank accounts.
- **payments for services disproportionate to effort** may also be an indication of fraudulent activity.

If management has established a strong system of internal control then the potential for fraud is greatly reduced.

It is up to the directors to decide what internal audit should do, but normally, where there is an effective internal audit department, the interna auditors will be given the responsibility to test the internal control system and to recommend improvements. The better the control system, the less likely it is that fraud will be attempted or will succeed if it is attempted.

The directors may also ask the internal auditors to carry out a specific investigation into situations where fraud has been discovered, to learn lessons for the future and ensure that such a fraud cannot be repeated.

There is a spectrum of **implications of fraud**, from the immaterial to the critical. These include:

- Loss of shareholder confidence
- Loss of assets
- Financial difficulties
- Collapse of the company
- Fines by tax and other authorities

Once a fraud has been identified, internal audit should be sent to the department to investigate the circumstances and to make recommendations to improve the controls in the area to deter future fraud. Internal audit should report their findings to the audit committee who can monitor whether the recommendations are swiftly implemented by management.

Limitations of internal audit

- Internal auditors have an unavoidable independence problem. They are employed by the management of the company and yet are expected to give an objective opinion on matters for which management are responsible.
- There is an argument that to overcome some of the problems of independence (or lack thereof), that internal audit should be completely separate to the finance function. However, although this may be feasible in, say, a large multinational organisation, resource constraints tend to prevent this in smaller organisations. In these organisations, internal audit and the finance function are still inextricably linked.

- Internal audit will only succeed if it is properly staffed and resourced.
- If internal auditors identify fraud, they may be unwilling to disclose it for fear of the repercussions (which could involve the collapse of the company and the loss of their jobs).

These limitations can be reduced if an **audit committee**:

- sets the work agenda for internal audit
- receives internal audit reports
- is able to ensure the internal audit is properly resourced
- has a 'voice' at main board level.

2.6 Recent changes in finance operations

As was touched upon in Chapter 3:

- Over the last two decades **shared service centres** (SSCs), whether in-house or outsourced, have taken control of the management of many of the rules-based finance operations of an organisation.
- More recently the scope of the SSCs work has expanded to handle all of the processes of finance operations from end to end.
- In addition, the quality of service or level of expertise, and the value they can contribute has become more important than being low cost.

Technology (such as robotic process automation, cognitive computing and blockchain) has also had a big impact on finance operations. It has resulted in the creation of '**smart finance factories**' at this level (i.e. level 4) of the diamond shape of the finance function.

Test your understanding 8

Which of the following statements about changes in finance operations is true?

A A shared service centre is also referred to as outsourcing

B The quality of work produced by an SSC is lower than if it were outsourced

C Establishing an SSC enables a business' processes to be standardised

D Shared service centres can only produce work at the lowest level (level 4) of the finance function

3 Digital centres of excellence (level 3)

3.1 Introduction

In this section we are going to look at the specialist areas that exist within an organisation. The **specialists are experts who provide insight** derived from the information that has been handed over to them (by level 4) in their specialist areas. Their insights create the building blocks of the organisation's value creation. The specialist areas include:

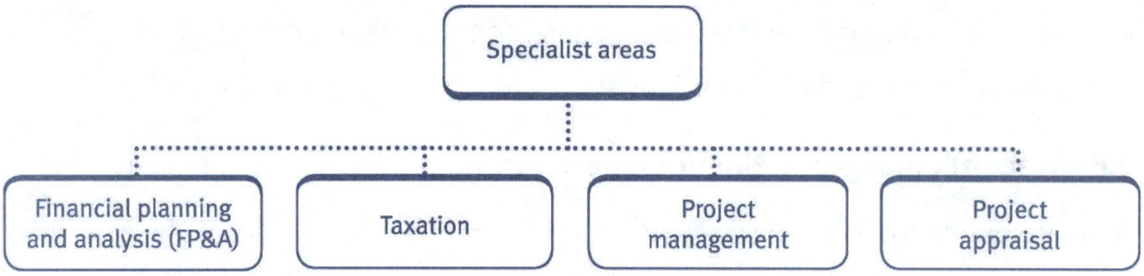

We will briefly introduce each of these specialist areas and will look at **how the finance function works with these specialist areas** to provide further insight to decision makers about value creation/preservation in areas of specialism.

3.2 Financial planning and analysis (FP&A)

Careful financial planning and cash flow management is an important tool in ensuring an organisation is consistently profitable and continues to grow.

FP&A specialists play a crucial role in organisations by performing budgeting, forecasting and data analysis that supports the major organisational decisions of the board.

The specialists utilise both quantitative and qualitative analysis of all the operational aspects of the organisation to evaluate its progress towards its goals and to map out future goals and plans.

The specialists consider economic and business trends, review past organisational performance, and attempt to anticipate obstacles and potential problems, all with an eye to forecasting the organisation's future results.

e.g

Illustration 5 – Examples of responsibilities of FP&A specialists

- Looking at the effectiveness of the organisation's current investments and comparison to other ways it may utilise its cash flow (for example, other investments or an increased dividend payment).
- Gauging the organisation's overall financial health using key financial ratios (for example, current ratios).
- Identifying which products or product lines are most profitable.
- Working with independent departments to prepare budgets and consolidate them into an overall budget.

3.3 Taxation

Taxation specialists play an important role in an organisation in **minimising risk** and **creating value**. They do this by focusing on two main areas:

- **Tax compliance** – following current legislation, regulation and procedures to **minimise risk**. For example, they will complete and file timely tax returns and produce and required supplementary reports or calculations.
- **Tax planning** – this focuses on ensuring the organisation is working in the most tax efficient manner to reduce the total tax paid and **create value**. Taxation specialists will help the organisation to achieve its goals, playing an important role in:
  - lowering the amount of taxable income
  - reducing the tax rate
  - allowing greater control of when taxes get paid
  - maximising tax relief/tax credits available.

3.4 Project management

A **project** can be defined simply as an activity, which has a start, middle and end, and consumes resources. It will:

- have a specific objective
- have a defined start and end date (timescale)
- consume resources (people, equipment and finance)
- be unique (a one-time-only configuration of these elements)
- have cost constraints that must be clearly defined and understood to ensure the project remains viable
- require organisation.

Examples include the development and launch of a new product/service, expansion into a new market, investment in new premises, machinery or equipment and investment in a new IT system.

Project management is the integration of all aspects of a project, ensuring that the proper knowledge and resources are available when and where needed, and above all to ensure the expected outcome is produced in a timely, cost effective manner.

Project teams will be put together for the sole purpose of achieving the project goals and objectives.

Projects may run for anything from a few weeks to many years depending on their size and complexity.

Illustration 6 – Project management stages

There are **five stages** to the project management process:

Stage	Explanation
1 Initiation	A project is initiated when a need or organisational objective is identified. The project identified is appraised to ensure it is feasible.
2 Planning	The drawing up of detailed plans. For example, communication of what must be done, when and by whom, identifying the resources needed and establishing measures of success for the project.
3 Executing	The project team members will perform the tasks they are responsible for, and the project manager will provide leadership and co-ordination.
4 Controlling	Projects progress, costs and performance will be tracked against the project plan and any corrective action necessary will be taken.
5 Review and close	Once the project work is finished, the project will be signed off and the team disbanded. A project review meeting will be held.

3.5 Project appraisal

Project appraisal takes place as part of the first stage (initiation) of the project management process and will involve an assessment and evaluation of the many decisions and potential outcomes of a particular project.

One of the most important project decisions that will need to be appraised is the capital investment decision, since the organisation may commit a substantial proportion of its resources here and this commitment may be long-term or irreversible.

Many different capital investment projects exist including replacement of assets, cost reduction schemes, new product/service developments and product/service expansions.

To appraise a potential capital project:

- Estimate the costs and benefits from the investment
- Select an appraisal method and use it to assess if the investment is financially worthwhile
- Decide whether or not to go ahead with the project.

There are a number of appraisal methods which are used to assess how financially worthwhile investments are. These include:

- payback
- net present value (NPV)
- internal rate of return (IRR).

Based on the decision rule of the method used, a decision can be made as to whether the investment is financially worthwhile, although there will be other, non-financial considerations which must also be taken into account.

e.g

Illustration 7 – An example of an appraisal method: payback

JKL is considering purchasing a new machine. The machine will cost $550,000. The management accountant of JKL has estimated the following additional cash flows will be received over the next 6 years if the new machine is purchased:

Year 1: $40,000

Year 2: $65,000

Year 3: $140,000

Year 4: $175,000

Year 5: $160,000

Year 6: $70,000

JKL has a target payback period of 4 years.

Calculate the payback period for the new machine and advise JKL whether or not to proceed with the investment.

Solution

Note: The investment is shown in year 0.

Work out the **cumulative cash flow** for each year until the cash flow becomes positive. This will highlight when payback has been achieved.

Year	Cash flow	Cumulative cash flow
	$000	$000
0	(550)	(550)
1	40	(510)
2	65	(445)
3	140	(305)
4	175	(130)
5	160	30
6	70	100

You can see that payback is achieved between years 4 and 5. JKL have a target payback period of 4 years. The payback is after this target, so the advice to JKL would be to **not undertake the investment**.

Test your understanding 9

Kazim, Paul, Belinda and Saira all work in a business partnering role, supporting the specialist areas of their organisation.

Match the type of work they do to the specialist area that they support.

- Part of Kazim's role is to manage and minimise the tax risk that the organisation is exposed to. Amongst other things this involves compliance and planning
- Paul is heavily involved in using techniques such as calculating net present values and payback
- Belinda performs budgets and forecasts and data analysis, as well as using key financial ratios
- Saira is in charge of managing resources to achieve a specific objective

A Financial planning and analysis

B Taxation

C Project management

D Project appraisal

Test your understanding 10

A finance member who is working in the area of project management would typically undertake which FOUR of the following activities?

A Feasibility study

B Tax mitigation

C Resource identification

D Leadership and co-ordination

E Net present value analysis

F Cost control

G Liquidity ratio calculations and analysis

3.6 How the finance function works with these specialists

The finance function offers expertise in accounting and financial matters.

Their subject matter expertise can be harnessed and developed by different specialist areas.

However, rather than working separately, the finance function works alongside these specialists providing expert support for decisions and projects and helps to formulate strategies so that the business can adapt to the ever changing environment.

The finance function can question and investigate, to constantly improve the shared understanding of how the business **generates value**.

e.g

Illustration 8 – How the finance function works with FP&A

FP&A specialists have a number of responsibilities, such as the calculation of key financial ratios for presentation to decision makers to gauge the organisation's overall financial health. These responsibilities will only be fulfilled by the **provision of accurate information** from the finance function (at level 4 of the diamond shape).

The FP&A specialists will own and be held accountable for the process that generates that data. The finance function can act as an 'expert' from outside of this specialist area ensuring the process is subject to the necessary rigour required. The finance function can **assemble and validate** the analysis presented to decision-makers and is able to provide further insight.

3.7 Recent changes to specialist areas

The shape of the finance function is now evolving to a diamond shape:

- This has expanded the opportunities for business partnering between the finance function and specialist areas.
- It has also increased the number of tasks present within these specialist areas that are offered by shared service centres. This has enabled experts from different disciplines to work together on the same team to better support the business.
- Technology has been used by the specialist areas, and by the finance function to improve their productivity in working alongside these specialists.
- The use of advanced technology and the creation of shared service centres have resulted in '**digital centres of excellence**' at this level (i.e. level 3) of the diamond shape.

Illustration 9 – Technology developments and FP&A

Technology has had a significant impact on the work carried out by the FP&A specialists and the finance function staff who work alongside them. For example:

- The production of routine management information is being automated.
- Managers across the organisation may have access to user friendly, self-service, computer dashboards so they can monitor current performance.
- These self-service tools allow interrogation, so managers are empowered to identify the root cause of problems and address these problems promptly.
- Advanced data visualisation and analytics can provide improved forecasting.

However, rather than posing a **threat** to the work carried out by the FP&A specialists, and the finance function employees who work alongside them, these developments can be seen as an **opportunity**.

Finance professionals can harness the value of the data generated and increase their focus on supporting bigger decisions and projects.

Test your understanding 11

Harry, a finance professional, is concerned that due to advancements in technology his job will be under threat. Moira, Harry's boss, is doing her best to reassure him that there are many advantages of the modern finance function that have been enabled due to the increased use of technology.

Which FOUR of the following could Moira use to explain the benefits to Harry?

A Technology can improve the productivity of the finance team

B There are more opportunities for partnering with specialists in the business

C Technology means the finance team have less work to do and therefore, will have more time to pursue their own interests

D Automation of routine tasks means the finance team can focus on more value adding analysis for the benefit of the organisation

E Technology used to support data analytics can provide improved forecasting enabling employees to make better business decisions

F Advances in technology mean Harry will have no new skills to learn, making his life easier

4 Strategic business partnering (level 2)

Level 2 involves:

- communicating insight to influence users
- business partnering

4.1 Communicating insight to influence users

As discussed previously:

- Finance operations will **generate information** and **preliminary insight** (level 4)
- The finance function will work with specialists to provide **further insight** to decision makers (level 3)

At the next level (of the diamond shape), the insights that level 3 provide will be passed on to finance professionals working as strategic partners. These strategic partners will interpret and use financial statements along with other data to communicate this insight:

- in an appropriate format
- and required frequency
- to internal and external stakeholders such as senior managers, colleagues in other functions (for example, marketing or operations), shareholders and regulators.

to **influence** users of this information in their decision making and implementation and control activities.

The evolving shape of the finance function means that more people will be needed here, and the finance function will need to develop the **competencies** required to adequately carry out this activity.

e.g

Illustration 10 – Communicating insight to influence users: Budgeting

The finance function's value adding role is often underplayed but it has an important role in communicating insight to influence the effectiveness of the decisions made by the users of the information.

For example, an organisation's budget is often out of date before it is even complete, takes significant time to produce and the numbers can be of questionable value.

However, the process of budgeting sets aside time from day-to-day activities for managers to think about risks to their plans, strategies to develop growth and to reduce costs.

Importantly, **the process can add value even if the output does not**.

The finance function could therefore consider an alternative output that would be more valuable itself, whilst still capturing the value of the process.

Test your understanding 12

Level 2 of the contemporary shape of the finance function involves Strategic Business Partnering. **Which of the following statements are true and which are false?**

Statement	True/False?
The finance function will communicate their insights once a month	
The finance function communicates their insights only to internal stakeholders	
Fewer people are required at this level of the finance function than previously	
Insight means the capacity to gain an accurate and deep understanding of someone or something	
New competencies need to be developed by the finance function to be able to effectively generate and communicate insight	

4.2 Business partnering

Strategic business partnering will be an increasingly important activity of the finance function.

The finance function will act as a business partner **influencing** the organisation's decisions to achieve the desired organisational **impact**.

The focus of the finance function's work is shifting from reporting historic performance to challenging management thinking and driving decision making to influence future performance.

The chief financial officer (CFO), as head of the finance function, works closely with the chief executive officer (CEO) to support him or her in the running of the organisation. Organisations develop and use finance function professionals as business partners to cascade the CFO's influence throughout the business.

Business partnering services may be provided by:

- individual finance function employees deployed to work alongside departmental mangers
- a multi-disciplinary team in a centre of excellence
- a mix of both with some local support but also an expert team tackling a particular problem or guiding a major initiative.

The expectation for finance to add greater value to the business is growing. Successful finance business partners are seen as leaders that can influence the decisions that a business makes to maximise value.

The CFO must have a team of highly credible finance executives who can act as a link between finance and the rest of the organisation.

The team's role will include helping to align the work of the analytics teams with business priorities, and helping leaders understand the implications of their data.

e.g

Illustration 11 – Finance business partnering at Disney

Business partnering between the finance function and Disney's other functions occurs regularly. One example of partnering between the finance function and the sales and marketing function is given below.

Disney's brand licensing business (where franchise characters are licensed to third-party merchandise brands) was facing pressure from a key customer for substantially lower royalty rates and improved terms for a contract renewal because of growth in volume of business over the years.

The finance business partner team partnered with the sales and marketing team to examine the merits of the customer's request and put together a well-substantiated and compelling counterproposal by:

- Doing a market analysis to verify the importance and potential of this customer.
- Working internally to aggregate information on ongoing and planned investments to increase the appeal of the particular franchise characters.
- Collecting market intelligence on estimated royalty pricing by competitors, for benchmarking purposes.
- Helping the sales and marketing team come up with a well-substantiated counteroffer that was compelling to the customer yet equitable for the company, and supporting the sales and marketing team by participating in the actual negotiations.

As a result, the contract was renewed at the rate originally proposed by Disney.

Success in this role requires a mix of commercial acumen, analytical skills, an ability to build relationships, to communicate effectively and persuade.

Illustration 12 – The finance business partner: skills needed

Amongst the many skills needed, people skills are critical. The effective finance business partner is adaptable and can deliver information in a digestible way to their particular audience.

This is particularly important when the message is one that the audience may not wish to hear, for example informing the sales function that they have overstated their margin.

Finance business partners must also be able to identify and win over key stakeholders, to build relationships and to persuade stakeholders in order to achieve the organisation's objectives.

Test your understanding 13

Which of the following would be useful as a definition of business partnership? Choose all that apply.

A Involvement in strategy formulation, implementation and communication

B Involvement in commercial decision making and negotiations

C Leading on business analysis

D Being a sounding board, trusted adviser, critical friend and facilitator of productive business discussions

5 Senior finance team (level 1)

The final activity is strategic leadership of the finance team.

The head of the finance function is the CFO and it is their responsibility to lead the finance team to achieve the desired organisational **impact**:

- leading key initiatives that support the organisation's goals
- executing and funding strategies set by the CEO
- liaising effectively with internal and external stakeholders.

To do this they will need to put a team in place that has the appropriate knowledge, skills and experience to effectively execute all of the finance function activities already discussed in this chapter.

CFOs are increasingly taking a more active leadership role working alongside and with the CEO as a 'co-pilot' in the success of the business.

Illustration 13 – The CFO's changing role: from navigator to co-pilot

CIMA have illustrated well the changing role of the CFO using the analogy of traditional versus modern aviation.

If we think about the cockpit of a large passenger plane (such as the Boeing 707) that flew in the 1950s:

- we would have had a pilot (left), a co-pilot (right) and a small instrument cluster
- plus a wooden chair for the navigator who was an essential part of the crew and who had access to a lot more instruments.

The CFO would have traditionally viewed their role as **navigator** to the business.

If we fast forward to a modern large passenger plane:

- we still have a pilot (left) and co-pilot (right), and they now have a large instrument cluster
- there is no longer a seat (or a need) for the navigator.

The navigator's role has become redundant meaning that the CFO has had to learn to 'fly the plane', using the large cluster of instruments available to them, to act as the **co-pilot** to the CEO.

Today's CFO needs a wider skill set:

- possessing strong analytical and communication skills
- and mastering areas outside of finance such as regulation, risk management, business transformation, supply chain management and IT.

The CFO is increasingly relying on automation of key business processes and is relying more on technology to transform data into actionable insights that can influence and impact the organisation's achievement of its goals.

Test your understanding 14

Which of the options can be best used to correctly fill the blanks in the following sentence?

'It is the responsibility of the CFO to lead the finance team to achieve the desired organisational _____. This involves leading key initiatives to support organisational _____, as well as liaising effectively with internal and external _____.'

	Gap 1	Gap 2	Gap 3
A	profit	efficiencies	stakeholders
B	impact	goals	shareholders
C	mission	norms	reporters
D	impact	goals	stakeholders

6 The impact of technology on the activities of finance professionals

6.1 Introduction

The finance function can view technology as both:

- an **opportunity** and
- a **threat**.

It can be viewed as an **opportunity** and used to improve the efficiency and productivity of the finance professionals in the areas discussed in the previous section of this chapter. It can also free up the finance professionals time to work on more interesting, challenging, value-adding work. This may require the finance function to build new capabilities.

However, automation and new technology can also be viewed as a **threat** to finance professionals since it can be used to reduce or replace many of their traditional roles and activities.

e.g

Illustration 14 – Technology and automation of jobs

The World Economic Forum Future of Jobs report (2025) concluded that the 7th top declining role by 2030 would be 'Accounting, Bookkeeping and Payroll Clerks'.

Note the word 'Clerks' – the dictionary defines this as an 'assistant'. The job of the accounts assistant is predicted to be automated in the future and clerks will need to retrain in analytical techniques to remain employed. There is anticipated to be a huge need for analysts – analysing and advising on the data the 'automation' has produced.

Just as with any other opportunity or threat, the organisation and its finance function must embrace the opportunities that the new technology offers and find a way of eliminating the threat or, even better, turning it into an opportunity.

6.2 Technology and the information to impact framework

Firstly, let's remind ourselves of our discussion from Chapter 2:

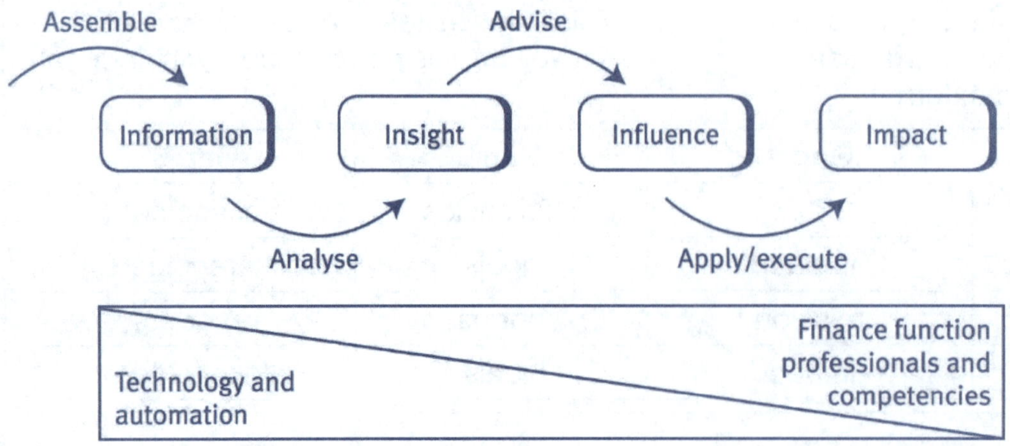

The information to impact framework clearly shows that:

- **Technology and automation** will play an important role in all of the activities of the finance function but will have the largest impact on the '**assembly**' and '**analysis**' activities.
- This will 'free up' the resource of the **finance function professionals** who can now place greater focus on the '**advising**' and '**applying/executing**' activities.
- The finance function will need to develop its **competencies**:
  - firstly, so that they are able to **use the up to date technology** and
  - secondly, so that they have the **necessary skills to provide the influence and impact required**.

Organisations are using technology to support the automation of management information processes and to provide reporting to the rest of the business on a self-service basis:

- This is resulting in a narrowing of the level 4 activities (diamond shape) of finance operations to generate information and preliminary insight.
- It has also increased the need for skills and talent at level 3 (working with specialists to provide further insight) and level 2 (communicating insight to influence users and business partnering to influence and impact the organisation).

Technology and its impact on the finance function will be explored in depth in the next few chapters. However, it is worth noting briefly that there have been two main technological changes that have impacted the finance function:

- New data sources and analysis methods
- Automation and cognitive computing

e.g

Illustration 15 – Opportunities offered by technology

Finance professionals might anticipate the technological advancements of the 4th Industrial Revolution with fear. However, the use of machines to take over repetitive, time-consuming and dated tasks, will free the finance professionals to do higher level, value-adding work.

The opportunities offered to the finance function by technology will be explored in later chapters.

Here will take a look at just a few of the opportunities that are available to an organisation as a whole thanks to this digital transformation:

Accounts payable/receivable – artificial intelligence (AI) powered invoice management systems make invoice processing much more streamlined. They can learn accounting codes that are more appropriate for each invoice.

Supplier management – machines can vet new suppliers by checking their credit scores or tax information and set them up in the system without human involvement.

Procurement – the procurement process for many organisations is filled with paperwork and uses different systems and files that are not compatible with one another. As machines can be integrated and the unstructured data is processed, the procurement system will eventually become paperless. Robots are ideally suited to tracking price changes among several suppliers.

Expense management – reviewing and approving expenses to ensure they are compliant with the organisation's policies is time consuming. Machines can read receipts, audit expenses and alert humans when a possible infraction has occurred.

AI chatbots – these can be used to efficiently solve common questions or queries from customers including the latest account balances, when certain bills are due, the status on accounts and more.

6.3 New data sources and analysis methods

New data sources and advanced methods for analysing this data are providing opportunities for better informed decision making.

For example, predictive analysis has improved forecasting and reduced the need to rely on the personal judgment of the finance professional.

Analytics has/will extend to areas such as financial planning and analysis (FP&A) pulling demand for talent from level 4 of the diamond to level 3.

6.4 Automation and cognitive computing

Cognitive computing is designed to simulate the human thought process in complex situations. The computers are taught to 'think' about problems and come up with plausible solutions.

Automation and cognitive computing have created cognitive Robotic Process Automation (RPA) whereby software takes over tasks which would otherwise been performed by humans.

According to a McKinsey report businesses which do this can automate between 50-70% of their tasks and decrease labour costs by 20-30%.

Formerly, RPA could only deal with structured data or processes where little to no interpretation was required, but now perception, sentiment and judgement can be factored in to include understanding of speech and imagery (or unstructured data).

Illustration 16 – Cognitive automation

For example, Virgin Trains in the UK has used cognitive RPA which provides opportunities to automate many routine, clerical activities. This enables customers to be dealt with quickly, for example when train-delay compensation is required. Cognitive RPA understands the customers complaint, issues the refund via a software bot, and reduces daily processing time and labour time by 85%.

A step further than the example above, where perception and judgement are factored into this, is the advent of the driverless car. The autonomous vehicle must use computer vision and radar to 'see' its surroundings, identifying pedestrians, traffic lights and other cars to make real-time driving decisions.

Test your understanding 15

Which FOUR of the following may be considered to be advantages of automating much of the traditional work of the finance function?

A Reduced human input, and therefore human error

B Reduced paperwork, for a more sustainable organisation

C Faster processing, meaning more real time information is available

D Improved data integrity

E Fewer finance staff required, reducing headcount costs

F Less training required for finance staff, reducing training costs

Test your understanding 16

Stanley, a CIMA student, has been asked by his manager to summarise the various viewpoints of the contemporary finance function.

Complete the table below from the options below.

Level in diamond	Information to impact framework	Activity	Position in finance function	McKinsey's automated functions
Level 1				
Level 2				
Level 3				
Level 4				

- Impact
- Smart finance factory
- Apply
- Data collection
- Advise
- Strategic business partner
- Information
- Stakeholder interactions/applying expertise
- Influence
- Analyse
- Data processing
- Digital centre of excellence
- Managing others/stakeholder interactions
- Insight
- Assemble
- Senior finance team

7 Chapter summary

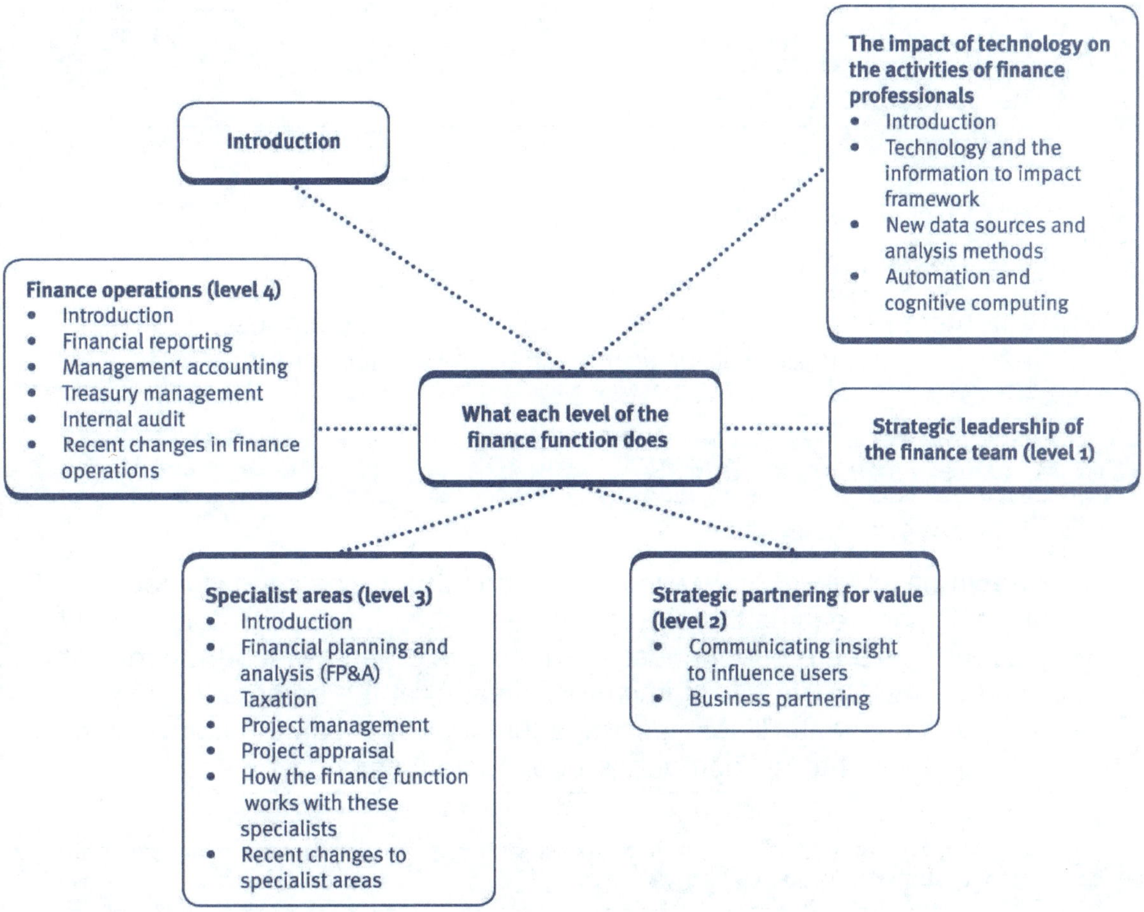

Test your understanding answers

Test your understanding 1

The correct answer is **A**

Test your understanding 2

The correct answer is **A**

Statement (i) is correct. However, statement (ii) describes a feature of financial accounting, rather than management accounting.

Test your understanding 3

The correct answer is **D**

Keeping a low level of receivables means that money is collected promptly, decreasing the chance of bad debts. Low receivables would also mean we are offering less credit to customers, which they may find unattractive. Low levels of inventory mean that the company is less exposed to inventory obsolescence, but it does mean the company may run out of inventory if demand is unexpectedly high.

Test your understanding 4

The correct answer is **B**

A is incorrect, as dividends are not tax allowable – interest is.

B is correct as, in the event of the product being a failure, AHG would not need to make unaffordable repayments to investors if it raises finance from equity.

C is incorrect as AHG only needs the money for 5 years. It could be argued that a 5 year loan would match the term of the project and therefore be more appropriate than equity finance, on which the company will have to pay dividends forever.

D is also incorrect as debt does normally require security from the company. Equity does not.

Test your understanding 5

The correct answer is **B – False**

The benefits of internal audit should exceed the costs. The IIA definition stresses that internal audit is a value-adding activity by helping an organisation to manage its risks and achieve its objectives. If an organisation believes that the costs of internal audit would exceed the benefits, then it shouldn't operate that internal audit function. This is a choice to be made by the directors of a company; there is no requirement to operate an internal audit department.

Test your understanding 6

The correct answer is **A – True**

Internal auditors can either be employees of the company being audited, or may be external experts brought in. Compare this with external auditors who have to be external to the company; employees of the company are not allowed to carry out an external audit of that company.

Test your understanding 7

The correct answer is **D**

Internal audit reports to the management of the company. In a smaller company, internal audit is likely to report directly to the board of directors of the company being audited. In a larger company where there is an audit committee, internal audit is likely to report to the audit committee, which will be made up of non-executive directors.

Test your understanding 8

Answer A is false – a shared service centre may be outsourced (internal outsourcing) but the two terms do not strictly mean the same thing.

Answer B is false – the shared service centre will view the business to be the customer. The more professional supplier/customer relationship should result in marked improvements in the quality of the service provided.

Answer C is true – establishing an SSC enables a business' processes to be standardised.

Answer D is false – in the diamond shape the level 3 tasks present within 'specialists generating further insights in their areas of specialism' are now offered by shared service centres.

Test your understanding 9

Kazim – taxation

Paul – project appraisal

Belinda – financial planning and analysis

Saira – project management

Test your understanding 10

The correct answers are **A, C, D and F**

Tax mitigation (answer B) would be carried out within the specialist area of taxation.

Net present value analysis (answer E) is typically performed by project analysts.

FP&A may use liquidity ratios to gauge the financial health of the organisation (answer G).

Test your understanding 11

The correct answers are **A, B, D and E**

Answer C – the finance team do not have less to do because of changes in technology, but the work they do is of a different nature.

Answer F – there are new skills to learn due to changes in technology and it is important that members within finance are up to date with these changes and have the necessary skills required to adapt.

Test your understanding 12

Statement	True/False?
The finance function will communicate their insights once a month	False – the insights will be communicated as frequently as required.
The finance function communicates their insights only to internal stakeholders	False – the finance function will communicate to both internal and external stakeholders.
Fewer people are required at this level of the finance function than previously	False – the evolving shape of the finance function will mean more people will be required at this level.
Insight means the capacity to gain an accurate and deep understanding of someone or something	True – by definition.
New competencies need to be developed by the finance function to be able to effectively generate and communicate insight	True – new competencies and skills will be required.

Test your understanding 13

The answer is **all of them**. There is no single definition of business partnership. Finance will support the organisation in all of the ways described.

Test your understanding 14

The best answer is **D**

"It is the responsibility of the CFO to lead the finance team to achieve the desired organisational **impact**. This involves leading key initiatives to support organisational **goals,** as well as liaising effectively with internal and external **stakeholders**."

Test your understanding 15

The four advantages are **A, B, C and D**

Whilst E and F appear to be advantages, it is not necessarily true that fewer staff will be required, merely that the type of work they are performing will be at a different level. Additionally, the transition to the contemporary finance function will require additional training to develop the new competencies required.

Test your understanding 16

Level in diamond	**Information to impact framework**	**Activity**	**Position in finance function**	**McKinsey's automated functions**
Level 1	Impact	Apply	Senior finance team	Managing others/ stakeholder interactions
Level 2	Influence	Advise	Strategic business partner	Stakeholder interactions/ applying expertise
Level 3	Insight	Analyse	Digital centre of excellence	Data processing
Level 4	information	Assemble	Smart finance factory	Data collection

Chapter

5

Technology affecting business and finance

Chapter learning objectives

Lead	Component
B1: Outline and explain the technologies that affect business and finance.	(a) Outline the key features of the fourth industrial revolution (b) Outline and explain the key technologies that define and drive the digital world

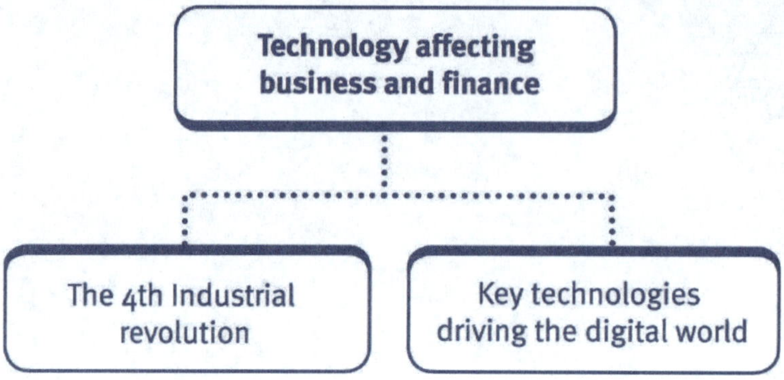

1 Introduction

In this chapter we will look at the technology driven changes facing the business world today. It considers the key technologies fuelling what is increasingly being viewed as a new industrial revolution. The aim is to create an awareness of the technologies (as outlined by major advisory firms and the World Economic Forum digital transformation initiative) that drive the digital world. It also looks at how the technologies interact with each other.

2 The 4th Industrial Revolution

2.1 What is an industrial revolution?

An industrial revolution can be generalised as **"a rapid and major change in an economy, driven by a shift in the methods and types of work undertaken"**.

Illustration 1 – Industrial revolutions

The **1st Industrial Revolution** in the 18th and 19th centuries saw a shift from rural, agricultural life to urban, industrialised societies. The growth in steam power and advancements in machinery transformed both agriculture and craft industries, and fundamentally changed the basis of the economy of the time for countries such as the United States, United Kingdom and elsewhere.

The period from 1870–1914 has been labelled the **2nd Industrial Revolution** by historians. Already industrialised societies driven by coal, steam power, iron and textiles were transformed by advancements in the electricity, petroleum and steel industries. This saw the growth of vast corporations and a wave of globalisation.

The **3rd Industrial Revolution** is popularly held as originating in the 1980s. It is known as the **Digital Revolution** and saw a move from mechanical and analogue technology to the digital technology of today. Developments and improvements in communications, computers and the introduction of the internet were some of the key drivers of this period of rapid change.

Technologies such as **cloud computing**, **big data, data analytics, process automation, artificial intelligence**, **data visualisation**, **blockchain**, **internet of things, mobile technologies** and **3-D printing** are some of the more commonly known developments predicted to drive the 4th Industrial Revolution.

2.2 Features of the 4th Industrial revolution

Each industrial revolution has impacted upon society in their own specific way. The characteristics predicted to define the **4th Industrial revolution** include:

- **Fusion** – cyber and physical systems will continue to fuse becoming increasingly autonomous
- **Employment** – robotics, automation and digitisation are predicted to fundamentally change many jobs
- **Artificial intelligence and machine learning** (see definition later) – improved computing speed and optimised supply chains, enables products to be customised more easily and more cheaply
- **Machine led manufacturing** – the shift from machines helping workers manufacture, to workers helping machines will accelerate
- **Improved asset management** – benefits to the natural world through more efficient use of natural assets, a shift to renewables, innovations in recycling, coupled with digitisation are anticipated to benefit the natural world.

e.g

Illustration 2 – A hypothetical vision of the future

An article from the BBC (October 2018 – Justin Rowlatt) discusses the impact of some of these emerging technologies and predicts how they may revolutionise our lives in the not too distant future.

The article titled **'why you have (*probably*) already bought your last car'** is written to provoke debate and is formed from the ideas of a number of tech analysts who predict within 20 years (so by 2038) we will have stopped owning cars altogether.

This idea is built upon the emergence of self-driving electric vehicles, enabled by tech including AI, internet of things and data analytics amongst others. The article claims that these vehicles will be operated in an '**Uber**' (the ride hailing technology company) style network that will be so cheap the idea of owning a car will become obsolete within a decade.

The idea of this sounds almost unbelievable when viewed through the norms of today, however the rapid emergence of the motor car just over 100 years ago is cited as evidence of how quickly things can change. Once mass production began, city streets changed from almost entirely horse and carriage to cars in the space of a decade.

So how will it all take hold?

The article walks through an example using an Uber style company as its backbone. Uber and their rivals have already transformed the face of urban transport, a driver can be hailed immediately using a smart phone and arrive within minutes, then for a modest fee, say $10, take us from A to B. These services have grown at a rapid pace and despite concerns and media criticism continue unabated.

Now, of the $10 cost, at least 50% is paying the driver a wage. Therefore, once **driverless tech** is available and licensed, which many believe could be within 5 years, the cost of your journey has immediately halved to $5. (This timescale is evidenced by every major motor and tech company fighting to take the lead of what will become a vast market worth billions of dollars annually).

The next thing to consider is the development and improvement of **electric powered vehicles**. The cost of purchasing electric cars is currently significantly higher than their fossil-fuelled counterparts. The emergence and growth of companies like Tesla, along with the threat of climate change and dwindling oil reserves, has seen major car companies shift their attentions to electric powered vehicles; they are ploughing billions of dollars in to refining and improving the technology. This level of investment will soon make electric vehicles accessible to the mass market and will ultimately bring the cost down to less than the cost of their fossil fuelled equivalents.

Further to this we must consider the running costs; fuel is one of the biggest costs for any fleet of taxis, a move to electric powered vehicles would see another significant cost removed. Additionally, **electric motors are much simpler** than a conventional engine, with only around 20 moving parts compared to 2,000 or so in the traditional engine. Therefore, electric cars are expected to last for at least 500,000 miles delivering a huge increase in the useful life of the asset.

Battery **technology continues to advance** and investments such as Tesla's 'gigafactory' are anticipated to see the efficiency and reliability of batteries improve, the cost and speed of charging will also continue to fall.

Statistics show that the average driver in England drives less than 10,000 miles annually meaning **95% of the time their cars are parked**, which makes for an expensive and somewhat inefficient lump of metal. Especially when compared with an autonomous and intelligently controlled taxi which could be utilised at near full capacity. Then on top of all of these factors, as adoption of this new service takes hold, it will fuel its own growth becoming cheaper and more efficient as more vehicles would be added to the network achieving **significant economies of scale**.

Influential analysts predict with all of these factors combined, the cost of your $10 Uber journey of today could be cut by as much as 90%, so down to just $1! This would be a huge saving on the cost of buying and running your own car.

Additional considerations include **time saved** leading to increased productivity i.e. that 1 hour commute becoming part of your productive working day for instance. Additionally, once self-driving technology is perfected the flow of traffic will become much **smoother and safer** as the most unreliable and unpredictable element, the human behind the wheel, is removed. In fact, the article goes on to suggest that ultimately humans will be banned from driving altogether due to the threat they pose to the efficient and safe running of the 'self-diving robo-network' of taxis.

If the potential upheaval of all these changes isn't enough, when you consider the array of industries and businesses built around private car ownership and how these could disappear or be radically changed, it makes you realise how far reaching such developments will be to the world of today in terms of **industrial and social upheaval**.

The fact that this sounds like science-fiction, is much like the idea of the light bulb and the motor car would have sounded to people only a handful of generations ago, prior to previous industrial revolutions. Much of the technology discussed above is well on its way so this could well become science fact sooner than we may imagine, and the **4th industrial revolution** will be in full swing.

3 Key technologies driving the digital world

In this section will we introduce some of the key developments and technologies driving the new wave of innovation and increasingly changing the world around us.

How these technologies are beginning to impact the world of finance and the role of the finance professional will be considered in more detail in later chapters.

3.1 Cloud computing

Cloud computing is defined as the delivery of on-demand computing resources – everything from applications to data centres – over the internet. (IBM)

The basic idea and application of cloud computing sees users log in to an account in order to access, manage and process files and software via remote servers hosted on the internet. This replaces the traditional method of owning and running software locally on a computer or networked server.

There are two main types of cloud setups:

- **Public cloud** – hosted by a third-party company. Specialist companies sell their cloud computing services to anyone over the public internet who wishes to purchase them, for example Amazon Web Services (AWS) Microsoft Azure or Google Cloud.
- **Private cloud** – sees IT services provided over a private infrastructure, typically for the use of a single organisation. They are usually managed internally.

e.g

Illustration 3 – Amazon and cloud computing services

Amazon's market value stands at $2.47 trillion in 2025. A large contributor to this was the continued growth of Amazon Web Services (AWS). They are the market leader holding 31% market share in cloud computing while Microsoft Azure have 20% and Google Cloud 11%. AWS controls a third of the market in an industry worth over $676 billion in 2025. The industry is expected to grow to $2,292 billion by 2032.

Significantly, their AWS business supports operations of other core areas of Amazon's business including e-commerce, Amazon Prime video and music and the Amazon home assistant. This was a gateway to the 'internet of things', another market which grew significantly.

Features of cloud computing

Advantages	**Disadvantages**
Flexibility and scalability – Cloud computing allows simple and frequent upgrades allowing access to the latest systems developments. A company doesn't become laden with expensive hardware and software that quickly becomes obsolete. This allows organisations to evolve and change, to adapt to new opportunities and working practices	**Organisational change** – Working methods and roles need to be modified to incorporate a move to cloud computing. It may also lead to job losses, primarily in IT support and maintenance roles
Cost efficient – Limited IT maintenance costs and reduced costs of IT hardware, sees capital expenses and fixed costs become operating expenses. Cloud technology also allows pay as you go computing, with charges based on what a company actually needs	**Contract management** – The cloud provider will immediately become a very significant supplier. Managing this relationship, monitoring performance and ensuring contractual obligations will introduce new challenges and costs

Advantages	Disadvantages
Security – Cloud service providers, like any outsource provider, are specialists. The security and integrity of their systems is fundamental to their business model and will be a strategic priority. Disaster recovery and backups are built in	**Security, privacy and compliance** – Whilst cloud providers will be specialists, they are bigger targets for malicious agents. This can threaten the security of sensitive information. Additionally, compliance with data regulations is put largely in the hands of a third party.
Flexible working – The increase in remote and home working is supported by cloud computing and the ability to access your 'desktop' from any location	**Reliance** – More so than with a standard outsource arrangements, the reliability of the cloud service provider is essential. Often the entire provision of information systems fundamental to the operation of a business is passed to this third party.
Environment – Less waste from the disposal of obsolete technology. More efficient use of scarce resources.	

Test your understanding 1

Which of the following describes a cloud service that can only be accessed by a limited number of authorised people?

A Management information system

B Private cloud

C Public cloud

D Big data

3.2 Big data

Big data describes data sets so large and varied they are beyond the capability of traditional data-processing

The key features of big data can be best captured using the **4Vs** framework:

Volume Considers the amount of data fed into the organisation	• Does the organisation have the resources available to store and manage this data? • Or does it have the financial resources required to invest in or upgrade IT/IS?
Velocity Considers the speed that data is fed into the organisation	• Are systems able to capture and process 'real time' data? • Does the organisation have the skills to provide timely analysis of this data?
Variety Considers the various formats of data received	• Are systems compatible and capable of accepting various forms of data? • Legally, is the data owned by the organisation or by the third party?
Veracity Considers the reliability of the data being received	• Can the organisation challenge data received from third parties? • Is the data received fully representative of the whole data population?

Sources of big data

Big data comes in two main forms. Structured data is deliberately produced and collected for a specific purpose and therefore exhibits a clear, deliberate structure. For instance, feedback data when people have been asked to rate a service or product. Unstructured data is captured passively without a clear purpose. Social media posts and 'likes' are an example of this. Its format is highly variable and non-standard.

The principal sources of these two forms of data are classified as follows:

- **Human-sourced data** – billions of data points are produced every day from social media, text messages, web browsing, emails etc.
- **Machine-generated data** – smart technologies and the internet of things (see later) is a growing source of data. Sensors are built into all aspects of modern technology, which log and upload data constantly. Home assistants, smart meters, TV boxes and cars are a small selection of items producing machine-generated data.
- **Processed data** – Traditional data is held on databases of businesses and organisations recording customers, transactions and company assets.
- **Open data** – Publicly available data stemming from sources such as governments, the public sector and national statistics agencies.

e.g

Illustration 4 – Big data in everyday life

The sheer volume of data we produce daily is vast and increasing all the time. It largely goes unnoticed as much of it we produce incidentally as we live our lives. Yet companies are desperate to collect this data as they hope to gain unique insights and information that could deliver a crucial advantage over their rivals.

If you consider a hypothetical morning routine for instance; woken up by your smartphone alarm, you pick it up to silence it before having a look at emails or messages received overnight.

Realising its a little cold you ask your smart home assistant to turn the heating up a few degrees and maybe even turn the lights on. As it's the weekend you decide to turn the TV on, digital of course, constantly firing data back to the service provider. What programme are you watching, how long do you watch for? Which adverts do you watch?

Next up you decide to have a quick browse on social media, a few likes and shares, time spent watching videos and clicking on an interesting advert or two, all adds a little more to this 'gold mine' of data.

So, without even leaving bed we have already generated multiple types of data. Not to mention the smart meter that is monitoring the power usage of all this technology and continually harvesting this data.

A quick drive to the shops will see the computer used to control all modern cars collect a wide array of data about the performance and condition of the car, both the cars sat-nav and your smart phone will be communicating data about your location and what the driving conditions are like on the roads you travel down. Monitors in traffic lights and in the roads themselves as well as cameras along the way will also track vehicles passing with data being used for traffic monitoring and surveillance.

You then pull up and park, the car park records your number plate and updates its information on the number of available spaces.

As you enter the shop your footfall is logged, the way we navigate the store, what causes us to stop and pick up certain items, all of this is of huge value to retailers so increasing attention is devoted to trying to capture this data to gain valuable insight.

Our card payment is logged by the provider as we pay for the basket of shopping, the contents of which is recorded and matched to our loyalty card profile which contains our shopping history as well as our profile info. This can be used to better understand customers, their habits and how they may be changing, what people want and when they buy it, what was the weather like when these purchases were made? And did this influence your choices?

Data on stock movements will also be generated, which is vital to the supply chain and inventory management systems of stores; these are often almost entirely automated.

So, from this simple example, without any deliberate actions or specific intent a surprisingly large amount of different data has been generated by one individual. If you multiply this across billions of different people doing their own morning routine, the result is a truly vast amount of data.

Test your understanding 2

A private educational college is looking at ways they can utilise data in their organisation. The managing director has suggested using the current system that has names of students, their student identity number, and the company they work for.

What kind of data would this be using?

A Public data

B Unstructured data

C Volume of data

D Structured data

3.3 Data analytics

Data analytics is the process of collecting, organising and analysing large sets of data (**big data**) to discover patterns and other information which an organisation can use to inform future decisions.

Collection of data
Organisations have access to greater quantities of data available from a number of internal and external sources.

Organisation of data
Once the data has been captured it needs to be organised and stored for future use, often using data warehousing facilities.

Analysis of data
Data mining software uses statistical algorithms to discover correlations and patterns to create useful information.

Uses of data analytics and big data – Understanding the potential value of data and its significance to an organisation presents a real opportunity to gain unique insight. This can be used to improve competitive position and potentially gain competitive advantage over rivals.

Business consultants McKinsey, summarised the following benefits an organisation can realise from effective data analytics:

- **Fresh insight and understanding** – Seeing underlying patterns through the intelligent use of data can reveal patterns and insight into how a business operates, revealing issues that they may not have known existed.
- **Performance improvement** – Data, processed and sorted into relevant management information in real time, can lead to significant operational gains and improved decision making and resource utilisation.
- **Market segmentation and customisation** (discussed further in Chapter 10) – Refining customer groups into ever more specific segments and understanding the wants and needs of those groups can lead to increased personalisation and customisation of products and services.
- **Decision making** – Real time information that is relevant can lead to faster decisions and decisive advantage over competitors.
- **Innovation** – Existing products can be improved from understanding the features and elements that customers enjoy and use. This can also lead to the development of whole new products.
- **Risk management** – Risk management and control are vital in the effective running of any organisation. The use of data can enhance all stages of the risk management process.

3.4 Process automation

The technology enabled automation of complex business processes. This can be entire processes or elements therein, aimed at improving consistency, quality and speed whilst delivering cost savings.

Traditional process automation – The traditional idea of process automation is that of a machine carrying out a simple repetitive task, replacing a job that would have been done by hand or in a semi-automated fashion. This type of automation is everywhere and has driven industrialisation, through the ability to produce ever higher volumes of products, with fewer problems and at less cost.

Modern process automation – Increasingly automation and process automation are focusing upon complex business areas, which were previously thought to be beyond the limits of technology.

Big data and the **internet of things** (see section 3.8) generate huge amounts of data; **data analytics** transforms this into useful information that supports **artificial intelligence** and **machine learning** (see section 3.5). Essentially process automation is becoming smarter and can make decisions using reasoning, language and learned behaviour.

Illustration 5 – Process automation

Customer contact centres are an area that many businesses are keen to automate. It is a business function deemed to be relatively low skilled in comparison to other business processes but is an area that customers value so must be handled with care.

This was evidenced by the wave of contact centres being offshored to countries with lower labour costs in the 1990s/2000s driven by the aim of achieving cost savings. Customers were however, often dissatisfied with the level of service received resulting in several companies ultimately bringing their contact centres back to the home country.

Companies were still keen to realise cost savings in this area but required a new approach to doing so. Developments in technology have led to significant improvements in process automation, contact centres are now typically heavily automated using the technology in conjunction with humans. The use of automation has been designed to use workers time more efficiently, through redesigning and streamlining processes as well as fully automating simple tasks and processes.

Developments in voice recognition technology and the ability of artificial intelligence allows contact centre calls to be answered robotically, they will typically ask the nature of the call, then place this on the right track. Many calls can be handled fully autonomously for instance making payments or tracing orders. Callers who do require a contact centre operative will then begin the security process; this will then interrogate the system to bring the customer and case information up on the operatives screen before they even speak.

More recently, many companies use 'chatbots' (a software application designed to have textual conversations) as they realise that many customers rarely call the company but instead use their computer to speak by text with the chat bot to resolve their query.

Data capture and analytics are also used to monitor and understand call types and chat bot interactions, monitoring for new or emerging trends and suspicious or potentially fraudulent activity. This will enable workers to be more prepared and trained specifically to deal with high risk call types or chatbot enquiries.

All of these improvements have led to both cost savings and service improvements through more targeted and efficient use of contact centre workers time, seeing them specifically used on activities where value can be added.

3.5 Artificial intelligence

Artificial Intelligence (AI) is an area of computer science that emphasises the creation of intelligent machines that work and react like human beings.

A common definition from Kaplan and Haenlein describes AI as a **"system's ability to correctly interpret external data, to learn from such data, and to use those learnings to achieve specific goals and tasks through flexible adaptation"**. This is often considered in the context of human-type robotics but reaches much further than this and is set to transform the way we live and work.

Some of the more advanced activities and skills artificial intelligence can now master, and therefore present huge opportunity for developers and companies alike, include:

- Voice recognition
- Planning
- Learning
- Problem solving

e.g

Illustration 6 – Artificial intelligence

Companies such as **Apple** and **Amazon** have developed and marketed voice recognition systems, either to be built into an existing product (such as Apple with its **Siri** system) or developed new products whose main function is voice recognition (such as Amazon and '**Alexa**').

There are many more complex examples of Artificial Intelligence, but a common factor to both the simple and the more involved is machine learning.

Data protection care must be taken with this kind of Artificial Intelligence use, as Amazon was fined $25 million in the U.S. for violating privacy laws by keeping recordings of children's conversations with Alexa. And Ring – the doorbell company, was fined $6 million for keeping recordings of visitor's faces.

Machine learning

Machine learning is a subset of AI where effectively AI computer code is built to mimic how the human brain works. It essentially uses probability based on past experiences through data, events and connections between events. The computer then applies this learning to a given situation to give a fact driven plausible outcome. If the conclusion the computer reaches turns out to be incorrect this will act to add more experience and enhance its understanding further, so in future the same mistake will not be repeated.

Essentially machine learning algorithms detect patterns and learn how to make predictions and recommendations rather than following explicit programming instruction. The algorithms themselves then adapt to new data and experiences to improve their function over time.

e.g

Illustration 7 – Artificial Intelligence: 'Move 37'

Go is a highly complex strategy game, believed to originate in China over 2,500 years ago. It is considered to be more complicated and advanced than Chess, with a larger board and more elements meaning each move has many more alternatives to consider.

In 2016 **Google DeepMind (GDM)**, an **AI** technology played a challenge match against Go world champion **Lee Sedol**. The match was won by **GDM** in what many considered to be a significant milestone in AI research and development.

Essentially the program had been built from uploading thousands of previous Go games, which allowed the software to learn moves, patterns and responses to moves, to become a Go expert.

One moment in the match, referred to as **Move 37**, is considered to be a particularly important moment in AI development. GDM played its 37th move which to all commentators and indeed Lee Sedol himself, appeared to be completely abstract and in effect a 'bad' move. It turned out to be an innovative new move never seen before. The significance of the move wasn't felt until much later in the game but it turned out to be the pivotal moment, which enabled GDM to win the match.

The fact the computer software, who's 'knowledge' was built upon past games of Go and the moves and permutations encountered, was then able to take this learning and build upon it, doing something completely new was a demonstration of the power of **AI** and **machine learning**.

Interestingly Lee Sedol the human world champion was later able to beat **GDM** by effectively identifying limitations in its coding. He then made moves that were outside of GDM's understanding and the system therefore struggled to respond appropriately. This is a useful illustration of why **AI** and human thinking will need to be used in a mutual and collaborative way to help achieve innovations.

Generative AI (GEN AI)

Generative AI is also a subset of artificial intelligence that specialises in producing new, original content (including text, images, audio, video, and code) by learning and copying the patterns, structures, and features present in existing data.

Using advanced machine learning techniques such as Generative Adversarial Networks (GANs), Variational Autoencoders (VAEs), and transformer-based models like Large Language Models (LLMs), generative AI not only copies but also innovates, generating outputs that can closely mimic or even surpass human-created work in complexity and creativity.

e.g

Illustration 8 – Types of Generative AI models

There are two types of Generative AI models:

Foundational Models

Generative AI relies on foundational models that provide the underlying techniques to generate new and innovative outputs. These foundational models include:

- **Generative Adversarial Networks (GANs)**
  GANs consist of two networks – a generator that creates new data and a discriminator that evaluates its authenticity. Through a competitive process, GANs improve the quality of generated outputs, making them particularly effective in producing realistic images and art. Clothing retailer H&M uses GANs to create highly realistic designs for its products.
- **Variational Autoencoders (VAEs)**
  VAEs learn to compress input data into a spare or hidden area and then decode it to generate new, similar data. This approach is useful for tasks such as image reconstruction and anomaly detection, as it captures the underlying structure of the data. For example, VAE is used in industrial quality control by identifying images of products on a production line that deviate from the image of a normal product. The abnormal product can then be removed.
- **Transformer-Based Models (Large Language Models or LLMs)**
  Models such as GPT-4 use transformer architectures with self-attention mechanisms (focussing on different parts of any input text during each processing step). This captures more context within the text and improves performance on natural language/text processing tasks. These models are widely used for text-to-text applications, producing content ranging from articles to conversational responses. For example, Google Translate uses transformer models to translate text from one language to another with high accuracy.
- **Diffusion Models**
  Diffusion models generate high-quality outputs by repeatedly refining random noise (decreasing unpredictable, irrelevant or erroneous data) into structured data, making them especially effective for detailed image generation. For example, diffusion models can process medical images such as X-rays and other scans more efficiently than people or traditional generative models, by ignoring parts of the medical image which are irrelevant.

Modality-Specific Applications

While foundational models provide the technical backbone for generative AI, the technology also extends into various modality-specific applications, demonstrating its versatility across different forms of data. Examples include:

- **Text-to-Text Generation**
  Using models like GPT-4, generative AI can transform given text prompts into new, contextually appropriate text. This capability is widely used in content creation, summarisation, and dialogue systems. For example, the summarisation function is used in many email systems now where you don't need to read a lengthy email chain anymore as AI will summarise it for you.

- **Speech-to-Text Conversion**
  In automatic speech recognition (ASR) systems, models such as Deep Speech convert spoken language into written text. Although primarily viewed as a conversion task, these systems use sequence-to-sequence learning – a generative technique – to produce accurate transcriptions. The BBC and other news channels use this type of system to add subtitles to their newsreaders verbal output. As many of you will know the written output is not always perfect yet!

- **Text-to-Speech Synthesis**
  Models like Tacotron and WaveNet transform written text into natural-sounding speech. These systems generate audio outputs by synthesising speech patterns learned from large datasets of human speech. Individuals living with Motor Neurone Disease (MND) can 'voice bank' their speech so that when their speech ability reduces or ends they can still communicate by typing text (or tracking their eyes to a keyboard) and this type of text to speech model then replicates the text into the individuals own voice from the voice bank data.

- **Image-to-Speech (Multimodal Applications)**
  Although less common, image-to-speech systems are typically built by combining image captioning models (which generate descriptive text from images) with text-to-speech engines. This multimodal (or multimedia) approach enables the conversion of visual information into text and then text into spoken language, broadening accessibility and enhancing user interaction. This is particularly useful for blind people.

Together, these foundational models and modality-specific applications illustrate the huge capabilities of generative AI. They highlight the theoretical techniques used to generate new, innovative content and also demonstrate practical applications which enable new forms of interaction, creativity, and automation.

Humans and Generative AI

Humans should not rely totally on computers and AI without some intervention.

- **Collaboration** – Generative AI works as a creative partner, augmenting human ideas rather than replacing them.
- **Review** – Humans provide context, evaluate outputs, and fine-tune models to ensure relevance and accuracy.
- **Skill enhancement** – AI frees up human time for higher-level strategic thinking and creative problem solving.

Features of Generative AI

- **Creativity** – AI learns complex patterns from vast data sets to produce new and innovative content.
- **Scalability** – AI can generate large volumes of content quickly and across multiple formats (text, image and audio).
- **Adaptability** – It is capable of repeating improvements based on new data and user feedback.
- **Interactivity** – It often includes user-friendly interfaces for real-time collaboration and adjustments.

Advantages of AI and Generative AI

As seen in the examples of foundational models and modality specific applications, there are huge advantages in the use of AI.

- **Improved productivity** – AI automates routine content creation, freeing up time for creative and strategic tasks.
- **Motivation** – Automation of repetitive tasks leads to more time to focus on the more stimulating/motivating and impactful aspects of work.
- **Availability** – unlike humans who need breaks in their working day and time-off, AI can work all day everyday thereby increasing productivity.
- **Efficiency** – AI can work much faster than the human brain speeding up processes such as report generation, design prototyping, and customer interaction.
- **Reduction in operational costs** – possibly by a reduction in staff numbers and therefore payroll costs.
- **Innovation** – AI can spark new ideas and creative designs by exploring diverse possibilities.
- **Personalisation** – AI can tailor outputs to specific contexts or user preferences, improving relevance and engagement.

Disadvantages of AI and Generative AI

- **Ethical concerns** – AI can raise issues around the authenticity of any material produced, intellectual property, and potential misuse.
- **Bias** – AI can inadvertently learn and increase biases present in the data. The output from AI is based on what is input and that input starts from potentially biased humans. This can lead to stereotyping, prejudice and outright lies.
- **Resource intensity and cost** – AI requires large data sets and significant computational power for training and operation.
- **Variable quality** – Outputs may sometimes be unpredictable or require human refinement for accuracy.
- **Lack of creativity** – Output is generated from statistical models and algorithms. It does not include the creativity of human professionals.
- **Lack of emotional intelligence** – AI can be programmed to recognise certain emotional cues and respond in predetermined ways, but it doesn't have empathy, nor is it able to manage complex human emotions (yet).
- **Encourages human laziness** – Humans may become dependent on AI to solve their work (or personal) problems. The solutions suggested may not be correct so any output from AI should be corroborated which takes time and money.
- **Risk to employment** – According to a study by Goldman Sachs in 2023, researchers estimate that two-thirds of current jobs in the US and Europe could be partially performed by AI and this could lead to the loss of almost 300 million full-time jobs.

Common uses of Generative AI

- **Content creation and editing** – Generating text, images, music, and videos for marketing, entertainment, and educational purposes.
- **Design and prototyping** – Assisting in the creation of design prototypes and innovative product concepts.
- **Personal and professional support** – Powering chatbots and virtual assistants to provide automated yet personalised support. Examples include general advice, writing/ editing/ business advice.
- **Data enhancement** – Creating synthetic data to increase machine learning training processes.
- **Research, analysis and decision making** – Specific search, enhanced decision-making, streamlining report generation, predictive analysis, and other routine tasks such as fact checking and evaluating can be performed quickly and accurately.

Test your understanding 3

Dollar Co is a chain of banks. It collects data from customers who visit the banks in person, and also from online transactions. For the online banking system, customers need to log in via the website using their login and password. Recently Dollar Co invested in a system that promoted certain products to customers when they were online, based on past transactions and banking history.

What is this is an example of?

A Traditional process automation

B Data visualisation

C Artificial intelligence

D Virtual reality

3.6 Data visualisation

Data visualisation allows large volumes of complex data to be displayed in a visually appealing and accessible way that facilitates the understanding and use of the underlying data.

The growing significance of data has seen a rise in the importance of being able to access and understand the data in clear, concise way. This is where **data visualisation** fits in. The tools of today's market leaders **Tableau** and **Qlik**, go far beyond the simple charts and graphs of Microsoft Excel. Data is displayed in customisable, interactive 3D formats that allow users to manipulate and drill down as required. Central to data visualisation is understanding and ease of use, the leading companies in the field look to make data easier and more accessible for everyone.

Essentially it aims to remove the need for complex extraction, analysis and presentation of data by finance, IT and data scientists. It puts the ability to find data into the hands of the end user, through intuitive, user friendly interfaces.

The most common use of data visualisation is in creating a dashboard to display the **key performance indicators** of a business in a live format, thus allowing immediate understanding of current performance and potentially prompting action to correct or amend performance accordingly.

An effective data visualisation tool should display these five features:

- **Decision making ability** – Results focused, it should aid decision making
- **Effective infrastructure** – The output is reliant upon sufficient quantity and quality of data
- **Integration capability** – With existing systems and the business overall
- **Prompt understanding and insight of data** – Live data is vital. A delay can limit the effective use of data for performance improvement or render any insight useless
- **Real time collaboration** – Users must interact with each other and the data

3.7 Blockchain

A **blockchain** has been described as a decentralised, distributed and public digital ledger that is used to record transactions across many computers. This means the record cannot be altered retroactively without the alteration of all subsequent blocks and the consensus of the network.

Alternatively, it has been defined by the **Bank of England** (in a more straightforward way) as a technology that allows people who do not know each other to trust a shared record of events.

e.g

Illustration 9 – Walmart's use of blockchain to improve food safety

Walmart is the world's biggest retailer. However, its supply chain was bogged down in manual processes, making it difficult and time consuming to track down issues, such as a recent E.coli (a potentially harmful bacteria) outbreak in one of its supplies of green, leafy vegetables.

Walmart has used blockchain to digitise the food supply process, making it more traceable and transparent. Before moving the process to the blockchain, it typically took 7 days to trace the source of food. With blockchain, it has been reduced to 2.2 seconds. This substantially reduces the threat that infected food will reach the customer.

Benefits of a blockchain

The main benefit of blockchain is security. In the digital era, cyber security is a key risk associated with the use of IT systems and the internet. This is because traditional systems have been 'closed', and so modifications to data have been carried out by just one party. If the system is hacked, there is little control over such modification to prevent it from happening.

A blockchain provides an effective control mechanism aimed at addressing such cyber security risks. It is a record keeping mechanism that is 'open' or public, as it utilises a distributed ledger; it has been described as a form of collective bookkeeping.

Key features of a blockchain

- In a blockchain system, transactions are recorded by several participants using a network which operates via the internet. The same records are maintained by several different parties; as a transaction is entered, it is recorded by not just two parties, but instead by all of the parties that make up the overall chain. This can happen because all of the records in the blockchain are publicly available and distributed across everyone that is part of that network.
- When a transaction takes place (for example, between a buyer and a seller) the details of that deal are recorded by everyone – the value, the time, the date and the details of those parties involved. All of the ledgers that make up the blockchain are updated in the same way, and it takes the agreement of all participants in the chain to update their ledgers for the transaction to be accepted.

- The process of verifying the transaction is carried out by computers; it is effectively the computers making up the network that audit the transaction. If all of the computers review the transaction and verify the details are correct, the systems of all participants in the blockchain have updated records. The computers work together to ensure that each transaction is valid before it is added to the blockchain. This decentralised network of computers ensures that a single system cannot add new blocks to the chain.
- When a new block is added to a blockchain, it is linked to the previous block using a cryptographic hash (this turns data into a format that can only be read by authorised users) generated from the contents of the previous block. This ensures that the chain is never broken and that each block is permanently recorded. It is intentionally difficult to alter past transactions in the blockchain because all of the subsequent blocks must be altered first.

It is this control aspect of blockchain technology which addresses the main concern of cyber security. If anyone should attempt to interfere with a transaction, it will be rejected by those network parties making up the blockchain whose role it is to verify the transaction. If just one party disagrees, the transaction will not be recorded.

Typical stages in a blockchain transaction

1. A transaction is requested

2. A block is created as a digital representation of the transaction

3. The block is sent to every node in the network (Distributed ledger)

4. The nodes validate the authenticity of the transaction

5. The nodes receive a reward for the proof of work i.e. some Bitcoin

6. The completed authorised block is added to the chain

e.g

Illustration 10 – Cryptocurrency

Bitcoin is a digital currency that was introduced in 2009. Its aim is to simplify online transactions by bypassing government control of currency. Other cryptocurrencies exist, such as **Litecoin, XRP** and **Ethereum**.

There is no physical version of Bitcoin; all Bitcoin transactions take place over the internet. Unlike traditional currencies, Bitcoin is decentralised, meaning it is not controlled by a single bank or government. Instead, Bitcoin uses a peer-to-peer (P2P) payment network made up of users with Bitcoin accounts.

Bitcoins can be acquired in two different ways: 1) exchanging other currencies for bitcoins; and 2) bitcoin mining.

The first method is by far the most common and can be done using a Bitcoin exchange such as **Mt.Gox** or **CampBX**. These exchanges allow users to exchange sterling, dollars etc. for bitcoins.

Bitcoin mining involves setting up a computer system to solve maths problems generated by the Bitcoin network. As a bitcoin miner solves these complex problems, bitcoins are credited to the miner. The network is designed to generate increasingly complex math problems which ensure that new bitcoins are generated at a consistent rate.

When a user obtains bitcoins, the balance is stored in a secure 'wallet' that is encrypted using password protection. When a bitcoin transaction takes place, the ownership of the bitcoins is updated in the network on all ledgers, and the balance in the relevant wallet is updated accordingly.

There is no need for a central bank to authorise transactions, since they are verified by those computers that make up the system. This therefore has the advantages of speed, reduced cost (transaction fees are small, typically $0.01 per transaction), and increased security.

Additionally, there are no pre-requisites for creating a Bitcoin account, and no transaction limits. Bitcoins can be used around the world, but the currency is only good for purchasing items from vendors that accept Bitcoin.

It is important to make the distinction that Bitcoin is not a blockchain itself. In many ways you can think of blockchain as the operating system and Bitcoin as one of the many applications that run on that system.

Illustration 11 – Which countries use Bitcoin?

Difficult economic conditions in Turkey have resulted in a continued fall in the value of the Turkish currency, the lira. Turkish investors are increasingly turning to cryptocurrency, and some predict that the regular Turkish currency will start to decline and be replaced by digital ones.

The country's businesses are reacting to this and taking action now to put them in a good position. For example, the neighbourhood teahouse is a focus of daily life across Turkey, a tradition that has endured across the centuries. At the Red Lightning Teahouse in Corum, the enterprising owners have one foot in the past and one foot in the future. It is the first teahouse in the country where customers can pay in Bitcoin.

On 9 June 2021 El Salvador made Bitcoin legal tender (in addition to the US dollar) followed by the Central African Republic on 22 April 2022.

In the US and UK, amongst many other countries, Bitcoin is used but is not legal tender.

Test your understanding 4

Which TWO of the following are advantages of blockchain technology?

A Anything of value can be transferred

B Everybody understands it

C Easy for management to override

D No need for an intermediary

3.8 Internet of things

The internet of things describes the network of smart devices with inbuilt software and connectivity to the internet allowing them to constantly monitor and exchange data.

What devices are connected to the internet of things (IoT)? Essentially anything with an on off switch can become a 'smart' device and be connected over the internet. This allows them to talk to us, applications and each other, which is at the core of their functionality.

Common devices currently connected as part of the internet of things include:

- **Smart meters** (contain in-home display screens that show how much energy is used in real-time) and **home control thermostat devices** (allow control of heating, electricity and hot water).
- **Doorbells and security** talk to your smart device. A live connection is established if the doorbell is pressed or the motion sensors activated, allowing immediate interaction.

- **Wearable tech** such as smart watches and fitness trackers capture and record an array of data to monitor and record your fitness.
- **Home appliances** such as smart lights, fridges, washing machines, ovens etc. The connectivity built in allows remote access and control of these devices, for instance turnings your lights on if you're out at night can be done using a smart phone.
- **Cars** – the computer systems used to control cars are increasingly sophisticated. They track and monitor thousands of parameters on every journey. This capability is central in the continued pursuit of autonomous vehicles.
- **Transport and infrastructure** – smart motorways are a common feature in many countries with traffic sensors monitoring the flow and build-up of traffic and responding to provide extra lanes or activate temporary speed limits.
- **Manufacturing equipment and plant** – monitoring of business assets facilitates efficient utilisation as it allows continual live feedback to track performance and flag maintenance requirements earlier.

The growth of the **internet of things** often termed '**smart technology**' is fuelled by improvements in broadband connectivity and the development of 4G and 5G communication networks. Coupled with the fact the people and businesses are increasingly comfortable with the idea and operation of this **smart technology**, it is anticipated that the **internet of things** will continue grow, becoming increasingly central to how we live and work as new and innovative applications for the technology emerge all the time.

e.g

Illustration 12 – Farming

Connected devices are becoming increasingly prevalent in the world of farming. It is an industry that is particularly vulnerable to adversity, through climate and weather effects, disease and pests. Therefore, the ability to monitor data on climatic conditions and the health of animals allows farmers to be forewarned of potential problems at an earlier stage. This allows farmers to take preventative action to fix problems or switch to alternative strategies, resulting in increased yields and importantly saving costs, wastage and loss.

A company called Allflex produce smart sensors, built into collars which are worn by each animal in a herd. These sensors monitor temperature, health, breathing, activity and nutrition of individual animals and the herd overall. Early warning signs can alert the farmer to potential problems and early preventative action can be taken such as veterinary care or isolating an animal showing markers of infection.

Test your understanding 5

X Co has created a brand of electronic toothbrushes that can sync with a mobile phone to let the user know the appropriate length of time they should be spending brushing their teeth.

This is an example of what?

A Big data

B Internet of things

C 3D printing

D Mobile technologies

3.9 Mobile technologies

Code-division multiple access (CDMA) is the technology that underpins mobile technology. It has developed rapidly over the last decade and increased the capability of mobile technology.

Developments in mobile technology have seen mobile phones progress from basic call and message devices in the late 1980s and 1990s to the **smart phones** and **tablets** we see today. These devices are more like computers than telephones and this is reflected in the prices of the latest models.

The rapid development in the capability of mobile technology has emerged at the same time as huge advances in internet technology and together the two technologies have been perfect partners.

All aspects of modern life are impacted by mobile technology, with major industries being completely transformed or new ones emerging, including:

- **Newspapers** – Physical sales of newspapers are in terminal decline. News is now consumed via mobile devices and is live rather than being a record of yesterday's news. Newspaper companies have attempted to evolve to maintain a presence in this mobile online world.
- **Advertising** – Closely linked with newspapers and other media, advertising is being transformed. Large scale mass advertising is in decline with a growth in smarter, targeted adverts.
- **Music** – CD's were replaced by MP3's which were seen as the future but have in turn have been replaced by music streaming services like **Spotify**.
- **Banking** – Increasingly people bank via mobile apps, designed for ease and convenience, the traditional high street branch continues to decline.
- **Socialising** – Social media has transformed how people socialise and communicate with friends using smartphones to post and tag and photograph their every move.
- **TV/Film** – Video streaming services such as **Netflix** and **Amazon Prime** as well as OnDemand TV and video sites like **YouTube** are designed for mobile internet technology and are transforming how we watch TV and films.

3.10 3-D Printing

3-D printing is part of a process known as **additive manufacturing** where an object is created layer by layer. It allows complex parts and components to be produced much cheaper, faster and in an entirely customisable manner.

How does it work? First a blueprint needs to be made; modelling software is widely available, catering for individual and industrial scale operations. Alternatively, objects created by others can be accessed on specialist communities.

Once a design is finalised it is ready to be printed. Printers can range from small desktop to industrial size. Most 3-D printers use thermoplastic composite type material. The printer follows the precise coordinates laid out by the design, building up the item layer by layer to produce a fully formed single piece 3-D object.

Applications range from producing **prototype parts** for manufacturing to printing human organs and bone using **bio-printing**.

What are the advantages?

- **Speed** – compared with conventional manufacturing such as injection moulds, 3-D printing gives significant time savings from prototype to finished article. Prototypes can be printed and tested in the same day, amendments made and reprinted immediately.
- **Cost effectiveness** – linked to the speed of the process, the labour cost of a conventional prototype process is high as designs need to be made into moulds which will then be tooled for manufacture, before a prototype can be made. Any changes need to follow the same lengthy and costly process.
- **Customisation** – the ability to easily amend designs and tailor them to an individual is a big draw for 3-D printing over traditional manufacture which is more focused on large volumes of identical products. This is a big selling point that can differentiate a business from its rivals.
- **Less waste** – 3-D printing sees the exact design printed and nothing else so uses raw materials much more efficiently than traditional manufacturing methods which see a lot of offcuts from the finished product.
- **Confidentiality** – 3-D printing allows continuous prototyping and manufacturing in-house, thus protecting intellectual property.

e.g

Illustration 13 – 3-D printing applications

Sports shoes

Several sports manufacturers such as Adidas, Nike and Reebok are using 3-D printing to produce customised footwear for elite athletes. 3-D foot scans are taken using either a scanner or an app which then allows designs and printing to produce a customised shoe. The shoe fits the biometrics and functional characteristics of the wearer, and the contours of their foot. Some athletes, e.g. Jack Bolas (US middle distance runner) report faster run times whilst wearing the 3-D printed shoes.

Healthcare

Because it can personalise devices and implants to individual anatomies and drastically reduce the need to buy items in bulk, there are numerous applications for 3-D printing in healthcare: hearing aids, facial reconstruction, personal prosthetics, dental crowns and surgical implants among them. More sophisticated printers, improved regenerative medicine, refinements in computer-aided design software and regulatory approvals are advancing its use in other areas, including drug production.

Houses

In May 2021, a retired Dutch couple became Europe's first inhabitants of a 3-D printed house. The two-bedroom boulder-shaped bungalow is the world's first habitable 3-D printed property with load-bearing walls. Proponents of the technology say it could result in sustainable and affordable homes, for example by reducing the amount of cement used in construction (cement is responsible for an estimated 8% of the world's CO_2 emissions) and that the technology could lead to homes that are tailor-made to the wishes of the resident(s).

4 Chapter summary

Technology affecting business and finance

The 4th Industrial revolution

- What is an industrial revolution?
- Features of the 4th industrial revolution

Key technologies driving the digital world

- Cloud computing
- Big data
- Data analytics
- Process automation
- Artificial intelligence
- Data visualisation
- Blockchain
- Internet of things
- Mobile technologies
- 3-D Printing

Test your understanding answers

Test your understanding 1

The correct answer is **B**

Private clouds are on a private infrastructure and managed internally. MIS may be limited in access but is not a cloud service. Public clouds are hosted by 3rd party. Big data is the term for data sets so large that necessitates cloud computing to allow more storage.

Test your understanding 2

The correct answer is **D**

Structured data is usually presented in some order and for particular uses. Public data is open data from governments. Unstructured data comes from a variety of sources, collected passively. Volume of data is a characteristic of big data.

Test your understanding 3

The correct answer is **C**

Artificial intelligence has algorithms that processes data and can use it to make recommendations. Traditional process automation is carrying out a simple repetitive task, which this is not. Data visualisation allows complex data to be viewed in a visually appealing way. Virtual reality is a computer generated experience in a simulated environment.

Test your understanding 4

The correct answer is **A and D**

Anything of value can be transferred, and it removes the need for an intermediary. Not everybody understands blockchain, and there may be some resistance to it. Blockchain technology makes it more difficult to interfere with transactions.

Test your understanding 5

The correct answer is **B**

Internet of things allows everyday objects to be connected to the internet and interact with us. Big data gets generated from products like this. There is no mention that this is done via 3-D printing (though toothbrushes could be!). Mobile technologies involve using them for the transactions, which is not the case here.

Chapter

6

How the finance function uses digital technologies

Chapter learning objectives

Lead	Component
B2: Examine how the finance function uses digital technologies to fulfil its roles.	Examine how finance uses the following to guide how it performs its roles: (a) Digital technology (b) Digital mindsets (c) Automation and the future of work (d) Ethics of technology usage

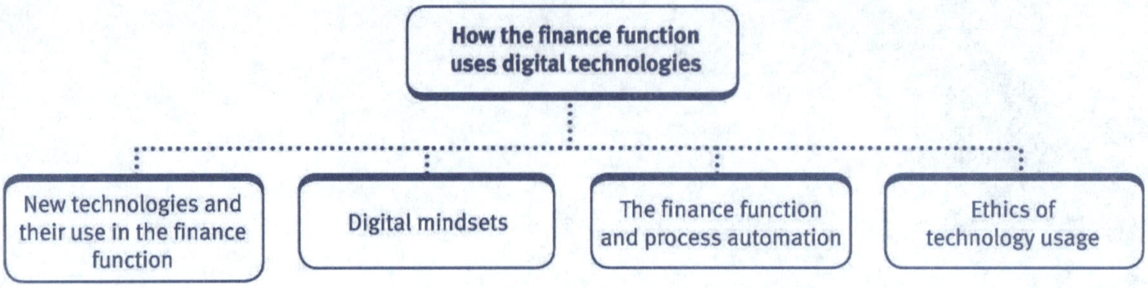

1 Digital technologies and the finance function

1.1 Introduction

In **Chapter 5** we considered the **4th industrial revolution**, including some of the key technological developments driving the changes that will increasingly impact on all aspects of modern life.

In this chapter we will look more specifically at how these emerging and developing technologies will affect the finance function of organisations and will shape future finance professionals.

We will consider the innovation and progress this technology can offer as well as investigating some of the ethical, legal and social considerations, through data protection and the idea of overall corporate digital responsibility.

Some of the technologies are anticipated to effectively update existing systems and improve capability; these have been termed **core modernisation tools** and are considered mainstream. Whilst others will deliver new capabilities, pushing the finance function forward, these are referred to as **exponentials** and are still at the early-adopter stage.

Core modernisation tools include:

- Cloud technology
- Data visualisation
- Blockchain
- Advanced analytics

Exponentials include:

- Artificial Intelligence

Illustration 1 – The changing face of the finance function

Essentially the finance function looks after an organisation's money. They ensure that a company's records are kept up to date, in order to understand, plan and ultimately control the money available within the business.

The finance function must establish sound systems which enable all financial transactions to be recorded. They must also be able to interrogate this data to provide meaningful information that is accurate, complete and timely.

Modern technologies introduced in Chapter 5 are impacting all areas of the finance function including:

- The hardware and software businesses use are being revolutionised with **cloud computing** transforming the way that accounting systems are owned, maintained and operated, leading to time and cost savings and more efficient ways of working.
- The **variety** and **volume** of data that is available to the modern finance professional has grown exponentially and brought about the concepts of **big data** and **data analytics** enabling greater insights into all areas of a business' operations.
- The information generated by the finance function, vital in managing all aspects of business can be brought to life through huge improvements in **data visualisation**.

2 New technologies and their use in the finance function

2.1 Cloud computing

Cloud computing as introduced in **Chapter 5**, involves the provision of shared computing services over the internet. Cloud systems can be **public** (shared) or **private** (closed) depending upon the needs and requirements of users.

Cloud computing and the finance function:

Cloud technology is impacting the provision of computing services within organisations including the finance function. This has wide ranging impacts on the way people and organisations work. The classic idea of office based work around fixed working hours within a physical team is becoming increasingly obsolete and the advent of **cloud computing** is one of the main drivers of this.

e.g **Illustration 2 – Cloud computing at the Royal Bank of Scotland**

The Royal Bank of Scotland (RBS) describes itself as 'customer obsessed'. To better serve its customers, the finance function is tasked with modelling various strategies and scenarios tied to the bank's products and services. These proved a challenge with legacy finance systems; the number of spreadsheets meant that the finance function was not able to model scenarios quickly.

To improve the speed of business, RBS decided to move a number of their finance function activities to the cloud – including planning and budgeting, forecasting, strategic modelling and profitability and cost management. As a result, RBS can now create its strategic models in minutes.

> RBS outlines five benefits that it achieved in moving to cloud:
>
> - Cost effectiveness
> - Better insight and control
> - Simplified processes
> - Continuous innovation
> - A move towards rolling forecasts

Cloud computing has driven the following changes in the structure and working of the finance function:

- **Collaboration** – File sharing and version control issues are minimised. Services such a Google drive for instance allow multiple collaborators to update documents in real time.
- **Flexible working** – Full access to all files and documents anywhere with an internet connection has facilitated increased flexibility to work pattern and arrangements.
- **Increased security** – Cloud service providers understand and acknowledge the security of data, especially financial data which is critical to their success.
- **Up to date** – Continually up to date software, helping to ensure compliance with regulations such as General Data Protection Regulation (GDPR).
- **Easier integration** – Cloud based accounting software can easily link with other cloud based software such as customer relationship management (CRM) software allowing an integrated approach to business in a cost effective way when compared with traditional software solutions.

Cloud computing, digital technology and financial reporting – The provision of services via cloud networks has revolutionised many industries. Physical products and the ownership of traditional physical assets like property, plant and equipment are becoming less important in the modern digital world. This has led to a growth in the significance of intangibles, which often aren't recorded on the **statement of financial position**. As a result, it is more difficult to determine the underlying value of digital businesses and to identify their sources of value creation using the traditional route of financial statement analysis. Using financial statements alone may significantly undervalue such entities as many intangible assets are internally generated and thus can't be recognised. This includes things like intellectual property and staff skills.

Illustration 3 – Cloud services impact on physical goods

Music streaming through services such as **Spotify, Deezer, Apple music** amongst others now dominate the music industry. While the buying of a physical product like a CD from a physical record store like **HMV** or **Virgin** is increasingly a thing of the past.

Other industries like hotels have seen the emergence of new players and business models. **Airbnb** for instance who act as an online broker, facilitating the short term lets of private accommodation between individuals is one of the largest 'hotel' companies in the world valued at around $80 billion (2025) yet they own no hotels or property.

Similarly, companies like **Uber** ($145 billion) who offer ride hailing services don't own a single vehicle yet dominate the transport industry and are valued beyond that of **Airbnb**.

All these businesses utilise cloud computing technology in the provision of their services and operate in a way that has revolutionised their industries.

They all have in common an absence of physical assets such as stock, property, plant, vehicles and equipment. Therefore, the financial reporting of these entities is a fundamentally different proposition compared to traditional bricks and mortar businesses.

2.2 Big data and data analytics

Computerisation has seen the role of finance professionals evolve over several decades from the traditional idea of 'bean counters' to a more strategic value adding position.

Technology has facilitated the ability to sort and analyse data to produce meaningful information far quicker than before, largely using **spreadsheet** and **database** software.

The development and use of ever more sophisticated digital technology means the role of the finance professional continues to evolve. Elements such as **big data** and **data analytics, artificial intelligence** and **data visualisation** present significant opportunities as well as challenges to both businesses and individuals.

Business partnering

Increasingly, management accountants are becoming embedded within functional departments of the organisation rather than operating from a central accounts department. The object is to provide real-time support and analysis to improve the operational performance of the functional department.

Big data and data analytics will increase the significance of the business partnering role, with the potential for new insights to be gained. It is anticipated accountants will act as the **interface between** data specialists such as **data scientists** (who have a background in statistics and computer science) **and the business**, essentially making the data generated commercially relevant thus transforming it into valuable information.

Other impacts of big data on elements of the finance function:

Management accounting	In management accounting, big data will contribute to the development of more efficient and insightful management control systems and budgeting processes.
Financial accounting	In financial accounting, big data will improve the quality and relevance of accounting information. This can enhance transparency and stakeholder decision making.
Reporting	In reporting, big data can assist with the creation and improvement of accounting standards. This will help to ensure that the accounting profession continues to provide useful information as the dynamic global economy evolves.

Internal audit and big data

Big data and data analytics are expected to enhance the quality and relevance of **internal audit** assignments. Technology advancements in big data and analytics are fundamentally changing how the review of internal controls and systems are carried out.

New technology is driving an expansion beyond sample-based testing to include analysis of entire populations of audit-relevant data, using intelligent analytics to deliver a higher quality of audit evidence and more relevant business insights. Big data and analytics are enabling internal audit to better identify anomalies, fraud and operational business risks and tailor their approach to target more business critical areas.

Test your understanding 1

The impact of big data in organisations will affect which elements of the finance function?

A Business partnering

B Management accounting

C Financial accounting

D Internal audit

E All of the above

2.3 Process automation

As discussed in **Chapter 5**, process automation involves the use of technology to automate processes previously carried out by human workers.

Developments in technology are enabling more complex activities to be automated and **process automation** is therefore becoming increasingly significant to the finance function of an organisation.

Repetitive, low skilled manual tasks such as data entry, duplication and processes that add minimal value to the end users of financial information are most likely to be automated by new developments in process automation software. Good examples include the automation of processes associated with the **financial close** and **regulatory reporting** and the automation of tasks associated with **account reconciliation**. This will free up time and resource for higher level value adding activities.

An organisation considering investing in **process automation** technology within the finance function would weigh up the following advantages and disadvantages:

Advantages	Disadvantages
Cost savings – reduction in headcount as routine aspects of finance work automated	**Uncertainty** – process automation changes the way the finance function works and can lead to uncertainty around job security and future prospects
Value adding – staff and management time is freed up to focus on higher level value adding (and more interesting) activities	**Relationship management** – for process automation software to be successful, time and resource is required for relationship management with IT support and software providers
Improved accuracy – automated processes will benefit from improved accuracy and efficiency with the removal of human error and working patterns	**Competence** – the automated process is built by IT staff who must also understand in detail the existing process as the automated process is only as effective as the coding that drives it
Positive return – well managed and implemented process automation software will provide positive returns on investment	**Training** – costs of training staff to understand how the new software works and interfaces with their roles can be significant
Adaptability – process automation can be used for existing processes or can form part of an overarching process improvement exercise	**Change management** – as with any significant changes made by the organisation the process must be managed carefully and led effectively for it to be successful

e.g

Illustration 4 – Process automation in the finance function

Process automation, when considered in the context of a large scale conglomerate organisation such as **Johnson & Johnson,** can generate time, cost and resource savings as well as generating significant efficiencies.

Compatibility issues between the multiple systems across Johnson & Johnson's many operating locations led the company to investigate the potential benefits process automation could deliver.

An initial project focused on simplifying their intercompany requests, recharges and postings process to test the capability of process automation and its potential for wider use in the business.

The automated process worked as follows:

- Requests for intercompany transactions are forwarded to an automated inbox instead of going to a member of the finance team.
- They are submitted following a standard and consistent template. This allows the software to open the email and process the details of the transaction.
- The details should be complete due to the standard template used enabling the system to verify the divisions involved, the general ledger codes, authorisation and narrative.
- Any omissions cause the request to be automatically rejected, and an email is generated to notify the sender of the reasons.
- Complete requests are then accepted and the details uploaded into the purchase order system automatically.
- The purchase order then needs to be approved.
- This approval triggers the next stage of the system and an invoice is automatically raised by the system in the division that initiated the process.
- All relevant postings are then automatically made in both divisions with sales and receivables in one division and expenses and payables in the other division.

The automation process has improved the consistency, accuracy and timeliness of the intercompany recharge process. Because all postings are controlled by the single process there are no longer issues with intercompany balances not agreeing. It also allows for simpler reporting and increased detail about workflows.

The work has freed up finance staff time to focus on more value adding activities and improved the understanding of the core process that has been redeveloped.

Test your understanding 2

Value Co, a chain of supermarkets, is taking action to increase process automation in the finance function for repetitive tasks such as intercompany transactions and reconciliations.

Which of the following is a disadvantage of taking such action?

A Free up management time

B Increased risk of human error

C Less training costs

D Resistance to change

2.4 Artificial Intelligence (AI)

AI and **machine learning** are anticipated to lead to significant impacts on the future of accountancy. **Process automation** as discussed above, will be enhanced by AI enabling automated reasoning, making automation more flexible and capable of dealing with complexity.

AI enables computers and machines to exhibit higher level, human style learning. A system can interpret data correctly and, over time, continually learn to interpret data better by understanding the differences between its interpretations and the actual outcomes.

Illustration 5 – Artificial Intelligence and forecasting – Salesforce

Saleforce.com a cloud based provider of customer relationship management (CRM) systems, has embraced the capability of **AI** to aid their revenue forecasts. The process of forecasting is built on data but with a very significant human input. Research has shown this human input is clouded by emotion and confirmation bias and often amounts to little more than hunches and gut feeling.

By investing in **AI** the data becomes the key driver of forecasting and treats the process of forecasting in a more scientific manner. Using a data driven approach allows for a solid rationale to be visible behind the forecasts that are produced.

For it to be successful the Chief Information Officer (CIO) of **Salesforce** asserts that data needs to be seen in the day to day operations of a business. This will act to aid understanding and buy-in to the process.

For instance, in a sales driven business forecasting often involves the assessment of leads and the likelihood these will be realised. Each salesperson's view and assessment of these leads will be impacted by their own opinion and disposition. Introducing a data driven approach to assessing sales leads, will be consistent and fact led, it will smooth the human inconsistency, enhance the forecasting and perhaps most significantly, improve the **AI** learning that can be achieved.

> This is done by the system interrogating and attempting to understand the differences between the forecasts and actuals. The data driving these differences is then 'learned' by the system and will not be replicated in future forecasts. So over time the process of forecasting will become increasingly accurate.
>
> The process of running this change at **Salesforce**, especially the human element wasn't smooth and took time, but the CIO insists the improved forecasting it has resulted in has been more than worth any hardship.

Artificial intelligence and accountancy

Although artificial intelligence techniques such as machine learning are not new, and the pace of change is fast, widespread adoption in business and accounting is still in the relatively early stages.

Increasingly, we are seeing systems that are producing outputs that far exceed the accuracy and consistency of those produced by humans. In the short to medium term, **AI** brings many opportunities for accountants to improve their efficiency, provide more insight and deliver more value to businesses. In the longer term, AI brings opportunities for much more radical change, as systems increasingly carry out decision-making tasks currently done by humans.

AI, no doubt, will contribute to substantial improvements across all areas of accounting, equipping accountants with powerful new capabilities, as well as leading to the automation of many tasks and decisions.

Examples include:

- Using machine learning to code accounting entries and improve on the accuracy of rules-based approaches, enabling **greater automation** of processes
- Improving **fraud detection** through more sophisticated, machine learning models of 'normal' activities and better prediction of fraudulent activities
- Using machine learning based **predictive models** to forecast revenues
- Recommending supplier specific discounts to **optimise cash at hand**
- Extraction of **insights** from huge amounts of real-time data (both financial and non-financial, structured and unstructured) without information overload.

Despite the opportunities that AI brings, it does not replicate **human intelligence**. There will be a need to retain the involvement of humans in many decision-making processes in accountancy due to the **limitations** of AI:

- Success relies on having **sufficient data of the right quality** to enable effective decision-making and for the machine to learn
- Models learn to carry out very specific tasks based on a given set of data and are **not particularly flexible**

- Although models can eliminate human bias, the data often reflects existing bias and prejudice in society and so **entrench societal bias** that already exists
- **Not every problem or task will be suitable for an AI approach**. For example, the task may be unique or novel or it may require other factors to be considered (such as ethical questions).

e.g

Illustration 6 – AI and the Serious Fraud Office (SFO)

In the UK, the Serious Fraud Office (SFO) has invested in an **AI** system called **OpenText Axcelerate**. One of the main operations of the system in the SFO's investigations involves interrogating huge volumes of documents. Connections between individuals and groups as well as key words and phrases can be identified and mapped in a way far beyond the capabilities of human workers.

This has not only saved countless hours spent trawling through and cross referencing documents, it has also been proven to actually improve the process, identifying more connections than the average human worker and crucially more complex and opaque connections that would typically not be spotted by the human eye. This has therefore enhanced the investigative power and effectiveness of the fraud agency.

2.5 Data Visualisation

This area of technology is of particular significance to the finance function of an organisation. The provision of information to help support the efficient and effective running of all functions within a business and the business overall is the **fundamental purpose of the finance function**.

Big data and data analytics are now mainstream in business. This growth in data and the need to communicate the information and insights to be found within the data makes **data visualisation** critically important to the finance function. The ability to make data relevant, accessible and easy for all end users is vital.

Key benefits of data visualisation

- **Accessible** – traditional spreadsheets and financial reports can be both difficult to understand and unappealing to look at. Modern data visualisation graphics and dashboards are designed to be user friendly and intuitive
- **Real time** – synchronising real time data with data visualisation tools give real-time, up to date numbers in a clear, informative style. This allows quicker response to business changes rather than waiting for weekly or monthly reports
- **Performance optimisation** – the immediacy and clarity of the information being displayed supports better decision making and proactive, efficient utilisation of resources as problems are identified promptly
- **Insight and understanding** – combining data and visualising it in a new way can lead to improved understanding and fresh insights about the cause and effect relationships that underpin performance.

Illustration 7 – Visualisation, key performance indicators

Key performance indicators are a set of metrics used by a business to monitor performance in areas where things must go according to plan for the business to be successful. These critical areas must first be identified, and then suitable metrics established to monitor performance, before finally setting targets to outline the level of desired performance.

The ability to receive real time information about critical areas and feed this back to staff allowing them to understand current performance and respond accordingly can be the difference between success and failure.

The collection and analysis of the data are underpinned by the ideas of **big data** however bringing this data to life in an easy to understand and intuitive fashion is the purpose of **data visualisation**.

Companies are increasingly using **dashboards** (a collection of key **infographics** displayed together) to display **key performance indicators** to staff in real time and to flag areas requiring improvement in order to hit the pre-determined targets and drive success. This instant feedback allows for action to be taken quickly to highlight and fix potential problems.

For instance, Kaplan's IT service desk uses key performance indicator dashboards to monitor and display performance for all staff and the department as a whole.

Metrics such as the number of support tickets logged, time taken to open support tickets, time taken to resolve support tickets and customer satisfaction would all be displayed clearly using graphics.

If performance in any of the areas is falling below target levels the graphics will clearly display this, prompting action to resolve the poor performance.

Test your understanding 3

Which TWO of the following are benefits of data visualisation for the finance function?

A User friendly and intuitive

B Regular monthly reporting

C Create fresh insights into the data

D Wider use of performance metrics

2.6 Blockchain

Blockchain is most widely understood in the context of cryptocurrencies such as **Bitcoin** as illustrated in Chapter 5. The illustration below compares a traditional payment to a payment using cryptocurrency, demonstrating the key differences of the blockchain transaction.

e.g

Illustration 8 – Cryptocurrency, how do they work?

First, consider a transaction using a standard currency like pounds or dollars for instance.

- Making a purchase, you present your payment card to the retailer, they then process the payment.
- In doing so the card payment machine essentially asks your bank if you have sufficient funds to make the purchase.
- The bank then checks its ledgers to verify whether you do in fact have the money to make the purchase.
- If so, the bank gives authorisation to the retailer, processes the payment and updates its ledgers. They also charge a small fee (usually to the retailer) for doing so.
- If other intermediaries such as credit card companies or PayPal are added to this process, they also take a small payment for their service.

Cryptocurrencies such as **Bitcoin** essentially act to remove the bank from the process, they use **blockchain** technology to both authorise the transaction and then also record it, in what is known as a distributed ledger. This replaces the single ledger that is held by a bank, with many separate or distributed ledgers which are all individually held by different people (or essentially computer servers). The separate ledgers all independently verify the transaction and record the movement of cryptocurrency at the same time. The fact that multiple different ledgers all support the same information acts to verify the legitimacy of the transaction. If one of these ledgers tried to record something different, this would not agree with the other ledgers and would be refused.

So, the process for the transaction using a cryptocurrency would be:

- I would present my payment details to the retailer, detailing my cryptocurrency account
- The retailer would then present this to the distributed ledgers, so effectively would ask all of these different independent ledger holders whether I had sufficient cryptocurrency to make the payment
- If they all agreed that I did, the transaction and the payment would then be authorised, and all of the distributed ledgers would update their records to reflect the movement

> - **Note:** It is here where an inaccurate entry would be rejected, if someone attempted to change their ledger it would be flagged up as different to all the other ledgers and would not be processed
> - The reward for the ledger holders is that one randomly selected ledger would be given some newly created cryptocurrency for each transaction.
>
> This distributed ledger approach removes the central intermediary i.e. the bank and distributes it in essence to everyone.

Blockchain and the finance function

Blockchain is the most notable example of distributed ledger technology. Its use will impact upon the current operations of the finance function of an organisation. Digital assets recorded and secured by blockchain technology such as cryptocurrencies, present both opportunities and challenges:

Financial reporting – Accounting for cryptocurrency is still a grey area for standard setters and exactly how they should be classified is subject to ongoing debate. Accounting standards were not designed with such technological developments in mind and therefore we do not have a specific standard (although in 2024 the US Financial Accounting Standards Board (FASB) issued an Accounting Standards Update addressing the accounting for and disclosure of crypto assets – considered to be intangible assets and need to be at fair value.) This topic is still under discussion.

Cross border payments – these remain complex, expensive and slow. The actions of intermediaries, the fees charged and the exact timescale is often opaque. Blockchain driven solutions such as **RippleNet** are growing in number and use. They aim to make the transfer of money like the transfer of data, easy and seamless by circumventing the traditional centralised intermediaries i.e. banks and payment providers.

Smart contracts – self executing contracts use blockchain technology built upon cryptography, digital signatures and secure computation. Theoretically money, property or any assets can be exchanged in a transparent manner. The document is created and agreed upon and then verified by the distributed ledger. The performance obligations, if met, execute at an agreed time and date and cannot be tampered with, without validation.

Security and traceability – the distributed ledger means all network participants involved in a blockchain hold a copy of the full ledger. Any attempts to amend a single block will become invalid and the peer to peer network will be immediately aware. All blocks are time stamped and secured through cryptography. This may fundamentally impact how finance functions record transactions with third parties.

Examples of how blockchain can enhance the accounting profession include:

- Improving the cash position by better managing resources
- Reducing the costs of maintaining and reconciling ledgers
- Providing absolute certainty over the ownership and history of assets
- Helping accountants gain clarity over available resources
- Freeing up resource to concentrate on value adding activities rather than record keeping.

Test your understanding 4

Lyric Co is a record company that uses music artists to record songs and produces the music itself. Revenues from sales of music come from physical sales in music stores, downloads from websites, and commissions from radio stations. Lyric Co wants the revenues to be distributed in pre-determined measures (i.e. a certain percentage) to the artist and the record company as long as agreed performance requirements are met.

Which one of the following areas of technology should they look to use?

A Artificial intelligence

B Cryptocurrency

C Blockchain

D Digital mindsets

2.7 Internet of things

The **internet of things** considers a network of smart devices with inbuilt sensors and internet connectivity. They collect and transmit data constantly and are an increasingly significant element of **big data**.

The ability to make virtually any asset a business owns and operates a 'smart' asset by building in some relevant sensors and internet connectivity can lead to some very useful data. It should facilitate better business planning, resource allocation and will help to optimise processes, minimise expenditure and give advanced warning of potential issues.

It is thought the finance professionals will work increasingly closely with the IT function of a business as the two functions overlap and require each other's mutual knowledge.

e.g

Illustration 9 – Internet of things - Rolls Royce

Rolls-Royce, manufacturer of aircraft engines, has embraced the capabilities of the **internet of things** and **big data** and this has fundamentally changed their business model.

Rolls-Royce engines are manufactured with hundreds of sensors built in throughout the engine unit. These sensors produce constant live data which is fed back to systems engineers at centres across the globe. Any anomalies are immediately flagged and the engineers can make an assessment from the vast array of data available as to the best course of action. Preventative maintenance can be scheduled much earlier than would ordinarily be possible through a system called 'IntelligentEngine' and can be planned for the most convenient and cost effective time and location.

AI has replaced human intervention to monitor the performance of their engines using an AI tool called 'IntelligentBorescope', and it has facilitated design improvements for new models.

2.8 Mobile technologies

Mobile technologies are a fundamental aspect of modern life, most notably **smartphones** and **tablet computers**. Their use continues to drive changes in how we live and work, creating both opportunities and threats as new ways of operating, and entirely new business models, emerge.

The impact of mobile technologies on the finance function remains modest. The focus of this technology and the bulk of investment has been on changing the way we communicate and interact with customers and ensuring we are in tune with customer expectations.

From the finance function perspective, the use of mobile technologies has centred on efficient communication within teams. There remains little practical day to day application of smart phones and tablets in the actual functioning of the accountancy operations (unless you are a small business operator, where your handheld device can be used to upload supplier invoices and send customer invoices using Xero, Quickbooks, etc.)

Some areas and efficiencies delivered or facilitated by mobile technologies include:

- **Communication and flexibility** – smart phones and tablets help deliver flexible working and facilitate improved communication between staff
- **Scalability** – mobile tech and cloud tech combined, overcome some of the obstacles traditionally associated with starting and growing a business, most notably the capital costs of setting up systems and IT

- **Less paperwork** – use of mobile technology has reduced duplication and data entry. For instance, new app software for logging and recording expenses has reduced manual processing, whilst delivering significant efficiencies and better quality management information
- **Instant data visibility** – accessing and communicating key data through data visualisation tools such as dashboards. Key metrics can be viewed live by all

2.9 3-D printing

3-D printing, as discussed in **Chapter 5**, is a process driven by computer-aided design (CAD) and computer-aided manufacturing (CAM) technology that allows almost anything to be printed to exact specifications as defined by the system. It has transformed the way products are prototyped and is anticipated to continue to increase in significance as technology develops and associated costs reduce.

The impact on the finance function is largely from a costing perspective, practically dealing with the changes in operations (operations will be discussed in Chapter 9) this technology allows:

- **Less waste** as the material is printed directly so no offcuts or by products
- **No overproduction** as products are made to exact specification as ordered rather than being produced in volume to a forecast demand level
- An increase in **direct costs** as the time spent setting up the systems, the materials used and the parts handling are all distinct to a specific job
- Minimal **tooling and set-up** costs make small production runs and bespoke products cost effective
- **Inventory** holding of finished goods should be zero and with effective supply chain management raw materials should be delivered following the 'just-in-time' principle meaning practically no holding of raw materials.

Test your understanding 5

3-D printing is classed as what type of manufacturing?

A Just-in-time

B Subtractive

C Lean

D Additive

3 Digital mindsets

3.1 Digital mindsets

A **digital mindset** is the concept of seeing beyond the individual elements of digital change, to understand the deeper all-pervading ways in which digital technology will ultimately transform every aspect of society and therefore impact an organisation.

A 'helicopter view' is a feature associated with strong visionary leaders. It is the ability to take a step back from an organisation and achieve a clear overview. It's about seeing the bigger picture, not getting stuck in the smaller detail and appreciating how all of the elements of the organisation interconnect.

A digital mindset is an extension of this idea and requires leaders and staff to see beyond the smaller incremental considerations of digital adaptation, instead thinking about the longer term vision for the organisation and how it will appear in a digital world.

The five following qualities, practices and approaches were identified by **Forbes** as being important dimensions of the **digital mindset**:

- **Provide vision** yet **empower others** – clear vision of how a business should evolve and transform in this digital age, whilst supporting the initiatives of employees in translating this vision into tangible action.
- **Give up control** yet **"architect" the choices** – empowering employees to adapt the organisation but maintaining sufficient oversight to shape and direct the process.
- **Sustain** yet **disrupt** – existing business practices must be sustained and enhanced where possible to ensure profitability. New ideas and concepts will disrupt and challenge the status quo but must be protected and nurtured for their potential to spark beneficial future change.
- **Rely on data** yet **trust your intuition** – data is a powerful tool in decision making but the digital mind-set is forward looking and change focused so looking beyond the numbers and using vision and intuition are important skills.
- **Be sceptical** yet **open-minded** – there are many new technologies and approaches that emerge and could potentially be the 'next big thing' or simply disappear. It is important to maintain a degree of caution yet to also consider and try things to learn lessons and see what fits.

3.2 Implications of a digital mindset on the finance professional

Acknowledging and accepting that technology will increasingly change and disrupt the ways in which society, organisations and therefore the finance function operates will be an important part of a finance professionals skill set.

Change adept organisations have the capability, capacity and readiness to deal with change, through flexible structures, lean processes and forward thinking. A key element of being **change adept** is having staff who share these attributes, so finance professionals must focus on having what Dr Carol Dweck described as a **growth mindset**. This is an appetite to continuously develop and learn. Feedback will be openly given and received and viewed as a tool for growth rather than criticism and confrontation, change will be embraced as a challenge and opportunity not seen as threat.

e.g

Illustration 10 – BP's growth mindset

BP is one of the world's largest companies, delivering energy products and services to people around the world. Such an evolving business and fast-moving industry requires a finance function that adapts to provide the professional support it needs.

One initiative focuses on the importance of a growth mindset. BP has created an environment that promotes continuous learning. For example:

- Using a variety of learning approaches from classroom to virtual instructor-led training to online courses; individuals are given the space to manage their learning.
- Some regions operate fortnightly 'Growth Fridays' where employees are encouraged to undertake online learning or to learn a new skill from their peers.
- Senior managers are also encouraged to take part in these activities and to share their experiences so that learning and growth are constant and that it occurs at all levels.

4 The finance function and process automation

4.1 Impacts on the finance function of increased automation

Technology and software developments are driving an increase in process automation across the finance function. Routine and transactional areas such as balancing ledger accounts and extracting trial balances and accounting summaries have been automated since computerised accounting packages came on to the market many years ago.

As technology continues to develop, more areas of finance are becoming automated or are likely to become automated.

> **e.g. Illustration 11 – New technology impacting finance - Expenses**
>
> The process of dealing with staff expenses has long been inefficient and unnecessarily complicated. New technology businesses like **Certify** or **Rydoo** allow staff to photograph receipts instantly on their mobile device, this uploads the receipt which is synchronised with their software account. The details are extracted, categorised and where required can be submitted for approval immediately. Exceptions can be flagged and reports can be generated showing line by line detail along with supporting receipts and mileage maps. Approved expenses can then be automatically reimbursed to the employee. The information from all employees is available in instant reports, allowing improved analysis and control.
>
> The process still involves human input but the software enabled automation of the compilation and submission of expenses, as well as the removal of manual receipts and the need for physical verification saves staff time and improves the efficiency of the process whilst also significantly improving the management information available.

4.2 Skills required by the future finance professional

Accountants and **finance professionals** in the future will see basic routine, transactional work reduced with a shift to higher-level skills. The following **skills** are anticipated to be fundamental to **future accountants**:

- **Analytical skills** – much of the data produced will come from automated processes and data specialists. Accountants will add value through analysing this data in the business context for meaning and insight
- **Business acumen** – having a wide understanding of all aspects of a business and the environment they are in is crucial to effective decision-making and the ability to provide insight to other functions
- **Judgement** – making decisions, evaluating data sources and applying knowledge to make sound judgements will be a key higher-level skill
- **People skills** – interpersonal skills including the ability to communicate, empathise and understand people will be increasingly important as accountant occupy more central business partnering roles, rather than just producing accounts and reports for others
- **Leadership** – accountants have a unique central position in organisations. This is necessary to be able to understand and question the numbers and information they are given. This provides them a wider understanding of the entire business and sees accountants increasingly occupying senior executive positions in companies.

e.g

Illustration 12 – Finance in the future

A report produced by Deloitte in 2025 gives their predictions on how the finance function in an organisation will change in the near future:

1. The finance factory

Transactions will be touchless as automation and blockchain reach deeper into finance operations.

2. The role of Finance

With operations largely automated, Finance will double down on business insights and service. Success is not assured. The skills required by finance professionals will change, likely dramatically, as new combinations of technology and human workforces permeate the workplace.

3. Finance cycles

Finance goes real time. Periodic reporting will no longer drive operations and decisions – if it ever did.

4. Self-service

Self-service will become the norm. Finance will be uneasy about this.

5. Operating models

New service-delivery models will emerge as robots and algorithms join a more diverse finance workforce – think about the integration of freelancers, gig workers, and crowds. Companies will assess the benefits of automation against onshore and offshore operations.

6. Enterprise resource planning (ERP)

Finance applications and microservices challenge traditional ERP. Big vendors will be prepared.

7. Data

The proliferation of Application Programming Interfaces will drive data standardization, but it won't be enough. Companies will still be struggling to clean up their data messes.

8. Workforce and workplace

Employees will be doing new things in new ways, some of which will make Chief Financial Officers uncomfortable.

4.3 The automation paradox

Increased **automation** of routine tasks takes them out of human control. This can result in the loss of these skills on a practical level, as the automated process takes over and is relied upon.

However atypical events can undermine an automated process as they are built by humans using code and algorithms that cannot accommodate all possible permutations. In this situation, where manual control is required, the deskilling of humans can see organisations unable to cope and therefore slow to respond.

Retaining expertise and ensuring knowledge and understanding of the basic functions of accounting systems and how they operate will be a challenge for the modern finance professional.

For example, the basic process of manually maintaining ledger accounts and balancing them off is fundamental to every bookkeeping course yet it is a task seldom undertaken by accountants today. Modern accounting systems perform multiple checks and balances automatically. Yet this underpinning knowledge is essential to ensure a full understanding of how the system functions and means an accountant can step in should the system fail.

5 Ethics of technology usage

5.1 Legal considerations of technology use

Data is a central aspect of the technology developments driving the 4th industrial revolution.

The amount of personal data available to and used by organisations means that the privacy, sensitivity and security of this data are very significant considerations in modern business.

A business must ensure it is compliant with all legislation but there are also considerations from an ethical and social responsibility point of view in terms of what is right and wrong in the eyes of the public.

Data protection – General Data Protection Regulation (GDPR) was introduced throughout the EU in 2018. It established certain principles about data that are best practice and are mirrored in legislation of countries outside the EU including the UK. It is a requirement that data is:

- Used fairly, lawfully and transparently
- Used for specified, explicit purposes
- Used in a way that is adequate, relevant and limited to only what is necessary
- Accurate and, where required, kept up to date
- Kept for no longer than is necessary
- Handled in a way that ensures appropriate security. Including protection against unlawful or unauthorised processing, access, loss, destruction or damage.

Data controllers within organisations must ensure adequate safeguards and controls to implement these data principles.

Background to GDPR

This new legislation was designed to overhaul the previous data protection act from 1995. This was written at a time when the internet was in its infancy, smartphones didn't exist and some of the largest and most influential companies in the world such as Facebook, Google and Amazon were barely even conceived.

The way data is used in 2018 and beyond required new laws that were fit for purpose and designed with the modern landscape in mind and are therefore able to safeguard the privacy and rights of individuals today.

Illustration 13 – Facebook and Cambridge Analytica scandal

Facebook received a £500,000 fine for its role in the Cambridge Analytica scandal. The fine was the maximum available under the data protection legislation in place at the time.

Facebook was found to have breached data protection legislation by allowing third party app developers access to users data without sufficiently clear and informed consent. They also failed to make suitable checks on apps and developers using the platform.

What was the Cambridge Analytica scandal?

A third party app designed as a personality quiz collected the data of 87 million Facebook users without their knowledge or explicit consent. This data was then sold on to third parties, one of whom was Cambridge Analytica.

They then used this data to profile voters in the US election based on personality and psychology before targeting advertising which took advantage of this information.

Around 1 million UK users' data was obtained in the scandal.

Test your understanding 6

GDPR legislation based on best practice attempts to ensure that organisations follow the principles about data.

Which TWO of the following are contained in those principles?

A Data is kept up to date

B Data is kept for longer than is necessary

C Data is used for implicit purposes

D Data is protected against unlawful access

E Data should always be in hard copy format

5.2 Ethical and social considerations of technology use

Ethics is a system of moral principles that affect how people and organisations make decisions. It involves acting in a way deemed acceptable by society.

Ethical and social considerations – Compliance with legislation such as the **GDPR** laws noted above is something that all companies should achieve.

However, the question of whether this is sufficient opens up ethical considerations as to what companies should do and how they should act.

When considering the way in which an organisation handles technology and data, **ethical and social considerations are important** for the following reasons:

- A company that handles technology and data in an ethical way will give investors confidence
- Customer confidence in data security is vital in the digital age and is an important element of brand confidence
- Consumers feel safer dealing with companies that are proactive and responsible in their use of data
- Employees are attracted to companies that exhibit a strong ethical stance when it comes to how they use technology and data
- Ethical handling of technology and data helps ensure long-term sustainability of an organisation through stakeholder confidence and trust
- It demonstrates a proactive awareness of the risks associated with data and technology

e.g

Illustration 14 – The ethics of artificial intelligence (AI)

AI has the capability to transform lives for the better but also raises certain ethical issues.

These include amongst many others:

- **Unemployment** – for example, what happens to delivery drivers' jobs if self-driving vehicles become widely available?
- **Inequality** – is it fair if AI driven companies make excessive profits at the expense of more traditional companies and/or consumers?
- **Discrimination** – AI systems are created by humans who can be biased and judgmental, for example with regards to race. Therefore, it can't always be trusted to be fair or neutral.
- **How it is used** – for example, is it ethical to use AI to monitor employees working from home/remotely? Another example would be is it ethical to use military AI capable of deadly force in modern warfare?

e.g

Illustration 15 – Microsoft's AI principles

Microsoft is one of several high profile technology companies to lay down a voluntary set of ethical principles surrounding its use of AI. It recognises that AI is an area of technology that presents some of the most challenging ethical questions.

Microsoft's AI principles:

Fairness – AI systems should treat all people fairly

Reliability and safety – AI systems should perform reliably and safely

Privacy and security – AI systems should be secure and respect privacy

Inclusiveness – AI systems should empower everyone and engage people

Transparency – AI systems should be understandable

Accountability – AI systems should have algorithmic accountability

Risks associated with the use of unethical data

The use of AI has incredible future potential, but it also has the potential for misuse including the spread of misinformation, fake news, and misleading content that can undermine trust and distort the public view.

Examples of the risks associated in using unethical data in AI and Generative AI applications include a broad range of harms to individuals, companies and society.

- **Data breaches and privacy violations** – Misuse of personal information without proper consent can lead to data breaches, compromising individual privacy.
- **Loss of trust and reputational damage** – Unethical data practices can erode user confidence and tarnish an organisation's reputation.
- **Legal consequences** – Violating data protection laws and intellectual property rights can result in fines, lawsuits, and other legal penalties.
- **Authenticity** – AI and GEN AI-generated content that is indistinguishable from human-created content can spread misinformation and reduce any trust in digital information.
- **Intellectual property concerns** – Unauthorised use of copyrighted material in training datasets can lead to intellectual property infringements.
- **Discriminatory practices** – Biased algorithms or flawed data can result in the unfair treatment of certain groups within society by maintaining or increasing existing inequalities and social injustices.
- **Potential misuse** – The creation of deceptive content, such as deepfakes, can facilitate malicious activities like fraud and misinformation campaigns.

Mitigation Strategies

- **Implement robust data governance** – Establish clear policies and procedures for data collection, storage, and usage to ensure ethical handling of information.
- **Ensure transparency** – Maintain transparency in data practices, allowing individuals to understand how their data is being used and providing options for consent.
- **Adhere to regulatory standards** – Follow relevant data protection laws and ethical guidelines (e.g. GDPR) to promote responsible AI and Generative AI development and usage.
- **Promote fairness and inclusivity** – Design algorithms that minimise bias and ensure equitable treatment of all individuals, fostering a fair and just AI ecosystem.
- **Enhance security measures** – Protect data against unauthorised access and breaches through advanced security protocols and regular audits.

5.3 Corporate digital responsibility

Corporate digital responsibility or **CDR** is a relatively new concept which extends the idea and ethos of **corporate social responsibility** (**CSR**) to the digital world.

It is a voluntary commitment by organisations to go beyond mere compliance with legislation, when it comes to how they handle technology and data. It considers the broader ethical values of organisations driving forward the advancement of technology to do so in a manner that is fundamentally leading toward a positive future.

CDR involves a commitment to protecting both customers and employees and ensuring that new technologies and data are used both productively and wisely.

The development of a **CDR strategy** is increasingly common in modern business and would include the following **5 key areas**:

- **Digital stewardship**, using data in a responsible and secure way that is in line with customers and employees expectations of what is reasonable
- **Customer expectations** around data use and the need for transparency are increasing. The ability to opt in and be rewarded for sharing data empowers the consumer
- **Giving back** means that companies can share data in a benevolent way to help society. For example, a bank with knowledge of financial information could help to inform a customer's choices to improve their financial management, even if it meant a loss of overdraft or credit card fees. Additionally, a pharmaceutical company sharing clinical trial data with university researchers for no gain

- **Data value** is becoming increasingly apparent to customers as well as businesses, so the need to reward and incentivise customers to give more data will become the norm
- **Digital inclusion** is about ensuring all members of society have the skills, tools and ability to access the online digital world, and are not left behind through lack of education or opportunity. Businesses need to be proactive to help and support users and reduce barriers and obstacles.

Test your understanding 7

Which of the following is not one of the 5 key areas of an effective approach to corporate digital responsibility?

A Digital stewardship

B Digital inclusion

C Digital sustainability

D Data value

Test your understanding 8

X Co is a traffic data management company, involved in town planning and transport logistics. They heavily invest in software to look at real time data on the impact of cycle lanes, new roads, types of cars etc. on traffic times in city centres. This wealth of knowledge has been built up for years, and recently X Co has looked at the possibility of sharing this information with hospitals and the emergency services, free of charge. This is to help the emergency services get to incidents quicker.

What is this project a specific example of?

A Corporate digital responsibility

B Corporate social responsibly

C Lobbying

D Artificial intelligence

6 Chapter summary

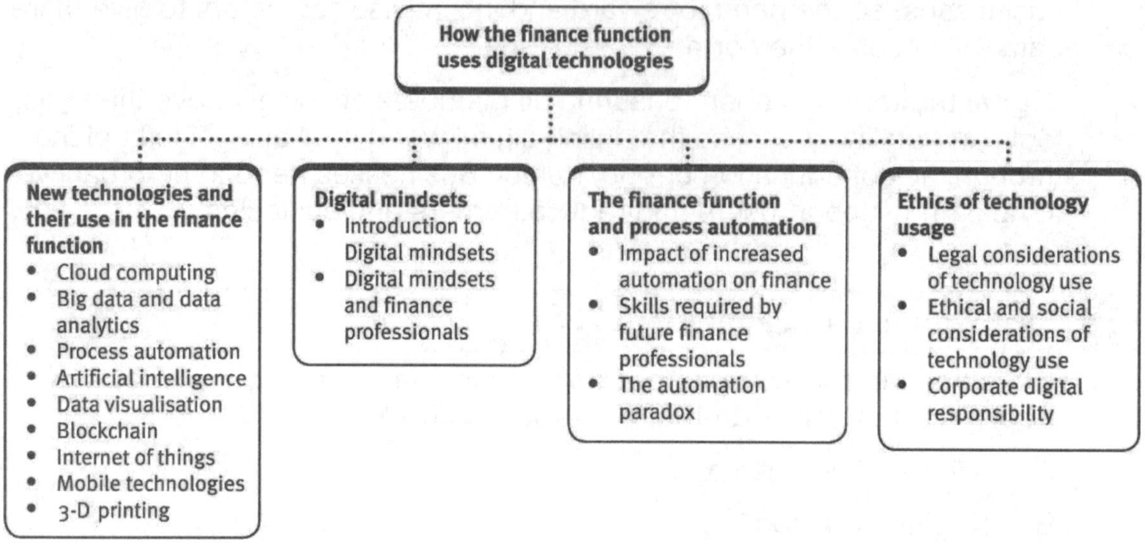

Test your understanding answers

Test your understanding 1

The correct answer is **all options**. They will all be impacted in some way by big data.

Test your understanding 2

The correct answer is **D**

Process automation brings uncertainty and change, which means employees, may resist change. Process automation brings advantages such as freeing up time for value added activities and improving accuracy by removing human error. It may involve more training costs to understand how the software may work.

Test your understanding 3

The correct answer is **A and C**

Data visualisation uses graphics and dashboard to be user friendly and intuitive. It also allows better understanding and fresh views on the data. Data visualisation can use real time data, to avoid monthly reporting. It does not necessarily involve a wider use of performance metrics, data visualisation just shows them in different ways.

Test your understanding 4

The correct answer is **C**

Blockchain would allow smart contracts to be used, which are self-executing and can't be tampered with. Artificial intelligence wouldn't be needed to make decisions. Cryptocurrency uses blockchain to underpin the digital transactions. Digital mindsets look at how technology may impact society.

Test your understanding 5

The correct answer is **D**

Additive manufacturing is creating additional layers to build up a structure, like 3-D printing. Subtractive manufacturing removes layers e.g. cutting sections. Just in Time generates raw material orders to coordinate with demand to reduce production cycles. Lean manufacturing concentrates on waste reduction.

Test your understanding 6

The correct answer is **A and D**

GDPR wants data to be kept up to date and protected. It also requires data to only be kept for as long as necessary and that it is used for explicit, specified purposes. Data can be stored in a variety of formats.

Test your understanding 7

The correct answer is **C**

The other two areas of effective CDR not listed are Giving back and Customer expectations. Digital sustainability is not a real concept and is a blend of elements of CDR and CSR.

Test your understanding 8

The correct answer is **A**

Corporate digital responsibility (CDR) goes beyond legislation when handling technology and data. Corporate social responsibility looks at maximising positive impacts on society and minimising the negative, and may incorporate CDR. Lobbying tries to influence the policies of government officials. Artificial intelligence is the creation of intelligent machines that work and react like humans.

Chapter

7

Data and the finance function

Chapter learning objectives

Lead	Component
C1: Describe the ways in which data is used by the finance function.	Identify the ways in which the finance function uses data: (a) In a general sense (b) Specifically in each of the primary activities of finance

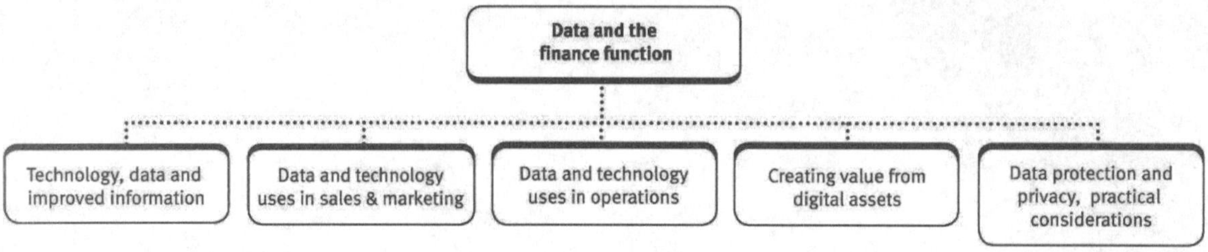

1 Introduction

We have introduced some of the key developments in technology which are transforming the world in which we work and live.

In this chapter we will look more closely at the growing importance of data and how this is both a key driver of new technologies, whilst also being a product of these same technologies.

We will also look at how data is used by the finance function to help the business across their various functions, for example to increase sales, generate new and innovative products, control costs and drive operational efficiencies. This relates back to our previous discussion (Chapter 2) on the basic primary activities of the finance function in that they will:

- Assemble information
- Analyse it for insights
- Advise to influence
- Apply for impact

2 Technology, data and improved information

2.1 The importance of information to decision makers

Decision making is a vital task in any business and takes place at 3 different levels in an organisation: strategic, tactical and operational.

Strategic – Long term, complex decisions made by directors and senior management. Decisions at this level impact the overall strategic direction of an organisation.

Tactical – Decisions are medium term and involve putting the strategic plan into action. This may involve selecting what products to stock in the current season or whether to open new branches.

Operational – Day to day decisions at junior levels of management concerned with the practical running of the business in line with plans set higher up the organisation.

Information

Firstly, let's recap what is meant by information from Chapter 2.

Information is data, processed in such a way that it has meaning to the person who receives it; this can then be used to improve the quality of decision making.

Accountants and the finance function are tasked with providing high quality information to support the successful operation of a business. The more **insight** this **information** can provide the more valuable it is to an organisation.

Some of the technological developments discussed in the previous chapters, are providing and utilising data on a new level, which if harnessed correctly can provide high value information, facilitating enhanced decision making across all levels of an organisation.

Some of the **benefits** of enhanced information include:

- Greater customer insights
- Potential for new sources of competitive advantage
- New business models and revenue streams
- Operational efficiencies offering significant cost savings as well as improved products and service for customers
- Quicker, more reactive decision making
- Early warning of potential problems
- Customised products specific to a customer needs

Test your understanding 1

Which of the following is the definition of information?

A A large store of data obtained from a wide variety of sources that can be used for decision making

B Raw and unprocessed numbers, facts or symbols that may contain valuable information if analysed effectively

C A structured set of data held in a computer

D Data processed in a way that it has a meaning to the person who receives it

2.2 Technology and data

As discussed in Chapter 2:

Data is raw and unprocessed numbers, facts or symbols that may contain potentially valuable information if analysed effectively.

Big data, data analytics and insight

Big data and **data analytics** are providing new **insights** and understanding of all aspects of the world around us. Accessing these insights is an opportunity for businesses but also a sizeable challenge and a potential threat should a business fall behind its rivals.

The main sources of **big data** are the technologies seen in the previous two chapters, the most significant being the **internet, mobile technologies** and the **internet of things**. These technologies facilitate software, applications (apps) and websites which generate vast amounts of data every second of every day.

e.g

Illustration 1 – The scale of big data

Internet – Globally there are 8.5 billion internet searches every day (or 100,000 per second) and annually around 2.77 billion people make online purchases (worth $6.3 trillion), with each individual search and transaction providing multiple data points

Mobile technologies – Smartphones have sound sensors, image sensors, touch sensors, an accelerometer, a light sensor, a proximity sensor and positional sensors for GPS. These are all used in the functioning of the smartphone but also produce enormous amounts of data continuously

Internet of things – there are in excess of 16 billion 'connected' devices, all with multiple sensors generating constant data about how devices are used and performing

Applications, software and websites – Facebook has over 3 billion monthly active users, and over 2 billion daily active users on the site. On average the user spends 23 minutes on Facebook. Users also generate 4 million likes every minute.

2.3 Improving information for decision makers

Decision makers at all levels of an organisation rely on good quality information to help inform and guide them. Whether it is an aged receivables report used by a credit controller or an investment proposal being considered at board level, the information used will be built from data.

In order to improve the information for decision makers, an organisation needs to improve the data being used to generate the information.

Internet of things, social media and the **internet** itself are three significant sources of data for organisations. Collecting this data and using it in a deliberate manner is hugely beneficial to decision makers for the following reasons.

- **Enhanced data transparency** – Improved systems for handling data allow new meaning to be found in data which may have previously been unviable to process. Technological developments allow data to be more easily integrated with other data sources across the business, generating greater insight.

- **Enhanced performance** – Real time monitoring of data, summarised into key metrics can enable corrective action to be taken immediately to improve controllable changes in performance.
- **Market segmentation and customisation** – Data can enable new market segments to be identified, which may previously have been lost within a broader market segment. Once identified, this segment can be more actively targeted with a customised message.
- **Improved decision-making** – Better understanding and insight into consumer behaviour through detailed data analysis can facilitate improved decision-making. Insights driven by deeper data understanding, for example, are which products to stock in a store. This is not just based on sales volumes but also related purchases they encourage and the type of customer they attract.
- **New products and services** – Understanding the various drivers that prompt customers to purchase a specific product or service over another can provide valuable insight into the development of new products or service offerings.
- **Operational gains** – Detailed insight into a business's operations can highlight potential efficiencies, cost savings and service improvements that can give a company an advantage over their rivals.

2.4 How the finance function uses data in its primary activities

The basic activities (the 5 A's) of the finance function can be summarised using the information to impact framework (covered in Chapter 2). The finance function will use data in each of its primary activities.

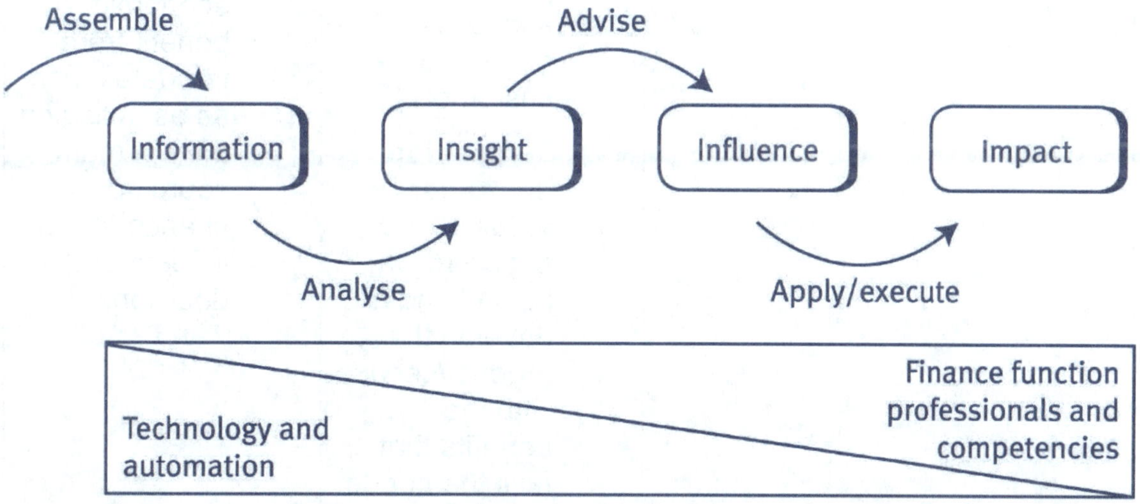

In the digital world, technology and automation will play a key role in collecting, processing and displaying information more efficiently than humans. This should be viewed as an opportunity for the finance function who can focus on using the information to create and preserve value for the organisation.

Assembling information and Analysing for insight	Advising to influence	Applying for impact
Technology and automation play a key role in, for example: • Collecting and processing data for costing and budgeting purposes. • Assembling information for inclusion in the financial statements. • Assembling information to assist with working capital management. This has freed up the resource of finance professionals but they do continue to have some role here. For example, the finance function will analyse the information for insight to **understand customers' needs** regarding which product features are desirable, the level of quality demanded or the price customers are willing to pay.	Technology and automation will have some role here but there is a greater opportunity for finance professionals to use their competencies, for example: • **Decision making** – analysed information is used to develop solutions and advise to influence, such as consideration of the optimum product mix (i.e. the selection of products or services offered to customers). • To **develop customer value proposition**, i.e. helping to develop the product/service with the benefits that fulfil the needs of customers.	The finance function will have a significant role, for example: • **Enhancing operational efficiency** by deploying solutions such as outsourcing production to a third party rather than making in-house, or changing suppliers after investigation into material variances. • **Monetising data** – actions taken to generate economic benefit from the data, such as establishing the optimum source of finance for an investment decision.

It is worth noting that many of the **reasons for collecting and processing information and the uses of this information are covered in other modules at the Operational level**. For example:

- **P1** includes topics such as costing, budgeting and control. It also decision making including product mix decisions and make or buy decisions.
- **F1** includes topics such as the preparation of financial statements and the management of working capital.

e.g

Illustration 2 – Data use in decision making

Consider a company that manufactures and sells protein bars for people who undertake a regular programme of exercise, and that the company makes its own peanut butter and uses cardboard packaging for its bars.

Suppose that the company is looking at ways to cut costs and improve margins.

The 'assembling information and analysing for insight' stages could include the following:

- asking customers to identify which features of the product they value the most and why. For example, if customers value sustainability enough, then it would be a mistake to consider substituting a cheaper plastic wrapper for the cardboard ones.
- looking at the costs of alternative ways of procuring ingredients, such as the costs of buying in peanut butter rather than making it in-house. These costs would include purchase and delivery costs and would save on internal salaries and other manufacturing costs.
- considering buying some ingredients in bulk to gain bulk discounts. Key data would include the impact on both purchasing and inventory holding costs.

3 Data and technology uses in sales and marketing

3.1 Sales and marketing

Marketing is the management process that identifies, anticipates and supplies customer needs efficiently and profitably.

Marketing is considered in detail in **Chapter 10**. In this section we are considering how the use of **technology and data** can help both the marketing and sales functions within a business.

Data use in marketing and sales – Big data and the use of smart technology, which collects relevant data, summarises it and presents the key findings, are driving real changes in the way businesses choose what to sell, the price to charge, when to sell it and when to discount.

The use of data is providing real, fact based insight into customers and competitors actions and thereby acting to remove a lot of the 'guesswork' from the business critical decisions made in the marketing and sales departments.

Pricing – Is a critical decision. Price too low and a business misses out on potential revenue, price too high and sales volumes will be low. Heavy discounting can reflect badly on brand image. Live market data allows a company to compare and benchmark prices across an entire industry, as well as seeing the rate of sales. This data indicates the right price point for a given product so the first price of a product can be set optimally.

Products – The days of retailers buying huge quantities of products in advance of distinct seasons are a thing of the past. Retailers test the market and constantly monitor what products and trends are selling both for themselves and their competitors. Short lead times allow products to be sourced almost immediately.

Segmentation – Analysis of buying patterns and social media trends and interactions can refine and identify new market segments by grouping similar data-points. This can be an opportunity enabling more targeted marketing; it may also provide data to show a segment isn't as significant as first thought and may not be viable.

Promotions – Data from past product launches and company promotions for an entire industry combined with the subsequent sales performance of those products provides huge insight into what promotions work best and when. This can reduce the guesswork by supporting companies with real data.

Customer relationship management (CRM) – Data on customers provides a profile which, together with their past buying trends, can make advertising and communications more personalised and tailored to meet their specific 'wants'. For instance, knowing a customer likes a bargain means offering them a discount on specific items and this may lead to a sale.

Targeting – By analysing market trends and seeing products, colours and designs that are on-trend and selling out elsewhere, a business can then push specific items to the front page of their website or a priority position in store and incorporate it in their advertising, targeted at specific consumers.

e.g

Illustration 3 – Data use in marketing and sales. Edited

Edited is a technology company that provides real-time **data analytics** software for retailers and fashion brands.

The software utilises **AI** and **SpiderBots** or **web crawlers** (these are automated programs which browse the web methodically extracting target data, such as pricing, styles, colours etc.)

The **Edited** software pulls together key industry wide metrics for the types of products being sold, those selling fast, the key colours and fashion trends and crucially pricing data. This information is available instantly and provides retailers with data on what products they should be designing or ordering, the pricing architecture of products and what products should be discounted and by how much.

All of this information is publically available but the process of searching for and sorting this data would traditionally be a laborious and time consuming task and by the time the data was available or usable it would be old. **Edited** cuts out the leg work and provides live data in a visually appealing and accessible way using **data visualisations** to highlight the key data points required.

The software is used by retailers such as **M&S, Shein, Puma and Under Armour** to name just a few.

Test your understanding 2

Which TWO of the following are ways in which data and technology can support the marketing function?

A Personalising communication with customers

B Scheduling production processes to alleviate bottlenecks

C Comparing prices with competitors

D Reducing the viability of a market segment

E Preventative maintenance of products

Illustration 4 – Data use and CRM

By harnessing technology and building a profile on customers, even small independent restaurants are incorporating data driven **customer relationship management (CRM)** in driving repeat custom.

Rather than taking a booking and it being a one-time only transaction, a restaurant will collect data such as an email address and/or phone number when taking this booking. This will then be used to create a new customer profile.

In addition, they will look at what the type of booking it is i.e. couple, group, family as well as the time and date of the booking. They may even try to find out if it is a special occasion which could also be used for future marketing.

The **data** collection continues as once the profile is established what food you order and the drinks you have will also be added to the profile giving them an insight into what you like and what in future may prompt you to return.

Then with all this data collected if the restaurant notices that you are a regular customer and you haven't visited for some time a marketing email can be generated; this can be tailored to hit the specific data held in your profile. For instance, if every time you visit you order the same starter the email may contain a picture of this dish to whet your appetite as well as offering a complimentary starter on your next visit. This may well be enough to convince you to make that next booking.

4 Data and technology uses in operations

4.1 Using data to enhance operations

Data and technology provide insights, and opportunity for businesses to drive sales growth and identify new revenue streams, but it is also playing a major role for businesses in changing and improving their internal operations and processes.

This can lead to multiple benefits for a business, these include:

- **Cost saving** – As with any efficiency gains, insights gained from the use of technology can generate significant cost savings through alleviating bottlenecks, reducing waste and reducing downtime.
- **Improved service** – Live data in operational processes can lead to significant service improvement and information availability for customers. Modern logistics companies allow live tracking of all deliveries through the use of data and connectivity.
- **Supply chain** – Big data is enabling increasingly complex supply chain networks through knowledge sharing and collaboration. Data sharing enables suppliers and customers to collaborate in order to modify either components or end products in the most cost effective manner.
- **Preventative maintenance** – Using an **internet of things** based approach, embedding sensors and connectivity in machines and assets facilitates continual monitoring of performance. Deviations from expected performance give early warning of potential problems and preventative maintenance can be scheduled at a convenient time and before an asset breaks down.
- **Forecasting** – Companies can use big data analytics to map the behaviour of customers, using sophisticated forecasting and predictive modelling techniques in order to schedule production processes for efficient utilisation and order fulfilment.

e.g

Illustration 5 – Data use in manufacturing

A case study from consulting firm **McKinsey** looked at the manufacturing processes of a leading pharmaceutical company.

The company manufactured vaccines and blood components, in which the need for purity is critical. Over 200 variables were monitored to inform on the level of purity, these would vary between batches impacting the ultimate yield of saleable vaccine or blood products achieved each time.

By analysing the huge amounts of data generated in the manufacturing process, 9 key parameters were identified. These were found to have a direct causal impact on the yield achieved in the process.

The company was able to then target improvements and consistency in these 9 specific areas to achieve increased standardisation and optimise these parameters, ultimately increasing the saleable yield. Output data from the process is now tracked and monitored against target levels.

The yield from the vaccine production process increased by 50% which led to savings for the business of over $7.5 million dollars per annum.

e.g

Illustration 6 – Data use in operations. DHL

DHL have invested heavily in an **internet of things** based tracking and monitoring system using embedded sensors in their various machinery, other assets and hand-held devices. This allows the business to track a huge range of metrics including vehicle behaviour and performance, the actual packages they are processing and environmental performance through sensors in their warehouses, hand-held devices and vehicles. All of this data is collected and harnessed to generate real time monitoring and process improvement as well as providing a huge array of data the business can mine to identify further insight that may drive future performance improvement.

This system at **DHL** is generating efficiencies, cost savings and service improvements.

Test your understanding 3

Core Co is a mining company. It extracts minerals from the ground using drills. Core buys drills that have software contained within them that records when each drill became operational; the hours used each day and the drill performance.

Which of the following would be the main benefit to Core Co of this software?

A Immediate cost savings

B Improved customer retention

C Preventative maintenance

D Reduction of accidents

5 Creating value from digital assets

5.1 Digital assets

Assets held by a business in digital form that do not have physical substance. This typically includes images, animations, audio, video and PDF files.

The volume of **digital assets** is rising rapidly in line with the increase in **internet** usage, **connectivity** and **mobile technologies**. These are the media upon which digital asset content is consumed and are now central to everyday life. Digital assets have become a significant part of modern businesses and must be managed in a deliberate and coordinated manner in order to leverage them to their maximum.

5.2 Digital asset management systems

A **digital asset management (DAM) system** is designed to coordinate the digital assets of a business, ensuring they are held centrally in an accessible, secure and logically designed repository. This supports the efficient running of the business, by facilitating availability and use of these increasingly important assets.

The **finance function** of a business would be involved in the process of building a **business case for investing** in a digital asset management system, coordinating the search for a suitable provider of a DAM system and managing the change in working practices to incorporate the system. This would need to be managed as a standalone project, outside of day to day activities.

Features of **DAM** system include:

- DAM systems are essentially a database specifically designed to manage digital assets
- Single central location for digital asset storage and access
- Often facilitated by cloud based software, supporting security and allowing access from any location
- Access levels built into the system, allowing access only to those with authorisation
- Assets categorised by format with associated metadata describing the content to facilitate search functionality

e.g

Illustration 7 – DAM system at the American Kennel Club

The **American Kennel Club** (AKC) invested in a DAM system from the specialist provider **Canto**.

The organisation is the authority on purebred dogs in the US, they maintain a registry of pedigrees and organise numerous dog shows. AKC hold a vast catalogue of digital assets, including photos, videos and certified documentation which is all held electronically. Organising these assets for efficient use was a significant challenge and countless hours of staff time was being spent scouring through a variety of locations on the network and hard drives trying to locate images or documents needed for promotional material, newsletters, their website and social media accounts.

The organisation recognised the need for a solution to this problem and considered a DAM system. **Canto** was the provider they ultimately opted for; they provided a cloud-based centralised library of digital assets tailored to their exact requirements. Assets are logged in the DAM system with numerous tags or metadata, which provides detailed information about the asset to facilitate easy searches, built on a user friendly platform with intuitive design. This had made the use of these assets more efficient and saved hundreds of staff hours searching for or duplicating content.

Benefits of a **digital asset management systems** include:

- Strengthen relationships across teams by facilitating the sharing of assets and content
- Improve service to customers and partners through easy asset sharing using web portals
- A standardised approach to metadata as prescribed by a DAM system eliminates wasted time spent searching for files and digital assets and prevents duplication and re-creation of content.
- Cost and space saving through use of cloud technology designed specifically for the purpose of managing digital assets
- Version control, watermarking and embargo dates allow increased security and protect assets from improper or untimely use
- Provides valuable data on the usage and access of digital assets that can provide insight and direct the production and type of digital assets that generate value
- Copyrighting and contact information can automatically be attached to every digital asset held. This provides consistency in publication and clarity to external users.

Test your understanding 4

Y Ltd is a newspaper and magazine publisher, established over 100 years ago. In that time, they have collected millions of photos to accompany their news stories. The Board have decided they need to make more efficient use of the photo bank.

Which of the following would be needed to utilise the photo bank?

A Augmented reality

B 3-D printing

C Non-market strategy

D Digital asset management system

6 Data protection and privacy, practical considerations

6.1 Data protection and privacy

In **Chapter 6** we introduced the ethical considerations of technology use, looking at legal elements such as **GDPR** and the ethical and social side of things through **corporate digital responsibility (CDR)**. Here we will consider some the practical considerations of data protection for a business.

Data protection can be defined as the process of safeguarding important information from corruption, compromise or loss.

Businesses as a minimum must ensure they are compliant with data protection legislation such as **GDPR** in order to avoid potential fines and legal recourse. Ideally a business should go above and beyond the requirements of **GDPR** by having a strong moral and ethical stance on how and why they handle data. This is covered by the concept of **CDR** covered in **Chapter 6**.

As a starting point to assess the adequacy of a business's data security, the UK **Information Commissioner's Office (ICO)** outlined the following key questions a business must address. Any questions that a business fails to answer should be immediately flagged as a critical weakness, with immediate action taken to correct the issues identified.

Key questions to assess data security capabilities

- Do you have a record of what personal data you hold? Do you know what you use it for?
- Do people know you have their personal data and know how you use it?
- Do you only collect the personal data you need?
- Do you only keep personal data for as long as it is needed?
- Do you keep personal data accurate and up to date?
- Do you keep personal data secure?

- Do you have a way for people to exercise their rights regarding the personal data you hold about them?
- Do you and your staff know your data protection responsibilities?

6.2 Features of sound data management

Traditionally data in organisations was not viewed with strategic significance both from a risk perspective i.e. **GDPR** and legislation, and as an opportunity i.e. **big data**. It would often be found under the umbrella of IT due to the obvious crossovers.

However, as data has grown in significance organisations are changing their approach to how data and data management fits within their overall organisation. The following are some of the features of modern organisational structures and their approach to data:

- **Chief Data Officer (CDO)** – This is an increasingly common executive role in larger organisations. The CDO holds overall responsibility for governance and protection of data as well as strategies to optimise the use of data as an asset
- **Data strategy** – Is now a deliberate and integrated part of overall corporate strategy. The **SAS institute**, a specialist in data analytics, identified the five following key building blocks of data strategy:
  - **Identify** – What data does a business have and require? What is its structure, origin and location?
  - **Store** – What structure and storage approach will enable easy sharing and access to data whilst ensuring it is adequately protected?
  - **Provision** – An overarching data strategy should ensure data is packaged to allow easy use throughout the organisation. Rules, guidelines and access levels will be essential.
  - **Process** – Current and existing data should be designed for easy clear and consistent processing. Unifying separate data stores to maximise the processing potential.
  - **Govern** – Establish clear, consistent user friendly policies on the use and storage of data to ensure correct use and minimise risk of data breaches.
- **Culture** – Promoting the significance of data at all levels of the organisation is essential. This must be led from the top of the business to show intent and commitment.
- **Training** – Additional to the areas such as health and safety and cyber security, data awareness training is increasingly mandatory to ensure compliance with legislation.

7 Chapter summary

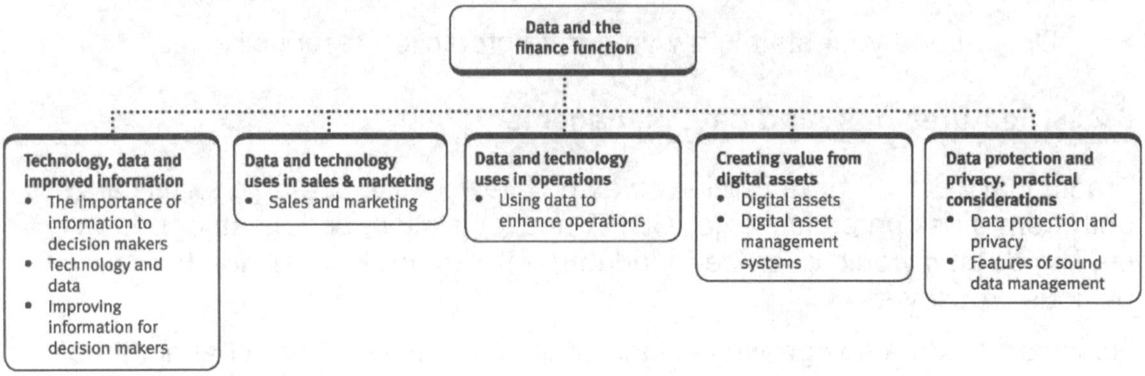

Test your understanding answers

Test your understanding 1

The correct answer is **D**

Information can be used by people for decision making, therefore must have some meaning. A large store of data is called a data warehouse. Raw and unprocessed numbers and facts is the definition of data itself. A structured set of data in a computer is a database.

Test your understanding 2

The correct answers are **A and C**

Data and technology could support the marketing function through personalised communication with customers (answer A), comparing prices with competitors (answer C) and assessing the viability of market segments (not reducing the viability of a market segment, as is suggested in answer D).

Answers B and E are ways in which technology and data could support the operations function, rather than the marketing function.

Test your understanding 3

The correct answer is **C**

Software/sensors can give ideas of when assets have reached their useful lives, or need to be replaced or improved. This may cost more initially, but leads to savings further down the line. Customers would not necessarily see the impact of this. Accidents may still occur due to the nature of the work.

Test your understanding 4

The correct answer is **D**

Digital asset management looks at all assets held in a digital format. Augmented reality is an interactive experience where a real world scenario is augmented by computer generated perceptual information. 3-D printing is an additive manufacturing process. Non-Market strategy looks at stakeholders outside of the normal commercial interests, such as governments.

Chapter

8

Data to create and preserve value for organisations

Chapter learning objectives

Lead	Component
C2: Explain the competencies required to use data to create and preserve value for organisations.	Explain the competencies that finance professionals need in: (a) Data strategy and planning (b) Data engineering, extraction and mining (c) Data modelling, manipulation and analysis (d) Data insight and communication

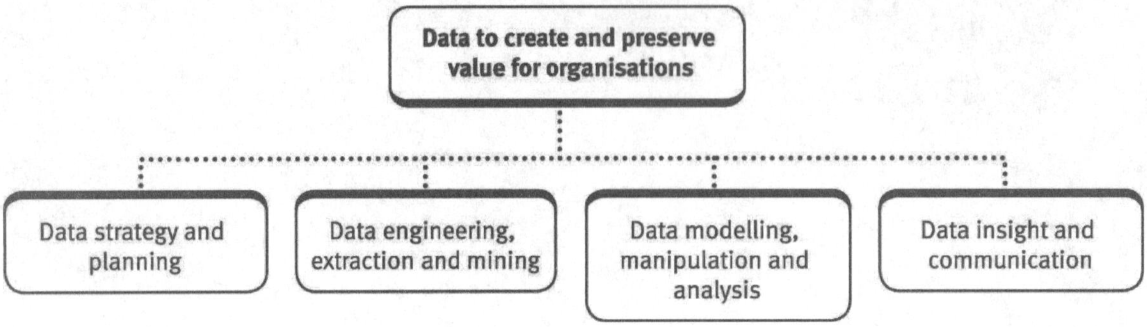

1 Introduction

Having considered data, and how it plays an increasingly significant role in modern business, this chapter looks at more technical elements of **data management** and how these impact the finance function.

We will consider the main stakeholders of the finance function, considering some of their data needs, before taking a closer look at the data strategy of a business as introduced in **Chapter 7**.

To underpin this discussion, we also need to consider the **competencies** required by finance professionals in the digital world in order for them to **use data to create and preserve value for the organisation**. Finance professionals will require competencies in:

- Data strategy and planning
- Data engineering, extraction and mining
- Data modelling, manipulation and analysis
- Data insight and communication

These four areas are discussed in Sections 2–5.

Some of the skills required by the **future** finance professional were briefly discussed in Chapter 6.

The CGMA (Chartered Global Management Accountant) 2023 competency framework outlines the skills needed by finance professionals in **current and future** roles. They can be grouped into four types of competency, all underpinned by **ethics, integrity and professionalism**.

Competency	Explanation
Technical skills	The finance professional will be required to **apply accounting and finance skills**. Technical skills will enable finance professionals to collect, store, process and analyse information to be shared with various stakeholders. As discussed previously, activities such as data collection and processing are increasingly automated. However, the finance function will still be required to act as a 'guardian' of the automated finance process; for example, retaining the skills required when faced with an unusual situation that requires a switch to manual control.

Business skills	**Understanding of the business and the environment** is crucial to effective decision-making and the ability to transform data into insight for use by the business and its functions to create and preserve value. Finance professionals will increasingly require good **knowledge of data sources**, **analytical skills** and **judgement**.
People skills	Finance professionals will need people skills and the **ability to communicate**. They will work alongside other parts of the organisation as a partner, collaborating to generate insight to influence decisions and improve performance. They will need to focus on **building empathy, understanding** and **interactions** with stakeholders.
Leadership skills	Finance professionals increasingly **occupy a central position in an organisation**, understanding and questioning numbers and information given. Leadership skills will centre on **team building**, **coaching** and **mentoring**, **driving performance** and **change management**, and the **ability to motivate and inspire**.

(**Note:** In the CGMA Competency Framework (2019) there was a fifth competency called Digital Skills. This has now been deleted from the Framework model as an 'individual' skill but instead it is of paramount importance across the other four skills in the Framework.)

Technological advancements are constantly changing the skills and knowledge organisations value in the finance professional. Therefore, the need for a **growth mindset** and **continued learning** is paramount.

2 Data strategy and planning

2.1 Data requirements and stakeholders

A **stakeholder** can be defined in many ways but is often summarised as being anybody who can affect or be affected by an organisation's actions. In this section, we are more specifically interested in the stakeholders of the finance function of an organisation. So, who would this typically include?

- Other departments and managers – The finance function of an organisation conducts the budgeting process and provides important management information and performance data to all functions of an organisation
- External stakeholders – Users of the financial statements include shareholders, lenders and investors. Auditors, customers and suppliers would be other significant external stakeholders of the finance department

- Employees – Staff in the finance department will clearly be a very significant stakeholder in the department and will need to be considered in all future strategies
- Directors – Key metrics and performance reports for the board are an important component of the finance department's work

The next consideration is what type of **feedback** we might receive from them and how could this impact the future **data needs** of the organisation. This would be an important element in generating an overall **data strategy**. Some examples are given in the table below:

Stakeholder	Feedback	Data needs
Sales department	Selling prices, sales volumes, customer feedback	Live data on competitors' pricing and market trends. Metrics on key customer feedback about products and services received.
Production department	Order levels, lead times, approved suppliers and unit cost information	Data collection and recording could be designed to support the collecting of cost data to enable more accurate understanding of costs and drivers of costs. Live systems such as smart shelves can automatically reorder stock.
HR department	Staff performance and development, the level of training planned and achieved. Appraisal process	Data system requirements would need to incorporate appraisal systems, productivity analysis as well as collecting data on internal progressions and training days. An integrated office management system could be considered.
Shareholders	Requirement for more information about impacts and future prospects of a business, over the standard annual report	A move to integrated reporting could see a shift in data needs and reporting. For instance, data about carbon footprint and water usage could be collected to report under the natural capital section of an integrated report.
Employees	Hands on users of systems and processes within finance	Unique position to flag inefficiencies in the system and potentially suggest improvements and test solutions.
Managers and directors	Seek insight and clarity from information provided by finance	Investment in improved systems to facilitate the use of data incorporating effective data visualisations to summarise key metrics.

3 Data engineering, extraction and mining

3.1 Data engineering and extraction

Data engineering is the practice of designing and building systems for collecting, storing and analysing large sets of data.

Extraction, transformation and loading (**ETL**) are the three stages in blending data from multiple sources into a destination system, for example a data warehouse.

- **Extraction** is the process of harvesting data from (typically multiple) source databases. Prior to extraction, the data needs to be analysed to understand its content, format and structure. This is **data profiling**.
- **Transformation** takes the extracted data and changes it into a format suitable for the destination database and ultimate, intended use. This is done using code and rules designed to interrogate the source data before converting it to a new format as per the code instructions.
- **Loading** is when the newly cleaned and prepared data is uploaded into the destination database (often a data warehouse) ready for use.

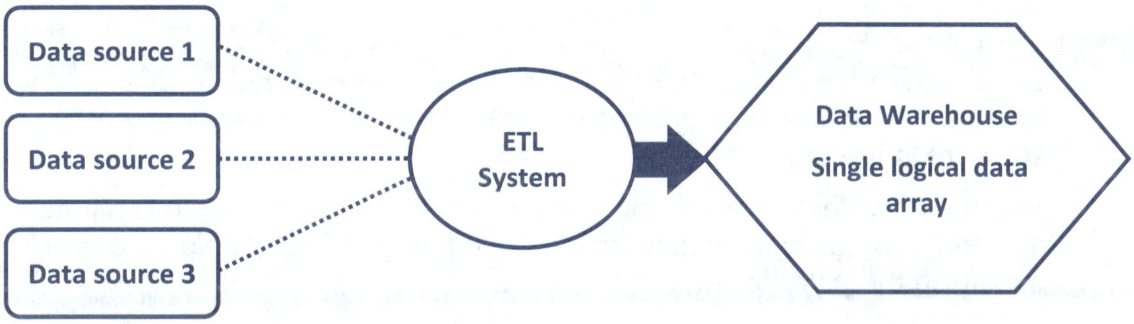

A **data warehouse** is a store for data that has been loaded in the ETL process. The data will be held in a systematic and logical way ready for further interrogation and analysis by the **business intelligence** function.

3.2 Business intelligence (BI) and data mining

Business intelligence (BI) is the technology driven process of analysing business data to create insightful and actionable information to help improve the operations or products of a business.

Data mining is an important component of BI. It is the process of uncovering patterns and other valuable information from large sets of data in the data warehouse.

As discussed, **ETL** systems provide data in a clean and ready-to-use format. BI systems access and analyse this data further and present the findings using **data visualisation** techniques as well as traditional summaries and reports.

BI software has evolved to become more user friendly and intuitive allowing users throughout an organisation to access data that may be of value without IT or finance assistance being required.

3.3 Big data, ETL and BI

Traditional **ETL** systems are not a new development and have been around since the 1970s. The modern digital world means these **ETL** or data integration systems are faced with fresh challenges. The main challenges include:

- **Rate of growth** – data volumes are growing at unprecedented levels
- **Types and sources** – traditional database integration is a thing of the past. Data for the modern business comes in all shapes and sizes and from an array of sources both internal and external (social media, connected devices, live streaming etc.)
- **New technologies** – **ETL** software is still a fundamental element of BI but new solutions such as **Hadoop** and **GoogleBigQuery** are designed for the modern landscape of big data. They use innovative techniques in order to handle the challenges presented by the volume, variety, veracity and velocity of big data.

e.g

Illustration 1 – Hadoop and modern data requirements

Hadoop is a name synonymous with **big data** and is an example of **BI** software in the digital age.

Hadoop provides a framework, using open source software, to facilitate distributed processing which enables companies to tackle big data and maximise the potential gains.

How it works

Put simply, Hadoop essentially breaks tasks down and then shares them between 'nodes' which are basically a series of servers. By breaking a task down, it allows the processing to be run in parallel, making a task much faster. It also has inbuilt failsafe's so if one node fails, its work will be picked up and processed elsewhere.

For instance, if I had a task that was going to take me 20 days to complete but it needed to be done more quickly, the obvious route would be to break the work down into blocks and get others to help. I would then reassemble the blocks of work and present the finished task.

Another advantage is that should one of the workers get ill (or fail from a computing perspective) their block of work could be shared between the other workers without any significant impact on the ultimate outcome.

Components of Hadoop

Hadoop Common: The common utilities that support the other Hadoop modules.

Hadoop Distributed File System (HDFS) – This is the part of the system responsible for breaking down a task into chunks of work and distributing them. HDFS operates following a similar logic to that on your personal computer, but scales this up to operate and arrange files across many machines.

Hadoop YARN: A framework for job scheduling and cluster resource management.

Hadoop MapReduce – Having broken the data into chunks, the MapReduce element of Hadoop then coordinates the actual distributed processing of this data to achieve an outcome.

For instance, if we were trying to interrogate a large data set looking for key words. The **HDFS** would take the large volume of data, break it into manageable chunks and spread this across multiple nodes. The **MapReduce** element would then find the instances of these key words in each chunk (mapping) and then summarise the outcome (reduce) to say how many instances we had overall.

Test your understanding 1

Which THREE of the following are reasons why traditional ETL systems may no longer be valid for an organisation today?

A Increased rate of data growth

B Wider sources of data

C More balanced composition of the Board

D Increased use of Corporate Social Responsibility

E Introduction of new big data technologies

F Restrictions in employee skillset

3.4 The finance function's role in data engineering, extraction and mining

Finance professionals **will use their unique set of competencies** to **act as an interface between data specialists** (such as data engineers and data scientists, who have a background in statistics and computer science) **and the business**, essentially making the data generated commercially relevant and transforming it into valuable information.

Linking this back to the **information to impact framework**, they will add value to the organisation through a process of:

- **Assembling information** – Unstructured data from a range of relevant sources is collected and cleaned from its raw format and assembled into meaningful information.
- **Generating insights** – Analysis of both financial and non-financial information leads to insights needed to improve the performance of the organisation.
- **Influencing decision-makers** – Insights are obtained and then used to advise and then influence relevant stakeholders within the organisation.
- **Achieving impact** – Will guide actions to help ensure the required impact is achieved.

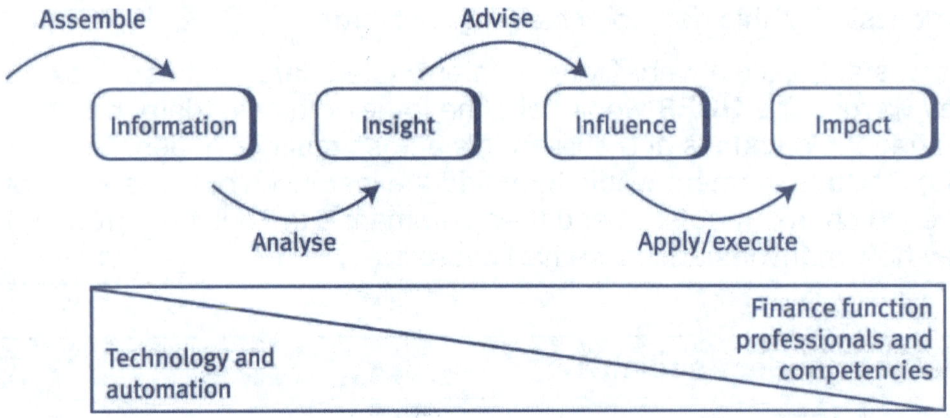

4 Data modelling, manipulation and analysis

4.1 Data modelling and the finance function

A **data model** considers the data of an organisation in a systematic way. This allows it to be stored and retrieved in an efficient and effective manner.

The process of data modelling involves laying out an organisation's data requirements in a way that can be easily and deliberately converted to computer code. The modelling process requires a clear and systematic plan of the key data being stored and how this should be organised to allow it to be retrieved, interrogated, linked and grouped.

The advantages of data modelling include:

- **Foundation** for handling data, it facilitates the effective use of that data throughout the organisation
- Enforces **business rules** and helps achieve regulatory compliance by ensuring data is complete and secure
- **Consistency** of naming conventions and values ultimately underpin a systematic and reliable database

- The **quality** of data is enhanced. Data modelling provides an organisation with a well-planned approach to its data, ensuring completeness and facilitating high quality data warehouses.

Three levels of a data modelling process

Conceptual – Business oriented and practical, considering the business data and its requirements.

Logical – This level begins to develop a technical map of rules and data structures, defining how data will be held and used.

Physical – This considers how the defined system requirements will be implemented using a specific database management system (DBMS).

Finance professionals understand the business data and the requirements of the organisation and so will have an important role in the **conceptual level** of the process. Using their **competencies**, they will work with data specialists to ensure the data and requirements are reflected at the logical and physical level.

4.2 Data manipulation

Data manipulation is the process of changing data to make it easier to read. It involves adding, deleting, querying and modifying data in a data-store using a **data manipulation language** or **DML**.

Data held in a database is held according to the parameters of the **data model** used to design it. This data can then be searched and interrogated using **data manipulation language** (**DML**) which essentially gives instructions to a database in a consistent and structured fashion.

Digital specialists develop the DML. They will be guided by **finance professionals** who have the skills and **competencies to identify and communicate what is needed by the business**.

From a finance perspective, the query function of **DML** is the most relevant feature, allowing users to ask the database questions about the data held. This is done in order to gather information required by management for things like analysis, reporting and decision-making.

Test your understanding 2

What are the THREE levels of the data modelling process?

A Rational, Time variant, Logical

B Conceptual, Irrational, Variety

C Conceptual, Logical, Physical

D Extraction, Transformation, Loading

4.3 Data analysis

Data analysis is the process of examining, transforming and arranging a given data set in specific ways in order to study its individual parts and extract useful information.

There are several methods available for data analysis. The methods can be used individually but are commonly used collectively:

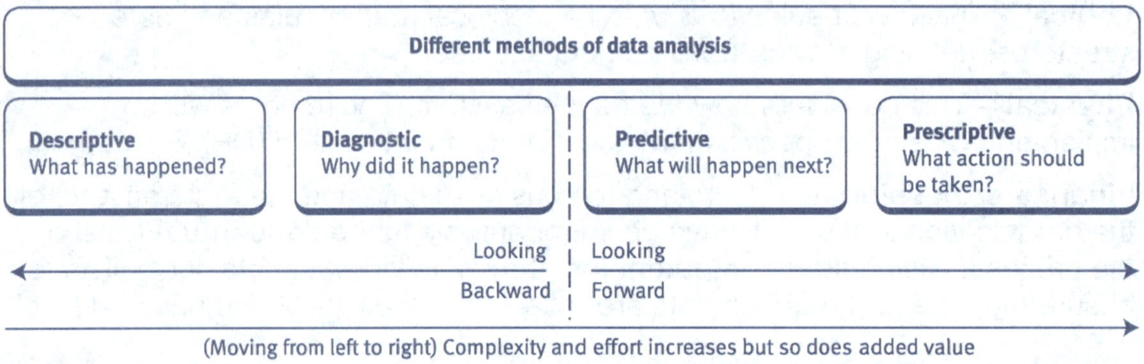

Much of the descriptive and diagnostic analysis is becoming a fully or almost fully automated process. This is releasing resource into the predictive and prescriptive activities that are of higher organisational value and where technology (such as advanced analytics and machine learning) combines with improved human capabilities, to reason, understand and learn together.

Data analysis techniques

A variety of data analysis techniques can be used. For example:

- Simple statistical and visual tools (such as the calculation of averages and the use of bar charts) for **descriptive analysis**
- Data mining to analyse the data and unearth unknown patterns or correlations in the data for **diagnostic analysis**
- More advanced statistical tools such as linear regression models, decision trees and simulation (Note: knowledge and understanding of these tools is not required) for **predictive analysis**
- AI and machine learning for **prescriptive analysis**.

Data analysis is a component of data analytics. Data analytics focuses on three areas – data collection, data organisation and data analysis.

5 Data insight and communication

5.1 Managing big data – the finance function

The role of providing management information in business has long been the remit of the finance function. **Big data** has seen the pool of data available to compile this management information increase exponentially. The finance function still plays an integral role in understanding and managing the data and information of a business.

Data strategy – the use of data is of fundamental importance to most modern businesses. In line with the concept of developing a **digital mindset**; digital technology and data must be considered at a strategic level within a business. Data is central to the overall strategic thinking of business and must be incorporated in strategic planning. An overall **data strategy** is a common element of overall corporate strategy and is defined by the Harvard Business Review as follows:

Data strategy is a coherent approach for organising, governing, analysing and deploying an organisation's information assets.

Developing a data strategy is a key part of the modern business landscape and an effective data strategy should consist of the 5 elements, **identify, store, provision, process** and **govern** as covered earlier. The strategy should provide a coherent, organisation wide approach, moving away from isolated data projects being conducted throughout the business in a haphazard fashion.

A key element of any data strategy from a value adding perspective is how to effectively capture and utilise big data.

To maximise the benefits it can deliver, a system must be designed that can cope with the attributes of big data, as outlined by the **4Vs**:

- **Volume** – The volume of data available from modern technologies is vast, the capability to handle and process the sheer quantity of data, which will continue to grow, must be a key consideration in any data strategy.
- **Velocity** – The stream of data coming into organisations is constant, transactions, web clicks, 'likes' on social media etc... occur in their millions every minute of every day. Data systems must have the capability to process this live data, providing up to date information as well as storing it for further use.
- **Variety** – Data comes from a range of sources both internal and external and in an array of formats. Traditional data use was largely internal and structured, but the growth in external sources such as social media and web cookies sees data in a range of unstructured formats. Systems must have the capability to handle this increasingly rich source of data.

- **Veracity** – This considers how trustworthy data is and is crucial to effective use of data. Systems must ensure data can be validated to reduce uncertainty to tolerable levels. Combining data with other sources can act as a check of data authenticity. For instance, GPS location data in cities suffers high levels of interference, this data could be validated by comparison to other data such as purchase data, accelerometer data (tracking motion) or social media updates.

Overall, an effective data strategy must address the challenges of big data considering how data is collected, held and incorporated across the business to maximise its value adding potential.

5.2 Data visualisations and the finance function

Data visualisation is an enabling technology that complements data analytics by facilitating user friendly and accessible presentation of key data through the following:

- **Information** – Providing information for stakeholders in and outside the business is core to the finance function's responsibilities, therefore data visualisation is a very important concept for the finance professional
- **Users** – Many users of the data finance departments produce do not have a finance background, so it is important to avoid data heavy presentations and technical jargon. Instead, the focus is on highlighting the key pieces of data the audience need and presenting these in an engaging and informative way
- **Simplicity** – Effective visualisations should be intuitive and involve practically no training for the end user

Prior to producing a data visualisation it is useful to consider some simple questions in order to improve its effectiveness:

- **Who are the audience?** Who are we producing the data for and what level of detail do they require are key considerations. It is also useful to consider the technical ability of the audience.
- **How do they want the data?** If, for example, it is for a sales force the data should be mobile friendly, summarised and quick to read, with the potential to drill down where required. Generally, the level of detail, the interface, medium and interactivity should all be considered.
- **What outcome do we want?** Ultimately what do they want to take from the data and how should it help enhance performance.

Illustration 2 – Data visualisation. Edited.

This is an example of a data visualisation from **Edited** the retail data analytics technology company discussed in **Chapter 7**. It demonstrates a summary of the stock movements, replenishment rates and price discounting across a range of retailers in the same sector of the market. The visualised data summarises a vast amount of data into a visually appealing and useful infographic that highlights just the key information needed by users.

	Sellout	Replenished	Currently discounted	Avg. Discount
La Redoute	22.4%	19.1%	63.4%	46.3%
Boohoo	8.7%	17.8%	44.2%	41.5%
Zara	42.1%	22.6%	28.1%	32.1%
Mango	18.2%	9.0%	52.2%	50.1%

Illustration 3 – Data visualisation. Accounts receivable (AR)

The **visualisation** below is an extract from an accounts receivable report; this simple pie chart gives the user a clear indication of the ageing of the receivables balances in a clear and concise way. The heavy detail of multiple pages of individual credit customers along with the breakdown of their balances is not needed by most users and this infographic directs users to the key headline information.

Here the figures of AR turnover and the AR turnover ratio are displayed clearly at the top and can be easily compared against budget to get an indication of performance.

A visualisation like this would typically allow users to drilldown into the detail behind the numbers, for instance by selecting the 90+ days segment of the pie chart, the user would access the customers and balances that make up this figure and further questions could then be asked upon these. This is the idea of layering data and making visualisations intuitive and simple to navigate.

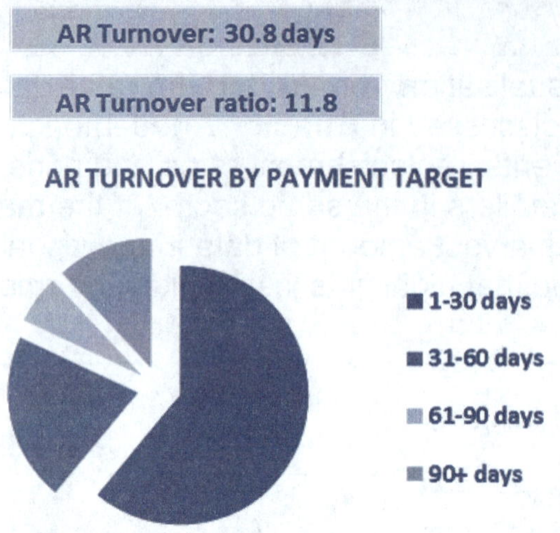

Test your understanding 3

Which TWO of the following are characteristics of effective data visualisation?

A Use of jargon

B Intuitive visuals

C Audience specific

D Extensive training used at same time

E High level only

F Paper format only

5.3 Business focused data

Data scientists are individuals with the ability to extract meaning from and interpret data, which requires both tools and methods from statistics and machine learning.

Data science is a very new field. It is an amalgam of data experts with a background in mathematics, statistics, programming and computer science. Organisations looking to capitalise on **big data** using **data analytics** are increasingly employing specialist data scientists.

In this data driven world it is important to maintain a coherent commercial, business focus to the work being undertaken by data scientists, this is where **management accountants** are ideally situated to take the lead. Partnering with data scientists to ensure the work they undertake is deliberate and targeted with clear objectives to ultimately support or enhance the business. Management accountants should also act to translate insights gained back to the wider business in a practical and commercial way.

Essentially **management accountants will act as an interface between the business functions and the data specialists**; they are uniquely positioned to do so for the following reasons:

- All activities have a financial consequence, so the finance function is central to an organisation with a unique understanding of the overall business picture.
- The information produced is already trusted and often audited.
- The management accounting function and the information produced provide the basis of performance management across the business.
- Finance is based on rational and measurable information. Finance professionals have credibility and ethical guidelines which underpin their objectivity and care in decision making.

6 Chapter summary

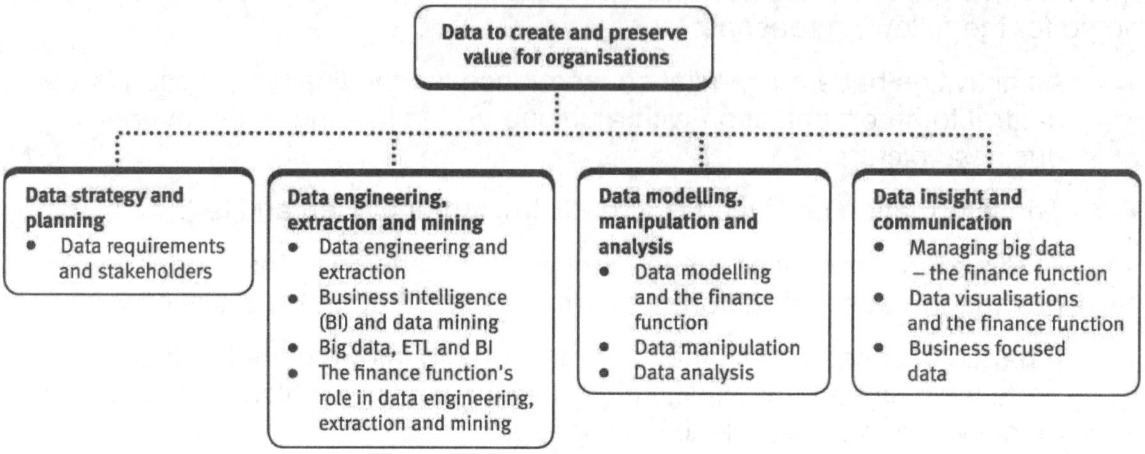

Test your understanding answers

Test your understanding 1

The correct answer is **A, B, E**

Growth of data, sources of data and new data technologies all mean traditional ETL programs may not be as valid today. The composition of the Board should not influence this, as the board have a duty to safeguard assets and manage risk, whatever era they are in. Employee skillsets will change but won't be the reason the systems are no longer valid.

Test your understanding 2

The correct answer is **C**

The three levels are Conceptual, Logical, and Physical. Extraction, transformation and Loading (ETL) are stages in transferring data into a single destination.

Test your understanding 3

The correct answer is **B, C**

Data visualisation should allow the audience to intuitively see results, and be focused at the right level for the audience. It should not use excessive jargon, need much training to understand. It can drill down into further depth if required, and be across several mediums, including paper copies.

Chapter

9

How the finance function interacts with operations

Chapter learning objectives

Lead	Component
E1: Describe how the finance function interacts with operations.	Describe: (a) Main role of operations (b) Areas of interface with finance (c) Key performance indicators

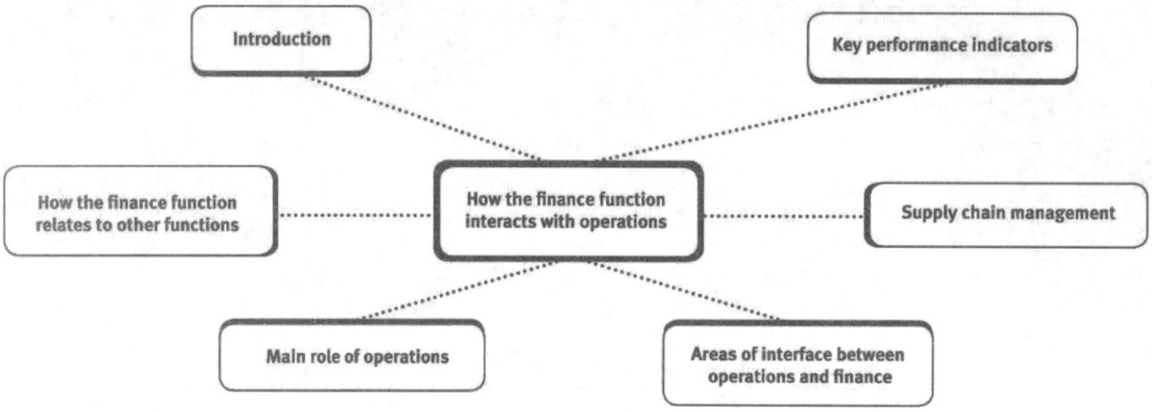

1 Introduction

Chapters 9 to 12 will cover syllabus area E '**Finance Interacting with the Organisation**'. We will bring together previous sections and describe how the finance function plays its role by interacting with the rest of the organisation.

The functions that need to be performed in a business depend on many variables, such as what industry it is in, how geographically spread it is, and what its plans are for the future. Most commonly, however, these **functions** are identified generically as follows:

- Operations
- Sales and marketing
- Human resources (HR)
- Information technology (IT)
- Finance

In today's interconnected organisations, finance will need to work collaboratively as business partners with other functional areas to achieve the objectives of finance, those other areas and crucially the objectives of the whole organisation.

In syllabus area E we will look at the main role of the first four of these five functions before understanding the areas of each function that interface with finance and, finally, understanding how the finance function helps to manage these functions.

Operations will be covered in this chapter.

Note: Candidates will not be required to have an in depth knowledge of all the techniques connected with the functional areas (operations, sales and marketing, HR and IT) of an organisation. Instead, they should have some understanding of certain key techniques and their financial implications, and hence the role finance can play in providing advice and helping develop relevant KPIs.

2 How the finance function relates to the other functions

This area will be explored in more detail in each of Chapters 9 to 12, but a short introduction is useful at this point.

The finance function's role in managing the financial resources of the organisation and providing information to help economic decision making will be integral to the effectiveness of the other functions (in this case, operations).

The finance function will:

- Assemble and extract data to provide **information** to the other function and **insight** about value creation/preservation
- Work with the other function (an internal stakeholder) and other stakeholders to **influence** and shape how this function creates and preserves value
- The CFO will work with the head of each function (for example, the chief operating officer (COO)) to achieve the desired organisational **impact** for this function.

3 Main role of operations

3.1 Definitions

Operations are those activities concerned with the acquisition of raw materials, their conversion into finished products and the supply of that finished product to the customer.

Contemporary thinking has broadened the definition to 'what the company does' to include service operations as well as manufacturing operations.

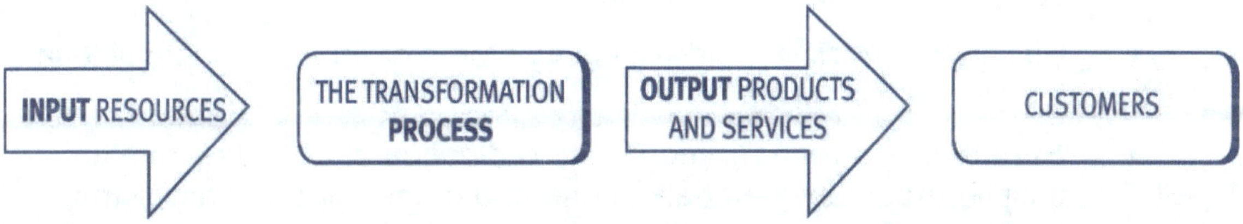

Illustration 1 – Examples of operations

Organisation	Operations function	Operation
McDonalds	Kitchen and serving staff	Selling fast food
Vauxhall	Production line	Making cars
Dell	Production line, internet	Making and selling computers
Real Madrid	Football coaches, training facilities	Playing football

Operations management is the activities involved in designing, producing and delivering products and services that satisfy the customer's requirements.

Illustration 2 – Operations management in IKEA

IKEA is the most successful furniture retailer ever. With 480 stores in 63 countries (2024), it has managed to develop its own special way of selling furniture. **Innovations in its operations** dramatically reduced its selling costs. These included the idea of selling furniture as self-assembly flat packs (resulting in reduced production and transport costs) and its 'showroom-warehouse' concept which required customers to pick the furniture up themselves from the warehouse (which reduced transport costs). Both of these operating principles are still the basis of IKEA's retail operations process today.

More recently Ikea has opened 8 small format high street shops focussing on home accessories and home furnishings. They are also experimenting with 'Plan and Order Points' which are smaller stores that help with planning kitchens, bedrooms and living rooms.

IKEA's **operations managers** are involved in a number of activities. These include:

- **Process design** – arranging the store's layout to give smooth and effective flow of customers
- **Product design** – designing stylish products that can be flat-packed efficiently
- **Job design** – making sure that all staff can contribute to the company's success
- **Supply network design** – locating stores of an appropriate size in the most effective place
- **Supply chain management** – co-ordination of activities from the supplier(s) of raw materials at one end of the supply chain to the customer at the other end
- **Transport and logistics** – to supply stores
- **Capacity management** – coping with fluctuations in demand
- **Failure prevention** – maintain cleanliness and safety of storage area
- **Inventory management** – avoiding running out of products for sale
- **Quality management** – monitoring and enhancing quality of service to customers
- **Operations improvement** – continually examining and improving operations practice.

These activities are only a small part of IKEA's total operations management, but they do give an indication of how operations management can contribute to business success.

Processes – All operations consist of a collection of processes. These are the building blocks of operations and connect with one another to form a network. The processes transform the input resources into output products/services.

e.g

Illustration 3 – Some operations described in terms of their processes

Operation	Inputs	Processes	Outputs
Airline	Aircraft Pilots and air crew Ground crew Passengers and freight	Check passengers in Board passengers Fly passengers and freight around the world Care for passengers	Transported passengers and freight
Department store	Goods for sale Sales staff Information systems Customers	Source and store goods Display goods Give sales advice Sell goods	Customers purchase goods for sale
Police	Police officers Information systems Public (law-abiding and criminals)	Crime prevention Crime detection Information gathering Detaining suspects	Lawful society, public with a feeling of security
Frozen food manufacturer	Fresh food Operators Process technology Cold storage facilities	Source raw materials Prepare foods Pack and freeze food	Frozen food

3.2 The different characteristics of operations processes

Although all operations processes are similar in that they all transform inputs into outputs, they do differ in several ways, four of which, known as the **4 Vs**, are particularly important. Each of these impact the way in which an operation will be organised and managed.

Volume of inputs and outputs

Operations differ in the volume of inputs they process. High-volume operations are likely to be more capital-intensive than low-volume operations, and there is likely to be a greater specialisation of labour skills.

e.g

Illustration 4 – The volume dimensions at McDonalds

McDonald's serves around 6.5 million burgers around the world every day (2025). Volume has important implications for the way McDonald's operations are organised. The first thing you notice is the **repeatability** of the tasks people are doing, and the **systemisation** of the work where standard procedures are set down specifying how each part of the job should be carried out. Also, because tasks are systemised and repeated, it is worthwhile developing specialised fryers and ovens. All this gives low unit costs.

Variety of inputs and outputs

Some operations handle a wide range of different inputs, or produce a wide range of output products or services. Others are much more restricted in the range of inputs they handle or outputs they produce.

Variation in demand

With some operations demand might vary significantly from one season of the year to another or from one time of the day to another, with some periods of peak demand and some periods of low demand. Other operations might handle a fairly constant volume of demand at all times.

Visibility to customers

Visibility refers to the extent to which an organisation is visible to its customers. When an operation is highly visible, the employees will have to show good communication skills and interpersonal skills in dealing with customers.

All four dimensions have implications for the cost of creating the products or services. Put simply, high volume, low variety, low variation and low customer contact (visibility) all help to keep processing costs down.

(**Note**: These should not be confused with the 4Vs of big data).

Test your understanding 1

Company A is an online retailer specialising in basic household cleaning products, it has a limited product range and sells many of its goods in bulk to cleaning companies.

Company B sells seasonal organic food stuffs from its local retail outlet. Its staff are expected to provide cooking and recipe guidance to its customers.

Requirement:

Using the 4 Vs, which company would be expected to have the lower processing costs?

3.3 Porter's value chain

The value chain model is based around **activities** rather than traditional functional departments (such as operations or finance).

It considers the organisation's activities that create value and drive costs and therefore the organisation should focus on improving those activities. **Many of the activities relate to the operations function**.

The activities are split into **primary** ones (the customer interacts with these and can 'see' the value being created) and **secondary** (or support) activities which are necessary to support the primary activities. Each activity is looked at to see if they give a cost advantage or a quality advantage.

Margin represents the value created. It is the difference between the cost of the activities in the chain and what the customer is willing to pay for the final product or service. (This might be seen as the profit).

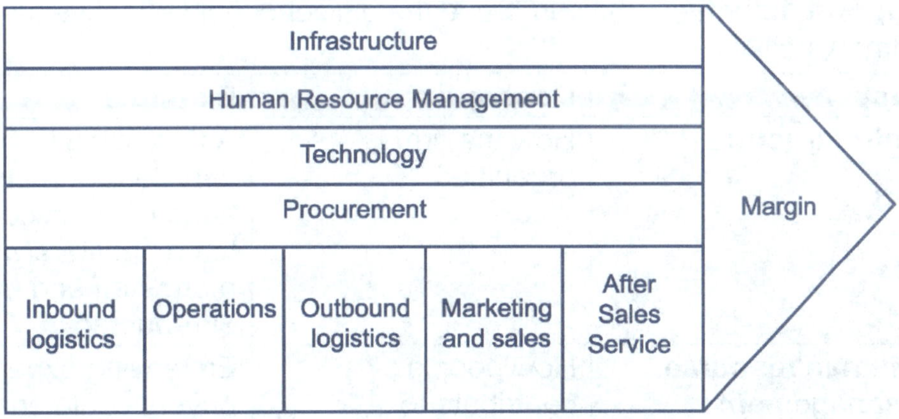

Value chain activities

Primary activities – directly concerned with the creation or delivery of a product/service.

Activity	Description	Example
Inbound logistics	Receiving, storing and handling raw material inputs.	A just-in-time stock system could give a cost advantage.
Operations	Transformation of raw materials into finished goods and services.	Using skilled employees could give a quality advantage.
Outbound logistics	Storing, distributing and delivering finished goods and services.	Outsourcing activities could give a cost advantage.
Marketing and sales	The mechanism by which the customer is made aware of the product or service.	Sponsorship of a sports celebrity could enhance the image of a product.
After sales service	All activities that occur after the point of sale, such as customer enquiries, returns and repairs/maintenance.	A friendly approach to returns gives it a perceived quality advantage.

Operations management is concerned with all of these primary activities apart from marketing and sales.

Support activities – help improve the efficiency and effectiveness of the primary activities.

Activity	Description	Example
Infrastructure	How the firm is organised.	A firm could have a very 'lean' structure at head office in contrast to competitors with more staff and more bureaucracy.
Human resource management	How people contribute to competitive advantage. Includes activities such as recruitment, selection, training and development and reward policies.	Employing expert buyers could enable a supermarket to purchase better wines than competitors.

Activity	Description	Example
Technology	How the firm uses technology.	The latest computer-controlled machinery gives greater flexibility to tailor products to customer specifications.
Procurement	Purchasing, but not just limited to materials.	Buying a building out of town could give a cost advantage over High Street competitors.

Operations management is directly concerned with procurement and some elements of firm infrastructure and technology development.

e.g

Illustration 5 – Value chain

One particular clothes manufacturer may spend large amounts on:

- Buying good quality raw materials (inbound logistics)
- Hand-finishing garments (operations)
- Building a successful brand image (marketing)
- Running its own fleet of delivery trucks in order to deliver finished clothes quickly to customers (outbound logistics).

All of these should add value to the product, allowing the company to charge a premium for its clothes. This is a differentiation strategy.

Another clothes manufacturer may:

- Reduce the cost of its raw materials by buying in cheaper supplies from abroad (inbound logistics)
- Making all its clothes by machinery running 24 hours a day (operations)
- Delaying distribution until delivery trucks can be filled with garments for a particular request (outbound logistics).

All of these should allow the company to be able to gain economies of scale and be able to sell clothes at a cheaper price than its rivals. This is a low cost strategy.

It is important to demonstrate consistency throughout the companies value chain – be either a low cost operator or a differentiator, otherwise Porter said you would be 'stuck in the middle' which would be disastrous.

Linkages connect the interdependent elements of the value chain together. For example, better quality production could reduce the need for after-sales service.

Test your understanding 2

Which value chain activity involves the purchasing of inputs such as material, supplies and equipment?

A Procurement

B Operations

C Purchasing

D Inbound logistics

Test your understanding 3

BB makes and sells freshly baked bread. It has recently developed an automated inventory control system for its finished loaves, which significantly reduces wastage.

Which one of the following value chain activities will BB's automated inventory system directly improve?

A Inbound logistics

B Operations

C Outbound logistics

D Marketing and sales

3.4 Process design

Process design is the method by which individual specialists seek to understand business processes and ensure that these processes are designed to be as efficient and effective as possible. The design of processes will go hand in hand with the design of new products and services.

Before any changes in processes are undertaken it is necessary to understand the organisation's mission, goals and customer needs and to carry out a detailed analysis of existing processes. Process maps can assist in such an examination.

A **process map** provides a visual representation of the steps and decisions by which a product or transaction is processed.

Illustration 6 – Simple process map for hiring process

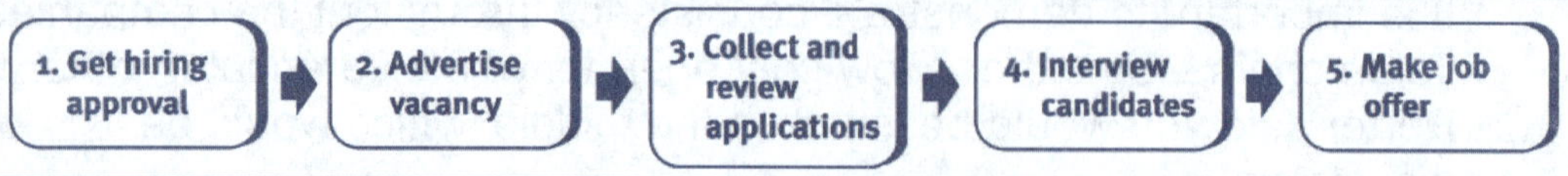

Advantages of process maps

- **Management understanding** – allows a better understanding of the basic processes that are undertaken, so providing management with a convenient overview demonstrating responsibilities and key stages in the operations.
- **Role understanding** – allows workers to understand what their job is and how their work fits into the whole process (and therefore the importance of undertaking their role effectively). Process mapping also allows consideration of role reallocation.
- **Standardisation** – highlights where opportunities exist to standardise processes.
- **Highlights inefficiencies** – visually highlights areas where inefficiencies are present through analysis of queues, value and location, so pinpointing areas of waste. This provides an agenda to tackle duplication of effort, the requirement to complete unnecessary paperwork, and misdirected queries that hold up production, etc.
- **Supports corporate initiatives** – mapping can be used as part of a corporate initiative such as customer satisfaction improvement programmes.

Example of a process map

Supply process map

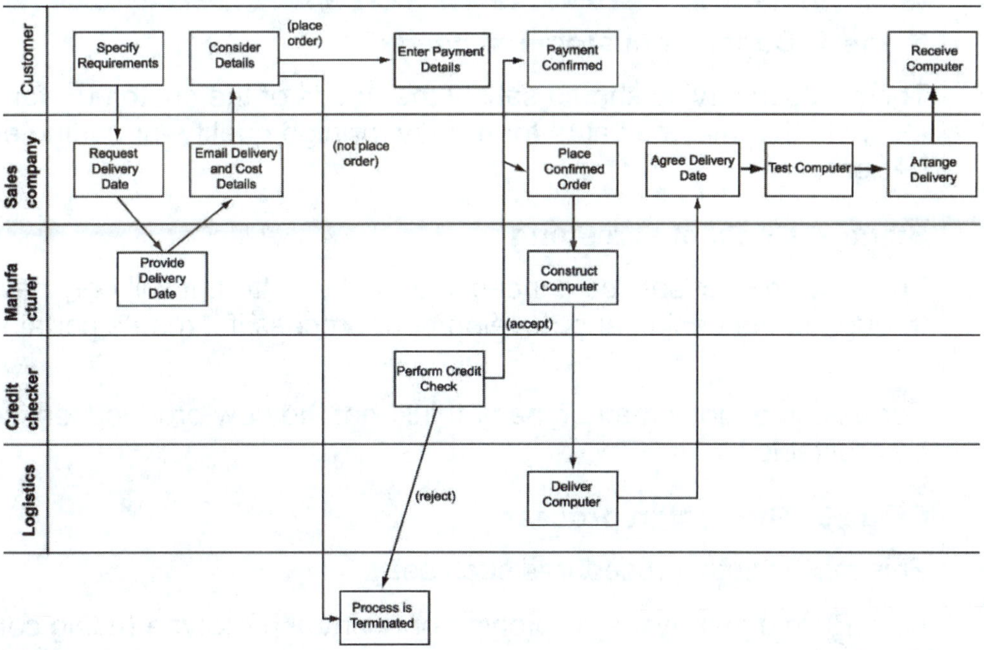

3.5 Product and service development

Companies need to continually look for new or improved products or services, to achieve or maintain competitive advantage in their market.

The stages of product/service development are as follows:

Illustration 7 – Considering customers' needs

The design of a new product/service should begin by understanding the needs of the customer. There are several ways to do this, for example:

- Customer relationship management (CRM) systems. Most CRM systems are based on a database (often in the cloud and maybe integrated with social media) that collects information about the organisation's customers and their needs.
- More radical solutions, e.g. Lego created Lego Ideas – a customer portal for idea crowdsourcing (where customers suggest ideas) and validation.

Product and service development

Stage 1: Consider customers' needs

The product/service should satisfy the needs of the customer, for example that may be value for money, or high quality, or cutting edge design, etc.

Stage 2: Concept screening

The new product/service concept should be vetted. It will only pass through to the design and development process if it meets certain criteria.

For example, does the company think that the new product/service will be profitable?

Stage 3: The design process

This may include procedures such as:

- Building a physical prototype or a virtual prototype (using computer aided design)
- Value engineering, i.e. ensuring that all components/features add value.

Stage 4: Time-to-market

A short time-to-market is desirable since:

- New product/service may be released ahead of competitors
- Development costs may be lower.

Stage 5: Product testing

The new product should be tested before it is released to the market:

- Does it work properly?
- Do customers like it?

4 Areas of interface between operations and finance

4.1 Introduction

Operations management will be an important contributor to effective and efficient purchasing, production and delivery of customer specific goods and services.

The operations function and the finance function should work in partnership to ensure this efficiency and effectiveness is optimised.

In this section we will examine how specific parts of an organisation's operations (i.e. purchasing, production and service provision) interact with the organisation's finance function. The **focus here will be on the operational level** tasks performed by the finance function.

Section 5 will explain how relationships in the supply chain can be managed and the interface with the finance function will be examined at a more **strategic level**.

4.2 Purchasing (procurement)

Purchasing is an important part of the operations function. It is responsible for placing and following up orders. It co-ordinates with the finance function as follows:

Establishing credit terms	The finance function will work with the purchasing to liaise with suppliers to obtain a credit account and to negotiate credit terms which are acceptable.
Prices	The finance function can advise the purchasing department on the maximum price that should be paid to maintain margins.
Payment	Payments may be approved by purchasing but are made by the finance function.
Data capture, for example, orders	Order details will be input by purchasing and details transferred to the finance function.

Inventory	Finance can help ensure that less cash is tied up in inventory and a philosophy of just in time, rather than just in case, is developed.
Budgeting	The finance function will consult with purchasing on the likely costs in preparing budgets.

e.g

Illustration 8 – Purchasing

XYZ Limited is a company manufacturing handbags.

Describe how **purchasing** liaises with the finance function when buying some leather to make handbags from DEF Limited, a new supplier.

Establishing credit terms	Purchasing will advise the finance function that the preferred supplier is DEF. The finance function contacts the credit controller at DEF and provides the information required to set up a credit account.
Prices	The finance function obtains the cost estimate for the handbag being produced. It discusses with purchasing how much can be paid for the leather in order to maintain margins.
Payment	The payment for the leather is approved by purchasing and then made by the finance function.
Data capture, for example, orders	Order details for the leather will be input by purchasing and details passed to the finance function to check that the price on the invoice is correct.
Inventory	Before placing the order, purchasing will consult with the warehouse staff to determine how much suitable leather is already in stock.

Test your understanding 4

Which of the following is an example of co-ordination between purchasing and the finance function?

A Establishing credit terms

B Determining sales prices

C Allocating costs

D Calculating pay rises

4.3 Production

Production is a core part of the operations function. It plans and oversees the production of goods. It liaises with the finance function as follows:

Cost measurement, allocation, absorption	Production measures quantities of materials and time used; the management accountant gives a monetary value to them. Costs are then allocated and absorbed to calculate production costs based on advice given by production.
Budgeting	Production will decide how many items of what type are to be produced. The cost of producing these will be determined jointly by the finance function and production and incorporated into the overall budget.
Cost versus quality	Production and the finance function will discuss the features that can be included in products and the raw materials that should be used. They should agree which better quality materials and features justify the extra cost, and discuss how to maximise quality and profit.
Production process	Finance can assist production in identifying inefficiencies in the production process (such as bottlenecks) and suggesting improvements.
Inventory	Production will liaise with the inventory section of the finance function to ensure that there are sufficient raw materials in inventory for the production that is planned.

e.g

Illustration 9 – Production

XYZ Limited is a company manufacturing handbags. The company has commissioned a designer to design a new style of handbag and discussions are taking place about the materials to be used and the quantity to be produced.

Describe how the finance function and **production** would liaise over this.

Cost measurement, allocation, absorption	Production would estimate the quantity of raw materials required and (in conjunction with purchasing) estimate their cost. Together with the finance function overheads will be allocated to determine the full cost of the handbag.
Budgeting	Production, the finance function and marketing will discuss how many bags are likely to be sold at what price and determine how many should be produced. A budget can then be produced.

Cost v quality	Production, the finance function (and marketing) will discuss the various grades of leather and the material that could be used, their costs, and the extra price that could be charged for better quality material. They will decide on the best combination of cost/quality/profit.
Production process	The finance function and production will work together to ensure that the newly designed production process is of optimum efficiency and avoids issues such as bottlenecks.
Inventory	Production will discuss with the inventory section of the finance function which materials are required. Some existing materials may be usable for the new product or entirely new materials may need to be acquired.

4.4 Service provision

Characteristics of services

Services are said to have four main characteristics.

- **Intangibility** – services are activities undertaken by the organisation on behalf of its customers and therefore cannot be packaged for the customer to take away with them. They often have few, if any, physical aspects.
- **Inseparability** – services are often created by the organisation at the same time as they are consumed by the customer. The service cannot therefore be easily distinguished from the person or organisation providing the service.
- **Perishability** – services cannot be stored for later.
- **Variability** – each service is unique and cannot usually be repeated in exactly the same way, making offering a standardised service to customers very difficult.

These characteristics must be considered when seeking to manage the performance of the service.

The relationship between service provision and the finance function

Examples of service organisation include hairdressing, healthcare and accountancy services.

In addition, some businesses may provide services to customers, at the same time as a sale of a physical product or afterwards. For example, a computer retailer may charge an extra fee to help customers set up their system, or a car dealer may provide car servicing.

Service provision will form an important part of the operations function.

There are several issues about which the service departments may need the input of the finance function.

Charge-out rates	This is the hourly rate which the company charges clients. It should be higher than the salary, as it should include a share of overheads, for example training, and any profit the company wishes to make. However, if the charge-out rate is too high customers will not use the service.
Estimating costs	Problems arise in determining the amount of overhead to be included in the charge-out rate. Also, if the service takes longer to provide than expected, the company may not be able to pass on the extra cost.
Problems measuring benefits	Market conditions may mean that the charge-out rate contains a very low profit element. The company may question whether it is worth carrying out these services. The problem is that the benefits are intangible and not easy to measure, but nevertheless real. A company with effective service provision has happier customers, and happy customers are more likely to buy from the company in future, therefore leading to lower selling costs. But it is very difficult to measure these benefits.

Test your understanding 5

Which of the following is a likely advantage of providing a good service?

A Greater customer satisfaction

B Higher payroll costs

C Higher inventory turnover

D Economies of scale

Test your understanding 6

'Most services provided by an organisation will be created at the same time as they are consumed.'

Which feature of services is being described?

A Intangibility

B Inseparability

C Perishability

D Variability

5 Supply chain management

5.1 Introduction

A **supply chain** consists of a network of organisations. Together they provide and process the necessary raw materials firstly into work in progress and then into finished goods for distribution and sale to the end customer.

The transformation of the product along the supply chain includes activities such as:

- production planning
- purchasing
- materials management
- distribution
- customer service
- forecasting.

More complex supply chains

The situation is usually more complex than is shown in the diagram above. Most businesses have several suppliers and several customers. Some businesses may compete for customers and have common suppliers. There may be several supply chains serving one group of customers and they may form complex webs.

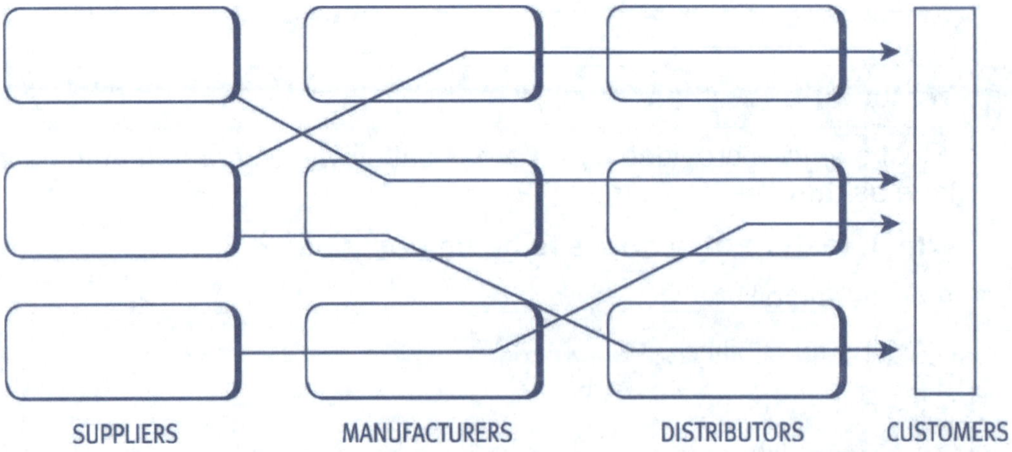

Supply chain management (SCM) involves the co-ordination of activities from the supplier(s) of raw materials at one end of the supply chain to the customer at the other end.

The idea behind supply chain management is that co-ordinating the activities of the different businesses in the supply chain can save costs while also adding value.

Technology can play a key part in effective SCM.

e.g

Illustration 10 – Use of blockchain in supply chain transparency

Start-up tech firm Provenance has developed technology which tracks the journey of organic food from farm to shop shelf. It is hoped that shoppers will be able to tap their smartphones on food, such as organic bacon, and instantly retrieve the product's complete supply chain journey.

The technology uses blockchain. This means the information of a product's journey and exactly what it means to be certified organic is now instantaneously accessible to shoppers with their smart phones, no app required. The technology will be available both on product packaging and on the shop shelf.

Traditionally, businesses within the supply chain operated independently. However, organisations are recognising that there are benefits associated with establishing links between different businesses in the supply chain. The objective of SCM is to achieve **synergies** (the sum of the group is greater than its individual parts) that benefit every player along the chain.

In this section we will understand:

- how the relationships within the supply chain can be managed and
- the interface between SCM and the finance function.

5.2 The strategic supply wheel – Cousins model

Traditionally, supply was viewed as an **operational issue**. Purchasing was seen as an administrative task with the emphasis being on price negotiations with suppliers. There was little awareness that supply could affect the firm's strategic goals or that it should be viewed as a key part of strategic planning.

Successful organisations in **today's competitive environment** have recognised that supply should be viewed as a **strategic issue**. The organisation's supply strategy should be aligned with the overall corporate goals and strategy and is integral to the organisation's competitive strategy.

Cousins' model emphasises the importance of viewing supply as central to the organisation and its effectiveness.

Cousins' thinking is based on the notion that an organisation's supply strategy should involve several key areas described as 'spokes' in the wheel. As such, the model can help an organisation concentrate on key areas for attention and action.

The wheel depicts the corporate supply strategy at the hub of the wheel and underlines the need for an **integrated approach** to supply strategy involving balancing all five 'spokes'.

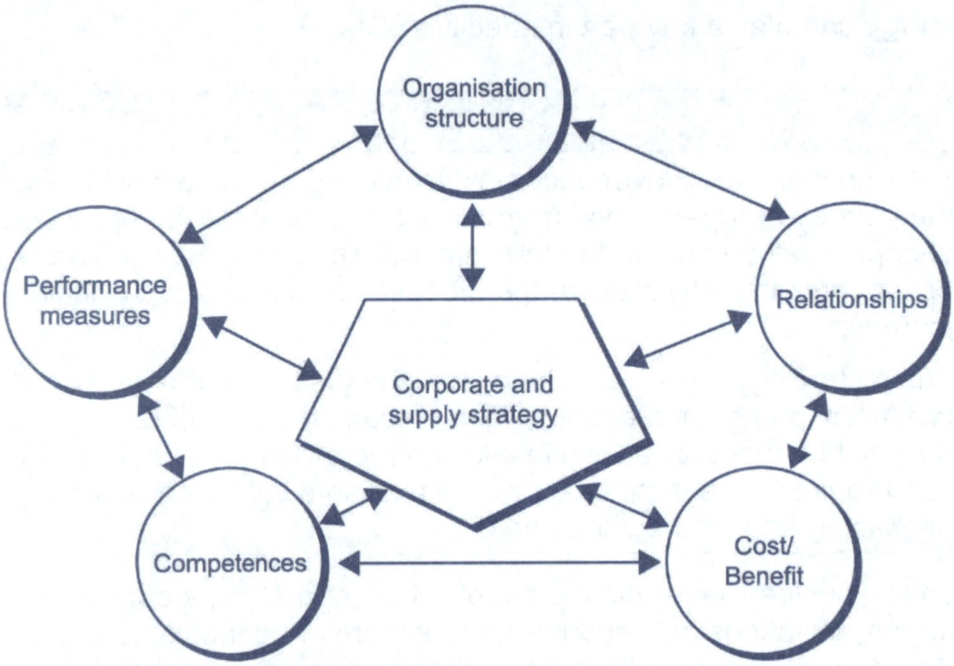

Spoke of wheel	Explanation
Organisation structure	The choice of structure (centralised, decentralised or a mix of these) impacts control and interaction. It should enhance rather than hinder the supply strategy.
Relationships with suppliers	Relationships can be: • competitive (contractual) – based on price deals, or • collaborative (relational) – a more positive relationship based on a joint quest to reduce costs and a sharing of technology and innovations to improve quality.
Cost/benefit	Supply decisions should be based on benefits as well as costs. Cost/benefit analysis should be at the heart of any strategic decision.
Competences	Do the skills exist to achieve the chosen strategy? For example, the development of long term supplier relations may lead to a need to retrain key personnel.
Performance measures	Necessary for monitoring and controlling the strategy chosen. Measures should extend beyond price and be aligned with the strategy.

There is an **interface between these spokes and the finance function**, more specifically in the areas of cost/benefit and performance measures.

Test your understanding 7

Which of the following statements about supply chain management (SCM) are true and which are false?

Statement	True/False?
The co-ordination of activities from the supplier(s) of raw materials at one end of the supply chain to the customer at the other end is known as supply chain management	
Cost savings are the only advantage of SCM	
The objective of SCM is to achieve synergies that benefit the customers at the end of the supply chain	
Cousins' supply wheel is a model used to look at the traditional supply function	
Cousins' supply wheel has five spokes	

5.3 Relationship with suppliers

Cousins identified two broad approaches to supplier relationships:

- competitive (also known as contractual) and
- collaborative (also known as relational).

Competitive (contractual)

In the past, the supply chain was typically defined by competitive relationships.

- The purchasing function sought out the lowest-price suppliers, often through a process of tendering, the use of 'power' and the constant switching of supply sources to prevent getting too reliant on any individual supplier.
- Supplier contracts featured heavy penalty clauses and were drawn up in a spirit of general mistrust of all external providers.
- The knowledge and skills of the supplier could not be exploited effectively. Information was deliberately withheld in case the supplier used it to gain power during price negotiations.

Hence, no single supplier ever knew enough about the ultimate customer to suggest ways of improving the cost-effectiveness and quality of the trading relationship.

Collaborative (relational)

Now there is increased recognition that successful management of suppliers is based upon collaboration and offers benefits to an organisation's suppliers as well as to the organisation itself. By working together and forming relationships, organisations can make a much better job of satisfying the requirements of their end market, and thus both can increase their market share.

- Organisations seek to enter partnerships with key customers and suppliers to better understand how to provide value and customer service.
- Organisations' product design processes include discussions that involve both customers and suppliers. By opening design departments and supply problems to selected suppliers, a synergy results, generating new ideas, solutions, and new innovative products.
- To enhance the nature of collaboration, the organisation may reward suppliers with long-term sole sourcing (only supplier) agreements in return for a greater level of support to the business and a commitment to on-going improvements of materials, deliveries and relationships.
- The nature of the collaboration needs to shift to reflect the constant change in the environment.

e.g

Illustration 11 – Recent changes in UK supply chain relationships

Partnerships within the supply chain must continue to adapt to reflect the unprecedented level of change in the external environment.

For example, several recent changes are impacting supply chain collaboration in the United Kingdom (UK). These changes include:

- a volatile political and economic climate
- increased urbanisation in the UK
- a dramatic change in consumer behaviour, for example with a preference for convenience, online shopping and smaller but more frequent shopping
- the growth in automation
- a shift towards digitisation.

The supply chain needs to address these changes, viewing them as an opportunity to reinvent itself and improve the effectiveness of collaboration across the supply chain:

- Changing technology combined with more accurate data is allowing for greater collaboration. For example, distribution is planned more effectively to minimise empty miles and waste.
- Today's consumers, driven by urbanisation, have moved away from the traditional large weekly shop in out-of-town retail parks and are now online shopping. The supply chain has collaborated to introduce new distribution models and retailing formats (such as meal delivery subscriptions and 'click and collect') in a cost effective manner.

5.4 Material requirement planning (MRP)

One important aspect of supply chain management is to ensure that materials are ready when they are needed. Several systems can be used to assist with this requirement.

MRP is a computerised system for planning the requirements for raw materials, work-in-progress and finished items.

MRP is designed to answer three questions:

- **What** is needed?
- **How** much is needed?
- **When** is it needed?

Functions include:

- Identifying firm orders and forecasting future orders with confidence.
- Using orders to determine quantities of material required.
- Determining the timing of the material requirement.
- Calculating purchase orders based on stock levels.
- Automatically placing purchase orders.
- Scheduling materials for future production.

Benefits of MRP

- Improved forecasting.
- Improved ability to meet orders leading to increased customer satisfaction.
- Reduced stock holding.
- The MRP schedule can be amended quickly if demand estimates change since the system is computerised.
- System can warn of purchasing or production problems due to bottlenecks or delays in the supply chain.
- A close relationship tends to be built with suppliers (it is consistent with just-in-time – see section 5.6).

However, MRP will not be suitable if it is not possible to predict sales in advance.

The following technology has been developed from MRP:

- **Manufacturing resource planning (MRPII)** – goes several steps beyond MRP and includes:
  - production planning
  - machine capacity scheduling
  - demand forecasting and analysis
  - quality tracking tools
  - employee attendance and
  - productivity tracking.
- **Enterprise resource planning (ERP)** is the next evolution of an MRP system. It integrates information from many aspects of operations (for example, manufacturing, inventory management, invoicing and management accounting) and support functions (such as human resource management and marketing) into one single system.

Benefits of ERP

Benefits of ERP to the organisation include:

- Identification and planning of the use of resources across the organisation to ensure customers' needs are fulfilled
- The free flow of information across all functions and improved communication between departments
- Aids management decision making due to decision support features
- Can be extended to incorporate supply chain management (SCM) and customer relationship management (CRM) software, thus helping to manage connections outside the organisation.

Test your understanding 8

Which THREE of the following are possible advantages of a collaborative relationship with suppliers?

A Increased market share

B Development of innovative products

C Better understanding of how to satisfy customer needs

D Improved quality is guaranteed

E The relationships will be harder to manage

F Relationship management will be more time consuming

5.5 Quality management

Introduction to quality

In today's competitive global business environment, quality is one of the key ways in which a business can differentiate its product or service, improve performance and gain competitive advantage. Quality can form a key part of a strategic supply chain management.

Quality can be defined in several ways:

- Is the product/service free from errors and does it adhere to design specifications?
- Is the product/service fit for use?
- Does the product/service meet customers' needs?

What is quality?

To control and improve quality, it must first be defined. Most dictionaries define quality as 'the degree of excellence' but this leaves one having to define what is meant by 'excellence'. Who defines what is excellent and by what standards is it measured? In response to this problem, several different definitions of quality have been developed.

In an industrial context, quality is defined in a functional way. Here, quality means that a product is made free from errors and according to its design specifications, within an acceptable production tolerance level. Such an approach also emphasises that every unit produced should meet the design specifications, so the idea of consistency becomes important.

However, this still leaves a problem. How should standards and specifications be set? Who decides what an 'acceptable' tolerance level should be?

An alternative approach to defining quality is to focus on the user.

- Japanese companies found the definition of quality as 'the degree of conformance to a standard' too narrow and consequently started to use a new definition of quality as 'user satisfaction'.
- Juran defines quality as 'fitness for use' (1988).

In these definitions, customer requirements and customer satisfaction are the main factors. If an organisation can meet the requirements of its customers, customers will presumably be satisfied. The ability to define accurately the needs related to design, performance, price, safety, delivery, and other business activities and processes will place an organisation ahead of its competitors in the market.

Taking these definitions together, Ken Holmes (Total Quality Management) has defined quality as 'the totality of features and characteristics of a product or service which bears on its ability to meet stated or implied needs'.

Quality is also normally seen in relation to price, and customers judge the quality of a product in relation to the price they must pay. Customers will accept a product of lower design quality provided that the price is lower than the price of a better quality alternative.

Illustration 12 – Pret A Manger's focus on quality

Described by the press as having 'revolutionised the concept of sandwich making and eating', Pret A Manger (Pret) opened their first store in the mid-1980s, in London. Now they have over 700 shops in the UK and other locations such as New York, Hong Kong and Tokyo.

They say that their secret is to continually focus on quality – not just of their food but in every aspect of their operations practice. They go to extraordinary lengths to avoid the chemicals and preservatives common in many other 'fast' foods which are often used by retailers to extend the shelf life of their products. Pret hopes to maintain the edge by selling food that simply can't be beaten for freshness. At the end of each day, they give whatever they haven't sold to charity to help feed those who might otherwise go hungry.

Pret rejected the idea of a huge, centralised sandwich factory even though it could significantly reduce costs. Instead, each shop has its own kitchen where fresh ingredients are delivered first thing every morning, and food is prepared throughout the day.

Pret have also worked hard to build great teams – taking reward schemes and career opportunities very seriously.

Customer feedback is also regarded as being particularly important at Pret. Examining customers' comments for feedback is a key part of weekly management meetings, and of the daily team briefs in each shop.

Test your understanding 9

Requirement:

Explain the reasons why quality may be important to an organisation.

The growth of global companies has resulted in dramatic improvements in the quality of products and services. Much of this impetus can be attributed to the efforts of **Japanese manufacturing companies** such as Toyota.

Key writers on quality

There are several key writers on quality.

Writer	Main contribution
W. Edward Deming	Believed: • managers should set up and then **continuously improve** the systems in which people work • managers should work with employees to gain feedback from those who do the job • workers should be trained in quality to identify what needs changing and how. Deming was credited with the creation of Total Quality Management (TQM) in Japan and developed 14 points for quality improvement.
Joseph M. Juran	• Drew on the Pareto principle and stated that **80% of (quality) difficulties arise from 20% of the items** and are due to the systems that employees work within rather than the employees themselves. • Therefore, the need to develop key projects for dealing with quality problems rather than concentrating on employee motivation. • He argued that quality should focus on the role of the customer. He believed that anyone affected by the product is considered a customer, so introduced the idea of internal customers (staff or departments) as well as external customers.
Phillip P. Crosby	• Introduced the concept of '**zero defects**'. • Believed that prevention is key and that the importance of quality is measured by the cost of not having quality. • He argued for worker participation and the need to motivate individuals to do something about quality.

Methods of quality measurement

- There are four main types of quality-related costs. The organisation needs to identify these costs.
- Monitoring the costs of quality is central to the operation of any quality improvement programme.
- Targets should be set for each of the quality-related costs.

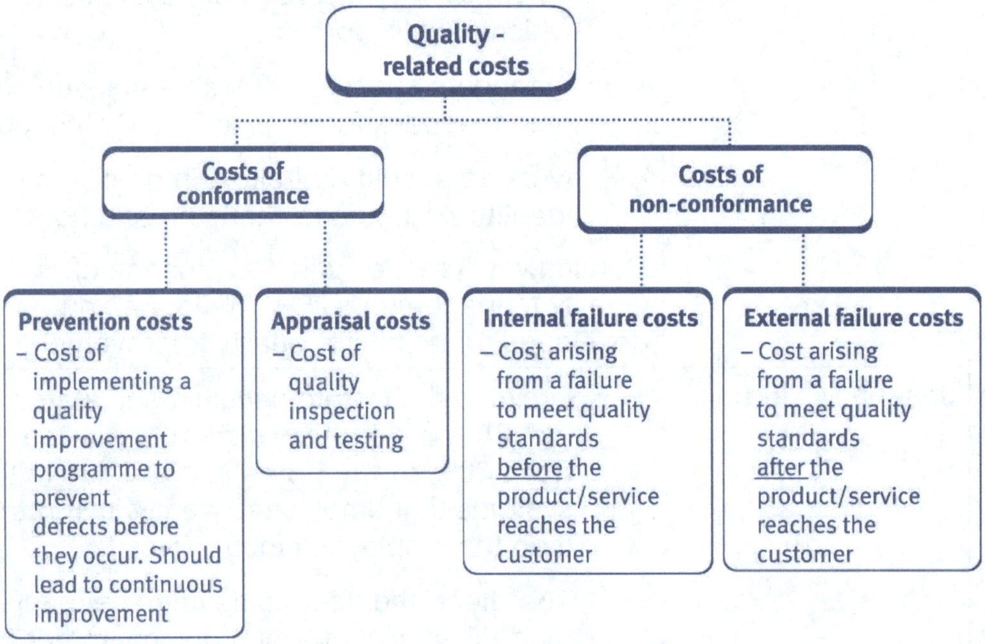

Illustration 13 – Examples of quality-related costs

Category	Examples
Prevention costs	• Cost of designing products and services with built in quality • Cost of training employees in the best way to do their job • Cost of equipment testing to ensure it conforms to quality standards required
Appraisal costs	Cost of inspection and testing, for example of purchased material or a service
Internal failure costs	• Cost of scrapped material due to poor quality • Cost of re-working parts • Re-inspection costs • Lower selling prices for sub-quality products
External failure costs	• Cost of recalling and correcting products • Cost of lost goodwill

Test your understanding 10

Which TWO of the following are examples of prevention costs of quality?

A Inspection of raw materials

B Routine repairs and maintenance of machinery

C Returns of faulty products

D Machine breakdown repairs

E Training costs of operational staff

5.6 Operational improvements

Introduction

There are several techniques that an organisation may use to improve the effectiveness of the supply chain and the management of relationships within the supply chain. These include:

- Statistical process control
- Total quality management (TQM)
- Just -in-time
- Kaizen
- Six sigma
- Lean thinking and
- Reverse logistics.

It is worth noting these techniques all have a **quality** focus and that the techniques are often be used alongside one another.

Statistical process control

Statistical process control (SPC) is a method for measuring and controlling quality during a process.

Quality data is obtained in real-time and plotted on a graph with a pre-determined target and control limits.

Data that falls within the control limits indicates that everything is operating as expected – any variation within the control limits is due to natural variation that is expected as part of a process.

If data falls outside of the control limits, the variation should be investigated and corrective action taken before a defect occurs.

Illustration 14 – Statistical process control and Mars Bars

Statistical process control may be used when many similar items, such as Mars Bars, are being produced. Every process is subject to variability, for example it is not possible to put exactly the same amount of ingredients in each Mars Bar.

A target weight is set for a Mars Bar (51g) and control limits assigned (1g above and below the target). The weight of the Mars Bars produced will be plotted on a chart and any points outside of the control limits (i.e. below 50g and above 52g) should be investigated and corrective action taken.

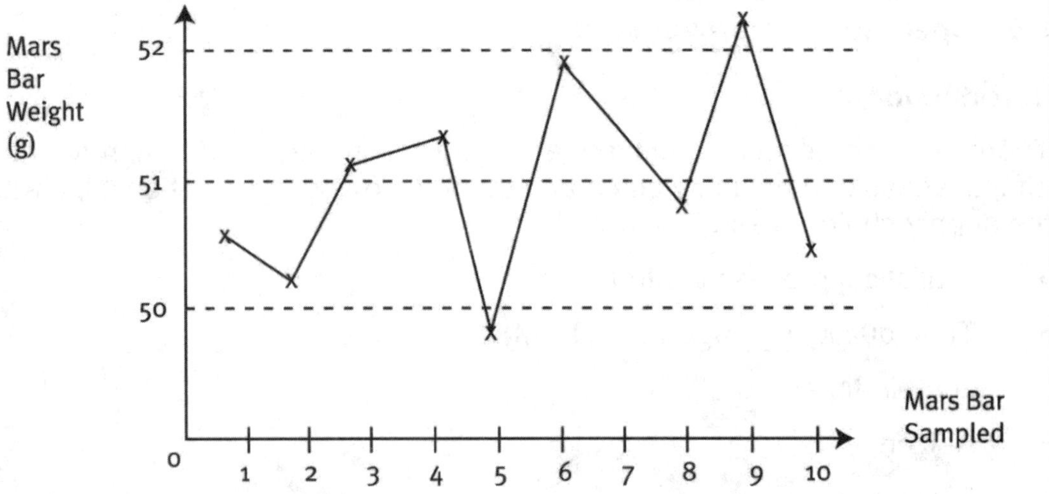

Total quality management

Total quality management (TQM) is a philosophy of quality management that originated in Japan in the 1950s.

TQM is the continuous improvement in quality, productivity and effectiveness obtained by establishing management responsibility for processes as well as outputs. In this, every process has an identified process owner and every person in an entity operates within a process and contributes to its improvement.

TQM is less of a single technique and more of a culturally shared understanding. The fundamental **features** of TQM include:

- **Prevention of errors before they occur** – the aim of TQM is to 'get things right first time'. TQM will result in a shift from quality control (detection costs, internal failure costs and external failure costs will fall) to quality assurance (prevention costs will increase).
- **Continual improvement** – quality management is not a one-off process but is the continuous examination and improvement of processes.

- **Real participation by all** – the 'total' in TQM means that everyone in the value chain is involved in the process. Collaboration internally and with suppliers and customers is key to the success of TQM:
  - **Employees** are encouraged to seek out, identify and correct quality problems. Teamwork will be vital. Employees should be empowered to decide how best to do their work and should be responsible for achieving targets.

    Quality circles may be established. These are small groups of workers of different levels in the firm who come together to discuss and solve quality problems that have been encountered. Everyone's opinion is valued and respected. Membership of quality circles is voluntary.
  - The quality and reliability of **suppliers** will play a vital role.
  - The goal is to identify and meet the needs of the **customer**.
- **Commitment of senior management** – management must be fully committed and encourage everyone else to become quality conscious. TQM is more of a shared philosophy and culture than a one-off exercise and a shift from quality control to quality assurance.

e.g

Illustration 15 – TQM success and failure

A TQM success story

Corning Inc is the world leader in speciality glass and ceramics. This is partly due to the implementation of a TQM approach. In 1983 the CEO announced a $1.6 billion investment in TQM. After several years of intensive training and a decade of applying the TQM approach, all of Corning's employees had bought into the quality concept. They knew the terminology – continuous improvement, empowerment, customer focus, management by prevention and they witnessed the impact of the firm's techniques as profits soared.

An example of TQM failure

British Telecom launched a total quality program in the late 1980s. This resulted in the company getting bogged down in its quality processes and bureaucracy. The company failed to focus on its customers and later decided to dismantle its TQM program. This was at great cost to the company, and they have failed to make a full recovery.

Implementation of a TQM approach

The implementation of a TQM approach may involve the following steps

Step 1: Senior management consultancy – Managers must be committed to the programme and should undergo quality training

Step 2: Establish a quality steering committee – The committee will guide the company through the process of implementing TQM

Step 3: Presentations and training – The steering committee should communicate the benefits of the change programme to employees in order to gain buy-in

Step 4: Establish quality circles – This will involve employees in the process of quality improvement

Step 5: Documentation – The actions carried out should be clearly documented

Step 6: Monitor progress – Actual results should be monitored against the standard set

Test your understanding 11

Requirement:

Discuss some of the common reasons for the failure of TQM programmes.

Just-in-time

Most inventory management systems assume that it is necessary to hold some inventory. An alternative view is that inventory is wasteful and adds no value to operations.

Just-in-time (JIT) is a system whose objective it is to produce or procure products or components as they are required by the customer or for use, rather than for inventory. This means that inventory levels of raw materials, work-in-progress and finished goods can be kept to a minimum.

JIT purchasing and JIT production

JIT applies to both production within an organisation and to purchasing from external suppliers:

- **JIT purchasing** is a method of purchasing that involves ordering materials only when customers place an order. When the goods are received, they go straight into production.
- **JIT production** is a production system that is driven by demand for the finished products (a 'pull' system), whereby each component on a production line is produced only when needed for the next stage.

Illustration 16 – JIT at Toyota

Toyota pioneered the JIT manufacturing system, in which suppliers send parts daily – or several times a day – and are notified electronically when the assembly line is running out.

Toyota's Georgetown plant in the USA is the largest of Toyota's manufacturing plants and has 20 suppliers based on-site. The rest are within a 3 hour drive of the plant, ensuring that supplies can be sourced the same day.

Requirements for successful operation of a JIT system

- **High quality and reliability** – disruptions create hold ups in the entire system and must be avoided. The emphasis is on getting the work 'right first time':
  - Highly skilled and well trained staff should be used.
  - Machinery must be fully maintained.
  - Long-term links should be established with suppliers to ensure a reliable and high quality service.
- **Elimination of non-value added activities** – value is only being added whilst a product is being processed. For example, value is not added whilst storing the products and therefore inventory levels should be minimised.
- **Speed of throughput** – the speed of production should match the rate at which customers demand the product. Production runs should be shorter with smaller stocks of finished goods.

- **Flexibility** – a flexible production system is needed to be able to respond immediately to customer orders:
  - The system should be capable of switching from making one product to making another.
  - The workforce should be dedicated and have the appropriate skills.
  - JIT is an organisational culture and the concept should be adopted by everyone.
  - Management should allow the work teams to use their initiative and to deal with problems as they arise.
- **Lower costs** – another objective of JIT is to reduce costs by:
  - Raising quality and eliminating waste.
  - Achieving faster throughput.
  - Minimising inventory levels.

Test your understanding 12

Requirement:

Explain the advantages and disadvantages to an organisation of operating a JIT system.

JIT and supplier relations

Many of the steps taken to improve the supply chain (and hence profitability) involve **improving the relationship between the manufacturer and its suppliers**. This will be of particular importance in a company operating a JIT system.

The advantages to a JIT company of developing close supplier relationships are as follows:

- **No rejects/returns** – a strong relationship should help to improve the quality of supplies. This should minimise production delays since there will be less inspection, fewer returns and less reworking of goods.
- **On-time deliveries** – the development of close working relationships should help to guarantee on-time deliveries of supplies.
- **Low inventory** – suppliers can be relied upon for frequent deliveries of small quantities of material to the company, ensuring that each delivery is just enough to meet the immediate production schedule.
- **Close proximity** – the supplier/portfolio of suppliers will be located close to the manufacturing plant. This will reduce delivery times and costs.

Kaizen

What is Kaizen?

Kaizen is a Japanese term for the philosophy of continuous improvement in performance via small, incremental steps.

Characteristics

- Kaizen involves setting standards and then continually improving these standards to achieve long-term sustainable improvements.
- The focus is on eliminating waste, improving processes and systems and improving productivity.
- Kaizen involves all areas of the business.
- Employees often work in teams and are empowered to make changes. Rather than viewing employees as the source of high costs, Kaizen views the employees as a source of ideas on how to reduce costs. A change of culture will be required, encouraging employees to suggest ideas to reduce costs.
- Kaizen allows the organisation to respond quickly to changes in the competitive environment.

e.g

Illustration 17 – Kaizen

Many Japanese companies have introduced a Kaizen approach:

- In Toyota each employee makes, on average, 10 suggestions each year.
- Around 700,000 suggestions are implemented across Toyota each year.

e.g

Illustration 18 – British cycling

British cycling's revolution through small, incremental improvements

When Sir David Brailsford became performance director of British cycling, he believed that if it were possible to make a 1% improvement in a whole host of areas, the cumulative gains would end up being hugely significant. He was on the look-out for all the weaknesses in the team's assumptions and saw these as opportunities to adapt and make marginal gains. For example:

- By experimenting in a wind tunnel, he noted that the bike was not sufficiently aerodynamic. Then by analysing the mechanics area in the team truck, he discovered that dust was accumulating on the floor, undermining bike maintenance. He had the floor painted pristine white, to spot any impurities.

- The team started using antibacterial hand gel to cut down on any infections.
- The team bus was redesigned to improve comfort and recuperation.

Many ridiculed both the approach and David Brailsford's ideas. However, recent performances in the Olympics have seen the team win an unprecedented number of gold medals.

Continuous improvement explained

Continuous improvement is the continual examination and improvement of existing processes and is very different from approaches such as business process re-engineering (BPR), which seeks to make radical one-off changes to improve an organisation's operations and processes. The concepts underlying continuous improvement are:

- The organisation should always seek perfection. Since perfection is never achieved, there must always be scope for improving on the current methods.
- The search for perfection should be ingrained into the culture and mind-set of all employees. Improvements should be sought all the time.
- Individual improvements identified by the work force will be small rather than far-reaching.

Six sigma

- Six sigma is a **quality management programme** that was pioneered in the 1980s by Motorola.
- The aim of the approach is to achieve a reduction in the number of faults that go beyond an accepted tolerance limit using statistical techniques.
- The sigma stands for standard deviation. For reasons that need not be explained here, it can be demonstrated that, **if the error rate lies within the sixth sigma of probability, there will be fewer than 3.4 defects in every one million**.
- This is the tolerance level set. It is almost perfection since customers will have a reason to complain fewer than four times in a million.

Illustration 19 – The six sigma approach

A hospital is using the six sigma process to improve patient waiting times. An investigation of the views of patients has revealed that:

- Patients do not want to be called before their appointment time as they do not want to feel that they must be at the hospital early to avoid missing an appointment
- The maximum length of time they are prepared to wait after the appointment time is 30 minutes.

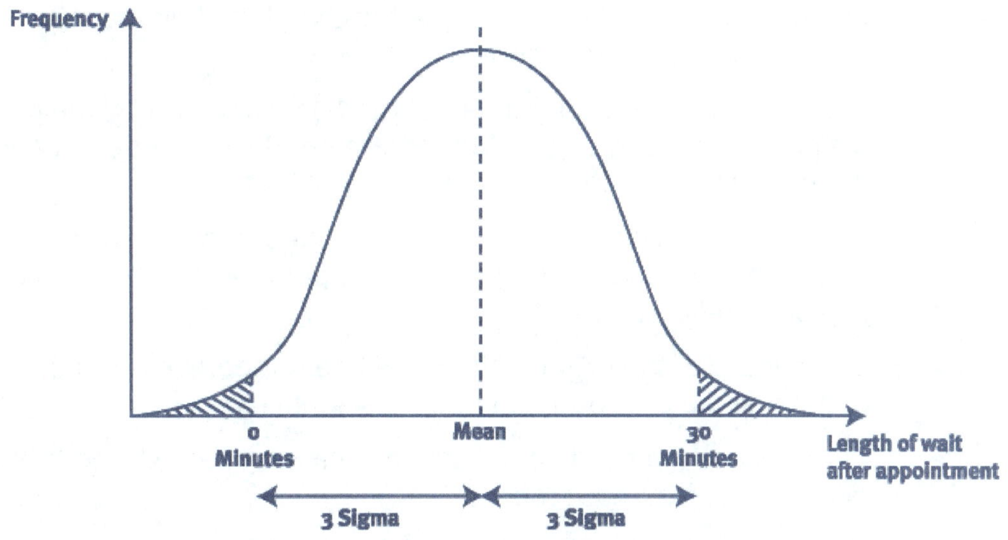

The aim of the six sigma programme will be to ensure that no more than 3.4 waits in every million occurrences exceed 30 minutes or are less than 0 minutes.

Further aspects of six sigma

Key requirements for successful six sigma implementation

There are several key requirements for the implementation of six sigma:

- Six sigma should be focused on the customer and based on the level of performance acceptable to the customer.
- Six sigma targets for a process should be related to the main drivers of performance.
- To maximise savings, six sigma needs to be part of a wider performance management programme which is linked to the strategy of the organisation. It should not be just about doing things better but about doing things differently.
- Senior managers within the organisation have a key role in driving the process.

- Training and education about the process throughout the organisation are essential for success.
- Six sigma sets a tight target but accepts some failure – the target is not zero defects.

Some criticisms and limitations of six sigma

Literature on six sigma contains some criticisms of the process and identifies several limitations as follows:

- Six sigma has been criticised for its focus on current processes and reliance on data. It is suggested that this could become too rigid and limit process innovation.
- Six sigma is based on the use of models which are by their nature simplifications of real life. Judgement needs to be used in applying the models in the context of business objectives.
- The approach can be very time consuming and expensive. Organisations need to be prepared to put time and effort into its implementation.
- The culture of the organisation must be supportive – not all organisations are ready for such a scientific process.
- The process is heavily data-driven. This can be a strength but can become over-bureaucratic.
- Six sigma can give all parts of the organisation a common language for process improvement, but it is important to ensure that this does not become jargon but is expressed in terms specific to the organisation and its business.
- There is an underlying assumption in six sigma that the existing business processes meet customers' expectations. It does not ask whether it is the right process.

Lean thinking

As the name suggests, **lean** is a philosophy that aims to **systematically eliminate waste** through the identification and elimination of all non-value adding activities.

e.g

Illustration 20 – Lean production at Toyota

60 years ago, the cars that Toyota was making were uncompetitive in both cost and quality terms. In a bid to catch up with its American competitors, it developed lean production. Lean production helped Toyota to become what it is now – the biggest car manufacturer in the world with a market share of 11.2% (11 million vehicles).

Wastes to be eliminated include:

- **Inventory** – holding or purchasing unnecessary raw materials, work-in-progress and finished goods
- **Waiting** – time delays/idle time when value is not added to the product
- **Defective units** – production of a part that is scrapped or requires rework
- **Effort or motion** – actions of people/equipment that do not add value
- **Transportation** – delays in transportation or unnecessary handling due to poor planning or factory layout
- **Over-processing** – unnecessary steps that do not add value
- **Over-production** – produce more than customers have ordered.

Characteristics of lean

Characteristics of lean include:

- **Improved production scheduling** – production is initiated by customer demand rather than ability and capacity to produce, i.e. production is demand-pull, not supply-push.
- **Small batch production or continuous production** – production is based on customer demand, resulting in highly flexible and responsive processes.
- **Economies of scope** – lean production is only achieved where 'economies of scope' make it economical to produce small batches of a variety of products with the same machines. This is in stark contrast with traditional manufacturing and its emphasis on mass production and economies of scale.
- **Continuous improvement** – the company continually finds ways to reduce process times:
  - A multi-skilled, trained workforce provides flexibility. Employees should be involved in and engaged with the lean philosophy.
  - The machines, tools and people used to make an item are located close together.
  - Quality at source reduces re-working.
  - A clean and orderly workplace.
- **Zero inventory** – just-in-time purchasing eliminates waste.
- **Zero waiting time** – JIT production means that the work performed at each stage of the process is dictated solely by the demand for materials for the next stage, thus reducing lead time.

The lean supply chain

The main objective of a lean supply chain is to completely remove waste to achieve competitive advantage through a reduction in costs and an improvement in quality. Other benefits are:

- reduced inventories (and thus increased cash flows and profits)
- shorter lead times, and thus faster deliveries to customers
- few bottlenecks, so better utilisation of resources, and further improvements in profit
- few quality problems, so less re-work, lower costs of quality failures, and happier customers.

However, disadvantages include the potential for large, powerful customers to dominate the supply chain and an over-emphasis on cost reduction rather than quality improvement.

Criticisms and limitations of lean manufacturing

- **High initial outlay** – It might involve a large amount of initial expenditure to switch from 'traditional' production systems to a system based on cellular manufacturing (a lean manufacturing process that organises production into self-sufficient units called cells). All the tools and equipment needed to manufacture a product need to be re-located to the same area of the factory floor. Employees need to be trained in multiple skills.
- **Requires a change in culture** – Lean manufacturing, like TQM, is a philosophy or culture of working, and it might be difficult for management and employees to acquire this culture. Employees might not be prepared to give the necessary commitment.
- **Part adoption** – It might be tempting for companies to select some elements of lean manufacturing (such as production based on cellular manufacturing), but not to adopt others (such as empowering employees to make on-the-spot decisions).
- **Cost may exceed benefit** – In practice, the expected benefits of lean manufacturing (lower costs and shorter cycle times) have not always materialised, or might not have been as large as expected.

Illustration 21 – Toyota versus a non-lean car manufacturer

	Non-lean manufacturer	Lean pioneer – Toyota
Production	Mass production requiring: • time to set up machinery and • skilled engineers	Produce smaller batches leading to: • quick set up • flexibility • production line staff trained to do set ups
Human resources	Cyclical nature of industry resulting in: • staff layoffs • unmotivated staff	• Job for life • Defined career path • Empowered staff
Employee roles	• Assembly worker • Foreman • Housekeeper • Engineer	Eliminates non-value adding activities so all workers trained on all aspects hence no indirect wages
Production problems	• Couldn't stop the production line • 20–25% defects	• Stops the production line and then the team works to solve issues quickly • Almost zero defects
Suppliers	Chosen on cost	• Use supplier expertise • Fair price • JIT
Sales	• Sell through dealers • Narrow product range	• Sell direct to customers • Customer feedback valued • Flexibility resulting in wide product range

Lean synchronisation aims to meet demand instantaneously with perfect quality and no waste.

Lean synchronisation overlaps to a large degree with the general concept of lean (elimination of waste) and just-in-time (which emphasises the idea of producing items only when they are needed).

Reverse logistics

Reverse logistics is the return of unwanted or surplus goods, materials or equipment back to the organisation for reuse, recycling or disposal.

The emergence of internet selling (some internet retailers estimate returns of 50%) and shorter product life cycles has led to many organisations focusing on their reverse logistics capability.

The main reasons for returns are as follows:

- The **customer is not satisfied** with the product and takes advantage of the organisation's return policy
- **Installation or usage problems** – a common problem if installation or usage is complicated, for example with IT equipment
- **Warranty claims** for defective products or parts
- Some manufacturers allow the **return of unsold stock** by retailers, for example this is common practice in the book industry
- **Manufacturer recall** program due to faults.

Attacking the returns challenge is a critical area of supply chain management. Steps should be taken to:

- **Minimise returns**, for example through the production of good quality products or parts, which meet customer requirements and have clear guidelines for installation and usage
- **Ensure the possible reuse or recycling of material**. This is closely linked to corporate social responsibility but should contribute to increased profitability.

Techniques include:

- Root cause analysis to understand the reasons for returns
- Creation of profit centres around the returns process to focus organisations on maximising the price that they will get for any returns
- Separation of the supply chain into separate forward and reverse logistics
- Centralising the returns centre to improve the speed and efficiency of handling returns
- Outsourcing the returns process to a competent and dedicated provider
- The use of technology such as enterprise resource planning (ERP) which supports reverse logistics processes.

The use of these techniques should reduce costs, improve customer service and increase revenue.

Test your understanding 13

Match the following techniques to their explanation.

Technique	Explanation
Statistical Process Control	The philosophy of continuous improvement via small, incremental steps
Just in Time	The return of unwanted or surplus goods, materials or equipment back to the organisation
Total Quality Management	An approach to achieve a reduction in the number of faults that go beyond an accepted tolerance limit
Six sigma	A method for measuring and controlling quality during a process
Lean thinking	A system whose objective it is to produce or procure products or components as they are required by the customer or for use, rather than for inventory
Reverse logistics	A philosophy that aims to systematically eliminate waste
Kaizen	The continuous improvement in quality, productivity and effectiveness obtained by establishing management responsibility for processes as well as outputs

Test your understanding 14

Lean thinking identifies seven wastes to be eliminated. **These include which FIVE of the following?**

A Over-processing

B Over-production

C Over-thinking

D Over-selling

E Transportation

F Effort or motion

G Human resources

H Inventory

e.g

Illustration 22 – Reverse logistics at Estee Lauder

A good example of a complete reverse logistics program is a project by cosmetics manufacturer Estee Lauder. The firm used to dump $60 million of its products into landfills each year, destroying more than a third of the name brand cosmetics returned by retailers.

Estee Lauder made a small investment of $1.3 million to build its reverse logistics system and apparently recovered its investment in the first year.

Estee Lauder has reduced its production and inventory levels through its increased ability to put returned goods back on the market and the availability of better data on the reasons for returns. In the first year Estee Lauder was able to evaluate 24 per cent more returned products, redistribute 150 per cent more of its returns, reduce the destroyed products from 37 per cent to 27 per cent and save about $0.5 million on labour costs.

e.g

Illustration 23 – Reverse logistics at Frasers Group plc

Jack Wills – a fashion retailer, was bought out of administration by Sports Direct in 2019 for £12.7 million. Sports Direct has since rebranded to Frasers Group plc.

Frasers Group operates a reverse logistics policy which embraces some of the 5R's – returns, resell, repair, recycle and replace.

For example, a customer orders a pair of Jack Wills jogging trousers in black. When they are delivered, they are navy blue in colour. The customer contacts customer services via the Jack Wills website where they are directed to a chatbot who asks for their order number and a photo of the garment, amongst other details. The chatbot then redirects the customer to an online customer service agent who has verified the trousers are navy blue and offers to deliver a black pair.

Crucially, when the customer asks what they should do with the navy blue pair, the agent tells them to donate them to charity. Whether they do or not is up to the customer. However, Jack Wills / Fraser Group do not want them back. They have worked out that it will cost more to restock the garment than it would to donate it to charity.

The company has saved on the restocking charge, the customer is satisfied, and charity has (possibly) received a valuable donation.

5.7 Supply chain management (SCM) interface with finance

Introduction

- Organisations with strong links between their finance function and supply chain teams are more likely to have effective supply chain management.
- A **collaborative relationship** between the CFO and the leader of the supply chain (either directly or through their teams) is advantageous for organisational growth and competitive advantage:
  - The role of the leader of the supply chain has become more prominent in recent years. The focus of supply chain management has moved away from cost reductions to creating a supply chain strategy that is aligned to the broader corporate goals of the organisation and is efficient in enabling the organisation to respond to new opportunities.
  - Meanwhile, the role of the finance function has been transformed. The finance function now collaborates more closely with other internal functions; not just from a monitoring, reporting and risk management perspective, but also as supporters and enablers of performance.
  - The result is that CFOs and supply chain leaders are working increasingly together to understand, analyse and address supply chain issues. CFOs are drawing on their skills and unique view of the organisation to provide insight to deliver more informed decision-making.

e.g

Illustration 24 – Supplier decision management

When it comes to supplier decision management, the operations function will make the decision regarding which supplier(s) to choose but the finance function would help with some aspects of the supplier relationship (mainly the financial side).

Opportunities for business partnering

The finance function has a unique end-to-end view of the organisation and is considered a trusted advisor. As a result, there are several areas where the CFO (and their team) has an opportunity to enhance performance through business partnering with the supply chain. These include:

- Stronger alignment between the supply chain and the broader strategy and consistency of strategy within the various parts of the supply chain.
- CFOs help to set the right growth priorities and pace of growth; they support and challenge the rationale for new investment, apply data analytics to support and challenge business decisions and ensure that tax is considered as part of operational decisions.
- Monitoring and enhancing performance through the establishment of appropriate KPIs that are aligned to the broader organisation.

- Managing risk and business continuity; the CFO has the opportunity to work with procurement and treasury to determine the extent to which risk is owned and managed by the company, and to what extent it is pushed further down the supply chain.

e.g

Illustration 25 – Business partnering to root out forced labour from supply chains

The finance function, as a business partner, have a significant role to play in preventing and detecting slavery in the supply chain. No one wants to imagine that the food ingredients their company has built an empire on may have been processed or picked by those getting no pay and having little choice in what they do. Nor does a retail chain executive want to find out shirts destined for the new collection were sewn by children too young to legally work. However, the reality is that many multinationals probably are taking part in forced, or slave labour – especially those with long, complex supply chains.

Forced labour is a big problem for companies all over the world. According to recent estimates by the International Labour Organisation, there are more than 152 million children performing child labour, and 40 million people trapped in forced labour – some of them in supply chains feeding into big companies.

However, with more governments getting serious about rooting out the practices through strengthening of legislation, companies are growing increasingly serious about addressing forced labour in their supply chains.

The finance function with their access to detailed financial information and the influence to make it a top company concern, have a major role to play through business partnering with the supply chain:

- The first step a CFO serious about addressing the issue of forced labour in supply chains should take is to have the company map out its supply chain in as much detail as possible.
- The finance function should work closely with the compliance and procurement departments to ensure that all the company suppliers sign a clearly worded code of conduct.
- One way in which the finance function can get involved in the fight against slavery is by raising awareness in their company about the issue. Additionally, everyone within the company should receive training about the risks and red flags of forced labour in supply chains.
- The finance function needs to be careful about the demands it puts on suppliers and ensure that they are not unintentionally creating pressures that may lead to the abuse of workers.
- Taking part in or actioning ethical audits (for example, of high risk factories).
- Developing and incorporating controls, for example on anti-trafficking of labour, into management accounting.

6 Key performance indicators

6.1 Introduction

Critical success factors (CSFs) are the vital areas 'where things must go right' for the business so they might achieve their strategic objectives.

Key performance indicators (KPIs) are the measures which indicate whether the CSFs are being achieved.

The achievement of the KPIs should be measured and any necessary corrective action taken.

e.g

Illustration 26 – CSFs and KPIs for supply chain management

The operations function will identify CSFs for its supply chain and may establish that it is critical for them to achieve a high level of quality, minimal level of waste and a reduction in supply chain costs.

The function will use techniques such as TQM, Kaizen, lean, JIT and reverse logistics management to optimise their performance in these areas.

KPIs will be used to indicate whether the CSFs are being achieved.

The **finance function will work with the operations function** to establish appropriate KPIs. For example:

- Defect/error rate, % product returns, amount spent on warranties will be used in a TQM environment
- Target costs will be used in a Kaizen environment
- Waste measurement and lean techniques will go hand in hand
- Inventory measurement will be important in a JIT environment
- % returns, reuse/recycling of returns will be used to monitor and measure the effectiveness of a reverse logistics strategy.

Characteristics of good KPIs include:

- KPIs should cascade from strategy to tactics, and to operational level.
- KPIs should cover all perspectives in supply chain management such as cost information and financial performance, quality of the supply chain, flexibility, resource utilisation, innovation, sustainability and competitiveness. This coverage will give a complete and well balanced view of
  - internal/external performance
  - short-term and long-term performance and
  - financial performance and non-financial performance.

- KPIs should be challenging but achievable and should enable employees to understand the performance measures they have control over and should motivate them to achieve KPIs through the establishment of appropriate rewards.
- KPIs should be SMART, i.e. **s**pecific, **m**easurable, **a**chievable, **r**elevant and **t**ime-bound.
- KPIs should be extended to include supply chain partners, because the objective of SCM is to create a supply chain that is much more competitive than the alternative supply chain providers' of that product or service.

6.2 Examples of KPIs for operations

Appropriate KPIs may include:

Example activity	**Possible KPI**
Inbound logistics	Percentage defect rate (supplies) Raw material inventory days = Raw material inventory ÷ Cost of sales (or Purchases) × 365 Payables days = Payables ÷ Purchases × 365
Production	Supply chain costs per unit sold Percentage defect rate Percentage wastage rate Asset utilisation rate Labour utilisation rate Queues and waiting times
Outbound logistics	Time taken to deliver a customer order Percentage on-time delivery to a customer Percentage of customer orders fulfilled Warehousing costs Transport costs Finished goods inventory days = Finished goods inventory ÷ Cost of sales × 365

Test your understanding 15

Ali is constructing some KPIs to measure whether or not the firm's CSFs are being met. He has been told that these KPIs should be SMART.

One KPI is as follows: Reduce the time taken to deliver a customer's order by three days. (The current lead time for deliveries is two weeks.)

Which of the SMART criteria is not being met in this KPI?

A Specific

B Measurable

C Achievable

D Relevant

E Time-bound

6.3 How the finance function manages operations using KPIs

Introduction

The finance function plays an important role in the performance management of the operations function, implementing a performance management approach that gives a complete and well balanced view of all supply chain activities.

Information to impact framework revisited

We can understand how the finance function helps manage operations by using KPIs and looking at the **information to impact framework**:

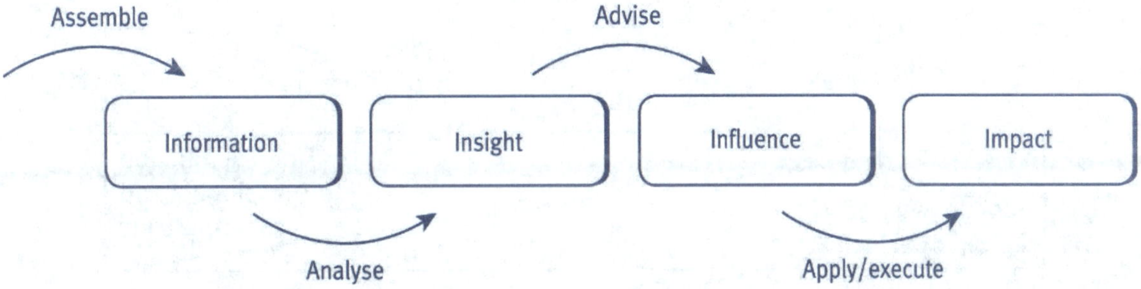

Finance function activity	Explanation of how the finance function helps manage operations using KPIs
Assembling information	The finance function works with operations to establish a set of appropriate KPIs. It then **assembles** data from a range of internal and external sources and processes this data to turn it into useful KPI information. This information is then **reported** to those people who need it within the organisation and across the supply chain.

Analysing for insights	The finance function analyses the KPI information to draw out patterns and relevant **insights** for those who use the information. This **questioning** may require individual KPIs to be broken down into several different performance measures so that the root cause of any deviations between the actual KPI and the target KPI can be established.
Advising to influence	The finance function then communicates these insights and contributes an objective and responsible perspective helping to **develop solutions** to any operational problems or areas for improvement identified to **influence** decision making in the operations function.
Applying for impact (also called **'execute'**)	The finance function applies the information to harness value for the operations function through its **impact**. **Solutions are deployed** such as changes to the operational strategy and future KPIs.

Impact of technology

The impact of technology and automation on the information to impact framework is shown below:

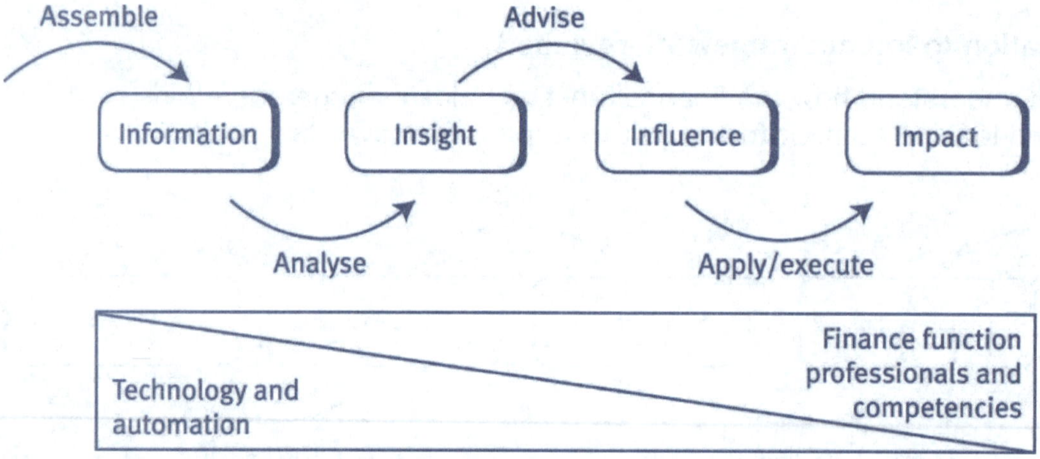

If we consider this in relation to how the finance function manages operations through the use of KPIs we can see that:

- **Technology and automation** will play an important role in all of the activities of the finance function but will have the largest impact on the **'assembly' and 'analysis' activities**.
  - Successful companies operate an enterprise data warehouse that acts as a single source to **assemble** 'clean' data (in-house data is seamlessly integrated with data from supply chain partners, usually via an extranet) and reports this in the form of a supply chain dashboard that is accessible and adaptable for relevant users across the supply chain and the organisation.

  - This integrated technology can draw out patterns and relevant insights for those who use the information, reducing the **analysis** role of the finance function.

- This will 'free up' the resource of the finance function professionals who can now place greater focus on the '**advising**' and '**applying/executing**' activities. However, even in these activities, technology will take on a role. For example, predictive algorithms may be used for advanced business intelligence and to determine timely corrective actions along the end-to-end supply chain.

e.g

Illustration 27 – Technological developments

Advances in technology offered by the 4th Industrial Revolution are giving organisations an opportunity to enhance performance management in the operations function. For example:

- Easier **linking of internal supply chain data with external sources** such as financial information about suppliers to improve supply chain risk management.
- Ongoing **digitisation of supply chains** and resulting exponential growth in data from connected devices (such as delivery vehicles).
- Use of **web mining** to report only the most relevant data and to quickly react to new events.
- A shift to real-time data enabled by sensors covering different locations.
- The most common use of **data visualisation** is in creating a dashboard to display the key performance indicators of a business in a live format, thus allowing immediate understanding of current performance and potentially prompting action to correct or amend performance accordingly.
- Increasing use of **predictive measures** to (for example) forecast sales, detect product quality issues, evaluate maintenance requirements and produce sound 'what-if' scenarios.
- **Improved analytics capabilities** (for example, using cloud technology) allowing for fast processing and analysis of large amounts of data.

Test your understanding 16

The finance function helps manage operations using KPIs.

Match the following KPI activities to the relevant stage in the 'information to impact framework'.

Assembling information	Deploying solutions such as developing future KPIs
Analysing for insights	Helping to develop solutions to any operational problems
Advising to influence	Establishing the cause of any deviations between actual and target KPIs
Applying for impact	Establishing a set of appropriate KPIs

Test your understanding 17

Which of the following statements is/are correct?

I Technology will have the largest impact on the assemble and analysis activities of the finance function

II Technology facilitates easier integration of internal supply chain data with external sources

III By analysing KPIs, the finance function can guarantee that CSFs are met

IV A primary feature of the interaction between finance and operations is performance management

A All of them

B I and IV

C I only

D I, II and IV

7 Chapter summary

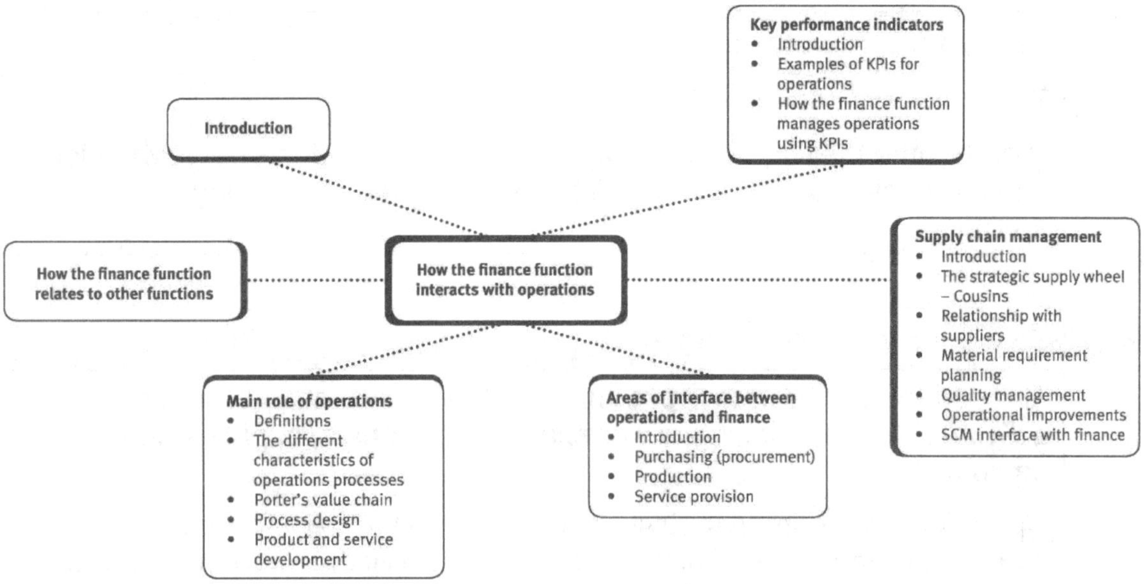

Test your understanding answers

Test your understanding 1

The answer is company **A**

High volume (selling in bulk), low variety (basic products), low variation and low customer contact (visibility) all help keep processing costs down.

Test your understanding 2

The correct answer is **A – procurement**. Procurement (a support activity) is the purchasing of, for example, materials, supplies and equipment.

Operations is a primary activity and relates to the transformation of raw materials or inputs into finished goods and services. Inbound logistics is also a primary activity and relates to the receiving, storing and handling of raw material inputs.

Purchasing is not one of the activities in the value chain model.

Test your understanding 3

The correct answer is **C – outbound logistics**

The new system helps manage the finished loaves, indicating that it refers to outbound logistics. It does not manage the raw materials (or ingredients), indicating that it will not help inbound logistics. It also is used after BB bakes the loaves of bread, so it cannot be part of operations. The system does not affect sales and marketing of the bread.

Test your understanding 4

The correct answer is **A**

B relates to marketing, C relates to production and D relates to human resource management.

Test your understanding 5

The correct answer is **A**

Note that provision of services would be unlikely to affect the sale of physical units, so inventory turnover would be unaffected.

Test your understanding 6

The correct answer is **B**

By definition.

Test your understanding 7

Statement	**True/False?**
The co-ordination of activities from the supplier(s) of raw materials at one end of the supply chain to the customer at the other end is known as supply chain management	True
Cost savings are the only advantage of supply chain management	False. Supply chain management can also add value to an organisation, for example in improved customer services.
The objective of SCM is to achieve synergies that benefit the customers at the end of the supply chain	False. The objective of SCM is to achieve synergies that benefit every player along the chain.
Cousins' supply wheel is a model used to look at the traditional supply function	False. Cousins' model examines supply in a strategic way. Successful organisations in today's competitive environment have recognised that supply should be viewed as a strategic issue.
Cousins' supply wheel has five spokes	True. The spokes are: Organisation structure, Performance Measures, Relationships with suppliers, Cost Benefit, and Competences.

Test your understanding 8

The correct answers are **A, B and C**

Answer D – improved quality is not guaranteed and therefore this is not an advantage.

Answers E and F – these are disadvantages.

Test your understanding 9

Higher quality can help to increase revenue and reduce costs:

- Higher quality improves the perceived image of a product or service. As a result, more customers will be willing to buy the product/service and may also be willing to pay more for the product/service.
- A higher volume of sales may result in lower unit costs due to economies of scale.
- Higher quality in manufacturing should result in lower waste and defective rates, which will reduce production costs.
- The need for inspection and testing should be reduced, also reducing costs.
- The volume of customer complaints should fall and warranty claims should be lower. This will reduce costs.
- Better quality in production should lead to shorter processing times. This will reduce costs.

Test your understanding 10

The correct answer is **B and E**

Prevention costs are those incurred in order to prevent poor quality.

Answer A – inspection of raw materials is an appraisal cost.

Answer C – returns from customers are an external failure cost.

Answer D – machine breakdown repairs are internal failure costs.

Test your understanding 11

Tail off – after an initial burst of enthusiasm, top management fails to maintain interest and support.

Deflection – other initiatives or problems deflect attention from TQM.

Lack of buy-in – managers pay only 'lip service' to the principles of worker involvement and communication.

Rejection – TQM does not fit in with the organisational culture and is therefore rejected.

Test your understanding 12

Advantages of JIT

- Lower stock holding costs means a reduction in storage space which saves rent and insurance costs.
- As stock is only obtained when it is needed, less working capital is tied up in stock.
- There is less likelihood of stock perishing, becoming obsolete or out of date.
- Avoids the build-up of unsold finished products that can occur with sudden changes in demand.
- Less time is spent checking and re-working the products as the emphasis is on getting the work right first time.

The result is that costs should fall and quality should increase. This should improve the company's competitive advantage.

Disadvantages of JIT

- There is little room for mistakes as little stock is kept for re-working a faulty product.
- Production is very reliant on suppliers and if stock is not delivered on time or is not of a high enough quality, the whole production schedule can be delayed.
- There is no spare finished product available to meet unexpected orders, because all products are made to meet actual orders.
- It may be difficult for managers to empower employees to embrace the concept and culture.
- It won't be suitable for all companies. For example, supermarkets must have a supply of inventory.
- It can be difficult to apply to the service industry. However, in the service industry a JIT approach may focus on eliminating queues, which are wasteful of customers' time.

Test your understanding 13

Technique	Explanation
Statistical Process Control	A method for measuring and controlling quality during a process.
Just in Time	A system whose objective it is to produce or procure products or components as they are required by the customer or for use, rather than for inventory.
Total Quality Management	The continuous improvement in quality, productivity and effectiveness obtained by establishing management responsibility for processes as well as outputs.
Six sigma	An approach to achieve a reduction in the number of faults that go beyond an accepted tolerance limit.
Lean thinking	A philosophy that aims to systematically eliminate waste.
Reverse logistics	The return of unwanted or surplus goods, materials or equipment back to the organisation.
Kaizen	The philosophy of continuous improvement via small incremental steps.

Test your understanding 14

The correct answers are **A, B, E, F and H**

The other two wastes to be eliminated under lean thinking are waiting and defective units.

Test your understanding 15

The correct answer is **E** – time-bound. There is no mention of by when the KPI needs to be achieved. Just because it mentions a number of days, does not make it time-bound.

The KPI is straight forward and, hence, specific, the time to deliver can be easily measured. Three days reduction seems achievable. The KPI is relevant to the CSF as delivery waiting times will be important to the customer.

Test your understanding 16

Assembling information	Establishing a set of appropriate KPIs
Analysing for insights	Establishing the cause of any deviations between actual and target KPIs
Advising to influence	Helping to develop solutions to any operational problems
Applying for impact	Deploying solutions such as developing future KPIs

Test your understanding 17

The correct answer is **D**

Option III is not correct as there is no guarantee that the CSFs will be met.

Chapter

10

How the finance function interacts with sales and marketing

Chapter learning objectives

Lead	Component
E2: Describe how the finance function interacts with sales and marketing.	Describe: (a) Main role of sales and marketing (b) Areas of interface with finance (c) Key performance indicators

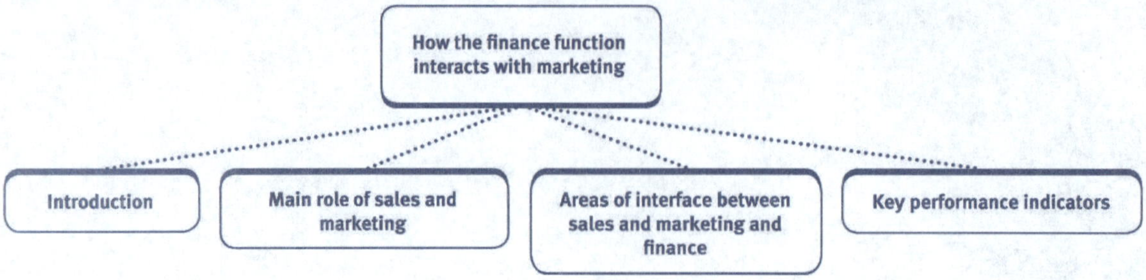

1 Introduction

In Chapter 9 we described the finance function's relationship with operations. In this chapter we will continue to describe how the finance function plays its role by interacting with the rest of the organisation and, more specifically in this chapter, the organisation's sales and marketing function.

We will begin by discussing the main role of the sales and marketing function; understanding the marketing environment, the marketing mix and the main techniques of sales and marketing.

We will then discuss the areas of interface with finance; understanding how the finance function interacts with sales and marketing and the role of big data analytics.

The final part of this chapter will discuss how the finance function helps to manage the sales and marketing function using key performance indicators (KPIs).

2 Main role of sales and marketing

2.1 Introduction

Marketing is defined by the Chartered Institute of Marketing (CIM) as 'the management process that identifies, anticipates and supplies customer needs efficiently and profitably.'

The key emphasis of the sales and marketing function is thus on **customer needs**.

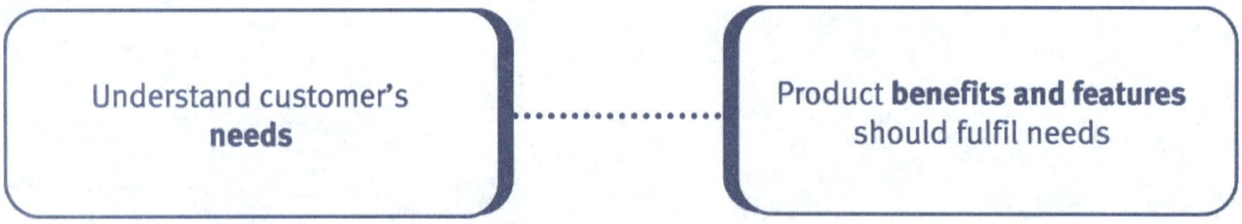

Four possible approaches to selling a product

There are four possible approaches to selling a product:

Marketing orientation: starts by understanding customers' needs and then produces products with benefits and features to fulfil these needs.

Production orientation: focus is on high volume production to achieve low unit cost.

Product orientation: focus is on continual improvement of products assuming customers simply want the best quality for their money.

Sales orientation: uses aggressive promotional policies to entice the customer.

Sales form only a part of the entire marketing process and philosophy. The sales aspect of marketing will be most prominent in an organisation that rejects the marketing orientation in favour of an alternative approach. Under these circumstances, the sales team will be obliged to 'find' customers and persuade them to buy the products that have been made. This may be an outdated approach, but it still exists in some industries.

Benefits of a marketing orientation

As the Chartered Institute of Marketing (CIM) point out:

"It is all about getting the right product or service to the customer at the right price, in the right place, at the right time. Business history and current practice both remind us that without proper marketing, companies cannot get close to customers and satisfy their needs. And if they don't, a competitor surely will."

Test your understanding 1

Marketing is mainly concerned with which one of the following?

A Increasing sales revenue

B Streamlining production

C Anticipating and meeting customer needs

D Maximising profit

The market planning process

A marketing action plan will be needed to ensure the effectiveness of the sales and marketing processes.

The following is an example of the different components that could be included in this plan:

Step 1: Situation analysis

Several techniques can be used. These include:

SWOT analysis – the organisation needs to understand its own strengths (S) and weaknesses (W) together with an appreciation of the wider environment in which it operates, i.e. the opportunities (O) and threats (T).

PESTEL analysis – The organisation should review the external environment for opportunities that may allow it to further meet their customers' needs. This analysis divides the business environment into six related sub-systems – Political, Economic, Social, Technological, Environmental/Ecological factors and Legal. Each of these factors can be applied to the marketing function.

Step 2: Review mission and objectives

The organisation will already have a mission statement and a set of objectives in place. These will underpin the marketing objectives.

Step 3: Set marketing objectives

Marketing objectives should be consistent with the organisation's overall mission and objectives.

Marketing objectives should be SMART – specific, measurable, achievable, relevant and time bound. For example, acquire 50,000 new online customers this financial year at an average cost per acquisition of $30 with an average profitability of $5.

Step 4: Devise an appropriate marketing strategy

There may be a gap between the current performance and the performance required to achieve the marketing objectives set. The organisation needs to consider how to close the gap. The following techniques can be used:

- **Market research** – focuses on understanding the market, consumer behaviour, and market trends
- **Marketing research** – requires an understanding of a broader range of activities including market analysis, product development and marketing strategies
- **Segmentation** – the market should be segmented, for example by age, social class or income. The needs of each segment should be established using market research

- **Targeting** – the most attractive segments in terms of profitability and growth should be targeted using an appropriate marketing mix
- **Positioning** – an appropriate positioning strategy, for example differentiation or cost leadership should be chosen for each market segment
- **Marketing mix** – the organisation should use the marketing mix to determine the correct marketing strategy.

Step 5: Implementation

The marketing action plan should then be implemented and appropriate KPIs established.

Step 6: Review

The plan should be monitored to gauge its success (or otherwise) and to identify any necessary changes required to achieve the marketing objectives set.

2.2 Understanding the marketing environment

The marketing environment is the content in which the organisation exists. The environment can have a considerable impact on the organisation.

The **macro environment** includes all the factors that influence an organisation but are outside of their control. Organisations will need flexible marketing practices to respond to this dynamic environment.

One popular technique for analysing the macro environment is **PESTEL** analysis:

PESTEL factor	**Explanation**
Political	Political factors can have a direct effect on the way an organisation operates. Decisions made by government affect our everyday lives. For example, the instability of many governments in developing nations has led several companies to question the wisdom of marketing in those countries.
Economic	All businesses are affected by economic factors nationally and globally. For example, within the UK, the climate of the economy can dictate consumer expenditure on luxury goods.

Social	Forces within society such as family, friends and the media affect our attitude, interests and opinions and, in turn, will influence our purchases. For example, within the UK people's attitudes are changing towards their diet and health. Over the past few years, the UK has seen a massive increase in demand for vegan food and food with reduced sugar and salt.
Technological	This is an area in which change takes place very rapidly and the organisation needs to be constantly aware of what is going on. For example, new technology has resulted in the production of new products, such as electric cars which reduce emissions.
Environmental/ Ecological	These have become increasingly important in recent years and influence a marketing orientated organisation in several ways. For example, using the example above, demand for vegan food has increased not only for health reasons but also due to the negative environmental impact of meat and dairy farming and fishing.
Legal	Laws and regulations governing businesses are widespread. These include laws on health and safety, information disclosure, the dismissal of employees, vehicle emissions, the use of pesticides and many more. For example, the UK smoking ban in public places has resulted in UK tobacco companies exploring new products, such as the legal, electronic cigarette (although the use of these has been banned in some countries .e.g. Argentina, and the sale of them has been banned in others .e.g. Switzerland.)

Test your understanding 2

Requirement:

Describe the changes that may be made to the marketing approach of a supermarket if the country goes into recession.

Social factors

According to Johnson and Scholes the following social influences should be monitored:

- **Population demographics** – a term used to describe the composition of the population in any given area, whether a region, a country or an area within a country.

- **Income distribution** – indicates how many people earn or receive various amounts of income and will provide the marketer with some indication of the size of the target markets.
- **Social mobility** – the marketer should be aware of social classes and the distribution among them. The marketer can use this knowledge to promote products to distinct social classes within the market.
- **Lifestyle changes** – refer to society's attitudes and opinions to things like credit, diet, fitness and health. Our attitudes have changed in recent years and this information is vital for the marketer.
- **Consumerism** – one of the social trends in recent years has been the rise of consumerism. This trend has increased to such an extent that governments have been pressured to design laws that protect the rights of the consumer.
- **Levels of education** – for example, in the UK the level of education has increased dramatically over the last few years and there is now a larger proportion of the population in higher education than ever before.

2.3 Understanding the marketing mix

The marketing mix is the set of controllable variables that a firm blends to produce desired results from its chosen target market.

It was originally based upon the 4P's – Product, Place, Promotion and Price, but then adapted for service based organisations to include People, Processes and Physical Evidence.

The 7 Ps

	Examples of elements
Product	This includes product features, durability, design, brand name, packaging, range, after-sales service, warranties and guarantees.
Place	Distribution channels and intermediaries, transportation and storage.
Promotion	Advertising, personal selling, public relations, sales promotion, sponsorship, direct marketing, e.g. direct mail and telephone marketing.
Price	Price level, discounts, credit policy, payment methods.
People	The role of employees in the service industry is particularly important because of the inseparability of the service from the service provider. Staff must be selected, trained and motivated to meet the needs of the target customer.

Processes	These are the systems through which the service is delivered. For example, the teaching methods used in a university or the speed and friendliness of service in a restaurant.
Physical evidence	Required to make the intangible service more tangible. For example, brochures, testimonials and the appearance of staff and of the environment.

The extension of the traditional marketing mix to include the three additional Ps acknowledges that there are fundamental differences between products and services and ,therefore, services marketing assumes a different emphasis to product marketing. However, although the extended mix is particularly relevant to service organisations, product based organisations would also do well to consider these aspects, particularly the competence of people and process efficiency.

Features of service organisations

Service organisations have certain distinguishing features that should be considered:

- Services are **intangible** and it is more difficult to measure their quality than it is for a physical product. Customers may be more reluctant to make a purchase due to uncertainty regarding what they will receive. Tools such as testimonials and brochures may help to address this problem.
- Services are consumed immediately and **cannot be stored**. Meeting customer needs depends on staff being available. Therefore, anticipating and responding to levels of demand is a priority.
- **Heterogeneity** – maintaining consistent, standard output can be difficult. In part this is due to the necessarily high levels of staff and human intervention. Organisations may attempt to moderate this through effective staff selection and training, and establishing standards for customer service and care.
- **Inseparability** of the service from the provider will again reinforce the need for high quality employee selection and training.
- Services **do not result in the transfer of propert**y and so it will be necessary to convince the customer of the benefits of what they are paying for. A tangible symbol of ownership, such as a certificate, may be used.

Each element of the traditional marketing mix will be reviewed in turn:

Product

There are two main product issues to consider:

- Product definition – The main issue regarding product is to define exactly what the product should be. This can be done on three levels:

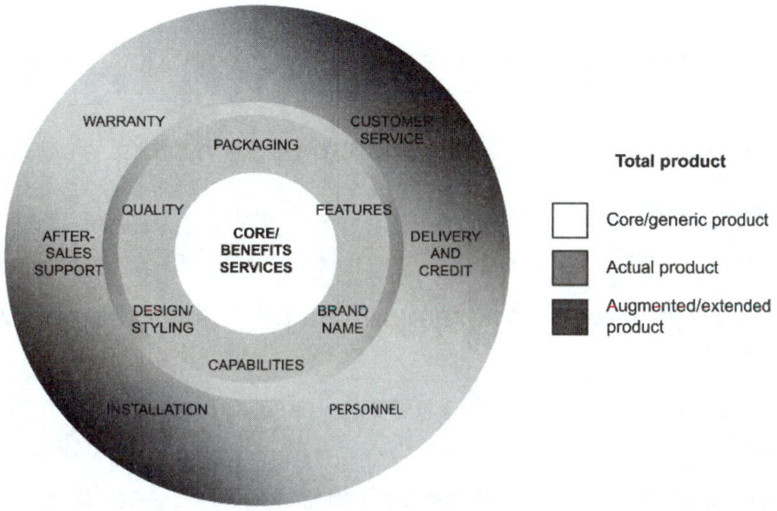

- Product positioning – With all of these factors the question of product positioning is critical – how does our product compare with the offerings of competitors? Is our product better? If so, in what way?

Illustration 1 – Product definition

A new car could be specified as follows:

- Core/generic product – personal transportation.
- Actual product – which brand, range of engine sizes, different body shapes offered, etc.
- Augmented product – manufacturer's warranty or dealer's discounted service contract.

Product – further considerations

The **core product** – what is the buyer really buying? The core product refers to the use, benefit or problem-solving service that the consumer is really buying when purchasing the product, i.e. the need that is being fulfilled.

The **actual product** is the tangible product or intangible service that serves as the medium for receiving core product benefits.

The **augmented product** consists of the measures taken to help the consumer put the actual product to sustained use, including installation, delivery and credit, warranties and after-sales service.

A product, therefore, is more than a simple set of tangible features. Consumers tend to see products as complex bundles of benefits that satisfy their needs. Most important is how the customer perceives the product. They are looking at factors such as aesthetics and styling, durability, brand image, packaging, service and warranty, any of which might be enough to set the product apart from its competitors.

Pricing

There are four key considerations (the '4 Cs') when deciding the price of a product:

- **Cost** – the price must be high enough to make a profit.
- **Customers** – how much are they willing to pay?
- **Competition** – is our price higher than competitors'?
- **Corporate objectives** – for example, the price could be set low to gain market share.

These issues can be blended to give a range of pricing tactics, including the following:

- **Cost plus pricing** – the cost per unit is calculated and then a mark-up is added.
- **Penetration pricing** – a low price is set to gain market share.
- **Perceived quality pricing** – a high price is set to reflect/create an image of high quality.
- **Price discrimination** – different prices are set for the same product in different markets, for example, peak/off-peak rail fares.
- **Going rate pricing** – prices are set to match competitors.
- **Dynamic pricing** – prices are altered in line with demand, for example this is used widely in the concert ticket, hotel and airline industries.
- **Price skimming** – high prices are set when a new product is launched. Later the price is dropped to increase demand once the customers who are willing to pay more have been 'skimmed' off.
- **Loss leaders** – one product may be sold at a loss with the expectation that customers will then go on and buy other more profitable products.
- **Captive product pricing** – this is used where customers must buy two products. The first is cheap to attract customers but the second is expensive, once they are captive.

Test your understanding 3

Companies with high costs may find it difficult to compete on the basis of price and so in terms of sales and marketing they would be well advised to do which one of the following?

A Reduce product prices

B Develop brand loyalty amongst customers

C Employ high pressure sales techniques

D Develop new products to replace current products

Promotion

Promotion is essentially about market communication. The primary aim is to encourage customers to buy the products by moving them along the **AIDA** sequence:

Awareness ⌦ **Interest** ⌦ **Desire** ⌦ **Action**

Towards this organisations will use a combination of different promotional techniques as part of their 'promotional mix', including:

- Advertising – for example, placing adverts on the Internet, TV, in newspapers, on billboards, etc.
- Sales promotion techniques – for example, 'buy one get one free'.
- Personal selling – for example, telesales.
- Public relations (PR) – building good relationships and a good corporate image, for example, by sponsoring sports events.

Test your understanding 4

Requirement:

Identify the advantages and disadvantages of following methods of promotion:

(a) Advertising

(b) Sales promotion

(c) Personal selling

(d) Public relations

Advertising

There are two opposing views on advertising:

- Advertising is ineffective and a waste of money, only adding to company (and hence customer) costs. Brands such as Rolls Royce and Zara see little use in advertising relying instead on other sources of information to form positive attitudes towards their products, such as word of mouth and social media. (The group of companies including Zara, Bershka, Pull and Bear, Stradivarius, etc. spend far less on advertising than other fashion brands.) In any case some might think that advertising demeans a particular product or company. In some cases, advertising may seem unethical. Lancaster and Withey (2005) conclude that some brands may be strong enough to sell on their own merits only if they are long established and have strong brand-loyal users.
- Advertising is so powerful and effective as to be essential. Consumers, it could be argued, will rarely purchase unadvertised brands so by not advertising, a company will be at serious disadvantage compared to its competitors. The results of advertising campaigns which have been undeniably successful include those for brands such as Walkers Crisps and John Lewis.

Some **new forms** of marketing communication include:

Type of marketing communication	**Explanation**
Viral	Encourages individuals to pass on a marketing message to others, so creating exponential growth in the message's exposure in the same way computer viruses grow.
Guerrilla	Relies on well thought out, highly focused and often unconventional attacks on key targets. This form of marketing is often low cost and has allowed organisations with small promotional budgets to be very effective.
Experiential	An interactive marketing experience aimed at stimulating all the senses, for example road shows, street theatre, product trials. The next time the consumer sees the product, it should trigger a range of positive memories making it the first choice.
Digital	The promotion of products or brands via one or more forms of electronic media, for example using email, social media, the organisation's website or Google search.

Type of marketing communication	Explanation
Search engine marketing	A form of digital marketing that involves the promotion of an organisation's website by increasing its visibility in search engine results pages, such as Google.
Social media marketing	A form of digital marketing, social media marketing refers to the process of gaining traffic or attention through social media sites.
Postmodern marketing	A philosophical approach to marketing which focuses on giving the customer an experience that is customised to them and in ensuring they receive marketing messages in a form they prefer.

New forms of marketing communication

Viral marketing

Notable examples typically involve posting humorous or extraordinary videos on YouTube in the hope that those seeing the videos will post them on to friends so spreading the message - for example, John Lewis Christmas adverts, or videos showing the ball skills of Lionel Messi wearing a particular pair of football boots.

Guerrilla marketing

IKEA created a massive scaffolding cover that looked exactly like their iconic blue and yellow carrier bag, generating widespread social media attention.

Experiential marketing

Carlsberg unveiled a billboard in Brick Lane, London, named 'Probably the best poster in the world' that had an actual working tap attached to the centre where people could pour themselves a pint of beer.

Place

A key decision under 'place' is between:

- **Selling direct** – here the manufacturer sells directly to the ultimate consumer without using any intermediaries. For example, rather than booking a holiday through a travel agent, the internet has enabled customers to go directly to hotel websites or airline websites and book their accommodation and flights themselves.
- **Selling indirect** – here there is a longer supply chain. The channel strategy could comprise a mixture of retailer, distributors, wholesalers and shipping agents. For example, food distribution will often involve distributors and retailers to get the product from farmer to consumer. Using the example above, customers could use online travel websites (such as Expedia) to book their holidays from a range of options that the website has sourced from flight and hotel reservation systems.

Variations in marketing mix settings

Different companies put different emphasis on each of the four components of the marketing mix.

For example, some companies place all the focus on making a good quality product; other companies place the emphasis on making it at a cheap price or emphasise the promotion and advertising to sell it.

A manufacturer of desks might wish to sell to both the consumer market and the industrial market for office furniture. The marketing mix selected for the consumer market might be low prices with attractive dealer discounts, sales largely through discount warehouses, modern design but fairly low quality and sales promotion relying on advertising by the retail outlets, together with personal selling by the manufacturing firm to the reseller. For the industrial market, the firm might develop a durable, robust product that sells at a higher price; selling may be by means of direct mailshots, backed by personal visits from salespeople.

An interesting comparison can be made between different firms in the same industry; for example, Avon and Elizabeth Arden both sell cosmetics but, whereas Avon relies on personal selling in the consumer's own home, Elizabeth Arden relies on an extensive dealer network and heavy advertising expenditure. A notable update to this difference in strategy is that Avon filed for bankruptcy in August 2024.

2.4 The main techniques of marketing

The marketing strategy discussed in section 2.1 touched upon the following marketing techniques:

- market research (this includes data gathering techniques and methods of analysis)
- market segmentation
- market targeting and
- market positioning.

These will be explored in turn below.

Market research

Market research is the systematic **gathering**, recording and **analysing** of information about problems relating to the marketing of goods and services. These problems will all relate to what customers and potential customers want, need and care about.

Data **gathering** techniques can be divided into two main types:

Data gathering technique	Examples
Secondary (desk) research – this is data that is already available and is therefore usually quicker and cheaper than carrying out primary research. However, the data may not be accurate and may not meet the exact needs of the organisation.	• Internal sources – accounts information, production records, order information, organisational website information, loyalty card information etc. Often sourced using an organisation's database. • External sources – such as the internet, trade and technical journals, published statutory reports, market research agency data etc.
Primary (field) research – this involves the collection of new (primary) information direct from respondents. As such, it is usually more expensive than desk research and is only performed if desk research fails to answer the questions asked. The sample chosen should be representative of the population in question.	• Questionnaires – can be done online, face to face, over the telephone or by self-completion. • Interviews – focus on a small group of individuals. • Focus groups – a trained moderator leads group discussion, such as feedback on a new product. Can be online or face to face. • Trial testing – for example, out of three chocolate bars which would you choose? • Observation – for example, use cameras to determine on average how long it takes to serve customers in a restaurant.

The data gathering techniques discussed above will be used to collect two main types of data:

- **Quantitative** (i.e. numerical) data – such as the total market size, market share percentage, segment information such as age and gender, location of existing/potential customers etc.
- **Qualitative** (i.e. non-numerical) data – such as the values and beliefs of existing/potential customers, trends in consumer preferences, growth opportunities for products sold etc.

e.g

Illustration 2 – Technology used in market research

Technology has had a significant impact on market research in both positive and, potentially, not so positive ways.

The **positive** includes:

- The ability to access a wide range of secondary research (research conducted by others) online.
- The ability to conduct qualitative research activities such as sentiment analysis (positive, negative or neutral emotions) and consumer perception analysis (asking customers what they think about a product or service, not just their emotionally reaction) through social media monitoring.
- Organisations can now also conduct focus groups online through technology allowing us to interact with people across wide geographic boundaries.
- Business insight can be gained faster and more comprehensively than before.

However, the use of technology for market research is not without its **disadvantages**. For example, online research can give the false impression that it is as statistically reliable as traditional research. It may or may not be. Organisations need to understand how to tell what is, and isn't, reliable or valid.

The data gathered will be recorded and then **analysed** to provide insights that will help to achieve the goals of the research. Large quantities of data must be summarised and presented in such a way that clearly communicates the most important features and conclusions.

The organisation may use an automated platform tailored to the specific needs of the organisation to do this. This technology will enable the organisation to filter, sort, highlight and present data visually (for example, using pie charts or bar charts).

Illustration 3 – Market research and analysis techniques for websites and apps

Market research and data analysis technology can be used to improve the performance of an organisation's website or app helping to track the behaviour of individual users, gather insights, test new ideas and tie the activities back to revenue.

Some examples of tools used include:

- Click analysis – tracks the actions of individual users within the website or app. For example, an e-commerce site may monitor items added to a shopping cart by visitors or a new app that relies on advertising revenue may monitor view time and clicks.
- Visual behaviour tools – reveal where users spend time looking at a screen (for example, using the number of taps and swipes on a mobile). Data may be presented as a heat map that highlights the most heavily trafficked or clicked areas.
- Search engine optimisation (SEO) tools – help the organisation understand how likely their site and content are to show up in online search results.
- Dashboard tools – consolidate market research into one interface so that the data can be quickly manipulated to gain insight.

Market segmentation

Market segmentation is the sub-dividing of the market into homogenous groups to whom a separate marketing mix can be focused.

A market segment is a group of consumers with distinct, shared needs.

Why segment the market?

- The key objective is to say that people falling into a particular segment are more likely to purchase the product than most.
- The company will choose a particular segment or segments to target. The total marketing budget can be split based on the likely return from each segment.
- The organisation may be able to identify new market opportunities or can try to dominate a particular segment because it will have a better understanding of customers' needs in each segment.

Kotler suggested that segments must meet **three criteria**. They should be:

- **Measurable** – it must be possible to identify the number of buyers in each market segment so that their potential profitability can be assessed. For example, the size of the segment of people aged 30–40, or who are married with children, can be accurately calculated but information about the number of people who are environmentally conscious is less readily available.

- **Accessible** – it must be possible to reach potential customers via the organisation's promotion and distribution channels. For example, some potential customers may be inaccessible if they are tied to other suppliers by long-term supply contracts.
- **Substantial** – small market segments may prove unprofitable to target.

There are several **different bases for segmentation**. Possible bases include:

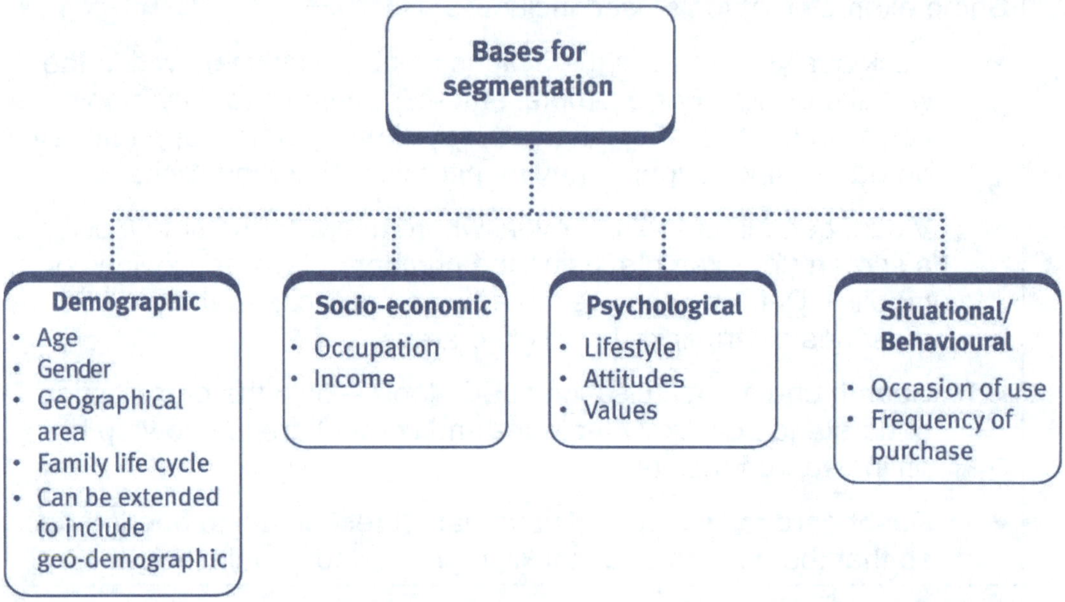

Bases for segmentation

Demographic

Market segments are frequently based on age, gender, geographical location or family life cycle.

This can be highly relevant with some products, for example, certain brands of breakfast cereal have regular sales to families with young children (for example, Coco Pops), whereas other brands (for example, Bran Flakes) sell almost entirely to adults.

In other areas, demographic influences seem to have little effect. For instance, own-label products are believed to sell equally to high and low income families and single people and across all age groups.

Family life cycle segmentation divides customers by their position in the family life cycle:

Life cycle stage	Characteristics	Examples of products purchased
Young, single individual	Financially well off. Fashion opinion leaders. Recreation orientated.	Cars, holidays, basic furniture, kitchen equipment.
A couple with no children	Still financially well off. Very high purchase rate, especially of durables.	Cars, furniture, houses, holidays, refrigerators.
A couple or individual with a very young child/children	Liquid assets (cash) low. Home buying at a peak.	Kitchen appliances, baby foods, toys, medicines.
A couple or individual with an older child/children	Better off. Some partners work. Some children work part time. Less influenced by advertising.	Larger size grocery packs, foods, cleaning materials, bicycles.
A couple or individual with a child/children almost old enough to leave home	Better off still. Purchasing durables.	New furniture, luxury appliances, recreational goods.
A couple or individual with a child/children who have left home	Satisfied with financial position.	Travel, luxuries, home improvements.
An ageing individual or couple who are not working	Drastic cut in income. Stay at home.	Medicines, health aids.

Geo-demographic segmentation combines demographic and geographic variables. This is a recent, but powerful, development in which geographical segmentation is undertaken at a much more localised level and linked to other demographic factors.

Socio-economic

One of the widely used forms of segmentation is socio-economic. While such class-based systems may seem out of date, the model is still widely used, especially in advertising. Socio-economic class is closely correlated with press readership and viewing habits, and media planners use this fact to advertise in the most effective way to communicate with their target audience.

Psychological

Lifestyle segmentation may be used because people of similar age and socio-economic status may lead quite different lifestyles. Marketers have segmented the market using terms such as 'Dinkies' (double income, no kids).

Attitudes and values can be harder to measure but can prove to be a useful basis for segmentation. For example, individuals may have a value based on caution and therefore purchase a safe, reliable car.

Situational (or behavioural)

Occasion of use – a product may be bought at different times for different uses. For example, workers may expect a lunchtime meal in a restaurant to be fast and good value for money, whereas those same individuals may be willing to pay more in the evening for a more relaxed dining experience.

Frequency of purchase – frequent buyers may be more demanding with regards to product features and may be more sensitive to price changes.

Test your understanding 5

Requirement:

Explain five variables that you think would be useful as a basis for segmenting the market for cars.

Targeting

Targeting is the process of selecting the most lucrative market segment(s) for marketing the product.

Having segmented the market, the organisation can now decide how to respond to the differences in customer needs identified and will reach a conclusion as to which segments are worth targeting.

The organisation may choose several different approaches. For example, the market for package holidays can be split into a variety of different segments – the family market, the elderly market, the young singles market, the activity holiday market, the budget holiday market, etc.

It would be virtually impossible to provide one single holiday package that would satisfy all people in the above markets. Because the people in the different segments will have different needs and wants, a holiday company has a choice in terms of its marketing approach. It can go for:

- **Concentrated marketing** (sometimes referred to as niche or target marketing) specialising in one of the identified markets only, where a company knows it can compete successfully. For example, Saga holidays offer a variety of holidays for the older market niche only.

- **Differentiated marketing** (sometimes called segmented marketing) where the company makes several products each aimed at a separate target segment. For example, Virgin Holidays offers a variety of family holidays, honeymoon packages and city breaks, each of which is targeted at a different group. Many retailers have developed different brand formats to target different groups.
- **Undifferentiated marketing** (sometimes called mass marketing) where there is the delivery of a single product to the entire market. There is little concern for segmentation. The hope is that as many customers as possible will buy the product. When Henry Ford began manufacturing cars he offered any colour 'as long as it's black'.

Positioning

Positioning involves the formulation of a definitive marketing strategy around which the product would be marketed to the target audience.

After the target market has been chosen, marketers will want to position their products in relation to the competitors for that segment. A variety of techniques are available.

For example, Porter identified four positioning strategies:

	Low cost	**High cost**
Broad target	**Cost leadership** – the organisation aims to be the lowest cost producer in the industry.	**Differentiation** – the organisation produces products which are different and appeal to customers on the grounds of, say, quality or design.
Narrow target	**Cost focus** – the pursuit of a cost leadership strategy but focused on one particular segment only	**Differentiation focus** – the pursuit of a differentiation strategy but focused on one particular segment only

Test your understanding 6

Undifferentiated marketing involves an organisation in offering:

A products based on market research

B a single product to the market as a whole

C multiple products to the market as a whole

D single products to segmented markets

Test your understanding 7

Segmentation involves identifying target markets that must be:

A measurable, accessible and substantial

B acceptable, feasible and suitable

C undeveloped, undiscovered and undifferentiated

D aligned to core competences

Test your understanding 8

Which of the following phrases explains concentrated marketing?

A The company produces one product for a number of different market segments

B The company introduces several versions of the product aimed at several market segments

C The company produces one product for a mass market

D The company produces one product for a one segment of the marketplace

3 Areas of interface between sales and marketing and finance

3.1 Introduction

The way in which finance interacts with sales and marketing will be explored in greater depth below. However, it is useful to begin by thinking about some basic ways in which the two areas interact:

Budgeting	Finance will discuss the likely sales volume of each product with the sales and marketing, to produce the sales budget.
Advertising	Finance will help sales and marketing in setting a budget, and in monitoring whether it is cost effective. For example, they could help in measuring new business generated as a result of different advertising campaigns.

Pricing	Finance will have input into the price that is charged. Often products are priced at cost plus a percentage. Even if sales and marketing determine the price based on market forces they need to consult with finance to ensure that costs are covered.
Market share	Finance can provide marketing with information on sales volumes for each product, to help the marketing department in determining market share.
KPIs	Finance will establish and monitor the KPIs for the sales and marketing function.

3.2 How the finance function interacts with sales and marketing

Introduction

- Finance and sales and marketing should interact to achieve organisational goals and their own individual functional goals.
- Traditionally, there may have been antagonism between the two functions over issues such as pricing and cost control.
- The modern approach is for the two functions to **collaborate** and to work in partnership.
- Effective interaction will be based on close working teams which possess a shared vision for the organisation and an appreciation of each other's specialisms.
- Technology is assisting this collaboration using tools such as cloud computing, data analytics and blockchain.

The finance function has a unique end to end view of the organisation and is considered a trusted advisor. As a result, there are several areas where the CFO (and their team) has an opportunity to enhance performance through business partnering with the sales and marketing. Two of these areas will be explored below:

- product/service development
- product/service life-cycles and costing

Product/service development

Organisations need to continually look for new or improved products or services, to achieve or maintain competitive advantage in their market.

The stages of product/service development are as follows:

Test your understanding 9

M Ltd are in the process of designing a new product to fit with the rapidly changing environment.

Which THREE of the following are activities that M may undertake during the first three stages of product development?

A Interviewing customers to determine what they want

B Analysing social media to gain an insight into customer tastes

C Testing the product to ensure it is durable

D Using computer aided design (CAD) to build a prototype

E Ensuring the product is released ahead of the competition

Given the rapidly changing nature of the modern consumer's preferences and expectations, this initial process of development can make or break an organisation. The finance function will work collaboratively with the sales and marketing function to evaluate new product/service lines or innovations. They have a sharp eye for the economic upside (or otherwise!) of a product/service.

Product/service life-cycles and costing

After product/service development most products/services go through several stages in their existence:

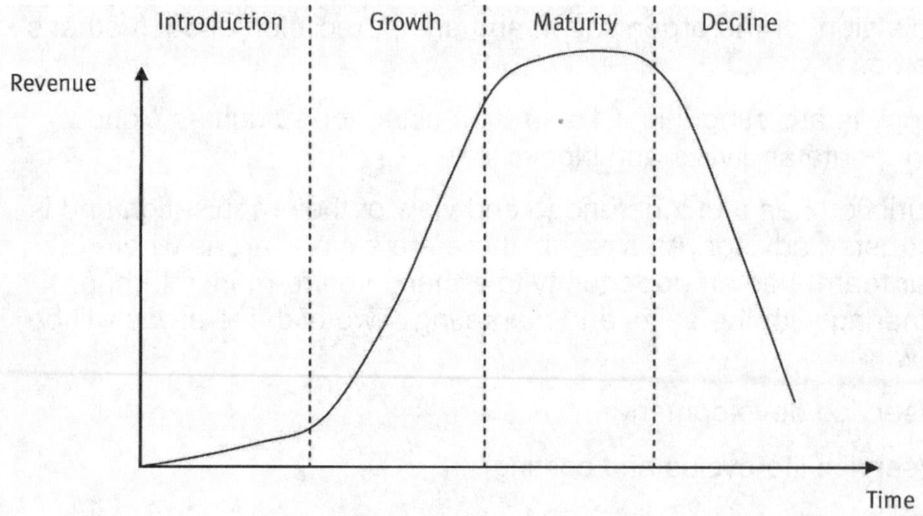

- **Stage 1: Introduction** – A small number of individuals will be prepared to pay a high price for a new, innovative product/service, for example, the latest mobile phone model. Revenues will be low and expenditure (including marketing costs) high.
- **Stage 2: Growth** – Revenue and profit grow as production and interest in the product/service increases. The firm will seek to differentiate its product/service and brand. Purchase costs and prices may fall due to economies of scale and increased competitive pressure. Investment costs will still be high.

- **Stage 3: Maturity** – This is usually the longest and most successful stage of the life cycle. Costs settle down into a pattern of repeat or replacement costs. Growth slows or halts as product consumption finally peaks. The price may be cut to attract a new group of customers.
- **Stage 4: Decline** – Few people will purchase the product/service at the end of the life cycle as superior alternatives replace it and promotional activity will drop. The firm will look to exit the market and find profitable alternatives.

The finance function will interact with the sales and marketing function in two main ways:

- **Life-cycle costing** – this considers the costs and revenues of a product/service over its whole life (including product/service development) rather than one accounting period. Therefore, the full cost incurred prior to, during and after production will be considered to ensure that the costs can be covered and/or any possible steps are taken to reduce the costs.
- **Balanced portfolio** – products/services at different stages in the lifecycle have different implications for resource requirements, risk and strategy. This would emphasise the importance of the finance function's involvement in portfolio management, helping to inform decisions about the organisation's overall product/service offering.

  For example, having too many products/services in the development stages will put a strain on finances as they will all require significant investment in marketing. On the other hand, if all products/services are at the maturity stage, then there may be a question over the organisation's long-term future – how long will it be before they move into the decline phase?

  An appropriate balance of existing products/services in a mature market, together with investment in new products in the introduction and growth stages is best.

Test your understanding 10

Are the following statements about the product life-cycle true or false?

Statement	True/False?
Economies of scale will be greatest during the introduction stage	
The growth stage is the longest stage	
Prices tend to increase during the maturity stage as this is when demand is highest and therefore, revenue can be maximised	
Product costs tend to be lowest during the later stages of the lifecycle	
All businesses will have a product at each stage of the lifecycle	

e.g

Illustration 4 – The use of technology in the life-cycle

Blockchain offers the prospect of designing a data structure from the perspective of the product; meaning that in a single chain all vital data about that product over its whole life-cycle can be captured. An accurate record of, say, inventory levels, costs and revenue is available by examining the current state of the block.

The internet of things (IoT) connects devices over the internet. Its applications can be used in the life-cycle in several ways:

- Maintenance and service – sensors can provide data on products for servicing purposes. This should help optimise future service schedules and reduce maintenance costs.
- Requirements management – providing visibility into how customers are using products. Knowing that some product functions are not in use and injecting this information in product modifications and future requirement analysis is of huge advantage.
- Product performance monitoring – providing real performance data from, say, the engine and other parts of a car, airplane, computer or even a toothbrush. This data helps inform future decisions.

3.3 Big data analytics in marketing

Introduction

Big data and data analytics have been discussed in detail in Chapters 5–8.

e.g

Illustration 5 – Big data analytics

An organisation and its sales and marketing function face several challenges when using its big data. For example, a lack of insight for targeted campaigns or an inability to support data growth.

Value is extracted from big data by the process of data analytics.

For example, **Google Analytics** tracks many features of website traffic.

Hadoop software allows the processing of large data sets by utilising multiple servers simultaneously. It enables instant analysis of social sentiment and customer feedback across digital, face-to-face and phone interactions.

The result should be a reduced time to obtain customer insight, an ability to make changes to campaigns or adjust product roll outs based on real-time customer reactions and an ability to offer incentives and new services to retail and grow its customer base.

Unlocking the potential value of big data using real-time data analytics and its significance to an organisation's sales and marketing function presents a huge opportunity to gain unique insight which can be used to improve competitive position and potentially gain competitive advantage over rivals. The finance function will work collaboratively with the sales and marketing function to provide this insight.

Examples of big data analytics in marketing

- **Market segmentation and customisation** – The volume and variety within big data enables organisations to create highly specific segments within its markets and to tailor its products and services precisely to meet those needs in real-time.

e.g **Illustration 6**

Biscuit manufacturer, Oreo

Many marketers consider Oreo's famous 'You can still dunk in the dark' marketing campaign during Super Bowl in New Orleans to be a landmark event in real-time marketing. During the third quarter of the game, the Superdome experienced a partial power outage, darkening the stadium and suspending play for 34 minutes. During this time, Oreo cleverly took advantage of the situation and tweeted its message out to thousands of loyal followers, receiving over 10,000 re-tweets and 20,000 likes on Facebook.

- **Product/service development** – Organisations can use data on customer behaviour and social trends to create new products/services to meet customers' needs or to enhance existing products/services so that they meet these needs more exactly.

e.g **Illustration 7**

Motor insurance

The availability of real-time location data, from satellite sensors, Black Box telematics and satellite navigation systems, can enable motor insurance companies to refine the pricing of their insurance policies according to where, and how, people drive their cars.

Health and life insurance

Health and life insurance company, Vitality, is offering its customers the opportunity to link their activity tracking device or app to their online Vitality profile. Points are earned for completing eligible activities such as a target number of steps, a gym visit or a park run. Customers can then redeem their points for treats such as Starbucks coffee or cinema visits.

- **Decision making** – The sophisticated analytics tools can also be used to improve decision making. For example, a retailer may use algorithms to optimise decisions about inventory levels and pricing (i.e. dynamic pricing) in response to current and predicted sales. Real-time data visualisation technologies (for example, dashboards) allow managers to adjust tactics based on, for example, live sales or inventory data.

e.g

Illustration 8

Dynamic pricing in action

The chances are that you've already seen dynamic pricing in action, even if you haven't realised you're being specifically targeted in this way. Perhaps you've viewed a flight or a holiday several times on a website but when you finally return to book it the price has jumped.

In 2024 the music band – Oasis, hit the news headlines when Ticketmaster used dynamic pricing to charge concert goers £355 for a ticket originally advertised for £148.

This kind of dynamic pricing is the result of ever increasing quantities of data giving retailers and service providers more insights into their own supply and customer desires than ever before. They can increase the price when demand rises or supply falls, or they can fill those last seats and sell out a service by dropping the price as the deadline comes closer. Some retailers can even work out how likely you are to make a purchase and either drop the price to give you an extra incentive to buy or hike it because they know you're ready to pay.

- **Obtaining customer feedback** – Organisations now have access to huge amounts of customer feedback in real or almost real time. For example, identifying what customers are saying in social media about an organisation's products or its customer service could help the organisation identify potential changes that may be needed.

Test your understanding 11

Using the options below, complete the following statements concerning big data analytics in marketing:

Tailoring products and services precisely to meet customers' needs in real-time is known as ____________________.

Using algorithms to optimise decisions such as those about pricing is known as ____________________ pricing.

What a consumer is saying about the product on social media can be a useful way of obtaining ____________________.

Options to choose from:

- Hadoop
- Criticism
- Feedback
- Dynamic
- Static
- Customisation
- Analytics

4 Key performance indicators (KPIs)

4.1 Introduction

In section 6 of Chapter 9 we:

- defined KPIs
- discussed their use in managing the operations function
- identified relevant KPIs for operations
- discussed how the finance function manages operations using KPIs and
- discussed the impact of technology in this area.

Much of this discussion can also be applied to the sales and marketing function.

In this section we will briefly discuss how the finance function helps to manage the sales and marketing function using KPIs before identifying some relevant KPIs for sales and marketing.

4.2 How finance helps to manage sales and marketing using KPIs

- The sales and marketing function will identify its relevant CSFs (i.e. the vital areas where things must go right for the function for them to achieve their strategic objectives).
- The KPIs are the measures that indicate whether the sales and marketing function is achieving these CSFs. KPIs are essential to the achievement of these objectives since 'what gets measured gets done', i.e. the things that are measured get done more often than the things that are not measured.
- The finance function works with the sales and marketing function to:
  - **identify** appropriate KPIs
  - **assemble** KPI data and information
  - **analyse** this for insight
  - give **advice** to the sales and marketing function based on this insight and

  - **apply** what has been learned to impact the achievement of the objectives of the sales and marketing function and the organisation as a whole.

- **Technology** will act as a key enabler in this, particularly in the 'assembly' and 'analysis' tasks.

e.g

Illustration 9 – KPI dashboards

One of the most common technologies used in this area is performance dashboards. The dashboard displays the KPIs of the sales and marketing function in a live format, thus allowing immediate understanding of current performance and potentially prompting action to correct or amend performance accordingly.

The dashboards assist with data visualisation. The simple and visually appealing layout can be understood by non-technical users. With just a few clicks interactive and versatile views can be built, providing, at a glance, relevant information and insights for different users.

This will 'free up' the resource of the finance function who can now spend more time on the 'advising' and 'applying' activities – a shift that makes better use of their skills and expertise.

Note: It would be useful to spend a few minutes looking at examples of sales and marketing dashboard images on the internet.

4.3 Examples of KPIs for sales and marketing

Example activity	Possible KPI
Overall sales and marketing activity	Growth in sales volume/revenue Market share Gross margins Customer retention rate Cost of customer acquisition Marketing spend per customer Customer lifetime value
Promotion	Promotion cost Awareness levels Website traffic to conversion rate % Social media reach (for example, Twitter followers) Email marketing performance (for example, unsubscribe rate) Sales team response times

Example activity	Possible KPI
Product/service	Product development time/cost Product life-cycle costs Repurchase rate Brand value Warranty claims
Pricing	Price relative to industry average Price elasticity of demand
Place	Transport costs Storage costs

It is important to note that the above is a generic list of KPIs for the sales and marketing function and that the function must identify the most appropriate KPIs for measuring the achievement of its CSFs. For example, one of the function's CSFs may to 'produce quality products'. The achievement of this CSF could be measured using several KPIs, for example 'warranty claims' (the number and value).These KPIs should be SMART.

Test your understanding 12

Match the following KPIs to the element of the marketing mix that it could measure.

A Brand value

B Packaging cost

C Lead times

D Price elasticity of demand

E Social media activity

F Number of 'clicks to buy'

Choose from the following options:

1 Product

2 Price

3 Place

4 Promotion

5 Chapter summary

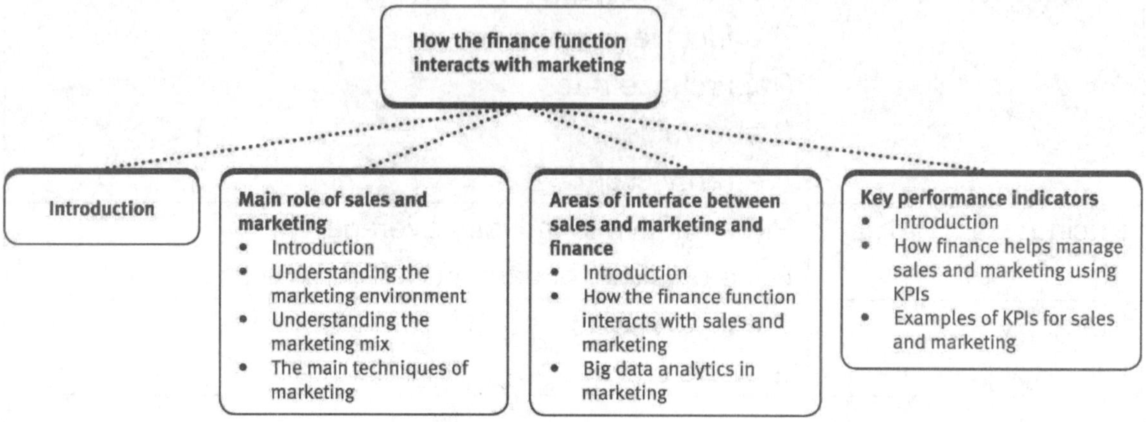

Test your understanding answers

Test your understanding 1

The correct answer is **C**

The key focus of marketing is customer needs.

Test your understanding 2

The changing needs of the population must be reflected in the product offerings. For example:

- The supermarket may reduce its range of luxury items in favour of lower priced, basic products.
- Special offers may be made on products, for example, discounts, buy one get one free offers, additional loyalty points on products.
- The supermarket may introduce more 'restaurant style' meals to reflect the trend that fewer people are eating out.

Test your understanding 3

The correct answer is **B**

The key focus of successful marketing is customer needs and therefore developing brand loyalty amongst customers would assist in this.

Test your understanding 4

Method	**Advantages**	**Disadvantages**
(a) Advertising	• Reach a large number of potential customers. • Low cost for each potential customer.	• Total cost can be very high. • Difficult to evaluate effectiveness.
(b) Sales promotion	• Can help gain new users. • Counteract competition. • Clear out surplus stock.	• Can be costly. • May not win customer loyalty.

Method	Advantages	Disadvantages
(c) Personal selling	• Can focus on needs of individual customer. • A talented salesperson can be very persuasive.	• Can be seen as pushy. • High cost per potential customer.
(d) Public relations	• Low or no cost. • Can be targeted. • Unbiased opinion.	• Negative review may damage reputation.

Test your understanding 5

Age

The age of the consumer will be of upmost importance. Teenage drivers may prefer a cheaper model, whereas drivers in their 20s, with more disposable income, may prefer a more expensive and stylish model.

Lifestyle

There may be a number of different lifestyles that could be targeted. Each group will have quite different needs. For example, a leisure user may be more interested in the style and design of the car whereas a commuter may want a safe, reliable car.

Income

The level of income will impact the make and the model that the user can afford and any optional extras that may be purchased.

Family life cycle

The life cycle stage will be important. For example, bachelors may prefer a higher priced, sporty, stylish model whereas those with a young and growing family may prefer a safe, reliable and family orientated people carrier.

Gender

It may be useful to segment the market based on gender. Females may be more inclined than males to purchase a car that is smaller, is available in bright colours and comes with fashionable accessories. Males, on the other hand, may be more inclined to purchase a more masculine looking and powerful car.

Test your understanding 6

The correct answer is **B**

Test your understanding 7

The correct answer is **A**

Test your understanding 8

The correct answer is **D**

Test your understanding 9

The correct answers are A, B and D

The first three stages are:

1 Consider customer's needs,

2 Concept screening, and

3 Design process

Interviewing customers and analysing social media will help to understand the customer's needs. Building a prototype is part of the design process.

The final two stages are:

1 Time to market and

2 Product testing

Test your understanding 10

Statement	**True/False?**
Economies of scale will be greatest during the introduction stage	False, economies of scale are greatest when higher volumes of the product are sold.
The growth stage is the longest stage	False, each stage can vary in length. However, it is the maturity stage that tends to be the longest.
Prices tend to increase during the maturity stage as this is when demand is highest and therefore, revenue can be maximised	False, prices tend to decrease during the maturity stage, partially in order to attract new customers to prolong the maturity phase.

Statement	True/False?
Product costs tend to be lowest during the later stages of the lifecycle	True
All businesses will have a product at each stage of the life-cycle	False, whilst a business may aim to have balanced portfolio, there is no guarantee that they will have products at each stage.

Test your understanding 11

Tailoring products and services precisely to meet customers' needs in real-time is known as **customisation**.

Using algorithms to optimise decisions such as those about pricing is known as **dynamic** pricing.

What a consumer is saying about the product on social media can be a useful way of obtaining **feedback**.

Test your understanding 12

A Brand value – **product**

B Packaging cost – **product**

C Lead times – **place**

D Price elasticity of demand – **price**

E Social media activity – **promotion**

F Number of 'clicks to buy' – **promotion**

Chapter

11

How the finance function interacts with human resources

Chapter learning objectives

Lead	Component
E3: Describe how the finance function interacts with human resources.	Describe: (a) Main role of human resources (b) Areas of interface with finance (c) Key performance indicators

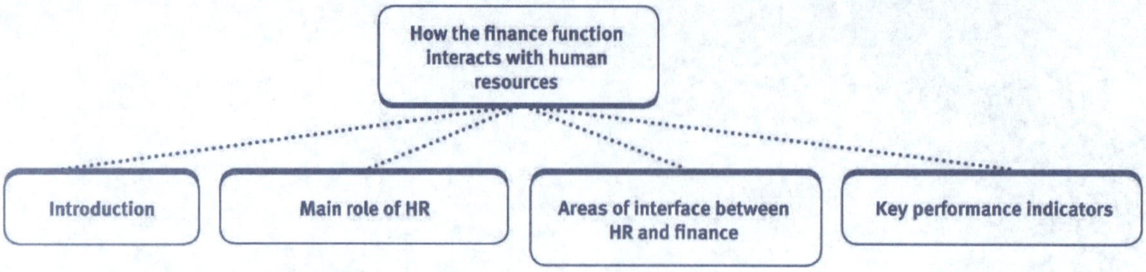

1 Introduction

In this chapter we will continue to describe how the finance function plays its role by interacting with the rest of the organisation (syllabus area E) and, more specifically here, the organisation's human resources (HR) function.

We will begin by discussing the main role of the HR function; understanding the different HR activities that exist. An effective HR function will view employees as a hugely valuable resource within the organisation and as a potential source of competitive advantage.

We will then discuss the areas of interface with finance before moving on to the final part of the chapter which will discuss how the finance function helps to manage the HR function using key performance indicators (KPIs).

2 Main role of HR

2.1 Introduction

The HR function is responsible for the management and development of human resources within the organisation. Their role includes the creation, development and maintenance of an effective workforce, matching the requirements of the organisation to the environment and responding to that environment.

Note: HR management and development is a responsibility shared between the HR function and line managers in charge of employees' day-to-day work. The degree of centralisation and size and power of the HR function will vary from organisation to organisation.

The HR plan

The HR plan is a strategy developed in the context of the organisation's overall strategic plan.

A typical plan will look forward 3-5 years and aims to identify and close the gap between the demand for labour and the supply of labour within the organisation.

Test your understanding 1
Requirement: **How can an organisation plan rationally in an unstable environment?**

Stages of HR planning

Stage 1: Strategic analysis

- The organisation's strategic objectives will have implications regarding the number of employees and the skills required over the planning period (e.g. development of a new product or expansion into a new market)
- The broader strategic environment should also be considered (e.g. trends in population growth, pensions, education and employment rights of women)

Stage 2: Internal analysis

- An 'audit' of existing staff should be carried out to establish the current numbers and skills
- Also consider:
  - Turnover of staff and absenteeism
  - Overtime worked and periods of inactivity
  - Staff potential

Stage 3: Identify the gap between supply and demand

- Shortages or excesses in labour numbers and skills deficiencies should be identified

Stage 4: Put plans into place to close the gap

Adjustments for shortfall

- Internal: Transfers, promotions, training, job enlargement, overtime, reduce labour turnover
- External: Fill remaining needs externally. Consider suitability and availability of external resource

Adjustments for a surplus

Consider use of natural wastage, recruitment freeze, retirement, part time working and redundancy

Stage 5: Review

Measure the effective use of the human resource and their contribution towards the achievement of the organisation's objectives

Test your understanding 2

The economic situation in a country (or specific area of a country) may have a marked effect on the ability of an organisation to attract suitable candidates.

Is this statement:

A True?

B False?

The HR cycle

A common approach to viewing the different HR activities is as a cycle:

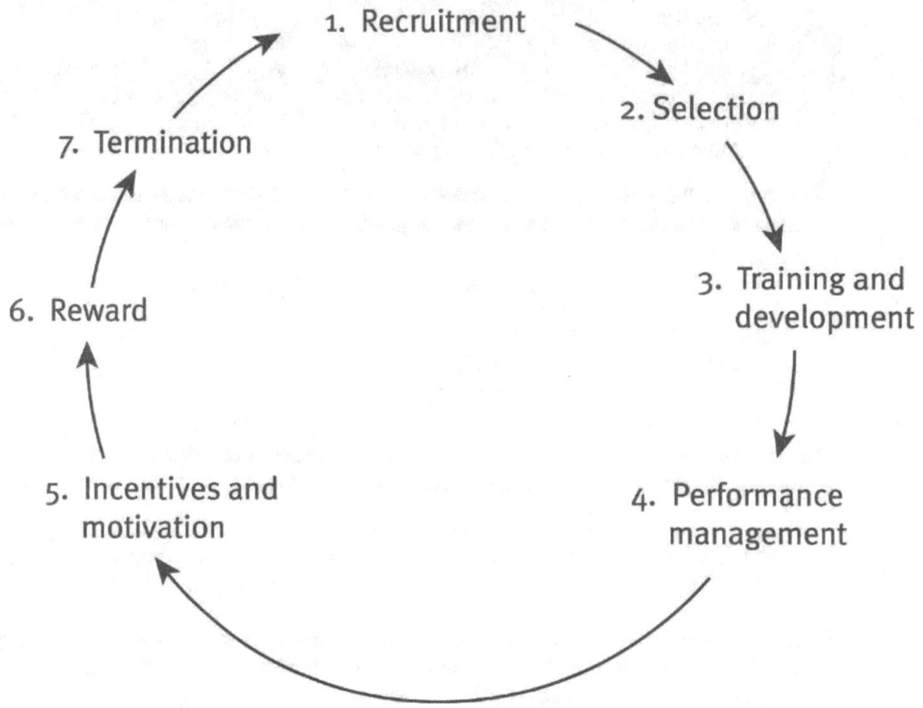

The first six of these activities will be discussed below.

2.2 Recruitment

Recruitment involves attracting a field of suitable candidates for the job.

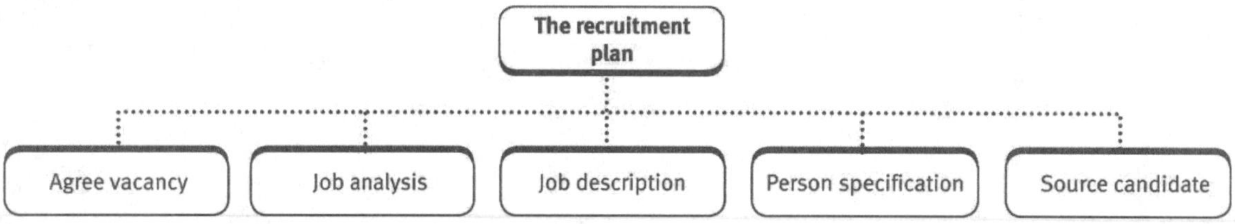

The best recruitment campaign will attract a small number of highly suitable applicants, be cost effective, be speedy and show courtesy to all candidates.

Illustration 1 – Recruitment in a downturn

In periods of economic recession, recruitment would appear to be less important, as large numbers of people will be looking for employment, meaning a field of candidates should be easy to attract.

However, even in times of high unemployment, organisations must ensure they only hire the correct people with the skills and abilities that they need. This can become more difficult when there are larger numbers of applicants.

Assessing the need to recruit

When considering recruitment, there are two questions that managers must address. The first is whether there is really a job, and the second is whether there is someone suitable who is already employed by the organisation. There are many alternatives to recruitment, for example:

- Promotion of existing staff (upwards or laterally)
- Secondment (temporary transfers to another department, office or country) of existing staff, which may or may not become permanent
- Closing the job down, by sharing out duties and responsibilities among existing staff
- Rotating jobs among staff, so that the vacant job is covered by different staff, on a systematic basis over several months
- Putting the job out to tender, using external contractors.

Agree vacancy – A vacancy may arise due to growth in the organisation, a change of direction or because an employee leaves the organisation.

Job analysis – This is the detailed study and description of the tasks that make up the job.

Job description – After a full job analysis has been carried out, a job description can be drawn up.

A job description is a broad statement of the purpose, scope duties and responsibilities of the job.

A typical job description will tend to include:

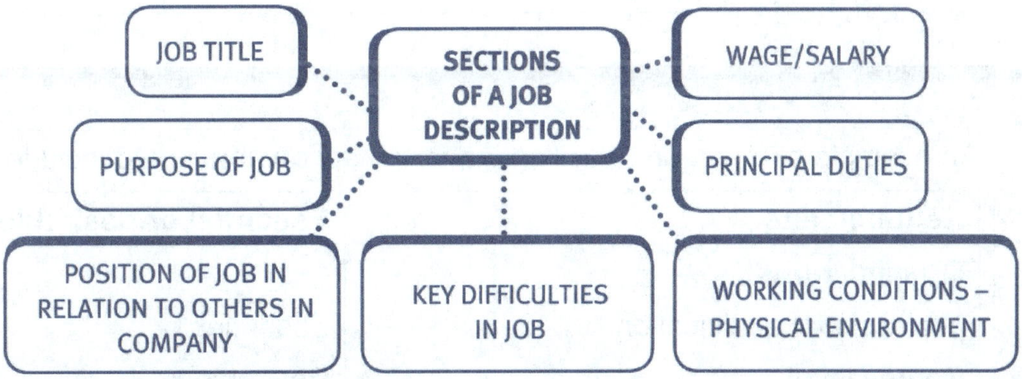

Test your understanding 3

Requirement:

Prepare a job description for a London based role as a Finance Director in an internet media company which is about to become a public company.

Person specification – Once management have a job description, they can attempt to define the key attributes and qualities that the jobholder should ideally have. Prospective candidates can then be compared to this specification as part of the selection process.

Alec Rodgers devised a seven-point plan which suggests the content of a person specification. You can remember this using the acronym **BADPIGS**.

Category	**Example**
B – Background/ circumstances	Details of previous work experience and circumstances – for example, criminal record or flexible working requirements.
A – Attainments	Details of qualifications and any relevant experience.
D – Disposition	The individual's nature (for example, can work calmly under pressure) and goals (for example, future ambitions).
P – Physical make-up	Personal appearance and level of health.
I – Interests	General interests and hobbies will be important. For example, being a member of a football team demonstrates teamwork skills.
G – General intelligence	Not necessarily academic qualifications but may refer to practical intelligence such as problem solving ability or whether the candidate is of average intelligence (or otherwise).
S – Special attributes	Skills such as the ability to speak another language or IT skills.

e.g

Illustration 2 – Person specification for an accountant

An example of a person specification for an accountant could include:

Requirement	**Essential or desirable?**
Qualifications	
Professional qualification	Essential
Degree level	Desirable
Experience	
Experience of working in a similar role	Essential
Experience of dealing with clients	Desirable

Requirement	Essential or desirable?
Skills and competencies	
Excellent communication skills	Essential
Ability to present complex information	Essential
Excellent numerical skills	Essential
Team player	Desirable
Ability to work flexibly	Desirable
Personal attributes	
Self-motivated	Essential
Able to use own initiative	Essential
Attention to detail	Essential
Prepared to learn new skills	Desirable
Other	
Ability to use Microsoft Word and Sage	Essential
Willing to participate in client meetings	Essential

Test your understanding 4

The purpose of a person specification is to provide details of which one of the following?

A Organisational size and diversity of activity

B The types of responsibilities and duties to be undertaken by the post holder

C Personal characteristics, experience and qualifications expected of a candidate

D Individual terms of engagement and period of contract

Test your understanding 5

Requirement:

Are there any circumstances when discrimination on the basis of physical make-up is acceptable?

Source candidates – this stage involves persuading relevant candidates to apply for the role the organisation wishes to fill.

The following methods may be used to contact and secure the application of appropriate candidates:

- internal sourcing
- internet and social media
- recruitment consultants
- newspaper and specialist journal advertising
- radio and television advertising
- job centres
- job fairs.

Illustration 3

Care must be taken not to transgress one of the laws relating to discrimination, as in the case of a job advertisement seeking 'a female Scottish cook and housekeeper', which was barred both on the grounds of race and sex discrimination.

2.3 Selection

Selection is aimed at choosing the best person for the job from the field of candidates sourced via recruitment.

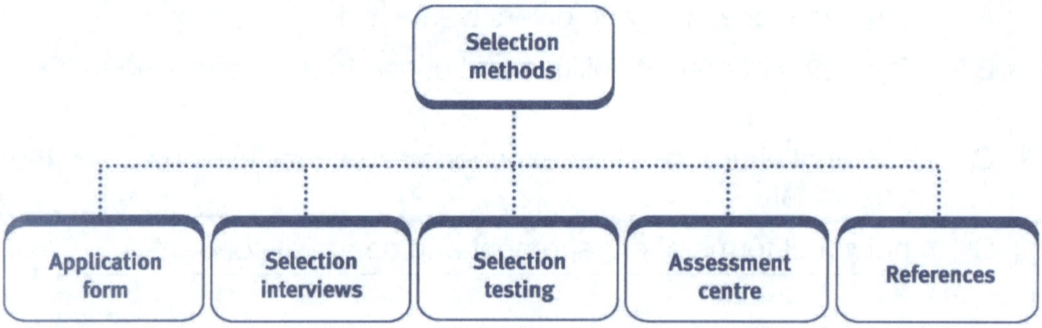

Application form

Application forms are used to obtain relevant information about the applicant and allow for comparison with the person specification of the job.

They should also give the applicants some ability to express themselves beyond the limited factual remit of the form.

A Curriculum Vitae (CV) or resume may be requested alongside the application form. This details the individual's unique skills, character, experience and achievements.

Selection interviews

Once the least appropriate candidates have been rejected using their application forms, the remaining applicants can be interviewed.

The purpose of an interview is to:

- find the best person for the job
- ensure that the candidate understands what the job involves and what the career prospects are
- make the candidate feel that they have been treated fairly in the selection process.

There are various types of interview that an organisation may use, including:

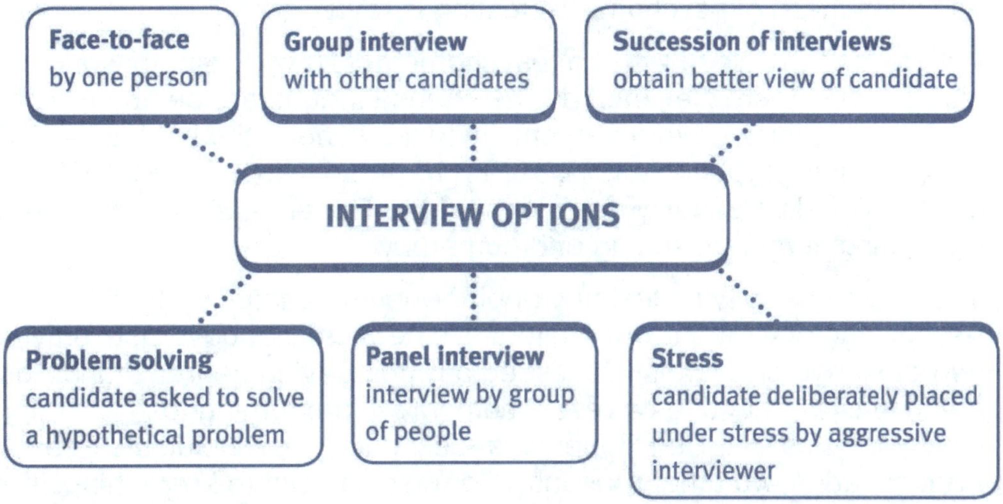

Test your understanding 6
Requirements: **(a) What are the key advantages and disadvantages of interviews as a way of selecting candidates?** **(b) For each of the interview options, identify one advantage and one disadvantage.**

Test your understanding 7
A has been asked to attend a job interview. He will be interviewed by the Finance Director first, followed by the HR Director. **What type of interview is A going to experience?** A Group B Panel C Stress D Succession

Selection testing

Testing can be undertaken either before or after the interview has taken place. The two basic types of test are:

- **Proficiency and attainment** – these are used to examine the applicant's competences, skills and abilities in areas that will be required in the job they have applied for.
- **Psychometric** – these are more general and test psychological factors, such as aptitude, intelligence and personality.

Psychometric testing

In the following extracts from an article by Bryan Appleyard the growth and usefulness of psychometric testing is reviewed:

Welcome to the weird world of psychometrics. If you want to work for a big company there's at least a 70% chance that before being given a job you will be subjected to a personality test by one of the big four – MBTI (Myers-Briggs Type Indicator), 16PF (16 personality factors), OPQ (occupational personality questionnaire) or Hogan – and an ability exam measuring verbal reasoning and numeracy.

These are basically IQ tests by another name...according to the Association of Graduate Recruiters, it's because nobody trusts university degrees anymore. It has just issued a report saying degree standards are inconsistent and, as a result, companies are turning to psychometrics. But Ceri Roderick at occupation psychologists Pearn Kandola adds two other reasons. 'Companies want to know things like the motivational characteristics of recruits and the technology is now available to do these things.' There's also a fourth reason: the need to compete for quality recruits. 'There's a war for talent,' says Professor David Bartram of the British Psychological Society (BPS), 'companies are fighting to get the best people.' All of which means there is now a rapid proliferation of psychometrics consultancies, most of them offering candidates the chance to do all the tests online…

Psychometrics works, but only if the tests are properly applied, rigorously interpreted and accompanied by traditional interviews. This means that they do not necessarily speed up the recruitment process. They might, however, help weed out unsuitables in advance, a huge benefit at a time when all companies are swamped with applicants for attractive jobs.

Source: Appleyard, B. (2007) Want a job? Let's play mind games

Assessment centres

Assessment centres involve candidates being observed and evaluated by trained assessors as they are given a selection of pre-programmed exercises or trials. These exercises may include:

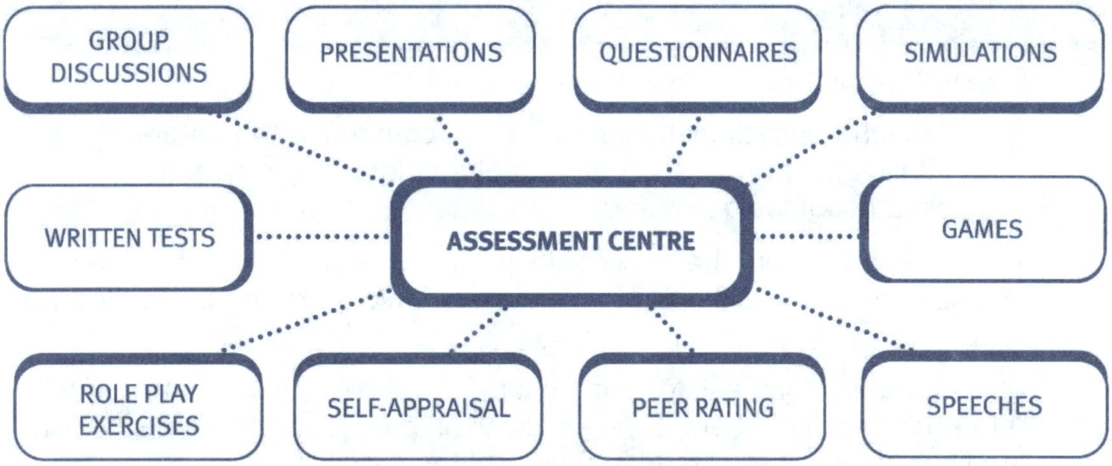

Assessors will be looking for evidence that candidates have certain abilities that are important in the job they have applied for. These criteria will change from job to job, but may include leadership or communication skills, for example.

Assessment centres

The assessment centre is really a combination of many forms of selection. Groups of around six to ten candidates are brought together for one to three days of intensive assessment. As well as being multi-method, other characteristics of assessment centres are that they use several assessors and they assess several dimensions of performance required, often for higher-level positions.

The advantages of assessment centres include:

- A high degree of acceptability and user confidence.
- Avoidance of a single-assessor bias.
- Reliability in predicting potential success (if the system is well conducted).
- The development of skills in the assessors, which may be useful in their own managerial responsibilities.
- Benefits to the assessed individuals, including experience of managerial/supervisory situations, opportunity for self-assessment and job-relevant feedback and opportunities to discuss career prospects openly with senior management.

References

The purpose of references is to confirm facts about the employee and increase the degree of confidence felt about information given during the other selection techniques.

References

References should contain two types of information:

- Straightforward, factual information, confirming the nature of the applicant's previous job, period of employment, pay and circumstances of leaving.
- Opinions about the applicant's personality and other attributes, though these are open to bias and should therefore be treated with caution.

Many organisations ask for a minimum of two references – including references from past employers as well as personal references (which are likely to be more biased in favour of the candidate).

References, while useful, must be viewed with caution. Allowances must be made for:

- prejudice (favourable or unfavourable)
- charity (withholding detrimental remarks)
- fear of being actionable for libel (although references are privileged, if they are factually correct and devoid of malice).

What happens next?

Once a suitable candidate has been found, a **job offer** can be made. It may be necessary to **negotiate** over some aspects of the employment contract, such as pay or hours of work.

On starting work with the organisation, the employee should be effectively assimilated into the organisation through a process of **induction**.

Illustration 4

The average UK employee turnover rate is 15% and the average cost of employee turnover is £30,614 (Source: Oxford Economics and Unum) for each employee earning £25,000 or more. A major reason why employees leave within the first six months to a year is a poorly planned induction process. Therefore, there are significant savings to be made from implementing an effective induction process.

2.4 Staff development and training

Introduction

Often the terms 'training' and 'development' are used inter-changeably. However, there are differences between the two:

Training is the planned and systematic modification of behaviour through learning events, programmes and instruction which enable individuals to achieve the level of knowledge, skills and competence to carry out their work effectively.

Development is the growth or realisation of a person's ability and potential through conscious or unconscious learning and educational experiences.

It is often argued that development is therefore more general, more future-oriented and more individually oriented than training.

Organisations should view training and development of staff as an investment.

Test your understanding 8

Requirement:

What are the benefits, for both the learner and the organisation, of training and development?

The training and development process

Due to the obvious importance of training and development, a systematic approach should be taken to maximise its effectiveness. To help with this, organisations may find it helpful to view training and development as a step-by-step process.

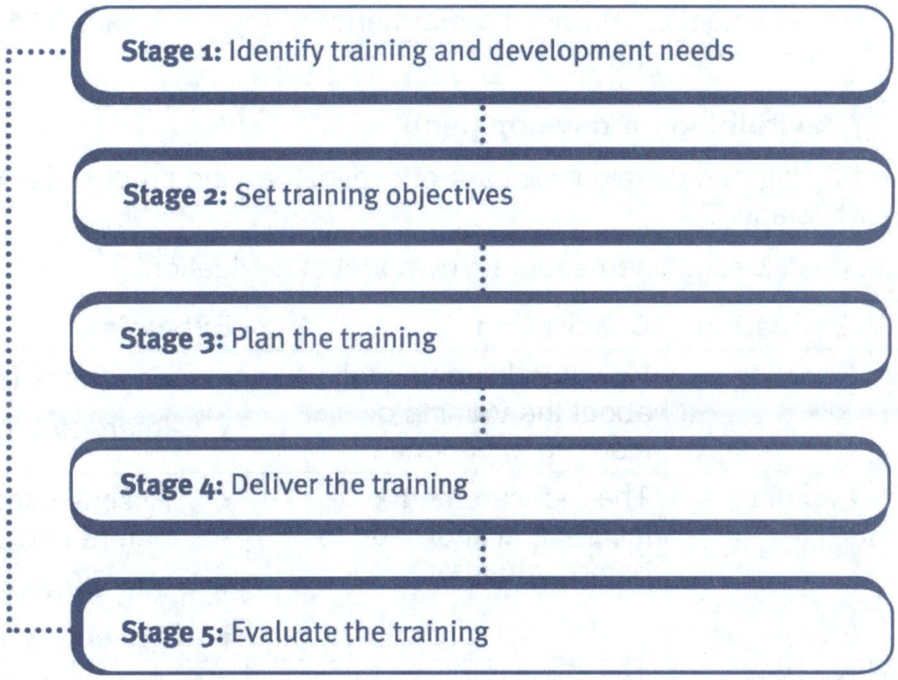

Stages in training and development

- **Identifying training (or development) needs** – this could include an investigation into the organisation's current performance as well as mapping the corporate skills base. It should drill down to the level of the individual to target specific needs.
- **Setting training (or development) objectives** – as with all objectives these should have clear, specific, measurable targets in relation to the standard of behaviour required to achieve a given level of performance.
- **Planning the training (or development)** – this covers who provides the training, where the training takes place and divisions of responsibilities between trainers, line managers or team leaders and the individual personally.
- **Delivering/implementing the training (or development)** – a combination of formal and on-the-job training programmes will be used.
- **Evaluating training (or development)** – assessment of cost versus benefit using feedback forms, end of course tests, assessment of improved performance in the workplace and impact on corporate goals.

Evaluating the training (or development)

To ensure training and development are effective, learning processes need to be evaluated (stage 5).

Donald Kirkpatrick suggested a four level model of evaluation.

Level	Evaluation	Description	Examples
1	Reaction	How the delegates felt about the training or learning experience	• Feedback forms • Interviews
2	Learning	The measurement of the increase in knowledge – before and after	• Assessment tests before and after • Interviews • Observation
3	Behaviour	The extent of applied learning back on the job – implementation	• Observation and interview over time
4	Results	The effect on the business or environment by the trainee	• Impact on existing KPIs

The evaluation should be completed by line managers in conjunction with the delegates themselves. Once completed, collated 'results' need to be interpreted by HR professionals and/or line managers to inform future decisions.

2.5 Performance management

Introduction

Performance management is used to assess and ensure that the employee is carrying out their duties which they are employed to do in an effective and satisfactory manner, which is contributing to the overall objectives of the organisation.

Organisations follow four main steps when managing the performance of employees:

- **Set targets** – at the start of the period, the manager and employee should agree on which SMART goals and targets the employee is going to work towards.

Setting targets

The targets usually include:

- Areas that the employee needs to improve (perhaps where the employee is currently making mistakes)
- Targets that link into the overall business goals (such as increasing activity by five percent)
- Development and training targets that will benefit the employee (and the business) and therefore increase motivation.

It is important that employees understand and agree to these targets. If they do not 'buy into' them, they will not put any effort in to accomplishing the goals set – especially if they do not feel that the targets are achievable. This can lead to demotivation.

- **Monitor** – during the period, the manager should monitor employee performance and provide regular feedback. Managers can offer rewards for good performance and support and help where it looks as though the employee is failing to meet their targets.
- **Review** – at the end of the period, the manager and employee will usually have a formal appraisal where they discuss the employee's performance and investigate how successful the employee has been at meeting the pre-agreed targets (appraisal is discussed in more detail below).
- **Action plan** – the manager and employee then agree on new targets that will be set for the coming period.

Appraisal

Appraisal is the systematic review and assessment of an employee's performance, potential and training needs.

Illustration 5 – Appraisal

Karl works for a call centre and is set targets for the number of calls he takes in the year, the number of customers who say they were satisfied with his performance and the number of complaints he receives in the year.

At the end of the year, the appraisal will allow both Karl and his manager to compare his actual performance against these targets. Any areas where he deviates from the targets (in either a positive or negative way) can be discussed and are likely to form the basis of Karl's annual bonus and pay rise for next year.

Any areas that Karl is struggling with or would like to gain additional skills and knowledge in, can be used to identify training and development opportunities for the coming year.

Finally, the appraisal can then be used to agree what Karl's targets will be for next year.

If not handled carefully, appraisals can cause demotivation for employees. Various studies have indicated that criticism of employees can have a negative effect on their goal achievement and self-confidence.

Lockett suggested that there are six main barriers to effective appraisals.

Barrier	Example
Confrontation	• Feedback is badly delivered. • Differing views regarding performance.
Judgement	• Appraisal is seen as a one-sided process – the manager is judge, jury and counsel for the prosecution.
Chat	• Lack of will from either party. • No outcomes set.
Bureaucracy	• Purely a 'form filling exercise'. • No purpose or worth.
Annual event	• A traditional ceremony carried out once or twice a year.
Unfinished business	• No follow up. • Points agreed not actioned.

Test your understanding 9

Which of the following is an objective of the appraisal process to an employer?

A It enables them to identify underperforming employees for punishment

B It helps the business to recruit the best possible employees

C It helps to identify employees' skills gaps

D It reinforces management authority over employees

2.6 The role of incentives and practices relating to motivation

Introduction

In an organisation, **motivation** refers to the willingness of individuals to perform certain tasks or actions. It is the incentive or reason for them behaving in a particular way.

In practice, motivation is taken as meaning how hard an employee is willing to work in their job. It goes beyond employees merely following rules and orders and looks at how **dedicated** they are.

Test your understanding 10

Requirement:

What are the benefits for:

- **the organisation**
- **the individual employee and**
- **the teams they work in**

of having motivated staff members?

As there are so many advantages to having motivated workers, motivation is a key issue for most organisations.

Unfortunately, motivation is difficult to measure directly, meaning that managers must look at other factors that may indicate the level of motivation within the organisation, often including staff turnover or productivity levels.

However, remember that these factors could also be caused by issues other than employee motivation. For instance, low productivity could be caused by poor working practices within the organisation, rather than unhappy staff.

Illustration 6 – Maslow's hierarchy of needs

A well know theory of motivation is Maslow's hierarchy of needs.

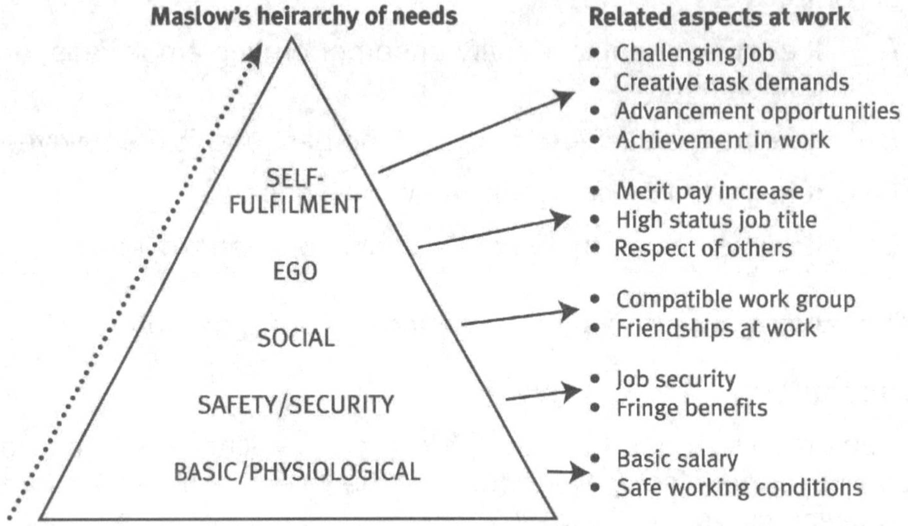

Maslow stated that people's wants and needs follow a hierarchy. As employees become progressively more highly paid, monetary rewards become less important as other needs such as recognition and an ability to achieve one's potential become more important.

Note: There are many different theories on motivation (many of them competing).

There are several different incentives and practices that can be used to assist in the motivation of employees. The role of the **psychological contract**, **employee involvement** and the use of **workforce flexibility** will be discussed below. Appropriate **reward systems** will be discussed in section 2.7.

The psychological contract

The psychological contract outlines the perceptions of the employee and the employer regarding what their mutual obligations are towards each other.

Unlike the employment contract, the psychological contract is highly subjective, not written down and not legally binding.

Key elements include the following:

	Employee	**Employer**
What do they want?	Want their needs to be satisfied	Want employee to work hard. Will have a set of expectations for each employee
What are they willing to give?	Will offer their energies and talents	Payment, benefits and other outcomes, e.g. a promotion

For managers to **motivate** and retain employees, they must understand the importance of the psychological contract and fulfil their side of the bargain.

Key elements include the following:

	Employee	**Employer**
What do they want?	Want their needs to be satisfied	Want employee to work hard. Will have a set of expectations for each employee
What are they willing to give?	Will offer their energies and talents	Payment, benefits and other outcomes, e.g. a promotion

For managers to **motivate** and retain employees, they must understand the importance of the psychological contract and fulfil their side of the bargain.

e.g

Illustration 7

Nikolina has worked as a trainee accountant with the same company for the past two years. She is ambitious and enjoys her work. Her manager asks her to produce a report that is outside of her normal role.

The report turns out to be difficult and time consuming and she must put in long hours to complete the report on time as well as carrying out her normal work.

She meets the deadline and sends the report to her manager. However, she receives no acknowledgement. The next day she finds out that her manager has successfully presented the findings of the report to his boss and has taken the credit for the report.

Nikolina is angry and has decided that she will never do any extra work for her boss again and has even started looking for another job due to the breach of her psychological contract.

Employee involvement

Employees should be empowered to contribute to the organisation. Relying on all employees for their ideas, intelligence and commitment to make the organisation successful should increase employee motivation and have positive financial benefits for the business.

Illustration 8 – Talent management at Apple

Apple's amazing product success is, in part, due to their (sometimes unusual) approach to talent management.

- Apple has an ability to move into and dominate completely unrelated industries. This is only possible because of extraordinary talent, the way it manages it and the creation of a culture that after succeeding in one task, employees will immediately move onto something different.
- A lean talent management approach enables Apple to achieve exceptional levels of employee productivity. Tight deadlines and lean schedules force everyone to work together and solve problems early on.
- The rewards and recognition programme is extremely attractive creating a performance culture and an element of internal competition.
- Rather than a work/life balance, Apple makes it clear that it is looking for extremely hard-working and committed individuals; the idea being that the satisfaction and reward achieved by the employee for their hard work is huge.

Illustration 9 – Employee empowerment and quality

Quality in operations management was discussed in Chapter 9. Many of the quality practices rely on the empowerment of employees. For example:

- In **TQM,** employees are expected to seek out, identify and correct quality problems (possibly as part of a quality circle) and are responsible for achieving targets.
- Highly skilled and well trained staff will be required for effective operation of a **JIT** system.
- With **Kaizen,** employees are encouraged to come up with small improvement suggestions on a regular basis.
- A **lean** culture will require a multi-skilled and flexible workforce.

Workforce flexibility

- **Flexible working arrangements** – these can be used to increase employee motivation. Flexibility in work patterns can be achieved in many ways:

Type of flexible working arrangement	Explanation
Remote working/ teleworking	Technology has enabled employees to work away from the office, usually at home
Flexitime	The need to work a standard set of hours but less restriction on when these hours are worked
Shift system	Working outside of normal working day patterns
Compressed week	Standard hours within fewer days in a shift rotation
Job sharing	Two employees share a standard hour week
Part-time	Fewer hours than the standard weekly number

Flexible working arrangements encompass one type of flexibility within organisations. Other types of flexibility are:

- **Task or functional flexibility** – employees can move between tasks as and when is required. This will allow an organisation to react to changes in production requirements and levels of demand and should result in better skilled and motivated employees.
- **Financial flexibility** – this is achieved through variable systems of rewards, for example bonus schemes or profit sharing. By linking rewards to performance, several improvements in performance should be realised.

2.7 Reward systems

A reward system refers to all the monetary, non-monetary and psychological payments that an organisation provides for its employees in exchange for the work they perform.

The aims of a reward system

Reward is not simply a benefit for the employee and a cost for the employer. Rather it is a fundamental aspect of HRM:

- It should support the overall strategy.
- It is a vital part of the psychological contract being adhered to.
- It influences the success of recruitment and retention policies.
- It must conform to relevant laws and regulations.
- It must be affordable.
- It affects motivation and performance management and should be managed accordingly.
- It must be administered efficiently and correctly.

Methods of reward

Rewards can be divided into two main categories:

- **Basic pay** – this is the minimum amount that the employee receives for working in the organisation. It can be determined in several ways, such as an hourly rate or an annual salary.
- **Performance-related pay** – pay is based on the level of performance. Rewards may be based on individual, group or organisational performance, all of which aim to motivate employees to work harder. SMART objectives should be set for employees so that it is clear the level of performance they are trying to achieve.

e.g

Illustration 10 – Types of performance-related pay

There are several different types of performance-related pay:

- **Individual performance-related pay** – a pay rise or bonus is given to an employee on achievement of pre-agreed objectives or based on the assessment by a manager (as part of their appraisal). Advantages include the ability to align individual objectives with organisational goals and the controllability of rewards by the employee. However, such schemes may result in a lack of teamwork and in tunnel vision (sole concentration on areas which are measured and rewarded).
- **Group performance-related pay** – rewards are based on the achievement of group targets. Encourages teamwork but may not be seen as fair by employees.
- **Knowledge contingent pay** – for example, an accountant may receive a bonus or pay rise on passing their exams.
- **Profit-related pay** – part of the employee's remuneration is linked to organisational profit. Can motivate employees to increase company profit and increase loyalty but may lead to short termism and lack of motivation if employees feel they have no control over organisational profit.
- **Share options** – they are often given to senior managers and should motivate them to increase share price. However, there is an argument that many of the factors that influence share price will be outside of the manager's control or that (previously risk averse) managers could be tempted to take risks in the hope of increasing the share price.
- **Commission** – normally used for sales staff and is based on a percentage of their sales. Can motivate staff but may lead to short termism and manipulation of results.

- **Piecework schemes** – a price is paid for each unit of output. Some employees, particularly in manufacturing industries, may be eligible for bonus payments as part of this agreement.
- **Benefits** – a wide range of rewards other than wages or pensions, such as company cars, health insurance or extra time off. These can provide additional incentives at a lower cost and can be designed in a flexible way to suit the individual employee.

3 Areas of interface between HR and finance

3.1 Introduction

In Chapters 9 and 10 we discussed the interaction between the operations function/sales and marketing function and finance. Much of the discussion below overlaps with what has already been said in that finance, as a trusted advisor, should collaborate with the other function to achieve organisational goals and their own individual functional goals.

3.2 Interaction between HR and finance

- **Traditionally**, the HR function and the finance function worked independently:
  - Finance very much viewed people as a **cost** whereas HR viewed people as an **asset**.
  - Collaboration between the functions was limited to, for example, establishing a budget for a reward programme.
- The **modern** approach is to view people as one of the greatest assets an organisation has. Finance and HR need to work more closely with the 'people as assets' as their focus.

e.g

Illustration 11 – Interaction between HR and finance

Fulfilling these responsibilities will require data analysis and financial projections from the finance function. For example, an increase in salary, bonus payments or benefits will result in an increased cost for the organisation but this cost needs to be considered in the context of the increased benefit to the organisation due to, say, increased motivation and productivity and reduced staff turnover. The finance function can provide this '**information**' and can then use it for '**insight**', '**influence**' and '**impact**'.

e.g

Illustration 12 – AI to replace doctors?

In the past, doctors were viewed as one of the greatest assets in the medical world, with highly prized training, skills and experience. However, there is a view that even in organisations that have previously viewed their employees as their key asset, technology will be able to replace many of the roles they previously carried out.

One example of this technology is the use of artificial intelligence (AI) systems in medicine.

According to Imperial College, London website:

New AI software can read the brain scans of patients who have had a stroke, to more accurately pinpoint when it happened and help doctors work out whether it can be successfully treated.

It is hoped that the new technology will ultimately enable faster and more accurate emergency treatment of patients in a hospital setting. Knowing the time the stroke started is important because standard treatments only work in the very early stages post-stroke – and may otherwise cause secondary damage.

The software, devised by researchers from Imperial College London, Technical University of Munich, and Edinburgh University, addresses two of the most difficult challenges in assessing stroke patients – identifying the onset time of the stroke and whether the damage can be reversed. The software has been found to be twice as accurate as the current method – a visual assessment of the scan by a medical professional, who considers how dark a stroke area appears on CT scans of the brain.

- Technology is freeing both functions from day-to-day duties in their respective fields. This combined with the increasingly competitive and fast changing global environment is leading to the functions having an increased role in the strategic direction of the organisation and an opportunity to work in a more joined-up way.
- Both functions will have overlapping responsibilities. For example, they must consider:
  - The cost and benefit of recruiting and selecting new employees
  - The impact of HR policies, such as reward policies, on the profitability of the business.

Test your understanding 11

Which of the following is an example of co-ordination between HR and the finance function?

A Establishing credit terms

B Determining sales prices

C Allocating costs

D Calculating reward packages

3.3 How technology is helping this interaction

- New technology has resulted in more compatible, joined up systems creating better information
- Some examples of this technology usage are illustrated below.

Illustration 13 – How the cloud is fuelling this collaboration

Sharing a finance and HR cloud system, integrating enterprise resource planning and human capital management systems will:

- Make it quicker and easier to track and to forecast key HR information
- Will aid collaboration to make effective decisions that will help achieve functional and organisational objectives.

Illustration 14 – Analytics technology fuelling better collaboration

Advances in analytics technology have helped in quantifying different HR activities or to measure the impact of a HR programme.

By demonstrating the value of investing in different HR activities, through measures such as employee satisfaction scores, HR and finance can work together to ensure they have the right information for responsible decision-making.

4 Key performance indicators (KPIs)

4.1 Introduction

In section 6 of Chapter 9 we:

- defined KPIs
- discussed their use in managing the operations function
- identified relevant KPIs for operations
- discussed how the finance function manages operations using KPIs and
- discussed the impact of technology in this area.

Much of this discussion can also be applied to the HR function.

In this section we will briefly discuss how the finance function helps to manage the HR function using KPIs before identifying some relevant KPIs for HR.

4.2 How finance helps to manage HR using KPIs

Let's begin by recapping our discussion from Chapter 10 but this time in the context of the HR function.

- The HR function will identify its relevant CSFs.
- The KPIs are the measures that indicate whether the HR function is achieving these CSFs.
- The finance function works with the HR function to:
  - **identify** appropriate KPIs
  - **assemble** KPI data and information
  - **analyse** this for insight
  - give **advice** to the HR function based on this insight and
  - **apply** what has been learned to impact the achievement of the objectives of the HR function and the organisation as a whole.
- **Technology** will act as a key enabler in this, particularly in the 'assembly' and 'analysis' tasks.

e.g

Illustration 15 – KPI dashboards

One of the most common technologies used in KPIs is performance dashboards. The dashboard displays the KPIs of the HR function in a live format, thus allowing immediate, visual understanding of current performance and potentially prompting action to correct or amend performance accordingly.

Separate dashboards may be used for areas such as:

- The recruitment and selection process – identifying bottlenecks and opportunities in the hiring process; to improve efficiency, reduce lost revenue and minimise costs
- Rewards – ensuring the system is fair (for example, females are not at a disadvantage compared to males) and competitive (for example, by benchmarking against competitor salaries)
- Employee turnover rate – to help prevent valued employees leaving the business and to minimise hiring and training costs.

Note: It would be useful to spend a few minutes looking at examples of HR dashboard images on the internet.

4.3 Examples of KPIs for HR

Example activity	Possible KPIs
Recruitment and selection	Cost per employee hired Selection method conversion rate Time to fill a position Female to male ratio
Training and development	Training and development costs Impact of training on existing KPIs Training feedback
Performance management	Appraisals completed on time Appraisal action plan agreed and subsequently followed up
Motivation	Turnover rate Employee absenteeism Employee productivity Employee satisfaction scores Flexible working arrangements offered
Reward systems	Cost of rewards Competitiveness of reward system Adherence to laws and regulations

It is important to note that the above is a generic list of KPIs for the HR function and that HR must identify the best KPIs for measuring the achievement of its CSFs. For example, one of the function's CSFs may be 'cost efficiency of the recruitment and selection process'. The achievement of this CSF could be measured using several KPIs, for example 'cost per employee hired'.

Test your understanding 12

Match the following CSFs of the HR function to the most appropriate KPI.

CSF	KPI
Diversity of workforce	Employee turnover
Motivated workforce	Training and development costs
Fair remuneration	Female to male ratio
Efficient recruitment process	Competitiveness of reward system
Suitably skilled workforce	Time to fill a position

Test your understanding 13

Fernando is constructing some KPIs to measure whether or not the firm's HR CSFs are being met. He has been told that these KPIs should be SMART.

One KPI is: 90% of all staff appraisals to be completed by the end of January each year. (Last year 50% of appraisals were completed by the end of January).

Which of the SMART criteria is not being met in the following KPI?

A Specific

B Measurable

C Achievable

D Relevant

E Time bound

Test your understanding 14 – KPI Case Study Question

Pop Up Limited

Pop Up Limited (PUL) is a business that provides a platform for pop up shops to run themselves a little more efficiently. Many pop-up shop owners have virtually no management experience and so, inevitably, mistakes are made along the way.

PUL provides an accounting system linked to a point-of-sale (POS) system along with the necessary equipment to record transactions. It also provides a performance management system to ensure that the staff have a clearer idea what is expected of them from the start.

PUL ask owners to complete an online form and questionnaire and from that, the basic understanding of the business is gleaned. Key performance targets are then generated and allocated to all staff members taking into account their individual roles. It is common that each staff member be allocated one KPI and the system will measure against this KPI every day, reporting to the owner accordingly.

Requirement:

Identify and explain three errors of the KPI setting process outlined above.

(15 marks)

5 Chapter summary

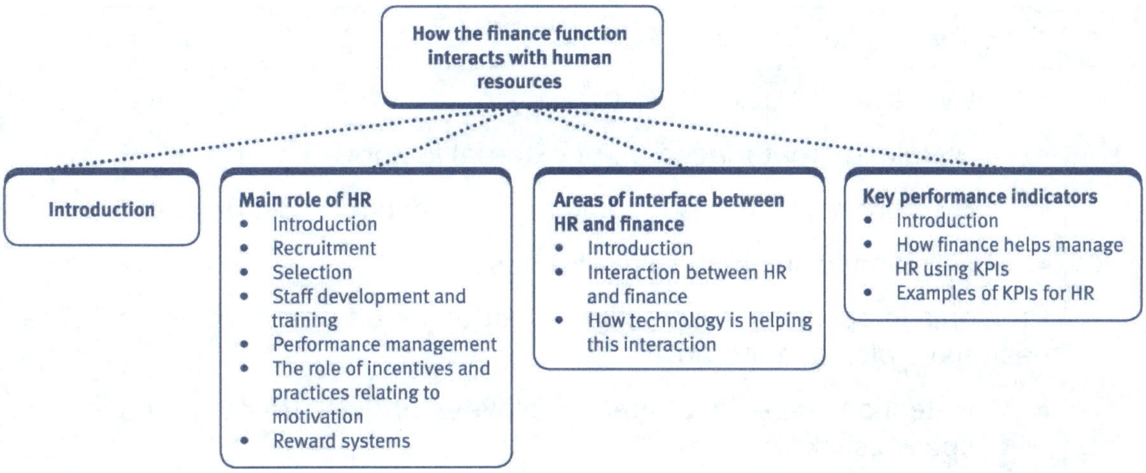

Test your understanding answers

Test your understanding 1

- By staying flexible.
- By taking greater account of external factors.
- By more sophisticated monitoring and control mechanisms.
- By planning in shorter time frames.

Problems in achieving plans might to a degree be predictable and, in the past, have also centred on:

- Retention, especially when employees are well trained or have specialist skills
- Slow promotion leading to staff turnover
- Unexpected vacancies arising in senior positions or vital skills areas.

Test your understanding 2

The correct answer is **A – True**

Economic uncertainty may cause people to remain in their present job and discourage them from moving elsewhere, particularly if finance from, say, building societies and banks is difficult to obtain. People with children may be less disposed to move and movement will mainly be among younger persons. Growth industries may therefore find it difficult to obtain people with the required experience.

Test your understanding 3

- Finance Director required **(job title)**.
- At least five years post qualified experience **(special requirements)**.
- Experience of a dynamic industry **(special requirements)**.
- Understanding of investor relations and pre-floatation requirements **(special requirements)**.
- Ability to manage change and form own department **(special requirements)**.

- Role includes **(brief description of role):**
  - Planning, monitoring and control of business and financial strategy.
  - Reporting and accounting as per the legal requirements.
  - Management of strategy for and liaison with stock market business press and the business analyst community.
- Excellent package including competitive salary and share options **(remuneration)**.
- Responsible for a growing team of 18 people **(number of staff directly supervised)**.
- Report directly to the Managing Director **(responsible to)**.
- Located in London with approximately 20% travel to other European locations **(location and special attributes, for example, shift systems, willingness to travel)**.

Test your understanding 4

The correct answer is **C**

Test your understanding 5

Discrimination may be acceptable in certain circumstances, for example:

- Army soldiers must be fit, healthy and be able to carry heavy kit.
- Firefighters must be a certain height so that they can reach the equipment.
- An Italian restaurant can choose to recruit only Italian waiters and waitresses.

Test your understanding 6

(a)

Advantages of the interview technique	**Disadvantages of the interview technique**
• Places candidate at ease. • Highly interactive, allowing flexible question and answers. • Opportunities to use non-verbal communication.	• Too brief to 'get to know' candidates. • Interview is an artificial situation. • Halo effect from initial impression.

• Opportunities to assess appearance, interpersonal and communication skills. • Opportunities to evaluate rapport between the candidate and the potential colleagues/bosses.	• Qualitative factors such as motivation, honesty or integrity are difficult to assess. • Prejudice – stereotyping groups of people. • Lack of interviewer preparation, skill, training and practice. • Subjectivity and bias.

(b)

Interview option	**Advantage**	**Disadvantage**
Face-to-face by one person	Good for establishing rapport between interviewer and candidate	Can be subject to bias
Group	A good opportunity to compare candidates	One candidate may dominate
Succession	Allows for a range of opinions about the candidate	Opinions about the candidate may vary and conflict
Panel	Allows comparison of the candidate in real time	May be more suited to confident candidates
Problem solving	Good for identifying relevant problem-solving skills	May be more suited to confident candidates
Stress	Good for judging how the candidate reacts under stress	Putting excessive stress on an individual may be considered unethical

Test your understanding 7

The correct answer is **D**

Test your understanding 8

The benefits for the learner and the organisation include:

For the individual:

- Improved skills and (dependent on the type of training) qualifications
- Increased confidence and job satisfaction.

For the organisation:

- Increased motivation of employees, leading to higher productivity
- Increased competence and confidence, meaning higher quality and fewer mistakes
- Low staff turnover, saving the organisation time and money
- Skilled workforce, leading to more innovation and a better customer experience.

Test your understanding 9

The correct answer is **C**

The appraisal process is certainly not designed to find employees that need to be punished and only applies to existing employees, meaning that it will not help the organisation with its recruitment. It is also designed to improve communication between managers and employees, not reinforce the differences between them.

Test your understanding 10

Having motivated staff members has a range of benefits – from the perspectives of both the organisation and the individuals or teams themselves. These include:

Organisation perspective	Individual perspective	Team perspective
Harder working employees	Greater job satisfaction	Increased cooperation
Fewer mistakes and errors	Improved health, due to less stress	More commitment to team needs
Less waste of time and resources	Improved career prospects	Better ideas generation and evaluation

More suggestions and ideas generated	Finding the job more interesting and enjoyable	
Increased job satisfaction and therefore lower staff turnover		
More customer satisfaction due to better service from staff		

Test your understanding 11

The answer is **D, calculating the rewards package**

Test your understanding 12

The CSFs should be matched to the KPIs as follows:

CSF	KPI
Diversity of workforce	Female to male ratio
Motivated workforce	Employee turnover
Fair remuneration	Competitiveness of reward system
Efficient recruitment process	Time to fill a position
Suitably skilled workforce	Training and development costs

Test your understanding 13

The answer is **Achievable**. It will be very difficult to increase this completion rate by 40%.

Test your understanding 14 – KPI Case Study Question

The PUL system has a number of flaws and only three are required:

Lack of discussion

It is sensible that KPIs are discussed with staff members in advance, but this is not the case here. This discussion would flush out practical problems that might exist and would ensure the employee fully understood what was expected of them. It is generally accepted that discussion and agreement prevent dictated standards. Employees will often buy in to targets more readily if they feel that they have had an input to them. This is clearly not the case here.

Incorrect level of difficulty

Equally, without due discussion, the level of difficulty set for the KPI could be wildly wrong. Setting a target that is too difficult can demotivate an employee meaning that they resent the target (and the employer who set it) and underperform. There is plenty of evidence to suggest that the level of output achieved is sub-optimal in this situation.

Equally the level of target could be too easy. Whilst this is then easily achieved an employee will often have a lack of respect for the setter as they will think of them a fool to set such an easy target. They may even feel patronised. As above, the output actually achieved will be suboptimal in most cases as the employee stops pushing once the target is reached.

Single KPI

Setting only one KPI keeps things simple and this may well have been the intention. However, single KPIs are notoriously easy to manipulate. Suppose a target is simply to make more sales volume. A staff member could quickly realise that this is achievable by deep discounting prices. This will destroy margin. Without a second KPI, perhaps on price level or margin achieved the consequences of a volume only target could be dire.

Unfairness between different members of staff

There is no evidence that the targets set are compared in terms of level of difficulty from one staff member to another. Resentment can quickly fester if a staff member feels unfairly treated.

Chapter

12

How the finance function interacts with IT

Chapter learning objectives

Lead	Component
E4: Describe how the finance function interacts with IT.	Describe: (a) Main role of IT (b) Areas of interface with finance (c) Key performance indicators

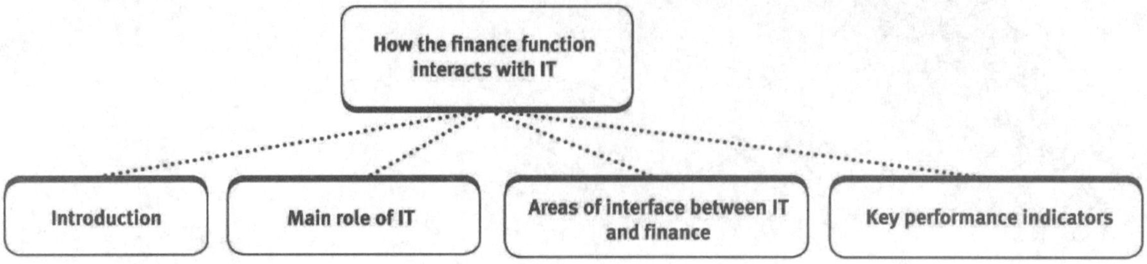

1 Introduction

In this chapter we will complete our discussion of how the finance function plays its role by interacting with the rest of the organisation (syllabus area E) and, more specifically here, the organisation's information technology (IT) function.

We will begin by discussing the main role of the IT function; understanding how IT systems can be used to support the rest of the organisation, how these systems can be best organised and managed and the costs and benefits of information systems.

We will then discuss the areas of interface with finance before moving on to the final part of the chapter which will discuss how the finance function helps to manage the IT function using key performance indicators (KPIs).

2 Main role of IT

2.1 IT systems support

The role of information systems in organisations

Organisations need information systems to enable them to capture and generate the information that managers need for **planning, control** and **decision-making**.

The hunger for information has never been greater than for today's organisations, likewise the value of information systems that deliver this information has never been so keenly felt. It follows that information technology (IT) and information systems (IS) assume increasing managerial importance within the modern organisation.

IT is becoming a strategic weapon which many organisations are using to improve their competitive position. This can come in many forms. For example, using IT can improve efficiency and reduce costs to compete better, it can help the organisation react more quickly to the changing environment or it can create new opportunities etc.

Before discussing the role of IT in more detail, it is useful to understand a few key **definitions**.

Information systems (IS) refer to the provision and management of information to support the running of the organisation.

Information technology (IT) is the supporting equipment (hardware) that provides the infrastructure to run the information systems.

The **IT function** is responsible for planning, evaluating, installing, operating and maintaining the hardware, software, networks and data centres required by the organisation.

A **management information system** (**MIS**) converts internal and external data into useful information which is then communicated to managers at all levels and across all functions to enable them to make timely and effective decisions for planning, directing and controlling activities.

There are several key types of MIS:

Type of MIS	Explanation
Executive information system (EIS)	An EIS gives senior management access to internal and external information. Information is presented in a flexible, user-friendly, summarised form with the option to 'drill down' to a greater level of detail.
Decision support system (DSS)	A DSS aids managers in making decisions. The system predicts the consequences of several possible scenarios and the manager then uses their judgement to make the final decision.
Transaction processing system (TPS)	A TPS is mainly used by operational managers to make decisions. It records all the daily transactions (for example, payroll or purchases) of an organisation and summarises them so they can be reported on a routine basis.
Expert system	Expert systems hold specialist knowledge, for example on law and taxation, and allow non-experts to interrogate them for information, advice and recommended decisions. Can be used at all levels of management.

e.g

Illustration 1 – EIS

A typical report from an EIS would combine many types of data on the same screen and make it easier for senior management to understand the performance of the business.

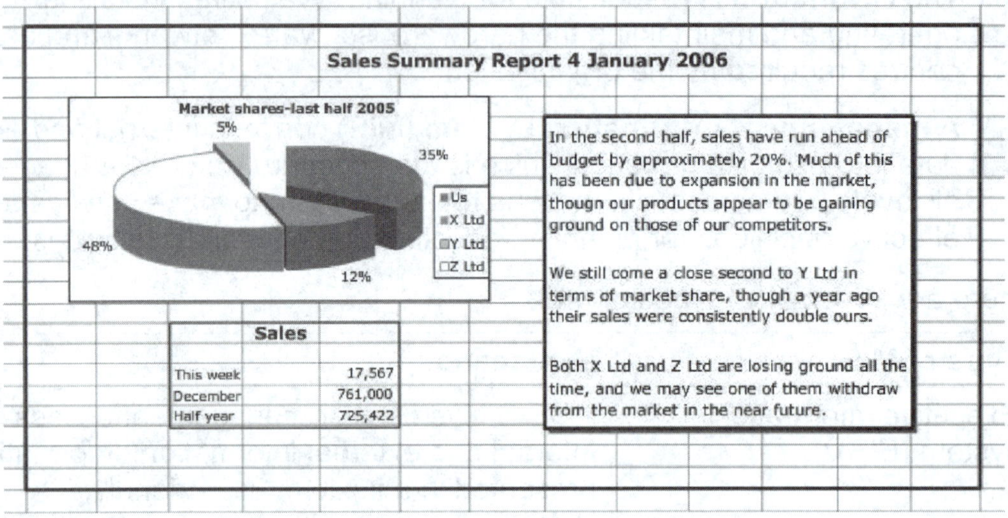

e.g

Illustration 2 – DSS

A supermarket chain is planning to start selling its goods online but is uncertain of whether it is appropriate for the organisation.

A DSS would gather information about the company itself – does it have the resources to start selling online?

It will also provide information about the online groceries market, such as the size of the market and who the competitors are.

The DSS will then present this information in a way that is easy to understand, helping the management to make the decision.

e.g

Illustration 3 – Expert systems

An accountant could use an expert system (ES) to calculate a client's personal tax liability.

The accountant will input the relevant information about the client's circumstances. The ES will then access its database of rules and regulations about personal tax, decide which rules apply to the client and then use them to calculate a tax liability.

How IT enables knowledge management between the functions

In Chapter 7 we discussed how:

- The finance function can use data and information to assist sales and marketing to better understand customers and to develop customer value proposition
- The finance function can use data and information to assist operations in enhancing operational efficiency
- The finance function can partner with other areas of the organisation to create value from digital assets.

As part of this discussion, we covered some examples of how IT enables knowledge management between functions.

Here we will look more specifically at knowledge management systems and how these enable knowledge management between the functions.

Knowledge is an important organisational resource. There is a difference between:

- **Data** – raw facts
- **Information** – processed, organised data
- **Knowledge** – the application of a cognitive process to the information so that it becomes useful.

There are two broad types of knowledge:

- **Explicit knowledge** – is knowledge that the company knows it has, for example customer information.
- **Tacit knowledge** – is personal knowledge and expertise held by people within the organisation that has not been formally documented, for example knowledge gained through the experiences of employees within the organisation.

Knowledge management is the process for the acquisition, sharing, retention and utilisation of knowledge.

In, what is increasingly referred to as a knowledge-based economy, it is evident that sufficient management attention should be given to this valuable organisational asset.

Organisations hold a huge volume and variety of information in different systems and people and therefore a knowledge management strategy is needed to unlock the value of this asset and improve organisational performance.

An important part of this strategy will involve a technology-based solution (a knowledge management system).

Knowledge management systems refer to any type of IT that helps to capture, store, retrieve and use knowledge to enhance the knowledge management process.

Examples include:

- Groupware – refers to technology designed to help people collaborate. Examples include email, file sharing technology and video/audio conferencing.
- Intranets – a private network within the organisation allowing the sharing of information and resources with employees.
- Extranets – an extension of an intranet to include suppliers, customers and other business partners.
- Data warehouses and data mining.
- Decision support systems (DSS).
- Content management systems – these make it easier to create content (for example, using templates), to edit content, to track changes allowing for version control and allow for collaborative and parallel work on content.
- Document management systems – often part of a content management system. They assist with, for example, the indexing and retrieval of documents.

It is important to note that technology is an important part of knowledge management. Technology alone, however, may simply increase the volume and management of unfocused data and analysed information. There is also a need for appropriate people skills and processes to convert this data/information into useful knowledge.

Test your understanding 1

The best working definition of information from the options below would be:

A Facts you can work with

B Facts

C Facts useful to the operations manager

D Facts useful to the decision maker

2.2 IT infrastructure

Introduction

IT infrastructure consists of the core networks, databases, software, hardware and procedures managed by the IT function.

The modernisation of IT infrastructure is necessary to take advantage of innovations such as data visualisation, AI and blockchain, which will all require the analysis of huge amounts of data.

In this section, we will discuss the ways of organising and managing IS in the context of the wider organisation including:

- The emergence of new technology
- Enabling transformation
- Geographically dispersed teams
- Enhancing internal and external relationships
- Ethical and social issues with IS and data.

Each of these will be explored in turn.

The emergence of new technology

Advancements in technology (as discussed in Chapter 5) are allowing organisations to do much more than they have in the past. However, many organisations are struggling with the pace of change, constantly having to react rather than lead with technological innovation.

There are several factors that influence the extent and the pace of technology adoption by organisations. These include:

- Technical feasibility
- The cost of developing, implementing and maintaining the new technology
- The economic benefits of the new technology
- The availability of labour skills to implement and use the new technology
- Regulatory and social acceptance.

By implementing an up to date and flexible IT infrastructure, the organisation can manage many of these factors – enabling technical feasibility, minimising costs and maximising the economic benefit and having the appropriate labour skills present – thus allowing them to embrace new technology and the opportunities it presents.

Enabling transformation

Technology is no longer viewed mainly as a vehicle for improved productivity but is seen as a key component of business transformation.

e.g

Illustration 4 – Cloud technology

The cloud is one transformational technology of IT infrastructure. Previously, organisations that wanted to increase their capability would have had to invest in new hardware which was time consuming and expensive. Now they can increase their capability at the click of a button (and a smaller payment).

Organisations are at different stages of their digital transformation but having a good IT infrastructure in place can enable organisational transformation in a huge variety of ways, such as:

- The adoption of new ways of working across the **business** and the **industry**.

e.g

Illustration 5 – Business Process Re-engineering (BPR)

BPR enabling new ways of working across the business

A company manufactures high quality women's clothing in its factory. The company is organised into traditional functional departments most of which have their own unreliable spreadsheet-based systems for planning and reporting. As a result, the company often fails to produce accurate, timely and consistent data to monitor its own performance, which contributes to failures in achieving the performance targets set by its retail customers.

The market is highly competitive. Retailers, who are the company's customers, have two key demands: they want lower prices to pass on to consumers and they also require suppliers to meet performance targets relating to lead times and quality.

To help them comply with the retailers' demands, the company have decided to use BPR to re-engineer the production process. It will close all their own manufacturing facilities and outsource all production to overseas suppliers, who have much larger factories and lower costs.

BPR will include a formal project, involving Finance, Operations and IT. IT will act as a key enabler in the re-engineering. To mitigate the cost of shipping goods over long distances, the company have invested in sophisticated software to consolidate orders so that each shipping container is completely full before despatch from their suppliers. Purchase invoice processing will also be automated by the integration of information systems into the suppliers' bespoke systems.

The changes will mean that staff from the company's functional departments will reorganise into multi-disciplinary teams, each serving a major customer account. Each team will perform all aspects of account management from taking sales orders and procurement through to arranging shipping and after sales service.

Illustration 6 – Disruptive technology

Disruptive technology and new ways of working across the hospitality industry

Airbnb, which was founded in 2008, is an online website. It allows hosts to post their homes on the site for short-term rent. Airbnb do not own the homes; it just acts as a broker and takes commission on every property that is rented. Versus a traditional hotel website which shows hotel rooms only, Airbnb has a range of accommodation types – from private rooms like a hotel, through to shared spaces (a room in someone's home), apartments, houses or even a campsite or boat.

Airbnb's focus is on cost savings, household amenities (like a living room, dishwasher, etc which you don't usually have in a hotel) and the potential for a more authentic experience ('living like a local').

Technology-wise Airbnb uses a microservices approach (all software is divided up into smaller, independent services such as the search service, the booking service, the message service, the review service and the notification service). These link up using Application Programming Interfaces which allows for easy scalability.

Airbnb also uses machine learning, understanding user preferences such as location, price range, etc. It also uses it to identify fraudulent listings and payments.

Innovative technology has been used, such as the use of cloud-based platforms to collect payments and the incorporation of algorithms to allow hosts to set the optimum price for their accommodation (which Airbnb calls 'Smart Pricing').

Also, Airbnb's website looks better than other accommodation companies, with maps, prices and notable locations.(However, Vrbo claims to have the best functionality for the traveller with a better filter and sort function. For example, the customer can filter by user reviews, including the property rated most highly for cleanliness, or 4 stars plus, etc.)

In the early years, Airbnb was only focusing on low-value customers, but eventually, it started focusing on high value customers as well. Renters can select homes or apartments based on location and the money they want to pay. Airbnb is tough competition for the hotels and other accommodation providers with 7.7 million active listings, 100,000 cities, 150 million worldwide users and 1.5 billion stays. The other accommodation websites are not able to match Airbnb on price, household comforts and the local experience offered. (Vrbo has just over 2 million active listings.)

- Productivity improvements

Illustration 7 – Technology improving farming productivity

In the United Kingdom and elsewhere, most farms would benefit from the application of digital and other technologies to increase farm productivity and help address climate change impacts. Some examples of how technology can be used to improve farm productivity include:

- Geographic information systems for agricultural mapping enabling better management of soil and irrigation.
- Digital technology can guide crop and input selection, provide weather, disease and pest-related advice, and real-time data on domestic and export markets.

- Multi-source data capture and analysis

Illustration 8 – Big data analytics use by supermarkets

In Chapter 5, we discussed big data and data analytics:

- Big data describes data sets so large and varied they are beyond the capability of traditional data-processing.
- Data analytics is the process of collecting, organising and analysing large sets of data to discover patterns and other information which an organisation can use for future decisions.

A supermarket can analyse this multi-source big data to improve its targeting of customers:

For example, a supermarket is able to take data from your past buying patterns, its internal inventory information, your mobile phone location data, social media as well as weather information to send you a voucher for barbeque food; but only if you own a barbeque, the weather is nice, you are within 3 miles of one of their stores and the barbeque food is in stock.

- The creation of shared service capability – shared service centres were discussed in Chapter 3. Globalisation and **technological advances** have meant that much of the routine processing of the organisation's functions (for example, the finance function) could be carried out by a shared service centre (i.e. the centralisation of this routine processing into one place).
- Digitisation of information

Illustration 9 – Digitisation within the NHS

The National Health Service (NHS) provides healthcare for all citizens in the United Kingdom. It is the fifth largest employer in the world. The government has committed billions of pounds to creating a 'paperless' NHS, recognising that making the best use of IT will deliver huge benefits and improved outcomes for patients.

> Digitisation was forced on to the NHS in some ways due to Covid 19, where doctors could not meet general practice (GP) patients face to face for several months. Swift steps forward in the NHS included:
>
> - The creation of electronic records for all patients (so patients will no longer have to repeat their medical history)
> - The creation of online booking and prescription ordering services
> - Access to healthcare apps for patients, for example, the Covid 19 app (now removed) and the NHS app where you can order repeat prescriptions and see your medical record including test results
> - Options for patients to choose to speak to a doctor online or via a smartphone or video link.
>
> However, digitisation is a huge challenge due to antiquated systems, the vast scale of the task and insufficient funding. However, although the modernisation is fraught with difficulty, the NHS continues to make progress.

- Flexible working practices (see discussion below)
- Virtual organisations (see discussion below).

Geographically dispersed teams

Technology developments have enabled the creation of new ways of working. Two significant changes include an increase in **remote working** (sometimes called homeworking or teleworking) and the formation of **virtual teams**:

- **Remote working** – IT developments (such as email and the internet), have enabled employees to work away from the office (for example, at home). The advantages and disadvantages for the organisation may include:

Advantages	**Disadvantages**
• Lower infrastructure costs • Increased employee motivation and productivity • Increased commitment to the organisation • Attracting individuals because of the availability of such conditions • Reduced absenteeism and staff turnover	• Difficulties in co-ordinating staff • Loss of control of staff • Dilution of organisational culture • Less commitment to the organisation • Set up costs, for example providing employees with equipment

Test your understanding 2

Requirement:

Consider your own employment. Would you like or dislike working from home? Discuss the reason for your opinion on this issue.

- **Virtual teams**

Before discussing virtual teams, it is useful to understand what is meant by a virtual organisation. This is because virtual teams are a key component of a virtual organisation.

A **virtual organisation** outsources most or all of its functions to other organisations and simply exists as a network of contracts, with very few, if any, functions being kept in-house.

Illustration 10 – Amazon, a virtual company

Many internet companies are examples of networks – Amazon being perhaps one of the best known on-line retailers.

- Amazon operates its website but relies on external suppliers, warehouses, couriers and credit card companies to deliver the rest of the customer experience.
- These partners are also expected to provide Amazon with information on, for example, stock availability, delivery times and promotional material.
- The customer feels that they are dealing with one organisation, not many.

Test your understanding 3

Which of the following statements regarding virtual organisations is incorrect?

A Virtual organisations occur when some or all elements of the organisation's functions are outsourced to third party organisations

B Information technology is usually a vital requirement for virtual organisations

C Virtual organisations usually face higher overhead costs

D Virtual organisations have more flexibility than traditionally structured organisations

Virtual teams are a key component of virtual organisations.

A **virtual team** is a group of people who interact through independent tasks guided by a common purpose and work across space, time and organisational boundaries with links strengthened by IT.

They are essentially teams of people who are not present in the same office or organisation.

The following challenges face virtual teams:

Challenge	**Explanation**
Forming a team	It may be difficult to establish a cohesive and trusting team.
Knowledge sharing	It may prove more difficult due to the absence of face to face contact.
Processes and goals	It may be more difficult to establish clear decision making processes and goals.
Leadership	This may be more difficult since individuals will be working at different times, in different locations and in different ways.
Cultural differences	Team members will be from different backgrounds and cultural differences may make working together more difficult.
Morale	Some team members may find this way of working isolating.

Test your understanding 4

Requirement:

Identify the ways in which the challenges faced by virtual teams can be overcome.

Enhancing internal and external relationships

Information systems provide an opportunity to build stronger relationships with stakeholders and to improve internal efficiency by providing convenient, easy to use, communication channels. For example, intranets and extranets, shared databases (these may utilise the cloud), email and live chat features.

e.g **Illustration 11 – Enhancing relationships with customers**

One example of a system that can be used to enhance relationships with stakeholders (in this case, customers) is a **customer relationship management (CRM)) system**.

CRM is the process the organisation uses to:

- Identify, attract and win new customers
- Retain existing customers
- Entice past customers back.

CRM systems refer to the technology that is used to gather the information needed to achieve the above. CRM systems range from simple spreadsheets and databases containing information about the customer to more complex online applications which are fully integrated with the organisation's other systems. A CRM system may include the following features:

Feature	**Benefit**
A central database that is accessible by all employees to view and update customer data.	Improved customer service, loyalty and retention.
Analysis of customer data including customer segmentation (existing and potential customers).	Improved marketing campaigns through customised targeting.
Customer web-based ordering.	Reduced order cost and customer service cost.
Identifying and tracking potential customers.	A wider customer base and more focused prospect tracking.
Reports generated with up-to-date information including revenue forecasting and trend analysis.	Better and more timely decision making.

Ethical and social issues with IS and data

In Chapter 6 we discussed how the increased use of technology impacts ethical and social considerations. In the context of IT infrastructure, the organisation must manage its information systems and data with these ethical and social issues in mind, including:

- **Data protection and data privacy** – the amount of personal data available to and used by organisations means that the privacy, sensitivity and security of this data is a very significant consideration in modern business. A business must ensure it is compliant with all legislation but there are also considerations from an ethical and social responsibility point of view in terms of what is right and wrong in the eyes of the public.

e.g

Illustration 12 – IT infrastructure and legal, ethical and social issues

An organisation must manage its information systems in the context of the legal, ethical and social issues that exist with IS and data:

Example of an issue	Possible intervention
Legal issue – data may be used or handled in an unlawful way, for example resulting in unauthorised access of data.	In the UK, the organisation's IS must be set up to comply with GDPR principles. This will ensure that the organisation's data is used lawfully. Data controllers within the organisation may be used to ensure that these adequate GDPR safeguards are in place.
Ethical issue – goes beyond legal requirements and considers what is right or wrong for the organisation to do. For example, just because an organisation's IS will allow the collection and analysis of an employee's social media presence, it may not be considered ethical to do so.	Organisations may create a written code of ethics and instruct employees to follow them. In the context of the example given here, it may contain a broad or more specific statement regarding the use of the organisation's IS to monitor an employee's social media presence.
Social issue – an organisation should make choices that are in the best interests of the society in which it operates (see illustration below).	The IT infrastructure within the organisation should be set up to collect, analyse and share data in an appropriate way. So, for example, a pharmaceutical company may align its systems so that it can easily share data and analysis with university research teams.

e.g

Illustration 13 – Social issues

In Chapter 6, we said that pharmaceutical companies may hold huge amounts of data and analysis from clinical trials. It may not make financial sense but from a societal point of view the company should consider donating this data and analysis to, say, universities for research purposes that could benefit society.

For example, Johnson and Johnson agreed to give its clinical trial data to Yale University to help advance science and medicine.

- **Corporate digital responsibility (CDR)** – as discussed in Chapter 6, CDR is a voluntary commitment by organisations to go beyond mere compliance with legislation, when it comes to how they handle technology and data. The social and ethical issues discussed above will be relevant here. The organisation's IT infrastructure should be aligned to it CDR strategy.

2.3 The costs and benefits of IS

Introduction

When an organisation sees a possibility for introducing a new IS, an evaluation of the new system should be made to decide whether the potential benefits are sufficient to justify the costs.

Cost-benefit analysis (CBA) can be used to assess the expected costs and benefits of the IS.

The **costs** of a new IS are:

Initial costs	**Running costs**
• Costs to design and develop system if software is bespoke. • Purchase price of software if it is not bespoke. • Purchase cost of new hardware. • Cost of testing and implementation of the new system. • Training costs.	• Cost of labour time to run the system. • Cost of materials, for example replacement parts. • Cost of service support, for example IT helpdesk. • Other ongoing costs such as the cost of quality or security adherence/failure.

The **benefits** of a new IS include:

- Speed – for example, in dealing with repetitive tasks such as data collection and payroll processing.
- Accuracy – the IS should reduce the incidence of human error and better information should be produced.
- Volume – the IS should be able to handle much larger volumes of data, 24 hours per day.
- Complexity – once systems are computerised and integrated, they can generally handle a greater level of complexity than humans.
- Collaboration – the IS can enable collaboration across the organisation due to better access and sharing of real-time information.
- Presentation – the IS may display information in a 'user-friendly' way.
- Lower costs – all of the above benefits mean that IS have become highly cost-effective providers of 'good' information.

The **finance function can assist the IT function** in this cost-benefit analysis.

We will now look more specifically at **the different costs and benefits of information systems** including:

- Privacy and security
- Systems architecture
- Data flows
- Big data information management.

Privacy and security

Information systems are exposed to privacy and security issues. The organisation must safeguard the privacy and security of data (considering legal, ethical and social factors and a wider sense of CDR) as well as ensuring complete and accurate processing of data.

There are different privacy and security risks that exist, together with solutions as to how the organisation can tackle each risk. Each of the solutions will have an associated **cost** (i.e. to implement the solution) and **benefit** (i.e. mitigation of the risk).

Potential threat	Solution
Natural disasters – for example, fire or flood	• Fire procedures – fire alarms, extinguishers, fire doors, staff training and insurance cover. • Location, for example, not in a basement area liable to flooding. • Physical environment – for example, air conditioning and dust controls. • Back up procedures – data should be backed up on a regular basis (ideally in real-time and on the cloud) to allow recovery. • Business continuity planning – to decide which systems are critical to the organisation continuing its activities.
Malfunction – of computer hardware or software	• Network design – to cope with periods of high volumes. • Back up procedures and business continuity planning (as above).

Potential threat	Solution
Unauthorised access, usage, damage or theft	• Personnel controls – includes segregation of duties, policy on usage and compliance with regulations such as GDPR, hierarchy of access. • Access controls – such as passwords and time lockouts. • Computer equipment controls – to protect equipment from theft or destruction.
Viruses – a small program that once introduced into the system spreads extensively. Can affect the whole computer system	• Anti-virus software – should be run and updated regularly to prevent corruption of the system by viruses. • Formal security policy and procedures, for example, employees should only download files or open attachments from reputed sources. • Regular audits to check for unauthorised software.
Hackers – deliberate access to systems by unauthorised persons	• Firewall software – should provide protection from unauthorised access to the system from the Internet. • Passwords and usernames – limit unauthorised access to the system. • User awareness training and a formal security policy so that employees are aware of the risks that exist and how best to mitigate them. • Data encryption – data is scrambled prior to transmission and is recovered in a readable format once transmission is complete.

Potential threat	Solution
Human errors – unintentional errors from using IS	• Training – adequate staff training and operating procedures. • Controls ensuring only valid data is input/processed.
Human resource risk – for example, repetitive strain injury (RSI), headaches and eye strain from computer screens, tripping over loose wires	• Ergonomic design of workstations should reduce problems such as RSI. • Anti-glare screens reduce eye strain. • Cables should be in ducts.

e.g

Illustration 14 – WikiLeaks

WikiLeaks is a not-for-profit organisation created to protect whistle blowers and journalists who have sensitive information to communicate to the public. WikiLeaks has dominated the news because of its steady drip feed of secret documents. For example:

- In 2010, the site released almost 400,000 secret US military logs detailing its operations in Iraq, 90,000 classified military records giving an insight into military strategy in Afghanistan and posted a video on its website showing a US Apache helicopter killing at least 12 people during an attack in Baghdad in 2007.
- In 2016, during the US presidential election, thousands of emails from Hilary Clinton's personal server were published by WikiLeaks. Some proved embarrassing and detracted from her campaign. Many were utilised by her opponent Donald Trump as part of his ultimately successful campaign.

e.g

Illustration 15 – Virus infection in the NHS

The NHS (National Health Service) faced a week of chaos after hackers demanding a ransom infiltrated the health service's computer system.

Operations and appointments were cancelled and ambulances diverted as up to 40 hospital trusts became infected by a ransomware (malicious software) attack demanding payments to regain access to vital medical records.

The attack was part of the biggest ransomware attack in history with 57,000 infections in 99 countries being observed.

Illustration 16 – Ransomware at the British Library (2023)

In October 2023, a ransomware attack rendered the British Library website inaccessible, and it remained down months later. Attackers stole personal data and threatened to sell it online, known as double extortion. By simultaneously encrypting and stealing data, targets faced additional pressure to pay the ransom. Rhysida, the group behind the attack, posted low-resolution images of the personal data on its leak site with a starting bid of 20 bitcoin (about £590,000 at the time).

Rhysida has also attacked a U.S. hospital group – Prospect Medical Holdings, and government institutions in Portugal, Chile, and Kuwait.

Systems architecture

Systems architecture is the way the systems infrastructure is organised together to support the organisation's functions and its overall goals.

The development of **network** technology has facilitated the transfer of information between different parts of the business. Organisations connect their computers together in **local area networks** (LANs), enabling them to share data (for example, via email) and devices (such as printers). **Wide area networks** (WANs) are used to connect LANs together, so that computer users in one location can communicate with computers users in another location.

There are **two broad approaches to systems architecture** – a centralised architecture or a decentralised architecture:

A **centralised** systems architecture is when the whole IT function or the entire IS is based out of a single, central location.

A **decentralised** systems architecture is when the IT function or the IS is spread out throughout the organisation's location.

The **costs and benefits of a decentralised approach** are as follows:

Costs	**Benefits**
• Higher costs due to duplication of equipment and effort: – analysis, design and implementation of IS – data gathering and administration – operation, support and maintenance of IS. • Barriers to sharing data between different parts of the organisation, for example, due to unaligned IS.	• Better ability to meet local needs. • Fewer staff relying on a single system. • Less reliance on a few key staff who plan, develop and run the systems. • Technology tends to be less complex making problems easier to diagnose. • Security breaches will have less of an impact.

Costs	Benefits
• Inconsistent data, for example, one version of the data may be more reliable or up to date. • Loss of control at a central level may result in common goals not being worked towards.	• Efficiencies since time is saved not having to collect information locally, process it and collate it centrally and then feedback down to a local level.

The **costs and benefits of centralised systems architecture are the opposite of those above**.

It is worth noting that an organisation may decide to **outsource IS** – the scope ranging from outsourcing of the development of a single system to total outsourcing when the vast majority of the organisation's IS and IT services and capabilities are outsourced.

Data flows

Data flow is the movement of data through a process or system. It includes:

- Data inputs (raw data)
- Data processing (turning the raw data into meaningful information)
- Data outputs ('good' information, i.e. accurate, timely, relevant, concise and cost effective, is produced for the user)
- Data storage.

There will be **costs** associated with data flows, i.e. the cost of collecting the data, processing the data, data output costs and the cost of the storage of data (much of this will rely on effective network technology). There will also be an upfront cost to produce a data flow diagram – this is a model used to map out the entire process of data movement.

However, there are **benefits** of having good data flows in place. Understanding the potential value of data and its significance to an organisation presents a real opportunity to gain unique insight which can be used to improve competitive position and potentially gain competitive advantage over rivals.

Big data information management

Effective big data information management will unlock the potential value of big data, but this will also come at a cost to the organisation:

The **benefits** are:

- Enhanced transparency
- Performance improvement
- Market segmentation and customisation
- Improved decision making
- Possible product innovation
- Effective risk management and control.

e.g

Illustration 17 – Big data information management at Netflix

Netflix has over 282 million subscribers worldwide. The company uses information gathered from analysis of viewing habits to inform decisions on which shows to invest in. Analysing past viewing figures and understanding viewer populations and the shows they are likely to watch allows the analysts to predict likely viewing figures before a show has even aired. This can help to determine if the show is a viable investment.

However, there are **costs** associated with big data information management:

- The **cost** of establishing the hardware and software needed. In addition, there will be a need to constantly **update** or **maintain** it to achieve competitive advantage.
- There may be **technical difficulties,** and therefore associated costs, with integrating existing data warehousing and, for example, Hadoop systems.
- **Incorrect data** (poor veracity) may result in incorrect conclusions being made. For example, data collected from social media may not be accurate. This wastes time and can result in poor and costly decisions.
- It is important to recognise that just because something can be measured, this does not necessarily mean it should be. There is a risk that **valuable time is spent measuring relationships that have no organisational value**.
- The **security of data** is a major concern in the majority of organisations and if the organisation lacks the resources to manage data then there is likely to be a greater risk of leaks and losses. There can be a risk to the data protection of organisations as they collect a greater range of data from increasingly personal sources (for example, Facebook). Current laws and regulations on the storage of personal information must be complied with to avoid legal action and/or reputational damage. This will all come at a cost.
- The nature of much of the data means that there is a risk that it will become **outdated and irrelevant very quickly** resulting in the need to constantly monitor databases.
- The **availability of skills** to use big data systems, which is compounded by the fact that many of the systems are rapidly developing, and support is not always easily and readily available. There is also an increasing need to combine data analysis skills with a deep understanding of the industry being analysed and this need is not always recognised. Recruitment and training of the right staff and provision of competitive remuneration to these staff can prove costly.

3 Areas of interface between IT and finance

3.1 Introduction

In Chapters 9 to 11, we discussed the interaction between the operations function/sales and marketing/HR function and finance. Much of the discussion below overlaps with what has already been discussed, in that finance, as a trusted advisor, should collaborate with the other function to achieve organisational goals and their own individual functional goals.

3.2 Interaction between IT and finance

- **Traditionally**, the IT function and the finance function worked independently:
  - Finance very much viewed IT as a cost whereas the IT function viewed itself as an asset
  - Collaboration between the functions was limited to, for example, establishing a budget for a new IT system.
- The **modern** approach is to view IT as one of the greatest assets an organisation has. Given the central role that technology plays in supporting modern business and their finance functions, the finance function and the IT function need to form a productive partnership.

  If a significant IT system is implemented, it will be treated as a project, be exposed to project management techniques and Finance will form part of the Project team.

  Examples of why the two functions need to interact include:
  - **Smarter investment in IT** – whether the business needs to implement a company-wide system or a solution that's for the finance function alone, the expert guidance of the IT function on which technology will help the company achieve its strategic goals and increase competitiveness will be of huge benefit to the finance function.
  - **Information security and compliance** – when it comes to data privacy and security, the finance function can work with the IT function on many fronts, including creating access policies and minimising the threat of data theft and loss.
  - **Data analytics** – organisations of all sizes are working to find ways to turn their data into actionable business intelligence. The finance function wants to make sure that only the most relevant and accurate data is used for decision making. This requires the business to apply the right combination of technologies, processes and strategies. The IT function is well equipped to lead and shape these activities.
  - **Cost-benefit analysis** (as discussed in Section 2.3).

4 Key performance indicators (KPIs)

4.1 Introduction

In section 6 of Chapter 9 we:

- Defined KPIs
- Discussed their use in managing the operations function
- Identified relevant KPIs for operations
- Discussed how the finance function manages operations using KPIs and
- Discussed the impact of technology in this area.

Much of this discussion can also be applied to the IT function and can therefore be referred back to.

In this section we will briefly discuss how the finance function helps to manage the IT function using KPIs before identifying some relevant KPIs for IT.

4.2 How finance helps to manage IT using KPIs

Let's begin by recapping our discussion from Chapter 10 but this time in the context of the IT function.

- The IT function will identify its relevant CSFs.
- The KPIs are the measures that indicate whether the IT function is achieving these CSFs.
- The finance function works with the IT function to:
  - **Identify** appropriate KPIs
  - **Assemble** KPI data and information
  - **Analyse** this for insight
  - Give **advice** to the IT function based on this insight and
  - **Apply** what has been learned to impact the achievement of the objectives of the IT function and the organisation.
- **Technology** will act as a key enabler in this, particularly in the 'assembly' and 'analysis' tasks.

4.3 Examples of KPIs for IT

Type of activity	Possible KPIs
Operational activities – KPIs are used to monitor the day to day activity and effectiveness of the IT function.	• Ticket response rates for IT issues sent to IT support • Resolution rates • System/technology downtime • Customer feedback/experience

Transformational activities – KPIs are used to measure the impact of IT initiatives in terms of better and more informed decision making.	• Cost of new technology • Time saved using new technology • IT spend per employee • IT utilisation • Security adherence/breaches
Strategic activities – KPIs are used to monitor the progress of the IT function towards long-term strategic goals.	• New/improved business opportunities using technology • Revenue generated by using new technology • Technology leading to competitive advantage • IT function as a leader in the marketplace

It is important to note that the above is a generic list of KPIs for the IT function and that the function must identify the most appropriate KPIs for measuring the achievement of its CSFs. For example, one of the function's CSFs may to 'provide skilled, technical IT support'. The achievement of this CSF could be measured using several KPIs, for example 'customer feedback' of the IT support service.

Test your understanding 5

Lamp Limited is introducing a new information system and given it is a large project the project manager has decided to set some key performance indicators for the team after discussion with them.

The project manager is concerned that the benefits from the project exceed the costs of it and that the project is completed on time with all the deliverables (outputs) of suitable quality.

Three KPIs have been selected for scrutiny, and you have been asked to comment.

KPI	**Background**
Volume of transactions Capable of processing up to 6,000 transactions per hour	This is an increase of 80% over the previous system
Labour Total labour spend on the project must not exceed $100,000	This is based on the original specification and scope of the project

Deliverables All originally specified deliverables (outputs) must be 100% delivered	This is based on the original specification and scope of the project

Requirement:

For each KPI listed above comment on the positives and the negatives you can identify in the measure suggested and comment on whether and how this measure could be manipulated.

(15 marks)

5 Chapter summary

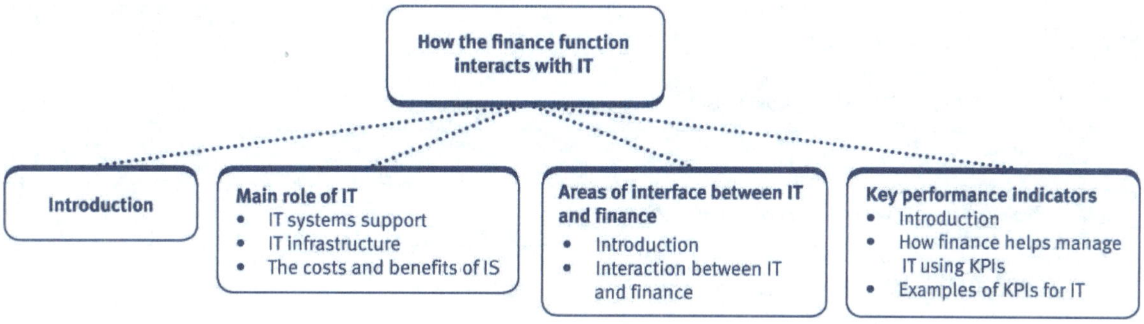

Test your understanding answers

Test your understanding 1

The best answer here is **D**

Test your understanding 2

Advantages

- Reduced travel time and hence cost savings.
- Reduction in stress due to the removal of the daily commute and the removal of the distractions of a busy office.
- Better work/life balance due to the removal of the daily commute and potential opportunities to work more flexible hours than the traditional '9 to 5'.
- Control – employees may feel an improved sense of control if they have more flexibility to decide their working patterns and hours.
- Employment opportunities for disadvantaged individuals, for example disabled people may now find it possible to work due to the removal of travel and the office environment.

Disadvantages

- May not suit those with poor personal motivation or who are not self-starters.
- May be distracted at home, for example by family members.
- Loss of learning/sharing of ideas from face to face contact.
- Loss of social interaction and stimulation.
- Difficultly in separating home and work life – an inability to 'switch off' from work may lead to 'burn out' or damaged personal relationships.

Test your understanding 3

The correct answer is **C** – virtual organisations usually have lower overhead costs.

Test your understanding 4

The challenges faced by virtual teams can be overcome by:

- training in technology and teamwork
- spending time getting to know each other, for example, team identity, jokes, occasional face to face meetings, team trips out
- clear roles and responsibilities
- detailed and timely feedback between the leader and team members
- regular and predictable communication matters. The benefits should be maximised, for example, the use of email, video conferencing, social networking sites and blogs could all assist in overcoming some of the challenges. Time zone differences may mean that managers and employees may have to accept that response times may not be immediate
- paying attention to cultural differences. This may require training in cross-cultural appreciation
- choosing dependable and self-reliant employees but managers should still be on hand to offer support
- valued staff should be made to feel wanted and a sense of loyalty to the firm instilled
- managers may need to view their role differently, the emphasis being on co-ordination rather than leadership
- clear communication from managers of information coming from higher up in the organisation to ensure that employees are fully informed and share the organisation's vision.

Test your understanding 5

Volume of transactions

Positive aspects

This measure is clearly very specific and should be measurable. It could be that the capacity of the system may never be fully utilised and so the 6,000 could never be reached and which case the actual data may show a number less than this target, without there being any underperformance.

Negative aspects

It is unclear whether an 80% increase is achievable, although system upgrades do tend to result in big increases in potential speeds in the modern IT world.

There is no quality aspect and speed alone may not be what is needed or preferred.

Manipulation

The number of transactions processed in a given time space is a very factual matter and without any element of judgement it is more difficult to manipulate.

A determined employee could duplicate transactions in an order to get this figure higher but that would result in the need for reversal and the likelihood of being caught.

Total labour spend

Positive aspects

Providing a financial constraint is clearly relevant and this measure is clear and measurable. However, this is set based on the agreed specification and scope of the project and if these change at all during the project then this limit might have to be revisited.

Negative aspects

Setting cash limits can constrain decisions during the project. “We can’t do (sensible thing) because we will spend more than was allowed”. This can have very damaging effects on the project outcomes.

If the scope changes and the target is not adjusted it will become either too lenient, or more likely too harsh.

Manipulation

Costs incurred could be wrongly categorised to either another cost heading or another project thus under recording the cost in this project.

Deliverables

Positive aspects

This is a clear target that is incapable of being misunderstood.
It is relevant as the quality of work was a concern of the project manager.

Negative aspects

One questions the achievability of 100% perfection, if a target is too difficult it can be ignored or become a demotivating factor.
You could also question its desirability. If delivering perfection gets expensive the costs might exceed the benefits here.

Manipulation

Other than just lying it is hard to see how this measure could be manipulated. Either the system delivers, or it doesn't. However, if some of the deliverables have elements of subjectivity (the "good" appearance of a document) then it is possible to "stretch" the definition a little and say it delivers when some might believe it does not.

D

E

F

L

M

N

O

P

T

U

V

W

Z